Woodstock and Altamont: the Music Festivals that defined the 1960s

Brian Ireland

First published in Great Britain in 2019
by Wymer Publishing
www.wymerpublishing.co.uk
Tel: 01234 326691
Wymer Publishing is a trading name of Wymer (UK) Ltd

ISBN: 978-1-912782-19-2

Design by 1016 Sarpsborg
Printed by Clays Ltd, Bungay, Suffolk, England.

A catalogue record for this book is available from the British Library.

Woodstock and Altamont: the Music Festivals that defined the 1960s

Brian Ireland

WP
WYMER
PUBLISHING
Bedford, England

Table of contents

Introduction

Time has not been kind to the 1969 Woodstock and Altamont music festivals, nor more generally to the 1960s. In popular memory, much of the decade is obscured by a miasma of pot smoke, or drowned out in a purple haze of iconic music. Liberals tend to remember it as a decade when great strides were made in making the American Dream available to all; in contrast, conservatives point to the 1960s as the era when American values were undermined by left wing activism. Music was more than a soundtrack to these events: often it inspired them. It was a time when song lyrics could reflect the hopes, dreams and fears of a generation, and when musicians could be, to paraphrase John Lennon, more popular than Jesus. It was also the era of the outdoor rock festival, with approximately 300 large rock festivals held in the United States between 1967-1971, attracting a combined audience of around 3 million people.[1] On the fortieth anniversary year of the festivals, Country Joe McDonald, a notable performer at Woodstock, reflected: "Woodstock and Altamont seem like bookends to the great social experiment of the late 60s".[2] This neatly sums up the popular memory of both iconic music festivals. The former, the Woodstock Festival of August 15-18, 1969 — which of course turned out to be the major musical and cultural event of the year, and perhaps the decade, attracting many of the major musical artists of the day and an audience of around 400,000 — seemed to offer proof that hippie idealism about peace and love was possible. Conversely, the ill-fated Altamont Speedway Free Festival held on December 6, 1969 seemed to reflect the dark side of the hippie dream — the flip side of the coin that had a peace sign on one side and Charles Manson's face on the other. Marked by violence and deaths, Altamont appeared to provide the opposite experience to the peaceful idealism of Woodstock. While there is a certain amount of truth in this narrative, contextualising these events within their wider social, cultural and political context reveals a much more illuminating and more complicated story.

This book, a monograph about the Woodstock and Altamont festivals of 1969, tells that story. It is the first to treat both festivals equally, and it explores their organisation, promotion, and unfolding, as well as their immediate and enduring impact. The book is, though, also about the 1960s, particularly the political, social, and cultural changes that provided the context for these festivals. It is appropriate, as the 50th anniversary of both Woodstock and Altamont approaches, to revisit these events, take stock of their historical importance, and to note their influence not just on popular culture and society, but also as part of a new musical culture that developed in the late 1960s — a particularly vibrant temporal, political and geographical nexus in what *Life* magazine called the "decade of tumult and change".[3] Rock festival culture allowed tens of thousands (and on occasion, hundreds of thousands) of young people to gather and engage with similarly-minded people about issues that were important to them, among which were the conduct of the war in Vietnam, the military draft, free speech, civil rights, gender equality, drug use, spirituality, capitalism — even revolution. Rock and roll "is the only way in which the vast but formless power of youth is structured, the only way in which it can be defined or inspected", claimed *Rolling Stone* founder Jan Wenner in 1968, and with that in mind, this book will return the emphasis about Woodstock and Altamont back to the music festival culture in which they were initially understood.

The Woodstock festival was the product of four men and two ideas: music producers Michael Lang and Artie Kornfeld envisioned opening a recording studio and creating a musical community in the town of Woodstock in upstate New York; whereas their business partners John Roberts and Joel Rosenman were venture capitalists looking to fund a new investment opportunity. They thus formed the company Woodstock Ventures and the festival was therefore planned from the beginning as a for-profit event. In the wake of a number of large, commercial music events, and a new rock festival culture that was developing in tandem with a politically engaged counterculture, the promoters expected an audience of maybe 200,000 people, each paying between $18-$24 for a ticket to the three-day event. The festival was advertised not just as a music event but also a "be-in" or "gathering of the tribes", which added to its attraction. To an extent, this is what actually occurred, and much of the credit for that belongs to Hog Farm, the hippie commune hired by Woodstock Ventures to help with security and provide food. Led by Hugh "Wavy Gravy" Romney, the Hog Farm became almost the public face of Woodstock, and the originators of the image of good will and brotherly love for which the festival became known. The band line-up was spectacular: Jimi Hendrix, Janis Joplin, The Who, Jefferson Airplane, Creedence Clearwater Revival, Crosby, Stills, Nash & Young, The Band, and The Grateful Dead were perhaps the most celebrated of the 32 acts booked to perform over three days. While they represented some of the most successful live performers of the time, it was, however, still a surprise when at least 400,000 people turned up, less than half of whom had bought advance tickets. Such was the mass of humanity arriving at the festival site, combined with the disorganisation that meant ticket booths were not in situ or operational as the festival began, that the organisers declared it a free festival. Woodstock was, therefore, a triumph of promotion and advertising, but also a victim of its own hype.

Because the crowd was twice the size the organisers had expected there were not sufficient toilet facilities, water, food, or first aid tents. In addition, heavy rain and thunderstorms turned the venue into a muddy mess. However, instead of leading to the kind of violence that marred other recent rock gatherings, the event was mainly peaceful: there were two accidental deaths but no murders, no riots, and no gate crashing. The organisers had arranged a light-touch security presence that was more akin to the kind of stewarding one might find at modern festivals than was then the norm in 1969. There were drug overdoses and numerous medical problems caused by exposure to the elements, but these practical issues were eclipsed by something more intangible — the festival's remarkably friendly and tolerant atmosphere. Woodstock was advertised as "Three days of peace and music" and, by and large, it lived up to that promise. Essentially, the organisers had arranged for a "safe space" for young people to express themselves and that's what they did: for a few days they dropped out, got high, stripped naked, and hung out with their peers in a spirit of sharing and acceptance. When the rain turned the venue into a quagmire, the crowd chose to play in the mud. In the absence of sufficient bathing facilities, people bathed in local lakes instead. When food ran short, local people donated sandwiches and drinks. This was a generation united by its support for civil rights and its opposition to the Vietnam War: music was both a soundtrack to their lives, and also a way of expressing their views. Rock music festivals were the most visible expression of their way of life, and Woodstock was the largest such event in history.

Of course there were incidents that threatened this rosy view: for example, radicals threatened to burn down food concession stands in protest at high prices; and Pete Townshend of The Who visibly demonstrated the divide between music and politics when he denied the stage to radical activist Abbie Hoffman, in the process smashing him over the head with his guitar. Nevertheless, these were exceptions to the norm at Woodstock: moreover, the crowd displayed a degree of social harmony that was notably absent in wider American society. Almost immediately, Woodstock became recognised as a cultural event of some significance, and over time it was acknowledged as a watershed moment, the highpoint of the counterculture in the 1960s. It seemed to prove that the "Age of Aquarius" had arrived and a new "Woodstock Nation" had been born. Perhaps people might live in peace and harmony, even in adverse circumstances, just as the hippies had been advocating. The festival also provided links between the 1950s "Beat" generation and the new Woodstock Nation, suggesting perhaps that the newness of these ideas was overstated, and that the first shoots of the counterculture had emerged earlier as a reaction to the Atomic Age and the Cold War. Beat legend Neal Cassady and the "Merry Pranksters" — a group of political activists, performance artists, and LSD advocates — took their "Magic Bus" to Woodstock and its psychedelic design made it a symbol of the festival. The pranksters mixed with counterculture figures like Hugh Romney — "Wavy Gravy" — and his Hog Farm commune in a symbolic meeting of the tribes of the Woodstock Nation.

Perhaps surprisingly, Woodstock was widely reported in the press, which gave it a kind of mainstream endorsement: as one researcher has observed, "Virtually every consumer publication in America featured at least one Woodstock article in August or September 1969".[4] The main focus of that reporting dealt with the logistical and practical problems of the festival, and there was also much discussion of drug use at Woodstock. However, when it came to the music and the festival's youthful audience, much of the coverage was positive. The reportage in the *New York Times* is indicative of this. Initially the *Times* viewed Woodstock in a negative fashion: on Sunday (day three of the festival), the newspaper's coverage focussed on the festival's shortcomings, such as sanitation problems, heavy rain, and food shortages. However, it also emphasised the peaceful nature of the event, remarking on the absence of violence and noting how few arrests for drug offences there had been in the surrounding area. On Monday its editorial stance appeared to harden: with the headline "Nightmare in the Catskills", the paper questioned what kind of a culture could produce such a massive heap of garbage as was left at Woodstock. However, the next day the *Times* softened its position. In an editorial entitled "Morning After at Bethel", it heaped praise on the young festival goers, noting perceptively that they came to Bethel not just to hear music, but also because they wanted to be part of the wider culture that their generation had ushered in, making them akin to comrades-in-arms — this time "comrades-in-rock". A broad spectrum of views were aired in the underground press: the more radical, political papers tended to view the festival as a capitalist venture designed to rip off fans; others focused on the music and culture that united hundreds of thousands of young people and enabled them to gather and enjoy themselves in a peaceful setting.

But other darker news stories were also circulating. On August 8 and 9, 1969, less than a week before Woodstock, members of a cult led by Charles Manson murdered seven people in two brutal attacks at their homes in Los Angeles. These were the last of nine murders committed that summer by the "Manson Family" and they immediately became national news due to the prominence of the victims, particularly Sharon Tate, the actress and wife of director Roman Polanski. The savagery of the murders was shocking, but equally disturbing were words daubed in blood and left at the crimes scenes — "pig", "Death to pigs", and "Helter Skelter" — that seemed to link the murders with the counterculture and with its music. Later, one of the murderers, Charles "Tex" Watson, recounted that when asked by a victim who he was, he replied: "I'm the devil, and I'm here to do the devil's business".[5] Less than four months later, on December 6, 1969, the devil would appear again, this time at the Altamont Speedway Free Festival, near Livermore, California. Organised primarily by the Rolling Stones as a grand finale at the end of their 1969 American tour, the Altamont festival attracted an audience of perhaps 300,000 people, who were there to see the Stones final performance of the year, as well as other artists such as Santana, Jefferson Airplane, Crosby, Stills, Nash & Young, the Flying Burrito Brothers, and The Grateful Dead. Aside from the Stones and the Flying Burrito Brothers, all of these artists had performed previously at Woodstock, and Altamont was meant to be "Woodstock West". Unlike Woodstock, however, Altamont is remembered mainly for violence, including the death of a young African-American man named Meredith Hunter at the hands of Hells Angels, and three other fatalities (two due to a hit-and-run incident, and one drowning in a nearby canal).

As the story of Altamont is much less well-known that Woodstock, it is useful to pause here to look at how plans for the Altamont Festival came together. Unlike Woodstock, which was always planned as a three-day, for-profit music festival, the story of how Altamont came about is much more haphazard and is directly tied to the story of the 1969 Rolling Stones tour of the U.S., which they had undertaken to support their forthcoming album *Let it Bleed*. Autumn 1969 marked the first time the Stones had toured the United States since 1966; and since then, the nature of rock audiences had changed. In June and July 1966, the band had played primarily to screaming teenagers; but by the time of Altamont in 1969, their fans were largely hippies who grooved to the music and listened to the lyrics instead — they assumed that the Stones had something to say that was relevant to their lives. This reflected the changes the Stones had gone through: they were by now writing their own songs, and those songs were about more weighty issues than love and romance. Tracks such as "Street Fighting Man", which had been inspired by demonstrations and riots, seemed both to reflect what was happening on the streets, and also incite those events. As Norma Coates has pointed out, by the time of Altamont, the underground press had embraced rock stars like Mick Jagger and sought out their opinions on a range of social and political issues. In essence, rock stars had become spokespersons for the counterculture, and were expected to behave accordingly.[6] This was a burden that sat heavily on the shoulders of supergroups such as the Beatles and Stones. For example, John Lennon's uncertainty about the goals of the counterculture and his place in it was reflected in his 1968 song "Revolution" from the *White Album*, with its indecisive lyric "you can count me out, in". Of all the Stones, Jagger was the one who saw the band's potential as avatars for the counterculture.

Unlike the Beatles, who had ceased touring in 1966 to focus on recording, the Stones' reputation as a dynamic live act remained intact (notwithstanding their two-year break from live performances from the end of their spring tour in 1967 until their concert in Hyde Park in July 1969). In fact, despite giving a somewhat lacklustre performance at the Hyde Park free concert, such was the popularity of their studio releases from 1966 to 1969, along with their well-publicised and notorious personal lives, that they remained an incredibly sought after and popular live act. Demand was such that the concert venues of the 1966 tour — small halls, and medium sized arenas — were no longer suitable. In 1969, the band played large arenas such as the LA Forum, Madison Square Garden, Boston Garden, and Philadelphia Spectrum, and outdoor venues such as the Palm Beach International Raceway.

Given their huge popularity, the Stones' should have been riding high at this point in 1969: from 1966 to 1969, for example, they generated 17 million dollars in earnings. Yet most of that money was held in America by their manager Alan Klein.[7] Essentially, for practical purposes, they were broke and needed the 1969 US tour to be a financial success so they could pay their debts and begin living the lifestyle their musical success seemed to promise. They therefore began sidelining Klein, bringing in instead new management to oversee their finances and set up a new financial model for the 1969 American tour. Essentially, this meant high ticket prices and a demand for large monetary advances from promoters. Despite these obligations, promoters were still eager to book the Stones as there was plenty of money to go around. In fact, until this point, contracts had been so heavily weighted against touring bands that promoters were easily able to absorb the Stones' financial demands. Such was fans' eagerness to see the band, some venues even scheduled afternoon as well as evening shows. Notwithstanding the higher ticket prices, most venues sold out.

Yet not everyone was happy: some fans, critics, and political activists in the counterculture movement had been advocating free concerts as the way forward. Ironically, of course, the biggest festival, Woodstock, was not meant to be free, and only became so when fans scaled or kicked down the perimeter fence. But it did strike a chord with a younger audience now growing accustomed to voicing anti-consumer and anti-capitalist arguments. For example, after The Who's Pete Townshend demanded the band's fee for playing at Woodstock and thus encouraged other artists at the festival to do the same, he was "denounced as a 'Rock capitalist,' a pig, a foppish dilettante 'artist' who was more interested in counting coin and playing Tommy for furs and tuxedos in ruling class opera houses than he was in relating to 'the needs of the people.'"[8] In Woodstock's wake, the New Orleans-based underground magazine *NOLA Express* gave advice on how to scale or cut through a cyclone fence to get free entry into festival grounds.[9] This sentiment was echoed in other underground publications: "The sound is rock music. What's going down is money", claimed *Rat* magazine in a 1967 article decrying links between pop music and imperialism.[10] Tom Hill wrote a diatribe against the appearance fees charged by artists at the 1970 Atlanta Pop Festival. Hill said: "It would probably not break any of the 'big name' groups to give their concerts for free. After all, they do make bread off their albums. It would seem that they could appear in person just to express their appreciation to the record-buying public".[11]

It was against this backdrop then that the Stones drew criticism for the allegedly excessive ticket prices for their 1969 American tour.[12] Influential music journalist Ralph Gleason of the *San Francisco Chronicle,* for example, lamented that top-price tickets for the 1969 Doors tour were $7.00 whereas the Stones were charging $8.50.[13] In fact, the Stones' ticket prices were comparable to those of other popular bands touring in 1969. For example, tickets for the Stones' gig at Madison Square Garden were priced between $5.00 to $8.00; tickets for the LA Forum gigs were $4.50, $5.50, $6.50 and $7.50; tickets for the Auburn show began at $5.00; and tickets for the San Diego and Oakland gigs, which were Bill Graham promotions, were priced from $4.50 to $7.50. Gleason also questioned if there was a racial element at play, and asked: "If they really dig the black musicians as much as every note they play and every syllable they utter indicates, is it possible to take out a show with, say, Ike and Tina and some of the older men like Howlin' Wolf and let them share in the loot?"[14] There was not much mileage in the racial argument given the Stones' affection for black blues music and the fact they had helped resurrect Chuck Berry's career by taking him on tour: financially, however, the Stones weren't overly generous to their support acts, whatever colour they were,[15] and the contrast between what they earned and what they paid their support acts, left them open to criticism. "The Stones are great. We love the Stones", said *San Francisco Good Times.* "The question is do the Stones love us?"[16] The mood of the counterculture, even before Woodstock or Altamont then, was for free music, and the Stones' capitalism was viewed as a betrayal. Yet, as Norma Coates points out, *Rolling Stone* and voices in the underground or alternative press were "willfully blind" to the realities of rock music, and the practicalities of organising and creating a music festival, even a supposedly "free" one.[17] For most musicians who worked in the realm of popular music, their work was part art, and part commodity to be bought and sold in the marketplace.

It was partly in response to the criticism of high ticket prices that the Stones began to talk of ending their tour with a 'free concert' in San Francisco. For their part, the Stones saw no downside to a free concert. The tour had been a roaring success. Critical reviews were glowing, shows sold out, and fans reacted positively to new songs. Band politics had also improved: Mick Taylor had replaced Brian Jones, and his skilful playing added a new element to the Stones' sound. In addition, they had gained the seal of approval from San Francisco's hippest band, The Grateful Dead. The original plan was to work with the Dead in arranging a festival at Golden

Gate Park. This would have been one of many the Dead participated in at the Park, but of course the addition of the Stones to proceedings added a level of cool and complication to proceedings. Everything was to be done in secret, right up to the last moment, but when plans leaked, San Francisco authorities refused permits for the event. Instead, a deal was done to hold the festival at Sears Point raceway. "Final, official, and definitive last word on the Rolling Stones concert", said the *Berkeley Tribe*, "It will take place this Saturday, from 10 a.m. to 5 p.m., at the Sears Point Raceway in Marin County".[18]

The slightly mocking tone of this piece reflects the confusion and uncertainty of the proposed free concert at Sears Point. Jagger had first mentioned it at a press conference in New York late November 1969, stating that it would be held in San Francisco, but rumours had circulated for a while that a free concert was possible. The *Los Angeles Free Press* and *San Francisco Chronicle* reported that the concert would take place in Golden Gate Park.[19] The *Free Press* claimed, "The concert will feature the Grateful Dead, Freddy Neil and perhaps one other group in addition to the Stones".[20] Fuelled by these reports, tens of thousands of fans made their way towards the city. However, after word got out that Sears Point would now host the event, Stones fans began making plans to go there instead. Just four days before the concert was due to take place however, the Sears Point plans fell through: the owners, Filmways, claimed the Stones misrepresented their intentions about filming the concert, and about donating profits from a concert film to charity. Looking beyond the company's press statements, Ralph Gleason explained that Filmways were, in fact, exacting some revenge on the Stones:

Stones's management (for which read Jagger) made promoters all over the country grovel and sweat and agree to exorbitant guarantees and special ego-satisfying clauses for the privilege of promoting the Stones' concerts. The Los Angeles concert was promoted by Concert Associates. Like other promoters, they were savaged by the Stones' contracts and by the ego trips and power plays of the actual tour company itself. Filmways, the giant corporation, owns Concert Associates. Filmways also owns the Sears Point Raceway... Once Filmways had the Stones over the barrel (as last month the Stones had everybody else over the barrel) Filmways stated the conditions. This was Thursday afternoon in a meeting here. The Stones were to put $100,000 in escrow to pay for possible damage to the Raceway and were either to pay another $100,000 for use or, in lieu of that, Filmways was to get distribution rights to the flick the Maysles Brothers (taking over for Haskell Wexler) were to make of the event. On the Stones tour when they had the monopoly, the charged all the traffic could bear. Now with Filmways thinking it had a monopoly, the shoe was on the other foot and the Stones' management screamed holdup! It was delightfully ironic.[21]

The Stones refused Filmways' terms but they were now in a bind: they had promised a free concert and now there was nowhere to hold it. However, the angels were smiling on the band: when Dick Carter, owner of Altamont Speedway, heard of the Sears Point debacle, he offered to host the concert for free. The Stones agreed: frantic, and thanks to Chip Monck, successful efforts were made to move equipment already in place at Sears Point, to Altamont Speedway near Livermore. Carter was accommodating because his speedway was in financial difficulties and he thought the festival would garner exposure and good publicity. However, the venue was not suitable to host a large-scale rock festival. For example, it didn't have enough car parking spaces; it was barren of vegetation, so there was no shelter or shade for the audience; there were no camping facilities; the lay of the land made it difficult to place the stage in a safe and visible location; and the speedway was littered with wrecked cars, old tyres, motor oil stains, and broken glass. Ironically, Woodstock Ventures' Michael Lang, who had volunteered his services to the festival team, and Grateful Dead manager Rock Scully took a helicopter trip over the proposed new venue. Scully was horrified by what he saw: Lang, however, declared, "This is perfect. We can do it here".[22] Selvin made a harsh judgement about Jagger's rejection of Filmways' terms: "Jagger refused to… negotiate the matter. He would not give up a nickel of the film's profits".[23] Selvin maintains that if Jagger had been flexible, the concert could have proceeded at Sears Point, a venue much more suitable for the concert than Altamont.

Jagger, though, felt he had been ripped off more than enough already in his career. Klein had left him almost penniless and this tour would set him right back on the financial path he wanted to follow. Profits from the concert film would offset the cost of running a free concert, with cash to spare. It would be a great finale to the tour: the Stones would bring the house down; the concert film would outshine the forthcoming Woodstock concert film, and it would also be released first; and the Stones' generosity in giving a "free" performance would demonstrate they were in touch with the free music activists. But most importantly, the tour was a financial success; a week after their performance at Altamont, Jagger flew to Geneva to deposit $1.8 million into the band's account.[24] Mission accomplished, on all fronts. Yet while financially lucrative for the Stones due to the release in 1970 of a tour film called *Gimme Shelter*, the festival did not offer the sort of grand finale that they had been hoping for. It would not be remembered for the music, but would rather earn its place in American cultural memory as a counterpoint to Woodstock in the worst possible way.

Violence was endemic at Altamont: as well as the aforementioned deaths, there were numerous acts of violence. For instance, soon after the Rolling Stones arrived by helicopter a man ran up to Mick Jagger, shouted "I hate you! I hate you!" and punched the singer in the face. Hells Angels, who had been hired to protect the stage, were responsible for many violent acts, and also largely to blame for the festival's dark mood. Some arrived by driving their motorcycles through the crowd and parking them in front of the stage. During Santana's show, Angels beat a young man unconscious for trying to reach the stage. Photographer John Young captured some of these unprovoked attacks and when he refused to hand over his film to an Angel, he was so savagely beaten that he had to have 13 stitches put in his head. While Jefferson Airplane played their hit "Somebody to Love", singer Marty Balin noticed the Angels assaulting a black man in the crowd. Balin tried to intervene and for this act of valour he was beaten unconscious. During the Crosby, Stills, Nash and Young set, Angels beat people with pool cues with many victims being stretchered away to medical tents. When the Rolling Stones took to the stage, their set was disrupted by violence which culminated in the death of 18-year-old Meredith Hunter, beaten and stabbed to death by the same Hells Angels who were employed to provide stage security. In addition to this violence, there were also major medical issues at the festival including drug overdoses and bad trips. In the aftermath of these events, *Rolling Stone* magazine detailed ten main reasons why the festival turned out badly as it did. These included poor planning and promotion, a last-minute venue change, an unsuitable location, failure to engage with neighbouring landowners, inadequate parking and sanitation, poor stage location and design, which failed to protect the stage from potential crowd surges, an inadequate and poor quality sound system, and, finally, hiring Hells Angels to provide security.[25]

There were, however, other factors which contributed to Altamont's macabre image, and these were mainly to do with the presence of the Rolling Stones. The band had developed a notorious reputation for outlaw behaviour, and their concerts were often marred by crowd violence. In addition, they had dabbled with Satanic imagery and lyrics: in 1967, for example, they released an album entitled *Their Satanic Majesties Request*; then, in 1968, they composed a song called "Sympathy for the Devil"; and they provided music for two films with Satanic themes, namely *Invocation of my Demon Brother* (1969) and *Lucifer Rising* (1972). Adding to this sense of macabre, band founder Brian Jones had recently died in mysterious circumstances. Questions arose as to whether the Stones' reputation somehow factored into events at Altamont. Despite the notoriety of these violent events, Altamont was not deemed a major cultural event: it was a west coast "happening" that went barely noticed in the rest of the United States. It is only when compared to Woodstock that it took on deeper symbolic meaning: cultural commentators could not resist declaring Woodstock the highpoint of the counterculture and Altamont its nadir.

Moreover, critics at the time offered different visions of what constituted a successful festival: on one side, for example, *Rolling Stone* magazine and artists such as the Grateful Dead saw these events as "be-ins", places where like-minded people could meet in peace and harmony to tune in, turn on, and drop out; in contrast, organisers and financiers of these events saw them as an opportunity quite simply to make money. For instance, Lang and Kornfeld only became aware of the venture capitalists Roberts and Rosenman after the latter duo had placed an advert in the *New York Times* announcing themselves as, "Young men with unlimited capital looking for interesting, legitimate investment opportunities and business propositions".[26] These simmering tensions — as to whether these festivals were genuine "happenings" of the counterculture, or whether they were, rather, a calculated attempt to make profit from the counterculture, or an uncomfortable mix of both — were exacerbated when both festivals appeared on film: events at Woodstock were captured in a 1970 documentary movie called *Woodstock*, while Altamont was filmed for the tour documentary *Gimme Shelter*. Much of the popular memory of the festivals draws from these films, but some critics excoriated them for financially exploiting the culture from which they derived, and also for misrepresenting events.

Festivals such as Woodstock and Altamont cannot be fully understood by examining them as individual events: the cultural and political context for such mass gatherings of music fans was rooted in both the major demographic changes of the post-World War Two "baby boom" era and the development of the counterculture in the late 1950s and 1960s. In the two decades before the 1960s began, the number of young people in the United States aged between 15 to 24 remained stable at around 23-24 million; by 1970 however, there were over 35 million young people in the United States in that age group. In 1955, 8.5 million Americans were aged between 18 to 21; in 1965 that number had risen to 12.1 million.[27] This baby boom provided the foot soldiers for both the Vietnam War and the counterculture that opposed it. Moreover, this vibrant young generation shattered the consensus that had existed in the 1950s: many young people, particularly those in university communities, helped to forge the budding movement of the New Left, which looked to American values of freedom and democracy, but found them undermined by rampant consumerism, political assassinations, and by the horrors of the Vietnam War. Students for a Democratic Society (SDS) — a socialist student activist movement — was one of the foundational organisations of the New Left. Its manifesto, the Port Huron Statement, set out an agenda for political activism in the 1960s. It criticised political leaders for failing to achieve international peace; it critiqued the Cold War and spoke of the threat of nuclear war and the arms race; it advocated civil rights legislation, economic equality, increased government welfare, including a "program against poverty"; and it proposed nonviolent civil disobedience to achieve these aims.

This vibrant political activism often went hand-in-hand with another unique and new phenomenon which shaped the sixties: recreational drug use. Timothy Leary, Ralph Metzner and Richard Alpert's *Psychedelic Experience* (1964) provided a kind of "instruction manual" in summarising the teaching of *The Tibetan Book of the Dead* to advise how to use psychedelic drugs like LSD. Together with Ken Kesey's "Acid Tests" — a series of parties/musical events, at which Kesey and his buddies, The Merry Pranksters, encouraged those present to take LSD and "graduate" to a higher level of consciousness — these two developments could be said to have kick started the counterculture into embracing drug use to explore altered states of consciousness and attain higher spiritual awareness. These ideas took physical manifestation as love-ins, be-ins and happenings — gatherings of people for political, social or artistic reasons, that usually involved some degree of audience participation. Indeed, as spirituality, drug use and antiwar sentiment featured prominently at Woodstock, the festival might be considered as the last great "happening" of the counterculture. One critic even attributes the absence of unrest at Woodstock "to the elevated level of experience that the Woodstock audience had with similar crowded situations" such as marches and demonstrations.[28] Richard Neville, founder of the influential London-based underground magazine *OZ*, reached a more practical conclusion: at music festivals, he claimed, "drugs are virtually essential to survival — how else could most people endure planned traffic jams, hard hitching, 72 pre-dominantly sleepless hours, rain, wind, bad food".[29]

Moreover, as events unfolded at Woodstock and Altamont in 1969, the Vietnam War had reached a stalemate. The previous year's Tet Offensive seemed to suggest that the war would not end in victory for the United States, and by late 1969, over 40,000 Americans had died in the war, surpassing the 33,629 American deaths in the Korean War[30]; and more to the point, burning anti-War sentiment was raging amongst student and youth communities. The Civil Rights Movement also reached a turning point at this time: it had achieved a number of major goals by the mid-1960s, but its near-consensus in aims and methodology fractured with the assassination in 1968 of Dr Martin Luther King, and the movement lost focus and much of its impact. For a time, louder, angrier voices of the Black Power Movement became more prominent, and groups like the Black Panthers increasingly came into conflict with the forces of law and order. At the same time, however, factions of the Civil Rights Movement merged with other pressing social movements — such as those for sexual freedom, gender equality, gay rights and free speech — to form a broad social agenda for change that, by the end of the decade, had transformed how young Americans viewed themselves and their society.[31] For many young people at this moment in 1969, the personal was the political, and many young Americans turned on, tuned in, and dropped out. In how they dressed, the length of their hair, the drugs they took, and their attitudes towards authority, they formed a counterculture that — according to the mythology — met at Woodstock in a "gathering of the tribes" for "three days of peace, music and love". Music journalist David Hepworth summed up the feelings of many of his generation: he considered that the Woodstock crowd seemed to possess "magical cohesion as a group … they were qualitatively different from a mass of people gathered to watch football or displays of marching".[32]

Perhaps this "magical cohesion" that Hepworth described can be rooted in the fact that at Woodstock and Altamont, music was a unique conduit for social engagement and performance. And significantly, it was *rock* music that occupied this role. The emergence of rock music as a significant musical conduit for political and social protest was quite a shift in American music history: traditionally this space had been filled by the genres of folk and blues, rather than rock and roll. For example, Woody Guthrie wrote and performed songs about the hardship working class Americans faced during the Great Depression of the 1930s;[33] and blues music was often a record of the suffering of African-Americans.[34] Furthermore, in the post-World War Two years, Americans rediscovered blues and folk music and it went through a revival. Even in the 1950s, when there was a conservative backlash against folk music because of its association with left-leaning politics, the music remained popular. Pete Seeger linked folk music's popularity with the opportunity it provided to discuss social and political issues: he pointed out that folk songs didn't stigmatise or deride the social groups that it focused on and that the genre offered opportunities to discuss current events.[35] Bob Dylan, one of the most popular folk artists in the 1960s, wrote songs about the threat of nuclear war and in support of the Civil Rights Movement.

He appeared at the Newport Folk Festival in 1963, 1964 and infamously in 1965 when the crowd jeered him for using an electric guitar. (At later concerts in England, Dylan was booed and called "Judas" for switching to an electric guitar.) Clearly, both artists and audiences enjoyed folk music at least in part due to its political connections, and in this particular instance, some fans thought Dylan had cheapened the discourse by introducing an electric guitar, an instrument associated with supposedly non-political rock music.

Moreover, it was not just that rock was deemed non-political in the 1950s and 1960s, but that it was primarily concerned with hedonism — with girls, cars and surfing being recurring themes. Yet by the late 1960s, there was a clear shift; rock music and politics had become inextricably linked, and at both Woodstock and Altamont, artists and audiences appreciated rock music as a vehicle for political and social criticism. Although its organisers never intended Woodstock to be a political demonstration, it in fact turned out to be one of the largest protests of the decade, with the Vietnam War being a main target of criticism. For example, at Woodstock, Country Joe McDonald performed "I-Feel-Like-I'm-Fixin'-to-Die Rag", a semi-comic song which captures the fatalistic attitude of many conscripted to go fight in Vietnam. In addition, Jimi Hendrix's powerful performance of the American national anthem at Woodstock has been likened to the sounds of battle, with the guitarist using distortion and manipulating his guitar's tremolo arm to imitate gunfire and explosions. Hendrix also incorporated the American military song "Taps" into the performance. Music authority Pete Fornatale describes Hendrix's rendition of the Star Spangled Banner at Woodstock as "Hendrix 'playing' the Vietnam War on the strings of his white solid-body electric guitar".[36] Like Woodstock, Altamont was not planned as a political statement, but it did attempt candidly to emulate the atmosphere of Woodstock. And in announcing it as a free concert (unlike Woodstock, which only became free after organisers ran out of time to set up ticket booths at venue entrances) it more overtly appealed to extant anti-capitalist feeling. Of the festival's performing artists, aside possibly from Jefferson Airplane's performance of the song "Volunteers", the Rolling Stones most openly embraced the politics of the time, with a set consisting of two explicitly political songs, "Street Fighting Man", apparently written about the 1968 antiwar protests that took place in London and Paris; and the apocalyptic "Gimme Shelter", which was influenced by the Vietnam War.

The British contribution to these festivals rarely merits much attention from cultural commentators and historians, which is surprising given the transatlantic musical scene that developed in the 1950s and 1960s, and the cross-pollination in festival culture that influenced British events such as Isle of Wight, Glastonbury, Windsor, Reading, Bath and Great Western. The "British Invasion" is a term used to explain the unparalleled success of bands such as The Beatles, The Rolling Stones, The Who, The Kinks and The Animals in the United States from around 1964 to 1967. Successful tours and numerous chart-topping hits marked British artists and music as a major force in the United States, with the Beatles and Rolling Stones forming a musical aristocracy that would greatly influence the burgeoning counterculture. By the time of Woodstock and Altamont, this demand had lost its initial frenzy but British artists were still very popular, as demonstrated by the line-up for both festivals in which British artists and music featured prominently.

At Woodstock, for example, there were performances by The Keef Hartley Band, The Incredible String Band, The Who, Ten Years After and Joe Cocker. Most notable of the British bands by their absence were The Beatles, who had stopped touring in 1966 to concentrate on studio work. However, on January 30, 1969, they did perform a short set of five songs on the roof of the Apple Building in London. This gave hope that an appearance at Woodstock might be possible, but the Apple gig turned out to be their last ever live band performance. The Beatles were, though, represented at Woodstock when Richie Havens and Joe Cocker performed cover versions of "With a Little Help from My Friends". Havens, in fact, played a trio of Beatles' songs, adding "Strawberry Fields Forever" and "Hey Jude" to his set. In addition, Crosby, Stills & Nash (and Young) performed Paul McCartney's composition, "Blackbird" as part of their set. That these notable artists would choose to perform Beatles songs in the short time they had on stage and at one of the most important and visible festivals of the era, indicates how influential and popular the British quartet were. Also absent from Woodstock, due to scheduling conflicts and other logistical and legal issues were the The Rolling Stones. By this point in their careers it was the Stones' notoriety that added to their attraction. Compared to The Beatles, they were the "bad boys" of the British Invasion, and by 1969 they were performing songs such as "Sympathy for the Devil" and a version of "Love in Vain" by Robert Johnson, an artist who had allegedly sold his soul to the devil, and whose influence on Keith Richards, in particular, seemed to suggest some kind of Satanic connection.[37]

The international aspect of the Woodstock festival was further enhanced by the presence on the bill of Indian classical musician Ravi Shankar, as well as the unscheduled on-stage address given by Indian holy man Swami Satchidananda. To understand these curiosities, one has to consider the American "turn to the East" in the 1950s and 1960s, and its fascination, in particular, with Indian music and spirituality. While the British attraction to India can be understood as a product of colonial familiarity, no such connection exists between the United States and India. Instead, a more positive relationship formed in these years as American youth looked to Indian spirituality as an alternative to organised American religion. Many followed the Hippie Trail to India and Nepal, while others converted to Buddhism, practiced yoga, or lit candles and incense and meditated as they imagined Indians might do. In 1965, a handful of Western artists began to incorporate Indian instruments and rhythms into their music, and within a few years they became a staple of psychedelic hippie music. Such was the impact of these events, claimed historian Theodore Roszak, that soon, "No anti-war demonstration would be complete without a hirsute, be-cowbelled contingent of holy men, bearing joss sticks and intoning the Hare Krishna"[38] and no self-respecting rock festival would be complete without a performance from Ravi Shankar (most famously at Monterey in 1967 and Woodstock in 1969), or a festival opening address by an Indian holy man such as Sri Swami Satchidananda, who led the Woodstock audience in a chant of "Hari Hari Hari Om".

After addressing the social, political, and musical context of Woodstock and Altamont, it is also worth asking how both festivals have been remembered: how has popular memory of these festivals been shaped and by what sources? Why do so many people remember Woodstock as a hallmark of the counterculture, but equate Altamont with the limitations of it? And how will this book contribute to and reshape some of the current understandings about Woodstock and Altamont? It is telling that, despite a combined audience of perhaps 800,000 fans, most people know about Woodstock and Altamont from viewing concert documentaries about the respective festivals. Each played a significant role in shaping the cultural memory of the events. As one scholar put it, Woodstock has been chronicled "so extensively in print, radio, television and film that it was as much a media event as it was a hippy happening... As a media event, it gave rise to an imagined community of such mythical proportions that it quickly eclipsed the individual memories of those people who had actually participated".[39] This has meant that some aspects of the festivals have been immortalised, while others overlooked, and this has been a consequence of almost every cinematic treatment of Woodstock: for instance, the documentary *Jimi Hendrix Live at Woodstock* (1994) situates Hendrix at the centre of events and so arguably overstates the importance of his performance.[40] The most recent evocation of Woodstock is Ang Lee's *Taking Woodstock* (2009), which provides a toothless and depoliticised version of the festival for the millennial generation. These films raise questions about the depiction and representation of historic events such as Woodstock and Altamont, particularly how they shape cultural memory, and the consequences of that.

It is testimony to the huge space that Woodstock and Altamont fill in the popular memory of the 1960s that, 50 years after they unfolded, they remain well-known events to the point that their names serve as shortcuts for opposing views of the decade; moreover, both festivals have generated numerous publications, albeit far more attention has been given to Woodstock than Altamont. In his book *Woodstock Scholarship: An Interdisciplinary Annotated Bibliography*, Jeffrey N. Gatten lists nearly 450 published books, book chapters, and academic articles about just one of those festivals, and by his own admission does not include literally thousands of newspaper and magazine sources.[41] Not as much has been written about Altamont, the lesser-known and perhaps culturally less significant event, but it has still generated a significant quantity of publications. There are a few basic genres that predominate in the published works. These include personal memoirs, monographs dedicated to each individual festival, monographs about festivals in general, and edited collections of the three categories listed above. Many are released or re-released to coincide with significant anniversaries of the events.

In the memoirs category, most prominent are Michael Lang's *The Road to Woodstock* (New York: HarperCollins, 2009); Joel Rosenberg, John Roberts and Robert Pilpel's *Young Men With Unlimited Capital* (New York: Harcourt Brace, 1974), which was re-released as an anniversary edition in 1989 to coincide with that year's 20th anniversary events; and Abbie Hoffman's *Woodstock Nation* (New York: Vintage, 1969). All offer first-hand accounts and are valuable resources. Lang's work is probably the most useful as he also offers some analysis of the 1994 and 1999 anniversary events. Hoffman's memoir is perhaps unexpectedly honest: he comments on his mixed feelings about rock music, as well as his unsuccessful attempts to pick up women. Its value now is mainly as a historical curiosity, with Hoffman rapping about "Fascist clock time", "culture vultures" and "bad acid". As such, while it evokes the era in which it was written, it's also fairly inaccessible to modern readers as an analysis of that time period.

In the category of monographs about music festivals are works such as Marley Brant's *Join Together: Forty Years of the Rock Music Festival* (New York: Backbeat, 2008) and Robert Santelli's *Aquarius Rising: The Rock Festival Years* (New York: Dell, 1980). The former is a rather mundane account of the era; the latter is much more authoritative and insightful. Santelli was a music journalist with an eye for detail and his work is clearly the product of extensive research. Indeed, music journalists rather than historians, often provide the best writing about musicians and musical events. *Barefoot in Babylon: The Creation of the Woodstock Music Festival, 1969* (New York: Viking, 1979) by Robert Stephen Spitz is another example of excellent journalism, with the author providing well-researched analysis of the planning and execution of the Woodstock festival. Andy Bennett has also edited a collection of essays entitled *Remembering Woodstock* (Aldershot: Ashgate, 2004). The essays are informative but not particularly inspiring: they are aimed at an academic audience and, like many of these collections, there is some insightful analysis (for example, of contemporary press reports) but an overall lack of focus. The same can be said of Ian Inglis's edited collection, *Performance and Popular Music: History Place and Time* (Aldershot: Ashgate, 2006), which has an interesting essay by Norma Coates on Altamont, and another by Mike Daley about Jimi Hendrix at Woodstock.

Oral histories are useful resources, and Joel Makower's *Woodstock: The Oral History* (London: Sidgewick & Jackson, 1989) is perhaps the most authoritative example from this genre; it is a book of interviews stitched together, usually in single-paragraph chunks, and released in time for Woodstock's 20th anniversary. It is serious and enjoyable but something of a missed opportunity: Makower's stance is "if you want to know what happened, ask the organisers", and this type of institutional approach, while quite revealing in itself, offers little attempt to represent the ordinary festival goers' experience. Pete Fornatale's *Back to the Garden: The Story of Woodstock* (New York: Simon & Schuster, 2009) adopts a similar template, with lengthy quotation linked together by author comments that provide some context. In *Woodstock Revisited* (Avon Ma.:Simon & Schuster, 2009), Susan Reynolds edits a collection of stories/memories from audience members; this offers an interesting but scattergun account, with little analysis even though the author was present at Woodstock. This is a limited effort by a non-historian, but it's also enthusiastic and provides valuable first-hand accounts of the festival. There are also some illuminating collections of photographs of Woodstock, most notably two books by Elliott Landy, who was the first official photographer at the festival (see his books *Woodstock Dream* (teNeues Italy, 1999) and *Woodstock 1969: the first festival* (Horsham: Ravette, 1994)). Yet perhaps the best photo collection is Mike Evans and Paul Kingsbury's *Woodstock: Three Days that Rocked the World*, which is lavishly illustrated with pictures and memorabilia but also offers lively and provocative commentary. In contrast, Richard Havers and Richard Evans' *Woodstock Chronicles: 3 Days of Peace & Music* (London: Compendium, 2009) lacks analysis and is mainly a picture book.

In contrast to the variety of books on Woodstock, relatively few have been written about the Altamont festival. Jonathan Eisen's *Altamont: Death of Innocence in the Woodstock Nation* (Avon, 1970) is a collection of essays and interviews and was published soon after the event; it offers some valuable first-hand accounts. *Rolling Stone* magazine provided one of the most-quoted reports about Altamont. Provocatively titled, "The Rolling Stones Disaster at Altamont: Let It Bleed", and published in January 1970, the article placed the blame for violence at the festival solely on the Rolling Stones and on Mick Jagger in particular. Interestingly, in his 2010 memoir, the Stones' road manager, Sam Cutler, took issue with *Rolling Stone*'s interpretation of Altamont: in his *You Can't Always Get What You Want: My Life with the Rolling Stones, the Grateful Dead, and Other Wonderful Reprobates* (Toronto: ECW Press, 2010), Cutler might have been forgiven for excoriating the Rolling Stones for abandoning him to deal with the aftermath of the festival, which included Cutler taking part in a very tense meeting with the Hell's Angels. Instead, however, he remained loyal to the band and claimed they weren't responsible for events at Altamont.

Also on the topic of the Rolling Stones at Altamont, photo-journalist Ethan A. Russell, who accompanied the Stones on their 1969 tour of the United States, compiled some vivid photographs of the festival in his book *Let It Bleed: The Rolling Stones, Altamont, and the End of the Sixties* (London: Hachette, 2009). While the photographs capture a thrilling evocation of life on the road, as well as the excitement of various tour performances, the book hardly adds to extant knowledge of events at Altamont, perhaps because Russell does not have enough critical distance from his subject matter. Rich Cohen's *The Sun & the Moon & the Rolling Stones* (London: Hachette, 2016) offers a chronological retelling of the Rolling Stones story, including a chapter on the 1969 tour that reiterates various aspects of Altamont but also offers some new points-of-view based on interviews conducted by the author. It is well-written and knowledgeable, and Cohen never indulges in the kind of hagiography that undermines many accounts of the Stones. Perhaps the most informative account of Altamont is offered by music journalist Joe Selvin in his book *Altamont: The Rolling Stones, the Hells Angels, and the Inside Story of Rock's Darkest Day* (New York: HarperCollins, 2016). Selvin offers an extensively-researched account of events at Altamont, with insightful analysis of the preparation, planning, developments, and aftermath of the festival. He emphasises that there was enough blame to go around for the horrific violence on display at Altamont, but reserves particular ire for the Rolling Stones' disinterest in real-life, practical concerns such as security and crowd safety.

This brief bibliographical discussion provides indicative examples of how Woodstock and

Altamont have thus far been analysed and remembered. This book, *Woodstock and Altamont: the Music Festivals that defined the 1960s*, is unique in being the first historical monograph that considers Woodstock and Altamont equally. In so doing, it aims to return the discussion back to the musical context in which these festivals were first understood. However, to fully understand this musical context, it is also necessary to situate the festivals into wider social, cultural, and political frameworks. To achieve this, the book is drawn mainly from primary sources — first-hand, direct accounts such as newspaper reports, eyewitness accounts and, particularly in this instance, underground and alternative newspapers. This not only gives the reader access to authoritative sources from the time period, but also provides a vivid evocation of the era — the argot of the counterculture, as well as that generation's fears and hopes. Underground and alternative newspapers reached their peak in the 1960s as mainstream news sources became less credible. For the most part, this was due to the Vietnam War, when news reports often conflicted with eye-witness testimony of returning soldiers. Many young people turned to alternative media sources for what they deemed to be more credible information. Such was the popularity of these underground and alternative newspapers that by the end of the decade almost every city and university town had an underground publication of some sort. In 1970, journalism lecturer Robert J. Glessing compiled a list of 457 underground newspapers, with a readership of almost five million.[42] In appealing mainly to a youthful audience, the papers' subject matter reflected the concerns of that audience: these included topical political issues such as civil rights, gender equality, gay rights, rampant consumerism, and the military draft, as well as cultural matters such as sex, drugs and music. Secondary sources — those that analyse, evaluate and synthesise primary source material — are used here mainly to explore different interpretations of the era's events.

The book is organised thematically, with three chapters each devoted to Woodstock and to Altamont. In part one on Woodstock, my aim is not to re-tell the chronology of the festival in minute detail — this has been done many times before — but rather to look at aspects of Woodstock that have not previously been given much attention. Chapter One begins by exploring how a cross section of specific groups such as women, African-Americans, and political radicals "experienced" Woodstock — how they were treated, what the festival meant to them and how they coped with those experiences. Chapter Two explores international aspects of Woodstock, focusing on British and Indian performers. This chapter provides musical and cultural context for these performances, examines their critical reception and impact, and reflects on the consequences for their careers of their Woodstock appearance. Chapter Three considers the role of the Woodstock film in shaping how the event has been remembered. In the second section of the book focussing on Altamont, I consider in more depth some aspects of the festival which have been either overlooked or deserve closer scrutiny. Chapter Four considers the decision to use the Hells Angels as "security" at Altamont. This chapter looks at the relationship that developed between the Hells Angels and the northern California music scene, and will then show that the decision to use the Angels as "security" was not unprecedented, and that although it is now deemed a seemingly obvious error in judgement, it was not quite so clear cut in 1969. Chapter Five considers the role of the Rolling Stones in events at Altamont, and explores particularly their reputation as a magnet for violence, and also crucially their supposed links to dark magic and even Devil worship (which led many to believe that Altamont was a pre-planned Satanic Black Mass on an epic scale). The final chapter focuses on the tour documentary *Gimme Shelter* (1970), particularly the methods, aims, and motivations of film makers Albert and David Maysles. The Maysles brothers made particular claims as to *Gimme Shelter*'s objectivity, which drew criticism not just from film critics but also from the wider counterculture community who saw in the film elements of exploitation as well as whitewashing the Rolling Stones of any blame for how the event transpired. This chapter unpicks narratives on both sides of the debate. A final concluding section reflects on the enduring influence and meaning of Woodstock and Altamont.

Having said what the book attempts to achieve, it is necessary also to set some boundaries. For example, this book won't retell the story of these festivals in minute detail, nor will it provide encyclopaedic details of every song, performer, and occurrence. As indicated above, there are plenty of sources that already do that, and no doubt more will appear in the 50th anniversary year of 2019. My aim is to provide such information only when it is relevant to my analysis and helpful to the reader. (In addition, some basic facts can be found in the appendix.) Furthermore, this is not a photo book: a picture may indeed be worth a thousand words, but not if that picture is so common and has been seen so often that it has lost its impact. But what I will do is look afresh at these festivals and try to answer some nagging and rather intriguing questions: why, for example, did so many commentators make reference to the supernatural to make sense of Meredith Hunter's death at Altamont, to the point where some even maintained his death was a ritual sacrifice? Why were Hell's Angels hired to provide security? Why was Woodstock "blessed" by an Indian holy man? Why were African-American musicians and female artists under-represented in the Woodstock line-up, for a festival that has been understood typically as the counterculture's idea of a future utopian America? And what is the connection between Charlton Heston's schlocky science fiction/horror film *The Omega Man* (1971), Woodstock and Altamont?

Buy the ticket, take the ride...

[1] Robert Santelli, *Aquarius Rising: the rock festival years* (New York: Dell, 1980), p. 2.

[2] Sean O'Hagan, "The year of living dangerously", *The Observer*, May 17, 2009. Available online at: https://www.theguardian.com/music/2009/may/17/woodstock-altamont-40th-anniversary-hippie-generation

[3] "The '60s Decade of Tumult and Change", *Life Magazine*, Dec 26, 1969.

[4] David Paul Proctor, *A Critical History of American Rock Journalism in Popular Magazines, 1955-1976*. MSc University of Utah, 1981, p. 24.

[5] Christopher Sandford, *Polanski* (London: Century, 2007) p. 179.

[6] Norma Coates, "If anything, blame Woodstock. The Rolling Stones: Altamont, December 6, 1969" in *Performance and Popular Music: History Place and Time*. Ian Inglis, ed., (Aldershot: Ashgate, 2006), pp. 58-69. At p. 59.

[7] Joel Selvin, *Altamont: The Rolling Stones, the Hells Angels, and the Inside Story of Rock's Darkest Day* (New York: HarperCollins, 2016), pp. 15-17.

[8] Miller Francis Jr., "Talkin 'bout My Generation", *Great Speckled Bird*, Vol 3, Issue 24, Jun 15, 1970), pp. 12-13. At p. 13.

[9] "Zero Buck", *NOLA Express*, Issue 37, Aug 29 – Sep 11, 1969, p. 5.

[10] "Stop! Look! What's that sound?", *The Rag*, Vol 3, Issue 28, Aug 25, 1969, p. 5.

[11] Michael Hill, Untitled review of 1970 Atlanta Pop Festival at Byron. *Great Speckled Bird*, Vol 4, Issue 29, Jul 20, 1970, pp. 12-13. At p.12.

[12] The impression given by these critics was that the Stones were gouging fans and thereby deterring the poorest from seeing the band. In the run-up to Altamont, San Francisco promoter Bill Graham joined the chorus criticising the Stones. Graham, of course, had his own interests in mind: he was unhappy with the band's management after they refused to let him promote the whole tour. Instead, he promoted only three gigs, two at Oakland, plus one in San Diego. His contract with the Stones gave the band 65 percent of gross profits from each concert, and he stood to lose out if, in future, the Stones' new financial model of upfront financial deposits was copied by other artists. His contract with the band would still make for a tidy profit but rumours had been circulating that he was unhappy with these financial arrangements and angry at Jagger in particular. Graham had also brawled with Sam Cutler onstage at the Oakland gig and swore at Jagger in the dressing room afterwards. It seems clear Graham used the issue of ticket prices to exact revenge on the band (See Jerry Hopkins, "Kiss Kiss Flutter Flutter Thank You Thank You", *Rolling Stone*, Dec 13, 1969, pp. 1, 6, 54; and Selvin, *Altamont*, pp. 68-69.).

[13] Rich Cohen, *The Sun & the Moon & the Rolling Stones* (London: Hachette, 2016), p. 231.

[14] See Jerry Hopkins, "The Stones Tour: 'Is That A Lot?'", *Rolling Stone*, Nov 15, 1969, pp. 16-17; and Coates, "If anything, blame Woodstock", p. 61. These sources offer some contradictory evidence about ticket prices. Hopkins states, for example, that VIP tickets at the LA Forum gig were $12.50. For accuracy, I have referred also to concert advertising posters on Google images.

[15] For example, Jim Russmiller and Steve Wolf were the promoters of the Stones' LA Forum shows on 8 November. These were matinee and evening performances on the same day. Russmiller and Wolf estimated the band's 65% cut of the profits for that day's work would amount to approximately $170,000. The Stones' paid their support acts around $1200 each, which amounts to less than $10,000 in total ("No Satisfaction", *San Francisco Good Times* Vol 2, Issue 43, Nov 6, 1969, p. 5).

[16] "No Satisfaction", *San Francisco Good Times*, Vol 2, Issue 43, Nov 6, 1969, p. 5.

[17] Coates, "If anything, blame Woodstock", p. 59.

[18] "Free Stone Bash Here", *Berkeley Tribe*, Dec 5-11, 1969, p. 5.

[19] Ralph J. Gleason, "Stones' Plans for Free S.F. Concert", *San Francisco Chronicle*, Nov 24, 1969, p. 46; Ralph J. Gleason, "A Few Guesses on Rolling Stones", *San Francisco Chronicle*, Nov 28, 1969, p. 50;

[20] "Free Show Come Celebrate", *Los Angeles Free Press*, Vol 6, Issue 279, Nov 21-28, 1969, p. 10.

[21] Ralph Gleason, *Los Angeles Free Press* Vol 6, Issue 282, Dec 12, 1969, p. 33.
[22] Selvin, *Altamont* p. 115.
[23] Selvin, *Altamont* p. 112.
[24] Selvin, *Altamont*, p. 239.
[25] Lester Bangs, et al. "The Rolling Stones Disaster at Altamont: Let It Bleed", *Rolling Stone*, Jan 21, 1970.
[26] Joel Rosenman, John Roberts and Robert Pilpel, *Young Men With Unlimited Capital* (New York: bantam, 1989), p. 9.
[27] M. J. Heale, *The Sixties in America* (Edinburgh University Press, 2001), p. 134.
[28] Michael Ethen, "The Festival is Dead, Long Live the 'Festival'", *Journal of Popular Music Studies*, Vol 26, Issue 2–3 (2014), pp. 251–267. At p. 252.
[29] Richard Neville, "Stanley Baker's Barbed Wire Circus", *International Times* 132 (1972), pp. 26-31. At p. 28.
[30] Max Hastings, *The Korean War* (New York: Simon & Schuster, 1988), p.329.
[31] See, for example, George Lipsitz, "Dancing in the Dark: Who Needs the Sixties?", in *American Studies in a Moment of Danger* (University of Minnesota, 2001), pp. 57-82; and Ed Weedon's "Painting it Black" *American Studies Today* 16 (2007), pp. 14-17.
[32] David Hepworth, 1971: *Never a Dull Moment* (London: Bantam Press, 2016), p. 168.
[33] Will Kaufman, Woody Guthrie, *American Radical* (University of Illinois Press, 2011).
[34] Ron Eyerman and Scott Barretta, "From the 30s to the 60s: The Folk Music Revival in the United States", *Theory and Society*, Vol 25, Issue 4 (1996), pp. 501-43.
[35] Richard Crawford, *America's Musical Life: A History* (New York & London: Norton, 2005), p. 745.
[36] Pete Fornatale, *Back to the Garden: The Story of Woodstock* (New York: Simon & Schuster, 2009), p. 270.
[37] James Miller, *Flowers in the Dustbin: The Rise of Rock and Roll, 1947-1977* (New York: Simon & Schuster, 1999), p. 277.
[38] Theodore Roszak, *The Making of a Counter Culture; Reflections on the Technocratic Society and Its Youthful Opposition* (Berkeley, Los Angeles & London: University of California Press, 1995), p. 140.
[39] Marios Elles, "Chinese Whispers: Jimi Hendrix, Fame and 'The Star Spangled Banner'" *49th Parallel* 17, Spring 2006. Unpaginated. Available online at: "https://49thparalleljournal.org/"https://49thparalleljournal.org/
[40] Elles, "Chinese Whispers".
[41] Jeffrey N. Gatten, *Woodstock Scholarship: An Interdisciplinary Annotated Bibliography* (Open Book Publishers, 2016).
[42] Robert J. Glessing, *The Underground Press in America* (Bloomington and London: Indiana University Press, 1970), p. 178.

Chapter 1: Woodstock Experiences

The truth, alas, about what happened at Woodstock is in the eye of the beholder.

Abbie Hoffman[1]

As stated in the advertisement in the *North Carolina Anvil* in July 1969, "3 Music Festivals Planned for August". The first event mentioned was the Atlanta Pop Festival, to be held from August 1st to 3rd, featuring "everyone from the Airplane to the Mothers". The second was the Ann Arbor Blues Festival, featuring the cream of contemporary American blues bands, along with some older artists who had been "rediscovered" in the 1960s; among these were distinguished musicians like BB King, Howlin' Wolf, Muddy Waters, John Lee Hooker, Big Mama Thornton, and Son House. The third and final festival was one advertised for Wallkill, upstate New York, which would feature the Jimi Hendrix Experience, The Who, Joe Cocker, Joan Baez, and Blood Sweat & Tears; a further attraction would be "Round-the-clock poetry, music, craft and theatre workshops". This last festival was called the Woodstock Music and Art Fair.[2]

In hindsight, it is notable that the *Anvil* gave no special prominence to Woodstock, which of course turned out to be the major musical and cultural event of the year, and perhaps even the decade. It featured many of the major artists of the day, and it attracted a massive audience of around 400,000, many more than the organisers planned for. That these artists and fans still seemingly lived up to the festival's motto, "3 days of peace and music", was a major achievement for America's youthful counterculture. It was, however, an achievement not universally acknowledged or celebrated at the time. As the *Anvil* advertisement indicates, Woodstock was not considered a special occasion, given that it was one of many outdoor festivals held that year. Moreover, the shift towards larger music festivals was not welcomed by everyone. For example, left wing political radicals saw them as "bread and circuses" — entertainment to occupy the minds of young people and distract them from political and revolutionary activities. On the other hand, if those radicals were involved in the organisation of music festivals, like, for example, those occurring regularly in Golden Gate Park in San Francisco, they would then offer an opportunity for political activism. The organisers of the Woodstock festival made every effort to appear on the side of the radicals, while at the same time trying to keep them at arm's length.

The idea came originally from Michael Lang and Artie Kornfeld. Lang was an enterprising music manager and concert promoter, while Kornfeld worked for Capitol Records. They had it in mind to build a recording studio in Woodstock, Lang's hometown since 1968. The studio would also act as a retreat for musicians. This studio/retreat would benefit from its pastoral location, which tallied with the "back-to-the-garden" ruralism of the hippie movement. It helped also that some prominent musicians resided in Woodstock, including Bob Dylan and The Band. Lang and Kornfeld pitched the idea to two venture capitalists, Joel Rosenman and John Roberts. In hoping to generate investment opportunities. While there is no evidence that Lang and Kornfeld saw the advertisement, it did raise the profiles of Rosenman and Roberts as potential investors, and they came to the attention of Lang and Kornfeld through word of mouth. Initially however, Rosenman and Roberts were unenthusiastic: they considered that there was no pressing demand for another recording studio, nor was it an idea that particularly excited them. However, when Lang mentioned that the enterprise would be partially funded by a music festival, Rosenman and Roberts began to take an interest. When the cash figures were presented to him, Roberts was completely sold: "We can make a goddamn fortune!" he exclaimed.[3] Together, the men formed a company called Woodstock Ventures, and began the long and complicated process of organising a music festival.

Lang and Kornfeld knew that publicity would be key: choosing the name of the festival was vitally important if the message was to reach the intended target audience of young, hip music fans. After some debate, Woodstock Ventures settled for the following nomenclature: "Woodstock Music & Art Fair presents An Aquarian Exposition in Wallkill, N.Y. 3 Days of Peace and Music".[4] In calling it a fair rather than a rock or pop festival, the organisers hoped to avoid potential local opposition. In addition, the 1967 Fantasy Fair and Magic Mountain Music Festival at Mount Tamalpais, Marin County, California, demonstrated the value of providing activities for the audience between musical acts. Moreover, in declaring Woodstock an "Aquarian Exposition", the promoters probably intended to link the festival to the Broadway music show *Hair*, which opened in April 1968 and was hugely popular. Its opening song was entitled "Aquarius". Lastly, the phrase "3 Days of Peace & Music" not only linked the festival to ongoing antiwar activities, but also suggested what in today's language would be called a "safe space" where attendees could do their own thing without fear of the police violence that marred the last big "happening" in Chicago in August 1968. "Everyone thought that it would prove itself the slickest avant garde, hip capitalist venture ever launched", claimed *The Rag*, not entirely sarcastically.[5]

To help raise expectations that the festival might live up to its lofty title, Woodstock Ventures deployed two different promotional poster designs. The first, by David Byrd, was based on Jean Auguste Dominique Ingres' *La Source* (1820-1856). It featured an artistic rendering of a naked woman pouring water from a jug balanced on her shoulder, and was bordered with illustrations of cupids, hearts and flowers. This poster provided only basic information about the festival, including the name, location and dates. A second promotional poster by Arnold H. Skolnick featured what would become the iconic image of Woodstock, a white dove perched on the neck of a guitar, against a red background. Unlike Byrd's design, Skolnick's included the most up-to-date lineup of artists, including their order of performance on each day. Thirty five thousand copies of this poster were printed, and numerous advertisements featuring this design appeared in the underground press, along with details of the planned arts show, crafts bizarre, workshops, and amenities.[6] The adverts also promised "Hundreds of Acres to Roam on — Walk around for three days without seeing a skyscraper or a traffic light. Fly a kite, sun yourself. Cook your own food and breathe unspoiled air".[7] This rural, "back-to-the garden" vision was clearly an important selling point if the advertising was to reach its intended target audience of those young people who had largely rejected the 9-5 lifestyle, were anti-consumerist (in ideology if not entirely in practice), and who dreamed of dropping out. "There was to be enough space to allow the children of urban Amerika to lounge about in pastoral solitude", *The Rag* observed.[8] Nothing was left to chance: even the tickets were decorated with stars, crescents and rainbows in an attempt to lure in the Aquarians, although more practically, these designs also served as an anti-forgery measure to protect profits.[9]

Despite the promoters' careful calculations to woo Aquarians, in the run up to Woodstock a number of articles appeared in the underground press that either struck a note of caution or were openly cynical about the forthcoming festival. For example, in a piece entitled "Woodstock not all roses; poses thorny problems", Mark Kramer argued that rock music was a capitalist enterprise, and that music companies marketed their product to young people by adopting and using their hip language. He linked this to the military industrial complex and Vietnam War. "What has this got to do with Woodstock?", he asked. "You might go there and have a fine time, but just remember that someone is making a million on your fun, and it isn't the performers, many of whom come for little or nothing". Kramer pointed out that while Mike Lang and Artie Kornfeld looked and talked hip, the partners had invested heavily in Woodstock and were expecting "big returns from ticket sales, a cut of concession sales, and also from selling T.V. and movie rights".[10] Other commentators, like David Walley, wondered about the potential for violence at large festivals in general and at Woodstock in particular: in an article about the Newport Folk Festival, he noted that "this has already been the year of tear gassings at the Newport, California festival, of riotings and some destruction at the Newport Jazz Festival... the huge brontosaurus monster festival Woodstock [is] coming up [and] town fathers everywhere within one hundred miles [are] out of their minds with fear".[11] Writing in Washington D.C.'s *Quicksilver Times,* Terry Becker raised concerns about Wes Pomeroy, the man Lang and Kornfeld hired to oversee security at Woodstock. Becker was especially concerned about Pomeroy's law enforcement background. Calling Pomeroy a "mercenary", Beaker warned, "Know who you patronize".[12] These views, ranging from the disinterest of the *North Carolina Anvil*, Kramer's concerns about the promoters' capitalist motives, Walley's fear of potential violence, and Becker's cynical take on the employment of an ex-cop to oversee security at a "hip" festival, suggest that a substantial section of the counterculture — the very people one might assume would be most supportive of an event such as Woodstock — viewed it with suspicion and even hostility.

Given that debate within the counterculture was being thrashed out in the underground press even *before* Woodstock had taken place, it is illuminating to consider how Woodstock attendees and performers actually "experienced" the festival itself. So in the pages that follow, we will consider how different sections of this diverse, vibrant counterculture community experienced and related to the festival, and the impact they had on shaping its outcome.

Abbie Hoffman and the Yippies

Among the most vocal critics of the idea of the Woodstock festival was Abbie Hoffman. The Brandeis and Berkeley graduate had been involved in the Civil Rights Movement in the early 1960s but as American involvement in Vietnam deepened, Hoffman shifted his focus towards antiwar protests.[13] In early 1968, Hoffman, Jerry Rubin and a few other like-minded individuals formed the Youth International Party, with members calling themselves "Yippies" — political hippies. Their central tenet was that of the "New Nation", an idea based on cooperation rather than the competition between individuals that a capitalist economy required. In August 1968, Hoffman and the Yippies planned to picket the Democratic National Convention in Chicago but were prevented from doing so by Mayor Richard Daley and the brutal actions of the Chicago police. In its aftermath, Hoffman and six other organisers, all of whom were prominent political enemies of the state, were arrested and charged with offences under the 1968 Civil Rights Act, which stipulated penalties of up to five years in prison for anyone travelling or using interstate communication "to organize, promote, encourage, participate in, or carry on a riot".[14] The subsequent trial of the "Chicago Seven" became one of the most infamous events of the 1960s. The group was charged in March 1969 and the trial was scheduled to begin in September, so these events framed Hoffman's appearance at Woodstock and influenced his thinking. For example, during the Chicago protests, Hoffman had helped organise the "Festival of Life" music event not just to entertain protesters, but also because he saw the power of music to bring people together and to liberate minds. He claimed that rock groups "occupy such a special place in the revolution" and that they "provide the electrical energy needed to shake the walls of the city".[15] As one Yippie explained, music would help make this a Festival of Life instead of a "Convention of Death".[16]

Of course for the Festival of Life to liberate minds it had to have the right kind of music, not just rock and roll, which one underground press journalist called "the music of the youth international scene",[17] but also bands which either had a political agenda or who were at least acceptable among the underground — White Panther Bob Rudnick called them "I-will-not-kiss-your-fucking-flag" bands.[18] So the Yippies invited Country Joe & the Fish, and The Fugs, both of which were known for their antiwar stance, as well as other notable counterculture artists such as Pete Seeger, Arlo Guthrie and Phil Ochs.[19] The City of Chicago refused a permit for the festival and while around thirty rock groups had originally been scheduled to appear, in the end only the Detroit-based band MC5, managed by John Sinclair, turned up and performed.[20] Nevertheless, the intent of the Festival of Life, which was to celebrate and demonstrate the "new culture" envisaged by the Yippies, and "alternative lifestyle" of the hippies, in some ways prefigures the Woodstock ideal. The primary purpose of the Festival of Life was, however, political, as evidenced by the list of performers, as well as speakers such as Tom Hayden, Rennie Davis, and Allen Ginsberg.[21] So when Hoffman learned that Woodstock would adopt many of the characteristics of the Festival of Life, but with no political aim, and no time allocated for political messages or activities, he was determined somehow to insert the Yippie agenda into Woodstock.

To begin with, Hoffman met with Jeff Shiro, the editor of the New York-based underground newspaper RAT: *Subterranean News,* before confronting Michael Lang. As Shiro recalls, Hoffman asked Lang for $80,000, which he would use to secure "help with medical, a bad trips tent, free food, a place for movement city and free buses from New York". Lang became angry, accusing Hoffman of using blackmail tactics. Eventually, however, Hoffman prevailed, and Lang offered $60,000, which Shiro claimed was used for the purposes mentioned: "We bought sack after massive sack of brown rice for the Hog Farms free food kitchen, arranged the movement medical team… to provide services, leased some old hippie buses for free rides, rented a huge circus like tent for all the movement organisation to use, and even brought a printing press"[22] A slightly different, perhaps less noble version of events was provided by Ted Franklin in *Liberation News Service:*

Abbie Hoffman and a number of other street and political associations from New York's Lower East Side called the fair's promoters to demand that the people whose culture was being exploited get a share of the proceeds. The festival officials, not wanting any trouble, were happy to fork over $10,000-$20,000 immediately. The money was divided up between numerous movement organizations for transportation and equipment needed to establish a movement presence at the fair. The Yippies, the Conspiracy, SDS, MDS, Alternative U., the Crazies, the Motherfuckers, Movement Movers..., N.Y. Women's Liberation, Newsreel and the Rat all got a piece of the pie.[23]

The festival promoters reserved an area for these activists well away from the stage, but placed close to Hog Farm and arts and craft events: this became known as "Movement City" and consisted mainly of a large tent from which activists could distribute underground magazines. This was a similar set up to the 1967 Monterey Festival, which provided a booth for the Underground Press Syndicate.[24] Opinions vary as to Movement City's impact: a report in *Liberation News Service* claimed that Movement City was limited to "an area only 30 yards square" and that the "political presence" that the Movement envisaged at the festival was "relegated to being just another sandal-maker or hot dog stand".[25] While *San Francisco Good Times* praised Movement City for providing booths for the underground press, the White Panthers, SDS, Women's

Liberation, and Meher Baba (Pete Townshend's guru), the paper revealed that "few of the crowd showed any interest", preferring instead to direct their energies towards the Hog Farm, which the paper championed as "Movement City in action".[26] By Sunday night, one concert attendee said the tent was still filled with undistributed stacks of magazines, and was being used as a makeshift sleeping area.[27]

In spite of the uncertainty over the legacy of Movement City, after Woodstock, Hoffman wrote a piece in the *Los Angeles Free Press* in which he excoriated his critics. In this lament, he defended Movement City, criticised the promoters for exploiting the audience, and pointed to the elitism of the rock star performers. Hoffman claimed that activists helped arrange lawyers for around 1000 people who were arrested on their way to Woodstock. He claimed that Movement City activists, especially those who were veterans of Chicago 1968, organised hospitals and first aid centres at Woodstock. While Hog Farm helped those on bad trips, the first aid centres established by Movement City activists treated hundreds of people with medical injuries. Hoffman claimed that the promoters had made no provision for this and it was an entirely volunteer effort by activists.[28]

Perhaps Hoffman was frustrated by the lack of recognition Movement City received for its efforts at Woodstock. Moreover, there was one particular issue that burned him at the time, and that was the incarceration of White Panther John Sinclair: and Hoffman had been hoping to use the Woodstock Festival as a platform to raise awareness of Sinclair's plight. Sinclair had been arrested earlier that year for offering two marijuana joints to an undercover police officer, and was sentenced to ten years in jail for this minor offence, a punishment that caused outrage in the political side of the counterculture movement. Hoffman claimed that he had extracted a promise from Michael Lang to donate ten percent of the profits from the Woodstock movie towards Sinclair's defence. According to Hoffman, Lang agreed to announce this from the stage, but when he reneged on this promise, Hoffman took matters into his own hands, and took to the stage during The Who's performance to make the point for him. Hoffman's intervention immediately drew the ire of Who guitarist Pete Townshend: already high after accidentally consuming a hallucinogenic substance, Townshend screamed at Hoffman to get off the stage before smashing him over the head with his Gibson SG guitar. Luckily for Hoffman, the SG was light in comparison to the solid-body Gibson Les Paul which, until the previous year, had been Townshend's preferred stage instrument. Hoffman escaped with just a headache and bruised pride.

Journalist Ellen Sander was with Hoffman immediately before he ascended to the stage. She first met Hoffman in December 1967 and they were on friendly terms, so when she saw him at the corner of the stage, she made her way over to him and they embraced. Both were on acid: Sander was in ebullient mood, but Hoffman looked "grim and bewildered". It did not take long for them to start arguing over the meaning and impact of Woodstock. "This is horseshit... There's no morality here", Hoffman proclaimed, before declaring himself the conscience of the Movement.[29] In response, Sander called Hoffman a "megalomaniac" and articulated what would become the standard, mythical view of Woodstock: "This is a glimpse of what's to come, this is what is what is going to change the generational resentment, not Molotov cocktails".[30] Later, Sander penned an open letter to Hoffman in which she claimed violence was counterproductive and that Woodstock was a "revolutionary crucible", its mantra of "peace and music" a new and powerful force for change. She told Hoffman that Woodstock was:

far beyond the lame kind of political activism you proselytize. You don't kill a legislator because you hate anti-marijuana laws, just smoke dope. You don't create riot situations to protest establishment repression, you share and dance and get high for three days. Or ninety days. Or forever. Abbie, the age of politics is over. The revolution is finished. It served its purpose and its irrelevant now. To hit out with violence is just plain stupid, you'll get your upraised fist shot off. The only way you get freedom is by deciding that you're free. If you fight authority, you acknowledge it, you give it power. If authority is ignored, it doesn't exist any more... You can't carve a new society with old tools.[31]

Miller Francis Jr., music reviewer for the Atlanta-based underground magazine *Great Speckled Bird*, was at Woodstock and witnessed Hoffman's altercation with Townshend. Francis heard Hoffman say, "I think this is a pile of shit while John Sinclair is rotting in prison!" which is supported by audio recordings.[32] This contradicts Hoffman's recollection of events whereupon he claimed to speak about raising funds for Sinclair's defence fund. Like Sander, Francis saw this incident as an example of the divide between music as entertainment and music as political statement. Francis explained it as the "ugly, self-defeating split between 'politics' and 'culture,' between politicos and hippies, between students and street people".[33]

The incident illustrates the strength and weakness of the "Woodstock Nation", as Hoffman called it: while music festivals were the most visible iteration of a new generation that did not share all or even most of the previous generation's values, much of the energy of this "nation" was focused on "doing their own thing". Sander and Francis note, for example, that at the festival of peace and music, the crowd cheered at Townshend's violent response to Hoffman's intrusion onto the stage. This was a point not lost on Hoffman either: "It was an interesting sight to see a rock musician defend his thing with violence beneath a thirty-foot high peace symbol".[34] For activists like Hoffman, the Woodstock crowd's "thing" was apolitical or even supportive of mainstream systems of power. John Sinclair himself, in a powerful letter from prison, was even more disparaging in his assessment of Woodstock. Mirroring views typical of the radical left, he noted: "right now the bands exert a lot more influence than we do, and it's a bad influence too... The rock and roll industry is just Amerikan capitalism in microcosm".[35] Sinclair spoke caustically of Townshend and Janis Joplin backstage at Woodstock drinking champagne: "Let them eat cake is their cry, as they drop flowers on the people starving in the mud".

If opposing some backstage refreshments was the extent of the argument against the Woodstock idea, it would carry little impact. However, Hoffman and Sinclair's critiques were emblematic of the different approaches within the counterculture to achieving change. In addition, these criticisms complicate the traditional narrative that rock music was the "soundtrack of the sixties" because clearly a section of the counterculture movement saw rock music as part of the problem rather than as a force for revolutionary change. Hoffman was torn between his love for the music and his distaste for the financial privileges rock musicians earned at the expense, he believed, of "his" people, the Woodstock Nation. Hoffman's immediate reaction to events at Woodstock was to write a book about it, which he called *Woodstock Nation: A Talk-Rock Album*. In it, Hoffman claimed that his skirmish with The Who symbolised his "amity-enmity attitude towards that particular rock group and the whole rock world in general. Clearly I love the music and sense in it the energy to liberate millions of minds", he explained. "On the other hand, I feel compelled to challenge their role in the community, to try and crack their plastic dome".[36]

Women at Woodstock

If Abbie Hoffman and the Yippie movement felt torn between an "amity-enmity" interpretation of Woodstock and what it represented, so too did another huge section of the counterculture movers and shakers — the women of Woodstock. At this point in 1969, the rising feminist movement and battle for "women's liberation" was ascending. In September 1968, for example, eleven months before Woodstock, around two dozen activists from the New York Radical Women collective had disrupted the Miss America beauty pageant. Outside the venue, on the boardwalk, they threw bras, high heels, and other symbols of femininity into a bin; inside the venue they set off firecrackers and shouted slogans. These protesters were mostly veterans of the civil rights movement and that day, for the first time, they were protesting for women's equality.[37] A few months after Woodstock, Robin Morgan wrote: "it hurts to understand that at Woodstock or Altamont a woman could be declared uptight or a poor sport if she didn't want to be raped".[38] If Woodstock was indeed the birth of a new "Woodstock Nation", as many claimed, it may be asked what role did women play in it? What exactly did women experience at Woodstock, and did the women's rights agenda affect that experience?

The Miss America protest was sorely needed. While the Twentieth Century saw gradual progress in women's rights and sexual equality in the United States, progress had been slow and grudging, and in the 1960s women were still seeking a double victory over sexism and inequality. The "first wave" of women's rights, fought for and won by women in the early part of the century, was mainly concerned with suffrage (a battle won in 1920 with the passage of the Nineteenth Amendment to the United States Constitution), but was also rooted in campaigns for contraception and reproductive rights. In 1916, for example, activist Margaret Sanger opened the nation's first birth control clinic. Five years later, Sanger founded the American Birth Control League, which provided contraceptive advice. This was a significant moment, as Sanger challenged the ban on contraception advice put in place by the Comstock Act of 1873. In this era, women attained the right to vote, and won some control over their own bodies, but there were other battles to come.

The "second wave" of women's rights activism took shape in the post-World War Two era, and was led by prominent figures such as Betty Friedan, Rosa Parks, Germane Greer, Gloria Steinem, Robin Morgan and Valerie Solanas. This second wave moved beyond suffrage and birth control to focus on issues such as equality in the workplace, civil rights, removing legal obstacles to equality, as well as more openness about family life, marriage and divorce rights, and sexuality. Yet, in the 1950s and early 1960s, many women remained excluded from male spheres of influence. A post-war "baby boom" fuelled economic growth and demand for more schools, universities, and housing led to the suburbanisation of America: by 1960 as many Americans lived in suburbs as in the cities.[39] This in turn led to more focus on family and gender roles. Yet in spite of new economic and social opportunities that arose during the war (personified in the character "Rosie the Riveter") in the post-war years women were expected to stay home and have children. Like the previous generation of women, they played out roles as girlfriends, wives, mothers and home-makers. Children and chores tied them to the home, while men were free to pursue a fuller role in society.

In addition, a variety of local, state and federal laws set limits for women's sexual and reproductive choices. Across America, one could find laws prohibiting extramarital sex, cohabitation of unmarried couples, or using any form of birth control except natural. There was a social stigma against public breastfeeding, which was often viewed as lewd or shameless behaviour. Pregnant teens could find themselves expelled from High School. Abortion was illegal, and would remain so until the Supreme Court judgment in *Roe v. Wade* (1973). Where race was a factor, laws about sexual relations were more rigidly enforced: for example, inter-racial marriage was forbidden in most states. In the South especially, extra-judicial vigilantes enforced separation of white women from black men, while at the same time white men lusted after black women for their supposed primitive sexuality. Widespread sexual assault of black women by white men in the South often went unreported and was hardly ever prosecuted. This was a world away from what often happened to black men: often a black man in the South had only to be suspected of disrespecting a white woman and he faced mob justice or lynching. For instance, in 1955, 14-year-old Chicagoan Emmett Till was visiting family in Mississippi when he was kidnapped, brutally beaten, shot, and his body dumped in a river. His alleged offence was that he whistled at a white woman.[40]

Yet in spite of this, there were significant landmarks of change in the 1950s and 1960s. The Kinsey Reports, particularly *Sexual Behavior in the Human Female* (1953), indicated that American women were more sexually adventurous in private than society permitted. In 1963, Betty Friedan's *Feminine Mystique* sent shockwaves through American society, with its powerful arguments about the system of power that kept women oppressed, while advice books such as Helen Gurley Brown's *Sex and the Single Girl* (1962) encouraged and showed women how to pursue sexual relationships before and outside marriage. Women activists fought hard for greater control of their reproductive rights, and they scored two huge victories in this field: in 1960, the Food and Drug Administration approved the use of the Birth Control Pill; and in 1965, the United States Supreme Court (in *Griswold v. Connecticut*) decriminalised contraception. The National Organization for Women, formed in 1966, borrowed directly from the language of the African-American civil rights movement in advocating a Bill of Rights for Women and an Equal Rights Amendment (to the U.S. Constitution) to end "Jane Crow".

Mark Hamilton Lytle identifies the 1968 Miss America pageant as a watershed moment in the campaign for women's rights.[41] The conflict between old and new gender expectations can best be seen in the juxtaposition between the participants in the 1968 Miss America beauty pageant, and those demonstrating outside against the objectification of women. Although the protesters thought the contestants were complicit in, or perhaps victims of a patriarchal society, the contestants no doubt believed they were in charge of their own destiny. The reality, perhaps, is that both groups were where they chose to be at that particular point in time. The movement for equality gave women more control over their own destiny and a wider range of options with regard to choices in behaviour, education, career, marriage and family. Many chose to exercise their sexual freedom: as Thornton and Young-DeMarco note, the 1960s "were years of remarkable changes in the freedom of unmarried individuals to be sexually active" and this was the result of a society that had become, by the late 1960s, more tolerant in its attitude towards sexual freedom, and more accepting of the notion that women had the same sexual rights as men.

Therefore, by the time of Woodstock in 1969, many young American women were aware of a new era of dawning political equality and many became activists in various counterculture, feminist, civil rights and anti-war movements. Yet for many women activists, it was a struggle to reconcile seemingly conflicting ideas of political activism and/or marriage and family. Rebecca Klatch points out, for example, that some married SDS activists faced criticism from unmarried activists for their choice to marry and have children.[43] In addition, not everyone in the counterculture was progressive in their views about women, and many women bristled at the yawning gap between the rhetoric of equality and the reality of rampant sexism that continued to thrive. Todd Gitlin notes, for example, that many underground newspaper papers were "stupidly sexist".[44] The activist Marilyn Webb recalled being shouted down when she spoke about sexism at a political rally. And when Marjory Tabankin, a young female activist at the University of Wisconsin, met Tom Hayden, the leader of the SDS, for the first time, Hayden asked her to do his dirty laundry.[45]

Moreover, while in theory the newly developing culture of "free love" in the 1960s meant men and women could more openly express their sexual needs and explore their sexual desires, for some men, however, it was an excuse to berate women to get over their supposed sexual hang-ups and to be more open to male sexual advances. One female activist called this the "most insidious device of all for brainwashing females", referring to the "contemporary demand for people to 'let go of their defences,' to 'relax,' 'stop being so uptight,' to 'groove.'"[46] For her, this was simply another extension of male privilege and another way of pressuring women into unwanted sexual encounters. These experiences caused many activist women to become disillusioned with the "Movement" and to take control over events. For example, in 1970 Robin Morgan published an influential article in the New York-based radical magazine, *Rat,* entitled "Goodbye to all That", which condemned sexism in the counterculture. Soon after, Jane Alpert, Morgan, and other female journalists took over the magazine in response to its sexist and pornographic content.[47]

It was this confusing matrix of raised aspirations, bitter experience, and tarnished hopes, that shaped the views and behavior of the young women who performed, worked at and attended Woodstock. Perhaps the first question to ask is whether there was a "glass ceiling" that existed at the festival? Interestingly, there is little evidence for this. Indeed, one of Woodstock Ventures' main concerns was to create a line-up of music acts that would draw the size of audience they needed to turn a profit on the festival. As none of the promoters was particularly well-known, and none had the clout to attract top acts, the only way to ensure top-draw artists would play was to pay them handsomely. In the main, it seems that the artists at Woodstock were paid a fee that reflected their popularity and therefore their potential to attract fans to the festival. For instance, by the end of April 1969, Michael Lang had booked folk singer Tim Hardin for $2,000, Canned Heat for $13,000, blues guitarist Johnny Winter for $7,500, and he had also secured two big bookings that would ensure the festival's success, Janis Joplin and Jefferson Airplane, for a fee of $15,000 for each.[48] By mid-May, Lang had secured The Band, also for a fee of $15,000.[49] By the end of May, for a fee of $4,500 each, The Incredible String Band and Ravi Shankar agreed to perform at Woodstock.[50] In early June, Blood, Sweat & Tears were booked for a fee of $15,000[51]. Joan Baez finally agreed to appear on the bill for a fee of $10,000[52]; while the then-unknown group Santana was booked for a fee of only $1,500.[53] Joe Cocker, also almost unknown before Woodstock, was brought onboard for $2,750. Lang negotiated with the talent agency Premier Talent a combined fee of $18,000 for their acts Ten Years After and the Jeff Beck Group to perform at the festival (although the latter would eventually decline to perform due to illness).[54] The Who, one of the biggest rock groups in the world at that time, agreed to appear for an almost miserly fee of $12,500. To put that in perspective, Hendrix was holding out for $50,000.[55] These figures show clearly that less well-known artists received a fee much lower than popular artists, and that gender played no role in this reckoning. For example, as a popular and celebrated artist, Joplin received more than Hardin, Cocker, The Incredible String Band and Ravi Shankar combined.

Yet at the same time, women, like black artists, were under-represented on the Woodstock stage. Only Joan Baez and Melanie Safka performed solo. Grace Slick was, of course, the lead singer for Jefferson Airplane and therefore a prominent female performer. Janis Joplin played with her new band and, like Slick, she was also in the foreground at the festival. Nancy "Nansi" Nevins would have been the first female vocal performer at Woodstock if her band Sweetwater had made it to the venue on time, but they got stuck in traffic and finally appeared onstage later on Friday evening. In addition, Rose Simpson and Christina "Licorice" McKechnie performed with the Incredible String band. Sly and the Family Stone was a mixed race and mixed gender band. Rose Stone — Sly's sister — sang and played keyboards; Cynthia Robinson played trumpet and sang backing vocals. Finally, Maya Kulkarni played the tambura for Ravi Shankar. And that was it: so in total, only a handful of women performed at the counterculture's biggest musical happening. There were some practical reasons for this: for instance, Joni Mitchell, who in 1970 would release the song "Woodstock" about the festival, chose to appear on the Dick Cavett Show rather than make her way to White Lake. She had performed at the Atlanta Pop Festival earlier in August and left the stage during her set, apparently annoyed that no one in the audience had noticed she had mistakenly repeated a verse. So she may not have been that keen to perform again so soon in front of another massive festival audience. In any event, she wasn't that well-known in the summer of 1969, and a television appearance would give her much-needed exposure. Most of the mainstream rock and pop performers in the United States were male, thereby limiting the choice Woodstock Ventures had when considering the festival line-up. Yet some prominent female artists such were not invited to perform at Woodstock. These include Dionne Warwick and Aretha Franklin, who were successful at the 11th Annual Grammy Awards held in March 1969, and other best-selling female artists such as Diana Ross and The Supremes, or Ike Turner & The Kings of Rhythm, with Tina Turner on vocals. The exclusion of these female artists, all of whom are of course African-American, remains a puzzle.

It is notable that in addition to the paucity of women performers and those best-selling female artists *not* invited, that the women who did perform at Woodstock were also excluded from post-Woodstock album and film. The *Various Artists Woodstock* triple vinyl album (1970), for example, which offered a compilation of music from the festival, entirely omitted any of the female performers at Woodstock. In the same vein, Michael Wadleigh's 1970 Woodstock film removed Melanie Safka, Sweetwater, Janis Joplin, and The Incredible String band from the festival altogether. In a similar vein, the journalist Bobbie Goldstone, in a review of the Woodstock movie, noted that women "appeared to have generally the same old roles and the male derived status as in the American nation".[56] Nina Sabaroff, a radical journalist who worked for *Liberated News Service* was also critical of the Woodstock movie's portrayal of women. She complained, for example, that Joan Baez was the only female performer in the film. She questioned the film's portrayal of gender roles, pointing out, for example, that men are depicted as active agents who build the stage, perform onstage, and film the unfolding events. In contrast, women are passive: they get "balled", strip nude for the camera, or look after children while the men are off doing more important things. Instead of liberated women, Sabaroff remarked caustically, there were "liberated nipples": she asked, "How'd you like it women? Did the cameras lie? Was Woodstock you?"[57] Irwin Silber, who also reviewed the Woodstock movie for *Other Scenes* magazine, noted the "almost total male-ness of the Woodstock scene", on-stage and off. He argued that there were no notable differences between the gender roles of the Woodstock audience, and the wider society they supposedly were an alternative to. He explained: "some of the cultural mores of Woodstock, with their orientation to male-dominated social forms of the past — whether the mysticisms of the East or the primitive naturalism so celebrated as the response to technology — actually represent a step into the past in terms of the liberation of women. One can almost feel a "Me Tarzan, You Jane" mood rustling through the Woodstock grass".[58]

This was certainly the case among the employees of Woodstock Ventures, and the many volunteers who turned to help at Howard Mills' farm in Wallkill, which was the original venue for the festival. A few scores of volunteers and employees of Woodstock Ventures worked hard over the summer of 1960 to create an outdoor auditorium from abandoned farmland, infested in places with poison ivy. A mixed-gender group of young hippies worked hard during the day and partied in the evenings. As Spitz notes, "casual sex was neither frowned upon or refused".[59] While male and female workers alike comprised the field crews, it is notable that duties of cooking and food shopping fell to two teenage girls, Carol and Linda.[60] A similar gender divide was evident in Hog Farm's daily routines. The commune had agreed, for a fee, to provide some services at the festival, including security, a "bad trip" tent, a stage for those without tickets, and most importantly a free food kitchen.[61] However, menus and provisions were the responsibility of the commune's women, with Bonnie Jean Romney in charge of the kitchen while her husband Hugh "Wavy Gravy" Romney was a more visible presence on and around the stage, becoming a media celebrity in the process.

During the festival itself, among the crowd of revelers, the new holy trinity of sex, drugs and rock and roll proved as attractive to women as it did to men. Perhaps this was because Woodstock was a "safe space" wherein drugs could be ingested and nudity indulged without fear that the forces of law and order would intervene. For the most part, the state police stayed on the roads outside the festival venue, whereas there was little danger that Hog Farm "security" would intervene, unless it was to join in the fun. Teenager Susan Reynolds, who went to Woodstock with her brother and sister, remembers feeling safe among the vast crowd: "immersed in my generation's culture, one with the swelling crowd, and part of something so monumental, I couldn't form opinions about what it was for a long time afterward. I felt like an amoeba in a far larger organism, symbiotic and miniscule".[62] In *Quicksilver Times*, Dick Gregory compared Woodstock with Chicago the previous year: "Both gatherings attracted people of national prominence: In Chicago, such persons as Sen. Eugene McCarthy, Sen. George McGovern, Gov. Lester Maddox and Vice-President Humphrey, and in Woodstock, Jimi Hendrix, Richie Havens, Arlo Guthrie and the Jefferson Airplane. The difference between Woodstock and Chicago", Gregory argued, "was that in Woodstock those of national prominence were in tune with the sentiments of the youthful masses". Gregory then compared the peaceful security presence at Woodstock with the behavior of the riot police at Chicago, remarking that their very appearance was now likely to spark trouble.[63]

The knowledge that they would not be busted for nudity or illicit drug use allowed women at Woodstock a degree of freedom seldom in evidence outside the boundaries of Yasgur's Farm, and for a few female journalists present it resulted in some interesting reporting. Writing in the *East Village Other* Lita Eliscu admitted, "I got high: I got stoned", the result of which was a colourful report about Woodstock in which she describes the space between the backstage pavilion and the stage as a "long red-light dragon" and Woodstock "the navel of the world" from which she might look up at "stars, constellations, galaxies".[64] Ellen Sander was also high when she met Hoffman before his altercation with Pete Townshend; however, her article for the *Los Angeles Free Press* was written in a more matter-of-fact style than Eliscu's, with no dragons on the loose. A week after Woodstock, Hoffman showed up at her apartment: they talked for a bit and then "he balled me and split", she told her readers, a candid admission presented almost as an afterthought. Such openness was, however, only encouraged or tolerated when women were not a threat to male privilege. After Sander criticised Hoffman's particular brand of radicalism, he dismissed her as merely a groupie who passed herself off as a music critic, thus undermining her professional credentials and reducing her to a sexual plaything.[65] Given the hurdles women had to overcome to be taken seriously in a professional vocation, this was a very low blow indeed.

Depending on which source one consults Woodstock was either a vast, open-air orgy, or a fairly ordinary scene. *The Seed's* man-on-the-spot reported, for example, that "not all that much balling [went] down";[66] in contrast, journalist Andrew Kopkind claimed "balling was easier than getting breakfast".[67] There's a certain amount of irony in the fact that a bunch of "squares" — the few hundred off-duty policemen hired by Pomeroy to do security — seemed to be enjoying the festival's sexual freedom: at one point, for example, Pomeroy complained that instead of doing their duty these men were busy "dragging teen-age girls off to the barn for a quick lay".[68] While on the surface, the "free love" on display here seems like evidence of sexual equality, the language used betrays the latent sexism in aspects of this orgy culture. Pomeroy's choice of words is indicative of the imbalance of gender at Woodstock and in society in general at this time. It suggests also a degree of unwillingness on the part of these teenage girls who have to be "dragged off" rather than proceed willingly. The term "balling" is indicative of the same mindset in action. As Germaine Greer lamented around this time, sex was so often talked of in the sense of men being active and women passive — men "balling" or "screwing" women, who were assumed to be inert objects just existing to "receive" male organs. As Greer said, hardly anyone talked of women being proactive sexual beings themselves: "What happens is that the female is considered as a sexual object for the use and appreciation of other sexual beings, men. Her sexuality is both denied and misrepresented by being identified as passivity".[69]

Undoubtedly the amount of nudity on display at and around the festival gave the impression of a "love-in". A combination of circumstances such as the shortage or complete absence of facilities for ablutions, the stifling heat, and the opportunity for recreation led to festival goers swimming and bathing in the three bodies of water located near the site. A *Seed* journalist reported: "Lotsa suburban chickies get uptight about skinny-bathing in the lake but don't regret it when they finally take the plunge. Fair amount of public nudity, about half of which is the result of acid naturalism".[70] Visual images of this appeared in the *Time* magazine festival special. As Gina Arnold points out, however, there is much less nudity on show that in popular memory. For example, the Woodstock film features only a few long-distance shots of people bathing, and the *Time* special contains only one nude image. Arnold maintains that the concept of female nudity was mainly a "media construct".[71] While there is a degree of truth in that position, the social nudity on display was novel, and it set a precedent for the success or otherwise of future festivals.[72] If there was lots of nudity it was "happening": if there wasn't, it was a bummer.

To return now to the female artists performing at Woodstock, it is useful to look more closely at the three most prominent female performers at Woodstock: Joan Baez, Grace Slick, and Janis Joplin. Each has a distinct musical style, and therefore a distinct fan base, which makes it difficult to generalise about their experiences and impact at the festival, and what came after. However, if rock is "sexism set to music", as Marion Meade argued a year after Woodstock, and its message is "that it's a man's world, baby and women have only one place in it. Between the sheets", then how should the presence of Baez, Slick and Joplin in that world be considered?[73] The *Berkeley Tribe* expressed similar sentiments to Meade and offered an explanation as to why some female performers were accepted: in rock culture, the *Tribe* argued, there was a clear division of labour in which all women were viewed as groupies and that women who were successful in this culture — Grace Slick, Janis Joplin, Judy Collins and Joan Baez — were only tolerated because they were "not in any way a threat to male supremacy. They are seen as sexual whether it be virgin or whore".[74] However, the prominent profile of these women, the fact that they were successful across a broad spectrum of musical genres (acoustic, folk, acid rock, soul, blues), and that for the most part they negotiated their success on their own terms, served to challenge male supremacist dogma.

Baez had developed a reputation as a radical folk singer, political activist, with close links to Bob Dylan, the Woodstock Nation's spokesman and poet laureate. Baez was a serious performer (unlike, for example, Sha Na Na): six months pregnant at the time, she made reference onstage to her 22-year-old husband David Harris, who was in gaol for draft resistance. Moreover, her chosen genre was folk, which was imbued with all sorts of historic and political overtones. Her music was meaningful, and at times deeply spiritual. At Woodstock her set list consisted of fourteen songs, including "Joe Hill", the song dedicated to union activism that Wadleigh chose to include on the Woodstock film. During her performance of the Civil Rights anthem "We Shall Overcome", one audience member remembered people "linked arms with strangers and swayed back and forth, singing along".[75] The depth of Baez's performance, the fact that she helped distribute food to hungry festival goers, that she was the only "star" to perform on the free stage (part of the "Fair" aspect of Woodstock, the free stage provided space for amateur musicians to perform), together with the widespread exposure the film gave her, meant she remained a popular and influential artist throughout the next decade. Immediately after Woodstock, she performed at the Big Sur Folk Festival — "Woodstock without mud" claimed the *Los Angeles Free Press* in their September 19-26, 1969 issue. There were similarities: some artists performed at both events, there was some nudity, some bathing, and lots of wine, pot and LSD was imbibed. There were also dissimilarities: Big Sur was a smaller event (5-6 thousand people per day)[76] and there was, indeed, no mud as the weather was fine. However, the *Los Angeles Free Press* was incorrect in one important aspect: as well as Baez and Joni Mitchell, the festival line-up included Mimi Farina, Julie Payne, Carol Cisneros, Ruthann Freidman, Dorothy Morrison, the all-female California Youth Choir, and The Incredible String Band featuring Rose Simpson and Christina McKechnie.[77] Female performers therefore comprised a much higher percentage of the onstage talent than at Woodstock. In that respect, Big Sur was probably more representative of the alternative society than was Woodstock, with one caveat: like Woodstock, black artists were noticeably in short supply.

Grace Slick and her band Jefferson Airplane had the unenviable task of closing day two in the early hours of Sunday morning. This meant they had to follow Creedence Clearwater Revival, Janis Joplin, Sly and the Family Stone, and The Who (featuring Abbie Hoffman's cameo). "You've heard all the heavies, now listen to the morning maniacs!", exclaimed Slick, before starting a lengthy thirteen-song set.[78] Slick was a rare breed: a powerful female lead vocalist in an all-male rock band, operating in a male-dominated music business. Meade notes, for example, the prevalence of all-male groups and music critics, and the dominance of men in rock publications and as music festival organisers.[79] Moreover, the counterculture was only slightly less male-dominated than the mainstream society it opposed. For example, Tom Hayden viewed "Movement" leadership as dominated by aggressive, egotistic males and as a result of that, only a few women were able to come to prominence. When they did, they were still treated as objects of male desire. In this environment, Hayden argued, "Janis Joplin and Grace Slick are musical [sex objects], whereas Joan Baez and Judy Collins [are] 'beautiful and pure.'"[80] The *Berkeley Tribe* took a similar view, identifying these egotistical males as "the yippies, Abbie and Jerry and their entourage, Rock groups, Hells Angels, Leary [and] John Sinclair".[81] Slick was an attractive woman in this male milieu: she "doesn't smoke, she smoulders", as one observer put it.[82] It is perhaps a little unfair to observe that Slick often had to adopt traditionally male traits in order to be taken seriously in this environment, but by her own admission, she swore, slept around, and drank alcohol, eschewing pot and acid.[83] However, she made men take her seriously due to her song-writing ability, powerful and distinctive voice, and imposing stage presence.

Jefferson Airplane's performance divided critics: in his piece about the festival and Wadleigh's film, Miller Francis Jr., a witness in the crowd, wrote about Airplane's "long superlative set" and asserted that the performance of "White Rabbit" was Slick's "personal triumph done brilliantly".[84] Reviewing the film, he described the Airplane's set as a "two-hour Rock masterpiece" and bemoaned its absence.[85] In contrast, from Jim Marion's position in the crowd he thought they played "loose and sloppy".[86] The band seemed to agree: they weren't happy about their performance and while they allowed one short song, "Volunteers", to appear on the Woodstock festival album, they refused to appear in the film[87]. Moreover, the band's Woodstock appearance hardly added to their reputation. Before Woodstock, they had not only performed at Monterey in 1967, with two of their songs appearing on the 1968 *Monterey Pop* concert film, they were moreover a staple of the San Francisco music scene. In record sales, they had achieved one platinum and two gold records in three years, two top ten albums, plus a number of hit singles. Both "Somebody to Love" and "White Rabbit" became emblematic songs of the decade. So while their album *Volunteers* peaked at number 13 in the U.S. album chart by the end of 1969, it's unclear if Woodstock had any noticeable impact on sales. It may even be the case that the shift in tone in this album from psychedelic towards a more openly political stance actually hurt record sales.[88] This image was reinforced when Jefferson Airplane played at the Altamont festival in December 1969. Images of Marty Balin being beaten unconscious by Hells Angels seemed to suggest that the Angels, who were more at home among the hedonistic hippies of San Francisco rather than the political radicals of Berkeley, had no time for the Airplane's radical musical output. But of course this is only an impression: in reality, Balin was beaten because he put himself bravely or foolishly between an Angel's fists and the person the Angel was attacking in front of the Altamont stage. While this violence was unfolding, Slick talked to the crowd and the Angels, trying to take the heat out of the situation. Journalist Sandy Darlington called this "Whorehouse tactics. And brave. And smart. Lili Marlene".[89] In the wake of Altamont, Spencer Dryden quit the band and Jorma Kaukonen and Jack Casady set up a side project called Hot Tuna. They cut a live album together, which reached number 30 in the U.S. album charts when released in 1970. The success of this album may suggest a "Woodstock boost" but it did little for the cohesion and longevity of Jefferson Airplane. In 1971, Balin left the Airplane, who released one more album before breaking up the following year.

Along with the Grateful Dead and Jefferson Airplane, Janis Joplin — "Pearl" — was an integral part of the San Francisco hippie scene. She performed twice at the Monterey Pop Festival, and appeared in the concert film. From that point on, she was a national figure and she struggled to cope with the pressures of fame. She increased her drug intake, and in 1969 she split from her band, Big Brother and the Holding Company. Joplin arrived at Woodstock well before her performance was scheduled to begin. With almost half a day to kill, she took heroin and drank alcohol. She eventually took to the stage around 2am on Sunday morning and to some reviewers her performance was below expectations: Mike Jahn of the *New York Times* said, "She sang hard and loud and was well received but there were problems. Miss Joplin is a very emotional singer given to great outbursts of energy. Big Brother and The Holding Company was similarly inclined. Precision was dropped in favor of spontaneity and excitement, and it was a happy bargain. Her new band is 10 times more precise and technically correct than Big Brother, but much less exciting".[90] Miller Francis Jr. also thought Joplin performed with more vigour and spontaneity when she was with Big Brother and the Holding Company, although he still considered that she put in a great performance at Woodstock.[91] Joplin must have had some doubts: although her performance was filmed and recorded, she refused permission for it to be included in the Woodstock film or soundtrack album.

A few months after Woodstock, a radical high school student magazine called *Inquisition,* based in Charlotte, North Carolina, engaged in a confrontational interview with Joplin.[92] Interviewers asked her if she planned to take part in the October Vietnam Moratorium, and seemed surprised when she said no. The interviewers then referred to her new group, the Kozmic Blues Band, as a "back-up" band, which Joplin objected to. When asked about Woodstock, Joplin didn't seem to think it was anything special: she said she preferred indoor concerts as she had more connection to the audience. Seemingly frustrated by Joplin's less than enthusiastic response to their Woodstock query, the interviewers then inquired as to whether she would accept a smaller performance fee so that some of the profits could go to a "community fund for free concerts". Joplin responded evenly that she delegated business decisions to her manager. The interviewers changed tack and began to press her as to why her relationship with Sam Andrew of Big Brother and the Holding Company broke up: "Last year when you were in Durham you said the only reason you kept him around was that he was a good ball". Joplin denied she had said that, but the interviewers persisted: "You were pretty high at the time". At this point Joplin lost her composure and began to cry. She responded: "That's really funny, really funny. You think... Fuck?... You think people are... going to be your friends... and... all they do is figure out... little... screws they think will open you up... or something. Do something rude to see how you handle it". This exchange is revealing: The dynamic between Joplin and the *Inquisitor* interviewers reveals something of the gap between performers and the radical political activists in the Movement. For example, when the interviewers asked her about a local political issue, Joplin responded: "I'm sure you have a lot of things going, but can you understand that I'm going to be here 26 hours and I have my own problems?" In a similar vein, Joplin explained: "If I tried to get involved in everybody's problems, I couldn't dig what I do. To get involved in all that shit, man, it wouldn't be worth it for me to sing. If there's more grief than joy, you know, I'd quit". Less than a year later, Joplin was dead, caused by an accidental heroin overdose. She was just 27 years old.

These vignettes suggest that where gender is concerned, it may well be the case that the festival offered not so much an alternative to mainstream society, but instead held up a mirror to it.

The Black Experience

Monterey was not actually the first major rock festival of the Summer of Love, but it is better remembered than the Fantasy Fair and Magic Mountain Music Festival that occurred a week previously. One of the reasons it is more well-known is that it was filmed and therefore reached a wider audience than just the festival attendees. Craig Werner watched the film and noticed few black faces in the crowd and even fewer black artists on stage. "Janis Joplin blew the crowd away", he claimed, "partly because she didn't have to compete with Koko Taylor or Aretha Franklin".[93] Of course, Otis Redding, Lou Rawls, Hugh Masekela, Booker T. & the M.G.'s (one of ten racially integrated groups at the festival), and Jimi Hendrix did perform at Monterey — with Redding and Hendrix in particular, making a big impact — but prominent black blues and soul artists were notably absent, causing Robert Christgau to comment in his festival review in *Esquire* that the "paucity of Negro acts" at Monterey, was "most disturbing".[94] Dionne Warwick was on the bill but was a no-show. Chuck Berry was invited but refused to perform for free. When even Smokey Robinson, who was on the Board of Governors for the festival, could not persuade any Motown artists to appear, Monterey became as Christgau, notes, "whitey's festival".

What lessons did the black community learn from Monterey? Music writer James Miller has claimed that for them, Monterey Pop was a turning point, that despite the performances of Otis Redding and Jimi Hendrix, Monterey "confirmed the fact that 'real' rock and roll had become... music made by whites (like Janis Joplin) trying to sound 'black' — or just plain white music (the Bay Area bands were overwhelmingly white)".[95] If this is accurate then one must look for reasons other than musical to explain why. After all, black music was exciting and popular, as Hendrix's performance at Monterey demonstrated. In her thoughtful study of American popular music, writer Martha Bayles explains that white racism and black music were intertwined. Whites associated black music with primitivism, and when rock and roll music developed in the 1950s, both whites and blacks had to negotiate America's racial colour line. "Racism", Bayles opined, "isn't the sole motive behind cultural resistance to Afro-American music, but it's certainly an important one".[96] It was once thought that rock and roll helped break down the colour barrier. For example, Elvis Presley made his breakthrough with Sam Phillips' Sun Records in Memphis, a company which specialised in black music. Phillips hoped to find a white singer who could sing "black" music — rhythm and blues and gospel — and when he heard Presley sing "That's All Right" he knew the singer was that person. The career of another white artist, Jerry Lee Lewis, followed a similar trajectory: brought up listening to black music, he was a session musician at Sun Records and found popular success with recordings of his own songs. However, the argument that Presley and Lewis broke down colour lines cut no ice with Bayles, who argues instead that these white artists progressed due to white privilege, while Elvis distanced himself quickly from any association with black music when he began his Hollywood movie career. Bayles therefore takes issue with what she calls the "myth" of rock and roll as a racial revolution. Instead, she opines that rock and roll and the movement for black civil rights and racial equality merely occurred at the same time, causing some to confuse correlation with causation. Bayles believes, however, that rock and roll was revolutionary in that it exposed racial prejudice, particularly the baser lusts of white men towards black women, and the outrage when corresponding attraction took place between white women and black men.[97]

Yet the popularity of Presley in particular, opened the door for black performers such as Jackie Wilson, Sam Cooke, Ray Charles, Little Richard and Chuck Berry to sign record contracts with mainstream studios and to achieve crossover success in the 1950s and early 1960s. Other black artists and music promoters chose, though, to find their own route to success, and therefore to retain more control over their music. The most successful alternative to white control over black music was Detroit's Motown Records. Founded by Berry Gordy Jr., Motown gave opportunities to a steady stream of black artists during the 1960s, and it was responsible for hundreds of hit records. Yet as Bayles points out, while it helped develop black artists, becoming in the process the "Black David who slew the White Goliath of the record industry", Motown's purpose was to make money by producing hits that would appeal mainly to a white audience.[98] It was this popularity that grated with uber-hip white critics such as Nik Cohn, who accused Motown of making soul music boring, and soul artists virtually interchangeable. If soul music had become "Uncle Tom" by the late 1960s, argued Cohn, Motown had to shoulder much of the blame.[99]

Black artists therefore had to negotiate a music industry that was dominated by white people, and a society that was still racially prejudiced. They could seek to take control of their own music but, as Cohn's quote proves, critical approval would not necessarily follow. Of course, that the music industry was dominated by white people did not necessarily equate to institutional racism. For example, Atlantic Records was run by brothers Ahmet and Nesuhi Ertegun, who shared a love of jazz music: Ahmet was a particular fan of Duke Ellington. Both were interested in signing black artists to the new label, and they would secure contracts with artists such as Aretha Franklin, Ray Charles, Solomon Burke, Ruth Brown and Wilson Pickett, and bands such as the Drifters and the Coasters. In addition, many white performers were sympathetic to the black civil rights movement, most famously perhaps, Bob Dylan who performed at a Congress of Racial Equality benefit event in February 1962, and at the Freedom March in Washington, D.C. in August 1963, when Dr Martin Luther King Jr. gave his watershed "I Have a Dream" speech. In addition, Dylan composed songs sympathising with black activism such as "The Death of Emmett Till", "Oxford Town", "Only a Pawn in their Game", "Paths of Victory", "Chimes of Freedom", and "The Lonesome Death of Hattie Carroll". Furthermore, many artists insisted on contractual arrangements which ensured they would play to desegregated audiences in the American South, the most famous of whom was The Beatles who, on their first American tour in 1964, insisted that they would refuse to play at segregated venues such as the Gator Bowl in Jacksonville, Florida. Their threat not to perform at that venue ensured there was no segregated seating, and the gig went ahead as planned.[100]

It is impossible to overstate the importance of support from the music community to civil rights activists or of music to the movement. Faced with establishment violence and intimidation, music helped provide activists with the inspiration to continue fighting and the hope they might be successful. From the days of slavery, music helped slaves cope with their existential dilemma. Slave owners believed slaves were happy because they sang: they were unaware that slaves sang to keep their spirits up, and also as a type of code between themselves; for example, the lyrics of "Swing Low, Sweet Chariot" may well refer to the Underground Railroad network. In his famous slave narrative, Frederick Douglass explained: "Slaves sing most when they are most unhappy. The songs of the slave represent the sorrows of his heart; and he is relieved by them, only as an aching heart is relieved by its tears".[101]

A century later, the descendants of those slaves were still fighting for their rights. Until the can-Americans remained second-class citizens in their own country. It is perhaps difficult now to appreciate the enormity of that situation. Full citizenship meant access to the American Dream and all the economic and social benefits that entailed. There were, however, two Americas, divided by what black intellectual W.E.B. DuBois called the "colour line". African-Americans faced discrimination from kindergarten to the grave, in schoolrooms, in the criminal justice system, in higher education, and in employment practices. In most areas of the South, African-Americans were required to use separate facilities to whites. This meant separate drinking fountains, waiting rooms, public parks and toilets. Whites would enter public buildings by the front door, whereas blacks would use the back entrance. In at least one case, blacks and whites used separate Bibles when swearing an oath in court. Restaurants and cafes had separate eating areas for blacks and whites, and on most inter-state bus routes seating was segregated, with blacks having to sit at the back of the bus. In addition, a minority of blacks in the South was registered to vote, and often those who tried to register faced a range of hurdles from illegal "literacy tests" to intimidation and violence. In many areas, American society was separate but not equal.

The Second World War marked the beginning of the end of the doctrine of white supremacy in the United States. Black men who had fought in the war against Nazi fascism and Japanese imperialism, also fought for a "double victory" against racism at home. *Brown v. Board of Education* (1954) began the long, slow process of desegregating the public school system. In Montgomery, Alabama, Rosa Parks' calculated act of civil disobedience led to the Montgomery Bus Boycott and eventual desegregation of public transport in both the city and in wider Alabama. (This event also marked the beginning of Dr Martin Luther King Jr.'s involvement in the movement.) Other acts of disobedience beginning at Woolworths lunch counters in Greensboro, North Carolina in 1960, and then all across the South, led to the desegregation of many businesses. Black and white "Freedom Riders" faced such horrific violence from locals and police that President Kennedy set in motion policies that would ensure all interstate transport facilities were integrated by 1962. Individual acts of bravery and sacrifice were repeated across the nation: U.S. Air Force veteran James Meredith, with the help of hundreds of U.S. Federal Marshals, faced down a violent mob of racists to become the first African-American to enroll at the University of Mississippi. Meredith would later be shot and wounded at a civil rights march and whereas he survived the attack, others would not be so fortunate: in June 1963, for example, an assassin murdered NAACP leader Medgar Evers in front of his wife and children; a few months later, in Birmingham, Alabama, four little girls were killed when their church was bombed by white racists; in June 1964, three young civil rights activists, James Chaney, Andrew Goodman, and Michael Schwerner, were murdered by the Ku Klux Klan as they worked to register black voters in Mississippi during "Freedom Summer"; and in 1968 Dr Martin Luther King Jr., the main spokesperson and figurehead of the civil rights movement, and a man who espoused a policy of non-violence, was murdered by an assassin. By this point Dr King had, however, lived long enough to see the beginning of the end of state-authorised discrimination. While the stroke of a pen cannot change economic conditions overnight — as evidenced by riots in the Watts district of Los Angeles in 1965, Detroit 1967, and in South Central Los Angeles in 1992 — the Civil Rights Bill of 1964 and the Voting Rights Act of 1965 did much to level the playing field of equality and opportunity.

King, however, had his critics, as historian Howard Zinn explains: "King's stress on love and nonviolence was powerfully effective in building a sympathetic following throughout the nation, among whites as well as blacks. But there were blacks who thought the message naïve".[102] Ella Baker, a grassroots civil rights activist who believed that organising at local level was more important than waiting for national leaders to act, criticised King openly and obliquely, stating that he had "heavy feet of clay" and minimisimg his importance: "the movement made Martin rather than

Martin the Movement", she claimed, and "strong people don't need strong leaders".[103] Malcolm X was also critical of King's leadership: in October 1963, two months after King's successful March on Washington (which Malcolm called the "Farce on Washington"), Malcolm declared King a "Tom" and the march a "sellout".[104] While change was being affected, it was happening too slowly for some black activists, and via the wrong tactics: by the end of the 1960s, Black Power activists offered a powerful alternative to Dr King's nonviolence. The Black Panther Party for Self-Defense, founded in October 1966 by Huey Newton and Bobby Seale, were perhaps the most visible iteration of Black Power. The Black Panthers, as they came to be known, were separatists rather than integrationists; they were armed; and they scared the hell out of the white mainstream.

Music played an important role in this struggle for equality. In the early 1960s, white folk musicians proved dependable allies to the civil rights movement, with Phil Ochs, Pete Seeger, Bob Dylan, and Joan Baez the most prominent of many folk musicians who were publically supportive. Black folk and blues singer Odetta Holmes performed "Oh Freedom" at the 1963 March on Washington; Sam Cooke's "A Change is Gonna Come" documents his arrest for attempting to book into a whites-only hotel; Nina Simone's "Mississippi Goddam" reflects her anger and frustration at the murder of activist Medgar Evers in Mississippi and the deaths of four black children in a church bombing in Birmingham, Alabama; the bombing is also the subject of John Coltrane's "Alabama". Activists sang gospel songs such as "We Are Crossing Jordan's River" and "We Shall Overcome", folk songs like Dylan's "Blowin' in the Wind" and "The Times They Are a- Changin'", and rock songs such as "Eve of Destruction", which referenced Selma, Alabama, the site of recent civil rights struggles. "For a few years in the mid-Sixties", claims historian Craig Werner, "all but the least aware Top 40 fans knew a few Movement standards", and while most remained passive supporters of peace and equality, a "handful marched out and put their lives on the line".[105]

Given this socio-political context, where did Woodstock fit into these debates about race equality and the forming of a new, more inclusive society? Werner suggests a degree of antipathy on the part of black folk who "didn't care much about Monterey" and "cared even less about Woodstock".[106] However, that viewpoint by itself does not fully address Woodstock's racial deficit. There were, for example, fewer headlining black artists at Woodstock than at Monterey, and that lack of representation is unusual in that it is the reverse of gains made by blacks in wider American society. This raises the question whether the Woodstock organisers saw race and civil rights as an important aspect of the festival, or if there was a wider problem within the music industry and the new rock festival culture. Woodstock Ventures invited Richie Havens and Jimi Hendrix, as well as some racially integrated groups like Santana, Sha Na Na, the Paul Butterfield Blues Band, and Sly and the Family Stone. This short list meant the festival line-up was an overwhelming white affair, not just in terms of numbers, but also the styles of music represented. Folk and rock dominate, along with white funk and blues. Soul music was in short supply, as *Rolling Stone* magazine's Jan Hodenfield noted at the time: "As with most of the festivals, white was right. No Sam and Dave. No Wilson Pickett. No Stevie Wonder. No Aretha. No Temptations. No Fats Domino. Which is perhaps understandable when the audience itself is largely white".[107] Journalist Mike Bourne also noted the "whiteness of the chosen groups", which he claimed was similar to the Atlanta Pop Festival held earlier in August. According to Bourne, both events had "no black music of note".[108]

In the memoirs of Lang, Kornfeld, Rosenman and Roberts, and in numerous contemporary interviews they conducted, there is no indication that Woodstock Ventures approached any other black artists to appear at the festival, or that they considered there was some responsibility on them to increase black representation. In contrast, they mention on a number of occasions that the criteria for choosing the festival line-up was financial: the artist needed to be popular enough to boost ticket sales. Thus Hendrix was approached, and offered a substantial fee, not because he was black but because his appearance at Monterey and at subsequent festivals made him a star draw. The same motive applied to Sly and the Family Stone, who in 1969 had a number one hit single and an album that sold half a million copies. In Bob Dylan's absence, there was room on the bill for other folk performers and Richie Havens was both popular and reliable. There is, therefore, no evidence of any racial animus in the behavior of Woodstock Ventures, or indeed that race was even a consideration.

To refer back to Abbie Hoffman, in spite of his painful experience at the hands of Pete Townshend, and his misgivings about the promoters' lack of enthusiasm for political action, Hoffman did see Woodstock's potential in the formation of a better world. For example, he called it "the most remarkable event in *our* history (as opposed to *their* history), the creation of WOODSTOCK NATION. It was a phenomenal burst of human energy and spirit that came and went like a tidal wave up there in White Lake, Bethel, Woodstock… I took a trip to our future. That's how I saw it. Functional anarchy, primitive tribalism, gathering of the tribes. Right on!"[109] Yet if the meaning some counterculture activists took from Woodstock was that it represented an alternative utopian vision of either the present or the future, it was also clear that the role of the black community in this supposedly inclusive vision is ambiguous at best. A reporter for The *Seed* noticed, for example, various "neighborhoods" in the Woodstock landscape: "We lived in a hard-core freak neighborhood. Up the hill was a mystic neighborhood, finger cymbals and huts made of straw. There was a biker neighborhood, a high energy freek neighborhood, even a black neighborhood of sorts".[110] The qualifying phrase at the end of that sentence is tantalising: what could it mean? Perhaps that there weren't enough black people present to qualify as a neighbourhood? That was certainly journalist Steve Lerner's impression: writing for the *Village Voice,* Lerner noted only a few black "kids" at the festival[111]. Furthermore, in reviewing the Woodstock film, *Ramparts Magazine* came to the conclusion that the "shining, happy faces at Woodstock are, almost to the 450,000th, white".[112] Nevertheless, even with relatively few black faces in the audience, and an underrepresentation of black artists on stage, it can be argued that their impact was out-of-proportion to their number. For example, black artists bookended the festival, even if that bookending was down to necessity rather than planning. Richie Havens opened the concert and appeared in the *Woodstock* movie, performing a powerful and moving version of the folk song "Motherless Child". Hendrix closed the concert with his incredible and disturbing performance of the "Star Spangled Banner". With this in mind, the following consideration of these artists, the reception they received at Woodstock, and what followed after, allows for some reflections about race relations in this period.

Although Richie Havens was not originally scheduled to be the opening act of Woodstock — he was only asked to perform first because the band Sweetwater got caught in the huge traffic jam of people trying to get to the event — it was his, "warm, lisping" voice (as later recalled by journalist Lita Eliscu who was in the audience) that opened the Festival.[113] Backed by Daniel Ben Zebulon on percussion and Paul Williams on guitar, Havens performed eleven songs, only one of which (the improvised "Freedom") made it onto Wadleigh's movie. Richard Gladstein arrived at the venue while Havens performed. Gladstein was fifteen years of age, but despite his tender age he had already hitchhiked across that United States that summer. He somehow managed to pick up tickets for Woodstock and travelled there with his girlfriend. Although they were far away from the stage as Havens performed, Gladstein remembers feeling very moved by Havens' music.[114] Michael Scuilla, in contrast, did not remember Havens for his mellow sound, but was instead struck by his "electrifying performance" which, Sciulla claimed, reflected the tenor of the era.[115] Reviewing Haven's performance in Wadleigh's film, Richard Green of the

New Musical Express claimed the singer was "his usual exciting self, parading about the stage clutching his guitar to his chest and rousing the audience to cheers and yells".[116] Given the confused and disorganised nature of the festival's opening day, Havens' bravery in volunteering to open the event, and his dynamic, mesmerising performance set the tone for the rest of the evening.

Richard Green was less impressed though with Sly and the Family Stone who, he said, "behave like irate chimps whose tea is late arriving".[117] Given that the band was an inter-racial funk rock ensemble, the unmistakable racial slur in Green's comments sticks out like a sore thumb, especially as Sly had been singled out by other reviewers and concert-goers as one of the highlights of the festival. For example, journalist Lita Eliscu recounted that Sly "absolutely shook the crowd apart, people start getting up and dancing madly, the platform feels like it will fall as we all bebop to the song Stand!"[118] And Miller Francis Jr. called Sly "one of the giant hits of the Woodstock festival".[119] Sly fused some of the best elements of rhythm and blues, with soul and psychedelia to get their funk rock sound. They had a number one hit single in the U.S. in 1968 with "Everyday People", which would appear on their hit album *Stand!* in 1969. They had performed at the Newport Festival in 1969 and were one of the most successful and popular bands with a young following. Despite Sly Stone's occasionally temperamental and unreliable personality, which was fueled by an on-off cocaine addiction, the promoters paid the band a $7,000 appearance fee, which made them the fifth highest paid act on the bill. They were worth the money: writing in the *New York Times*, journalist Mike Jahn gave the band a glowing review:

The innovative rock band from San Francisco... completely captured the audience's imagination. The group appeared early in the morning, and by the end of its hour-and-a-half stint had almost everybody within earshot dancing or clapping. Spotlights made great swoops across the crowd and people threw sparklers into the air every time the group shouted "Higher!" as part of one of their songs... The crowd here responded many times more warmly than to any of the groups or individuals that appeared earlier.[120]

Billboard's Danny Goldberg called Sly and the Family Stone one of Saturday's standout acts, "who brought the crowd to their feet".[121] Robert Spitz adjudged the band's performance "the most outstanding" of the entire festival.[122] The view from the crowd was just as good: nineteen-year-old Bob Brown of Hamilton Ontario made up his mind to travel to White Lake whenever he read that The Who and Sly and the Family Stone were on the bill. He spent the weekend there, enjoying what he called a "classic performance" from Sly and the Family Stone, before hitchhiking all the way home again.[123] And Greg Henry remembers that during the song "I Want to Take You Higher" everyone around him was "on their feet, clapping and stomping. I remember standing still; I could feel the ground beneath me rumble... and we just stood there with these huge smiles on our faces. It was amazing. Sly had everyone dancing and some with torches made by tying shirts on sticks and setting them afire".[124]

Sly and the Family Stone were one of the biggest acts of the late 1960s and, buoyed by positive reviews of their performance at Woodstock, as well as their inclusion in Wadleigh's film, their success continued in the early 1970s. Three months after Woodstock they played at the Palm Beach Pop Festival on the same bill as the Rolling Stones. However, due to Sly Stone's drug problems, the band more or less ground to a halt for nearly two years. They were booked but failed to appear at numerous concerts, including 1971's prestigious Festival of Life.[125] Nevertheless, despite Sly's increasing addiction, various line-up changes, and a shift in musical style towards a less pop-orientated version of funk rock, they continued to have hit records. However, internal arguments eventually caused the band to split up in the mid 1970s.

Although Sly and the Family Stone were probably the most conspicuous and most celebrated black artists at Woodstock, over time their performance has been overshadowed by that of Jimi Hendrix. Hendrix's ability to get distinctive and unusual sounds out of his guitar and amplifiers (for example to generate and control feedback), as well as his natural showmanship, song-writing ability, and distinctive singing voice, made him a popular choice at outdoor festivals. Considered by many to be perhaps the greatest rock guitarist of the era, Hendrix was nevertheless a divisive performer. At Monterey, for example, Pete Townshend picked a fight with Hendrix over top billing: Townshend believed Hendrix copied some of Townshend's distinctive stage performance antics, such as damaging guitars as a kind of nihilistic, alternative encore. By his own admission, Townshend was also uncomfortable around black blues players. He didn't have, for example, Eric Clapton's natural affinity for the music, nor Clapton's comfortable demeanour around black artists.[126] But this dispute didn't stop Hendrix from producing a remarkable performance at Monterey, one which included playing the guitar around his back, picking the strings with his teeth, and at one point spraying lighter fuel onto his Stratocaster and setting it alight. The crowd loved it, as did the cameras. Suddenly, after years of relative obscurity, Hendrix was a superstar in his home country.

But not everyone was a fan. Music critic Robert Christgau's review of Hendrix at Monterey is negative and counter to the prevailing popular memory of Hendrix it deserves to be aired almost in its entirety:

He came to Monterey recommended by the likes of Paul McCartney. He was terrible. Hendrix is a psychedelic Uncle Tom. Don't believe me, believe Sam Silver of The East Village Other: "Jimi did a beautiful Spade routine." Hendrix earned that capital S. Dressed in English fop mod, with a ruffled orange shirt and red pants that outlined his crotch to the thirtieth row, Jimi really, as Silver phrased it, "socked it to them." Grunting and groaning on the brink of sham orgasm, he made his way through five or six almost indistinguishable songs, occasionally flicking an anteater tongue at that great crotch in the sky. He also played what everybody seems to call "heavy" guitar; in this case, that means he was loud. He was loud with his teeth and behind his back and between his legs, and in case anyone still remembered The Who, Hendrix had a capper. With his back to the audience, Hendrix humped the amplifier and jacked the guitar around his midsection, then turned and sat astride his instrument so that its neck extended like a third leg. For a few tender moments he caressed the strings. Then, in a sacrifice that couldn't have satisfied him more than it did me, he squirted it with lighter fluid from a can held near his crotch and set the cursed thing afire. The audience scrambled for the chunks he tossed into the front rows. He had tailored a caricature to their mythic standards and apparently didn't even overdo it a shade. The destructiveness of The Who is consistent theater, deriving directly from the group's defiant, lower-class stance. I suppose Hendrix's act can be seen as a consistently vulgar parody of rock theatrics, but I don't feel I have to like it. Anyhow, he can't sing.[127]

Musical judgment aside for the moment, Christgau's sexualised language and resort to racial typecasting illuminates the stereotypes white men had of black men, such as the idea of the over-sexed black male "grunting and groaning" and "flicking his anteater tongue at that great crotch". It is a disturbing insight into the mind of a white male trying to describe the energy of a black, male performer, with recourse to crude sexual innuendo. He also applies a racial double standard, that The Who's destruction of their instruments was somehow authentic art deriving from their working class background, whereas Hendrix's similar performance in destroying his guitar was merely "parody", ergo fake and inauthentic. If this is how a professional music journalist writes about a virtuoso musician like Hendrix, it indicates perhaps why black musicians and black audiences might steer well clear of the "white" music world.

Turning to Christgau's musical judgment, his was a minority opinion: his superficial comment about the loudness of Hendrix's guitar, and crass remark that "he can't sing" was out of touch with hordes of rock fans who had a deeper appreciation of Hendrix's stagecraft and guitar virtuosity. Christgau has, for example, selectively quoted Sam Silver of the *East Village Other*: Silver's overall analysis was that "Jimi socked it to them" at Monterey.[128] Moreover, the *Berkeley Barb* called Hendrix "outstanding", claiming that the Monterey audience was "climbing all over itself just to get a look".[129] This acclaim increased when Hendrix appeared in the Monterey concert film released in 1968 as his blend of exciting music and flashy stage presentation was a perfect fit for the cinema's visual and aural dynamic. The audience was receptive to this mix because the visual aspect complemented Hendrix's music rather than deflected attention from it. His showmanship was not an attempt to hide any musical flaws: he was the real deal.

Previous to Monterey, Hendrix had gained success in the U.K. with three top ten single releases but it was his Monterey performance that gave him an American audience. As a result, his debut album *Are You Experienced* reached number five on the Billboard album charts just a few months after the festival. By the time Woodstock rolled around, Hendrix had a second top ten album in the U.S. charts in *Axis: Bold as Love* (1967), a number one album in *Electric Ladyland* (1968), and a hit single with his cover version of Bob Dylan's "All Along the Watchtower". In addition, he had been touring extensively in the U.S., U.K. and Europe, to great acclaim. By the summer of 1969 Hendrix's appearance at an outdoor festival almost guaranteed its financial success and that was regardless of how much he asked as a performance fee, so he performed that year at huge festivals at the Santa Clara Fairgrounds in May, Newport '69 in June, and the Denver Pop Festival also in June. Nevertheless, when Woodstock Ventures approached Hendrix to perform at the festival, Hendrix kept them waiting, apparently because he was concerned about the sheer numbers of people expected at White Lake. Although his manager Michael Jeffery eventually persuaded the guitarist to perform, as late as Sunday afternoon, a few hours before he was originally scheduled to close the show, Hendrix was still considering cancelling his performance.[130] However, the festival overran for the third day in a row, partially due to chaotic organisation, but also because the promoters realised that by providing music into the early hours of the next morning they could keep the crowd entertained and also distracted from the many existential problems that were unfolding around them, such as where to find food and clean water, how to keep dry, and where to sleep. By the time Hendrix was eventually ushered to the stage around 6:30am on Monday August 18, 1969, he had put his stage fright behind him. In any event, he had no need to be frightened over the size of his audience: by that time, the crowd had shrunk to around 25,000 people.[131]

Hendrix played a long set of sixteen tracks, including all his hits to that point, as well as his legendary rendition of "The Star-Spangled Banner". Despite his earlier nervousness, and the fact that he had not rehearsed much with his new band, he appeared relaxed and performed with his usual energy and innovation. Hendrix's eerie version of the American national anthem is transfixing: it remains the stand-out performance of the festival and of Wadleigh's movie, and is now remembered as one of the most iconic moments of the 1960s. After enduring four days of ankle-deep mud and rain, Barbara Greenough-Acker was drifting away from the festival site when she heard Hendrix play the first bars of the anthem. Immediately she considered it as something special: "It seemed a fitting end for a half million people who had been brought together by music—and the idea that we really could change just by loving each other and by opting for peace instead of violence or war".[132] Reflecting on the performance many years later, Michael Lang saw meaning beyond the festival: "Jimi has plugged into our collective experience: all the environmental turmoil and confusion we have felt as young Americans growing up in the sixties pours from the sound towers. His song takes us to the battlefield, where we feel the rockets and bombs exploding around us; to demonstrations and marches, confronting police and angry citizens. It's a powerful rebuke of the war, of racial and social equality, and a wake-up call to fix the things that are broken in our society".[133] Lang and Greenough-Acker's reflections are a reminder that Hendrix, a black man at a festival that was hardly representative of the black experience, provided this key point of unity.

The assumption that Hendrix's rendition of "The Star-Spangled Banner" was a political act of defiance, a protest, for example, against the Vietnam War, has become commonplace. However, Hendrix performed the anthem dozens of times prior to Woodstock, often in a very different way. Musicologist Mark Clague's research reveals, for example, that the earliest recorded live version was a full year before Woodstock. Near the end of that set in Columbia, Maryland, Hendrix played the opening bars of the anthem during the song "Wild Thing", before segueing into the military bugle song known as "Taps" — often played at funeral or memorial services to fallen soldiers.[134] As Hendrix had been a member of the 101st Airborne in the early 1960s, passing "jump school" before seeking discharge to pursue his musical interests, the exact meaning of his earliest performances of the anthem remain unclear. Clague traces the development of Hendrix's live rendition of the anthem over the next year. He notes that in October 1968, at a performance at the San Francisco Winterland Ballroom, Hendrix specifically linked how he played the song to how he felt, and he made reference to Owsley Stanley, the Grateful Dead's sound engineer, who was also a mass producer of LSD in the San Francisco Bay area in the mid-1960s. In other performances at the Winterland, Clague reads critiques of commercial culture and materialism into Hendrix's performances of the anthem. Ralph Gleason held a similar opinion: when Hendrix played "The Star Spangled Banner", Gleason argued, he did it "screwing the guitar" as a "revolutionary act surely as important as getting arrested at a... rally".[135]

Between Hendrix's first live rendition of the anthem in August 1968 and then his performance of it at Woodstock a year later, some momentous events had taken place. Peaceful protests at the Democratic Convention in Chicago resulted in a "police riot" against the protesters; Richard Nixon was elected president; news of the My Lai massacre began to circulate in the underground press and generated even more hatred of the Vietnam War; universities were in a state of unrest, with notable protests and confrontations at institutions as geographically and ideologically diverse as Harvard and Berkeley; and antiwar protests escalated, with particularly large demonstrations occurring in April 1969 in New York, Philadelphia, San Francisco, Chicago, Atlanta, and Austin. While the assassinations of Dr King and Robert Kennedy in spring and early summer 1968 immediately preceded Hendrix's first rendition of the national anthem, it seemed that in the run up to Woodstock the fracturing of the country was occurring before Hendrix's eyes. Hendrix's musical direction had changed too: just a few months back he played his last gig with the Jimi Hendrix Experience, believing it limited his potential to explore different types of music. He also grated against the popular music scene and his rock star image: in an interview with *Rolling Stone* in November 1969, he explained: "I don't want to be a clown anymore. I don't want to be a rock & roll star".[136] As Werner points out, his fans were mainly young and white, and he was frustrated that he never got the same level of appreciation from black fans. Playing at "white" festivals like Monterey, and later Woodstock, seemed to alienate him from what should have been his natural black audience. He recalled that while living in Harlem his psychedelic style and long hair provoked ridicule: "What is this, the circus or something?" said one neighbor, causing Hendrix to reflect, "God! Even in your own section. Your own people hurt you more".[137]

Hendrix had no specific plan to play "The Star Spangled Banner" at Woodstock, and it is therefore possible that he was affected both by these contextual events, and the alternative vision of hope offered by the festival's peaceful, appreciative crowd. In his now world famous rendition at Woodstock he used a variety of techniques and effects to achieve his desired outcome, including single-note picking, hammer-ons, string bends, tremolo bar bends, dive bombs, harmonics, string scraping, sliding, and feedback, as well as distortion and wah-wah pedals. But what was his intent? Some critics have labelled it unpatriotic or insulting. However, some indication of Hendrix's thinking may be evident when, as *Rolling Stone* journalist Loraine Alterman noted, at a gig at the Fillmore East on New Year's Day, 1970, Hendrix dedicated the song "Machine Gun" to "all the soldiers in Detroit, New York, Chicago and, oh yes, Vietnam".[138] The lyrics to this Francis Scott Key song had, of course, been inspired by war — in this case the War of 1812 when the British rained down bombs upon Fort McHenry in Maryland in 1814. And it is important to note that every Hendrix rendition of the anthem took place against the backdrop of the unpopular war in Vietnam. Undoubtedly, the two events were related: Hendrix biographer Charles Shaar Murray spoke of the irony of a black guitarist, playing a white guitar, with an almost white audience "wallowing in a paddy field of its own making".[139] Was it then a plea for unity? Rather than an unpatriotic statement, it is possible Hendrix meant his version to bridge the gap between the soldiers in Vietnam, including his ex-comrades in the 101st Airborne, and the Aquarians at Woodstock. After all, he attempted no visual tricks in this performance — no picking the strings with his teeth or playing the guitar behind his back. Compared to some earlier performances, where he integrated commercial jingles and television show theme tunes into the anthem, this was a respectful interpretation. The inclusion of a brief snippet of "Taps" might suggest a mark of respect for the Vietnam War dead, or it might be more symbolic perhaps of the death of the American Dream. If that is the case, then the suggestion might have been to start over with the "Age of Aquarius", which is what Woodstock meant for many who attended or who later watched the concert film.

In the context of performing "The Star Spangled Banner" in such a stylised way, Hendrix's blackness was a potential trigger for white animus. As Clague notes, "A black man performing the U.S. national anthem on electric guitar in a mixed-race band as part of psychedelic counterculture threatened American social constructs". Clague points out that at one gig in Dallas in April 1969, a group of white men warned Hendrix's tour manager Ron Terry that if Hendrix played the anthem that night he wouldn't get out of the venue alive.[140] How should that blackness be understood at a festival where whiteness was prevalent onstage, in Woodstock Ventures and its employees, in the audience, and in the surrounding community of Bethel? Perhaps Miller's analysis of Monterey is correct: perhaps rock and roll was either music made by whites, or by white artists "trying to sound 'black'". Jan Hodenfield's observation that Joe Cocker's performance was akin to a "darkie show" supports this conclusion, while also highlighting the absence of black R&B artists such as Ray Charles, the man Cocker based his career on trying to emulate. However, this position ignores Charles' legions of white fans. Moreover the festival audience was appreciative of black artists, as the reception of Richie Havens, Sly and the Family Stone and Hendrix proves. There is, however, a degree of irony in black artists opening and closing the festival, even if that was unintentional. It served mainly to highlight the whiteness of proceedings and — despite Hendrix's best efforts — to undermine the narrative that Woodstock offered a glimpse of an alternative, inclusive culture. Noting "hardly a black face in the crowd", journalist Craig McGregor of the *New York Times* reflected on what he termed the "cruelest paradox" of the Woodstock Nation, "that it has been liberated, primarily, by the black race from which it has borrowed its music, dance, language, style and much of its sense of brotherhood — but that so far it has done little to free those who freed it".

Conclusion

The diverse experiences of radicals, women, and African-Americans at Woodstock defy easy generalisation. They perhaps shared similar aims of a fairer, more equal society in which all could enjoy their country's liberties and opportunities. All were in "pursuit of happiness" — America's foundational statement of intent — and Woodstock Ventures provided the space for attendees to do their own thing, for a few days at least, without being judged, beaten up, or arrested. And all came to share their love of great music, in a time period in which outstanding musicians and performers embraced ideas as diverse and yet interconnected as peace, love and revolution. Peace and love seemed close but just out of reach, and revolution was, at any time, just a shot away. The festival mood, sharing of resources, and absence of violence led some to believe a new nation had been birthed at White Lake. However, the old society's hang-ups and prejudices were also in evidence at the festival, whether that was the for-profit nature of the event, the underrepresentation of female and black performers, the profiteering of concession stand owners, or the blackmail tactics and threats of the radicals. Largely though, the festival lived up to its promise of "3 days of peace and music", albeit for many that peace ended when they returned to eir everyday lives, and some, like Hendrix and Joplin, would only find peace at a very high price.

1. Abbie Hoffman, "Abbie answers Ellen Sander", *Los Angeles Free Press*, Vol 6, Issue 271, Sep 26 - Oct 2, 1969, p. 21.
2. *North Carolina Anvil*, Vol 3, Issue 112, Jul 12, 1969, p. 9.
3. Spitz, *Barefoot in Babylon: The Creation of the Woodstock Music Festival*, 1969 (New York: Viking, 1979), p. 22.
4 See advertisement in *San Francisco Good Times* Vol. 11, No. 28, Jul 24, 1969, p. 17. This ad predates the move from Wallkill to White Lake.
5 "Woodstock escape from Amerika", The Rag Vol 3, Issue 28, Aug 25, 1969, pp. 3 & 7. At p. 7.
6 Spitz, *Barefoot in Babylon*, p. 238.
7 *San Francisco Good Times*, Vol 2, Number 28, Jul 24, 1969, p. 17.
8 "Woodstock escape from Amerika", p. 7.
9 Joel Rosenman, John Roberts and Robert Pilpel, *Young Men With Unlimited Capital* (New York: bantam, 1989), p. 49.
10 Mark Kramer, "Woodstock not all roses; poses thorny problems", *Quicksilver Times*, Vol 1, Issue 4, Jul 21-31, 1969, pp. 4 & 16. At p. 4.
11 David Walley "Newport Folk Festival", *East Village Other*, Vol 4, Issue 35, Jul 30, 1969, p. 10.
12 Terry Becker, "Woodstock Cops", *Quicksilver Times*, Vol 1, Issue 4, Jul 21-31, 1969, p. 16.
13 Abbie Hoffman, *Woodstock Nation: A Talk-Rock Album* (New York: Random House, 1969), pp. 152-3.
14 Howard Zinn, *A Peoples History of the United States*, 1492-present (London & New York: Routledge, 2013), p. 461.
15 Abbie Hoffman, "Abbie answers Ellen Sander", *Los Angeles Free Press*, Vol 6, Issue 271, Sep 26 - Oct 2, 1969, p. 21.
16 Elliot Mintz, "Looking Out", *Los Angeles Free Press*, Vol 5, Issue 187, Feb 16-22, 1968, p. 24.
17 "MC5 set to kick off Yippie festival", *Sun* (Detroit), Issue 9, Aug 7, 1968, p. 1.
18 "MC5" *Ann Arbor Argus*, Vol 1, Issue 7, May 24-June 9, 1969, p. 12.
19 Elliot Mintz, "Looking Out", *Los Angeles Free Press*, Vol 5, Issue 187, Feb 16-22, 1968, p. 24.
20 "Yippies ready for Chicago assault", *Fifth Estate*, Vol 3, Issue 7 (59), Aug 1-14, 1968, p. 5.
21 "An Open Letter on Yippie", *The Seed*, Vol 2, Issue 11, Jul 1, 1968, p. 2 & 23.
22 Jeff Shiro, "Becoming Pirates for Woodstock", *Rat: Subterranean News*. Accessed Oct 16, 2018. "http://www.ratundergroundnews. com/?p=43"http:// www.ratundergroundnews.com/?p=43
23 Ted Franklin, "Woodstock: Youth Culture in the Wilderness", *Liberation News Service*, Issue 187, Aug 21, 1969 pp. 1-4. At p. 2. Joel Silverman claims the amount Hoffman asked for was $10,000, and he received only "a few thousand" of that. See Rosenman, Roberts and Pilpel, *Young Men With Unlimited Capital*, p. 94.
24 Sam Silver, "Monterey Pop Festival", *East Village Other*, Vol 2, Issue 16, Jul 15-30, 1967, p. 6.
25 "Woodstock Festival pledges space for Movement", *Liberation News Service*, No 183, Aug 2, 1969, p. 4.
26 "Wild East", *San Francisco Good Times*, Vol 2, Issue 32, Aug 21, 1969, p. 2.
27 Miller Francis Jr., "Woodstock", *Great Speckled Bird*, Sep 1, 1969, pp. 12-13, 18-19. At p. 19.
28 Hoffman, "Abbie answers Ellen Sander", p. 21.
29 Ellen Sander, "It's the Sound", *Los Angeles Free Press*, Vol 6, Issue 268 Part Two: Arts and Living, Sep 5, 1969, pp. 31, 41 & 47. At p. 31.
31 Sander, "It's the Sound", p. 41.
31 Ellen Sander, "Dear Abbie", *Los Angeles Free Press*, Vol 6, Issue 268 Part Two: Arts and Living, Sep 5, 1969, pp. 31 & 41. At p. 41.
32 For example, The Who, *Thirty Years of Maximum* R&B (Polydor 1994).
33 Francis Jr., "Woodstock", p. 18.
34 Hoffman, "Abbie answers Ellen Sander", p. 21.
35 "John Sinclair Letter from prison: Dear Abbie", *The Seed*, Vol 4, Issue 9, Nov 1, 1969, p. 16.
36 Hoffman, *Woodstock Nation*, p. 5.
37 Sara Evans, *Personal Politics: the Roots of Women's Liberation in the Civil Rights Movement & the New Left* (New York: Random House, 1980), pp. 213-4.
38 Robin Morgan, "Goodbye to all That", *Rat*, Feb 6-23, 1970, p. 7.
39 Terry H. Anderson, *The Sixties*. Second edition. (Pearson Longman, 2004), p. 2.
40 David Brown and Clive Webb, *Race in the American South: From Slavery to Civil Rights* (Edinburgh University Press, 2007), p. 309.
41 Mark Hamilton Lytle, *America's Uncivil Wars: the Sixties Era from Elvis to the Fall of Richard Nixon* (Oxford & New York: Oxford University Press, 2006), p. 270.
42 Arland Thornton and Linda Young-DeMarco, "Four Decades of Trends in Attitudes toward Family Issues in the United States: The 1960s through the 1990s", *Journal of Marriage and the Family*, Vol 63, No 4, (2001), pp. 1009-1037. At p. 1021.

[43] Rebecca E. Klatch, *A Generation Divided: the New Left, the New Right, and the 1960s* (Berkeley & Los Angeles: University of California Press, 1999), p. 189.
[44] Todd Gitlin, "The Underground Press and Its Cave-In", in *Unamerican Activities: The Campaign Against the Underground Press*. Anne Janowitz and Nancy Peters, eds. (San Francisco: City Lights Books, 1981), pp. 19-30. At p. 23.
[45] Gerald J. DeGroot, *The Sixties Unplugged: a Kaleidoscopic History of a Disorderly Decade* (Cambridge MA & London: Harvard University Press, 2008), pp. 290-91.
[46] Roxanne Dunbar, "'Sexual Liberation': More of the Same Thing", *No More Fun and Games: A Journal of Female Liberation*, Issue 3, Nov 1969, pp. 49-56. At p. 50.
[47] "Court in Contempt of Women, Busts Man from Rat", *The Spectator,* Vol 10, Issue 3, Feb 18, 1970, p. 7.
[48] Spitz, *Barefoot in Babylon*, pp. 80-81. Spitz does not provide sources for his figures. *Variety* magazine provided different figures based on the amounts agreed pre-festival between Woodstock Ventures and the performers. These figures are provided in the Appendix. It should be noted that some artists weren't paid at all, and some received different amounts. For example, The Who reproduced their original Woodstock contract in the sleeve notes of their album *Live at Leeds*. Whereas *Variety* claimed their fee was $6,250, the contract stipulates a fee of $12,500. See Robert Santelli, *Aquarius Rising: The Rock Festival Years* (New York: Dell, 1980), p. 153.
[49] Spitz, *Barefoot in Babylon*, p. 104.
[50] Spitz, *Barefoot in Babylon*, p. 112.
[51] Spitz, *Barefoot in Babylon*, p. 139.
[52] Spitz, *Barefoot in Babylon,* p. 178.
[53] Spitz, *Barefoot in Babylon*, p. 179.
[54] Spitz, *Barefoot in Babylon*, p. 182.
[55] Spitz, *Barefoot in Babylon*, p.185.
[56] Bobbie Goldstone, "Woodstock", *Off Our Backs*: A Woman's News Journal, Vol 1, Issue 6, May 30, 1970, p. 14.
[57] Nina Sabaroff, "How much wood can a Woodstock stock, if…", *Helix*, Apr 23, 1970, p. 19.
[58] Irwin Silber, "Woodstock: The Euphoria Was Real", *Other Scenes*, Vol 4, Issue 5, May 1, 1970, pp. 5 & 6. At p. 6.
[59] Spitz, *Barefoot in Babylon*, p. 213.
[60] Spitz, *Barefoot in Babylon,* p. 213-14.
[61] Spitz, *Barefoot in Babylon*, p. 334.
[62] Susan Reynolds, "Coming Around Again", in Susan Reynolds, ed., *Woodstock Revisited* (Avon Ma.:Simon & Schuster, 2009), pp. 1-6. At p. 2.
[63] Dick Gregory, "Woodstock", *Quicksilver Times*, Vol 1, Issue 8, Sep 10-21, 1969, p. 20.
[64] Lita Eliscu, "Thilm", *East Village Other* Vol 4, Issue 39, Aug 27, 1969 pp 9, 14 & 15. At p. 9.
[65] Hoffman, "Abbie answers Ellen Sander", p. 21.
[66] "Electric Mud: Twelve Takes on the Aquarian Exposition", *The Seed*, Vol 4, Issue 5, Sep 1, 1969, pp. 4, 5, 11, 16 & 17. At p. 4.
[67] Andrew Kopkind, "Woodstock at Yasgur", *Helix*, Vol 9, Issue 6, 1969, pp. 6-7. At p. 7.
[68] Spitz, *Barefoot in Babylon,* p. 434.
[69] Germaine Greer, *The Female Eunuch* (London: Paladin, 1970), Intro.
[70] "Electric Mud", p. 4. This same journalist was taken to task by "three Liberated Women" at the festival for referring to them as "chicks". At p. 11.
[71] Gina Arnold, *Half a Million Strong*: *Crowds and Power from Woodstock to Coachella* (Iowa City: Univeristy of Iowa Press, 2018), p. 108.
[72] See Michael Wm. Doyle, "Statement on the Historical and Cultural Significance of the 1969 Woodstock Festival Site", Woodstock Preservation Archives. Available online at: "http://www.woodstockpreservation.org/SignificanceStatement.htm"http://www.woodstockpreservation.org/SignificanceStatement.htm
[73] Marion Meade, "Women and Rock: Sexism set to Music", *Women: A Journal of Liberation*, Vol 2, Issue 1, Fall 1970, pp. 24-26. At p. 24.
[74] "Cultural Revolution, but not yet Revolutionary Culture", *Berkeley Tribe*, Vol 2, Issue 52, Jul 3-10, 1970, pp. 2-3, 20. At p. 3.
[75] Brad Littleproud and Joanne Hague, *Woodstock: Peace, Music & Memories* (Iola, WI: Krause, 2009), Chapter2: Please Walk on the Grass Day One — Friday, Aug. 15, 1969.
[76] Jean Raisler, "Encounter Monster From the Id", *Berkeley Tribe*, Vol 1, Issue 11, Sep 19-25, 1969, p. 5.
[77] John Carpenter, "Big Sur Folk Festival", *Los Angeles Free Press,* Vol 6, Issue 270, Sep 19-25, 1969, pp. 1 & 6. At p. 6.
[78] Francis Jr., "Woodstock", p. 18.
[79] Meade, "Women and Rock", p. 25.
[80] Tom Hayden, "The Limits of the Conspiracy", *Berkeley Tribe*, Vol 2, Issue 48, Jun 5-12, 1970, pp. 10-11. At p. 10.
[81] "Cultural Revolution, but not yet Revolutionary Culture", *Berkeley Tribe*, Vol 2, Issue 52, Jul 3-10, 1970, pp. 2-3, 20. At p. 2.
[82] Richard Havers and Richard Evans, *Woodstock Chronicles: 3 Days of Peace & Music* (London: Compendium, 2009), p. 162.
[83] See Grace Slick and Andrea Cagan, *Somebody To Love? A Rock And Roll Memoir* (New York: Warner, 1998).
[84] Francis Jr., "Woodstock", p. 18.
[85] Francis, jr., "Woodstock", p. 12.
[86] Pete Fornatale, *Back to the Garden* (NY: Touchstone, 2010), p. 206.
[87] Fornatale, *Back to the Garden*, p. 201.
[88] For an in-depth discussion of the Airplane's radical politics, see Patrick Burke, "Tear down the walls: Jefferson Airplane, race, and revolutionary rhetoric in 1960s rock", *Popular Music* Vol 29, No 1 (2010), pp. 61–79.
[89] Sandy Darlington, "Let it Bleed", *Great Speckled Bird*, Vol 3, Issue 2, Jan 12, 1970, pp. 20 & 17. At p. 20.
[90] Mike Jahn, "The Band, Sly & The Family Stone, Creedence Clearwater Revival, Janis Joplin: Woodstock Music & Art Fair, Bethel, NY", *New York Times,* Aug 18, 1969.
[91] Francis Jr., "Woodstock", p. 13.
[92] "Joplin", Reprinted in *Los Angeles Free Press,* Vol 7, Issue 292 Part Two, Feb 20, 1970, p. 33.
[93] Craig Werner, *A Change is Gonna Come: Music, Race and the Soul of America* (Edinburgh: Canogate, 2002 [2000]), p. 92.
[94] Robert Christgau, originally published as *"Anatomy of a Love Festival"*, *Esquire*, January 1968, pp. 64–66, 147. Available online at: "http://www.robertchristgau.com/xg/music/monterey-69.php"http://www.robertchristgau.com/xg/music/monterey-69.php
[95] James Miller, *Flowers in the Dustbin: The Rise of Rock and Roll, 1947-1977* (New York: Simon & Schuster, 1999), p. 269.
[96] Martha Bayles, *Hole in Our Soul: The loss of beauty and meaning in American popular music* (New York: Macmillan, 1994), p. 63
[97] Bayles, *Hole in Our Soul,* p. 139.
[98] Bayles, *Hole in Our Soul,* p. 153.
[99] Nik Cohn, *Awopbopaloobop Alopbamboom*: *Pop from the Beginning* (London: Pimlico, 2004), p. 120.
[100] Michael R. Frontani, *The Beatles: Image and the Media* (Jackson: University of Mississippi, 2007), p. 14.
[101] Frederick Douglass, *Narrative of the Life of Frederick Douglass An American Slave* (New York: Norton Critical Edition, 1997), p. 19.
[102] Howard Zinn, *A People's History of the United States, 1492-present* (London & New York: Routledge, 2015), p. 452.
[103] Charles M. Payne, *I've Got the Light of Freedom: The Organizing Tradition and the Mississippi Freedom Struggle* (Berkeley and Los Angeles: University of California Press, 2007), p. 93.

[104] Zinn, *A People's History,* p. 457.
[105] Werner, *A Change is Gonna Come*, p. 55.
[106] Werner, *A Change is Gonna Come*, p. 92.
[107] Jan Hodenfield, "Woodstock: 'It Was Like Balling for the First Time'", Rolling Stone, Sep 20, 1969.
[108] Mike Bourne, "Babycakes in New York", *The Spectator,* Vol 9, Issue 2, Sep 23, 1969, pp. 17-18. At p. 18.
[109] Hoffman, *Woodstock Nation*, p. 13.
[110] "Electric Mud", p. 5.
[111] *Steve Lerner,* "The 10th Largest City in the United States", *Village Voice*, Aug 21, 1969, p. 10.
[112] Joan Holden, "Woodstock: The Four Dollar Revolution", *Ramparts Magazine*, Oct 1970, pp. 60-64. At p. 64.
[113] Lita Eliscu, "Thilm", *East Village Other*, Vol 4, Issue 39, Aug 27, 1969, pp. 9, 14 & 15. At p. 15.
[114] Richard Gladstein, "Riding the Crest of the Wave", in Susan Reynolds, ed., *Woodstock Revisited* (Avon Ma.:Simon & Schuster, 2009), pp. 198-201. At p. 199.
[115] Michael Sciulla, "The Little Car That Could", in Susan Reynolds, ed., *Woodstock Revisited* (Avon Ma.:Simon & Schuster, 2009), pp. 153-56. At p. 156.
[116] Richard Green, "Woodstock — Best Film Ever Made About Pop", *New Musical Express*, May 23, 1970.
[117] Green, "Woodstock". When Green later reviewed the Woodstock vinyl album release, he said there was "[n]othing very special about" Sly and the Family Stone aside from the excitement they generate. See Richard Green, Review of Various Artists: *Woodstock* (Atlantic, stereo 2663001; 150s), *New Musical Express*, May 30, 1970.
[118] Eliscu, "Thilm", p. 15.
[119] Francis Jr., "Woodstock", p. 18.
[120] Mike Jahn, "The Band, Sly & The Family Stone, Creedence Clearwater Revival, Janis Joplin: Woodstock Music & Art Fair, Bethel, NY", *New York Times,* August 18, 1969.
[121] Danny Goldberg, "Woodstock: Peace Mecca", *Billboard* Aug 30, 1969.
[122] Spitz, *Barefoot in Babylon*, p. 462.
[123] Bob Brown, "Peace and Music in Wartime", in Susan Reynolds, ed., *Woodstock Revisited* (Avon Ma.:Simon & Schuster, 2009), pp. 75-79.
[124] Brad Littleproud and Joanne Hague, *Woodstock: Peace, Music & Memories* (Iola, WI: Krause, 2009), p. 125.
[125] Chet Flippo, "Life Celebration: A Report From the Front. Drugs, death and rock & roll at the Louisiana music festival", *Rolling Stone*, Jul 22, 1971. Available online at: http://www.rollingstone.com/music/features/life-celebration-a-report-from-the-front-19710722
[126] Werner, *A Change is Gonna Come*, p. 93. Unsurprisingly perhaps, Townshend remembers it differently. In his autobiography *Who I Am*, Townshend contends that he wanted Hendrix to play higher on the bill than The Who as he believed Hendrix had musically "surpassed" his band, plus he was worried that if Hendrix performed first his showmanship might overshadow The Who. See Pete Townshend, *Who I Am* (London: HarperCollins, 2012), pp. 118-120.
[127] Christgau, "Anatomy of a Love Festival".
[128] Silver, "Monterey Pop Festival", p. 6.
[129] Robert and Joanalee Hurwitt, "Pops Groove, Cry for More!" *Berkeley Barb*, Vol 4, No. 25, Issue 97, Jun 23-29, 1967, pp. 3 & 10. At p. 10.
[130] Spitz, *Barefoot in Babylon*, pp. 375 & 475.
[131] Marios Elles, "Chinese Whispers: Jimi Hendrix, Fame And 'The Star Spangled Banner,'" *49th Parallel: An Interdisciplinary Journal of North American Studies* 17 (2006): pp. 1-13. At p. 2.
[132] Barbara Greenough-Acker, "The Road That Was Taken", in Susan Reynolds, ed., *Woodstock Revisited* (Avon Ma.:Simon & Schuster, 2009), pp. 185-88. At p. 188.
[133] Michael Lang and Holly-George Warren, *The Road to Woodstock* (New York: HarperCollins, 2009), p. 2.
[134] Mark Clague, "'This Is America': Jimi Hendrix's Star Spangled Banner Journey as Psychedelic Citizenship", *Journal of the Society for American Music*, Vol 8, Number 4 (2014), pp. 435–478. At p. 437.
[135] Ralph Gleason, "Ralph Gleason: Outside Agitator", *Berkeley Barb*, Vol 7, No. 18, Issue 167, Oct 25-31, 1968, p. 14.
[136] Sheila Weller, "Jimi Hendrix: I Don't Want to be a Clown Any More", *Rolling Stone*, Nov 15, 1969.
[137] Werner, *A Change is Gonna Come,* p. 142.
[138] Loraine Alterman, "Hendrix's All-New Band of Gypsys: Fillmore East, New York NY", *Rolling Stone*, Feb 7, 1970.
[139] Charles Shaar Murray, *Crosstown Traffic: Jimi Hendrix and Post-war Pop* (London: Faber and Faber, 1989), p. 24.

[140] Clague, "'This Is America'", p. 459.
[141] Craig McGregor, "Woodstock: A Desperate Fear for the Future?", *New York Times* April 19, 1970, p. 99.

Chapter 2: International Woodstock: British and Indian Influences

If these pictures or the films are going to be shown in India, they would certainly never believe that this is taken in America. For here, the East has come into the West.

Swami Satchidananda's address at the Woodstock Music Festival in Bethel, New York on August 15, 1969.

In the last thirty years the East has been seeking out the West and vice versa. Indian culture has been exposing its wares, disciplines, music, religions and philosophies to American curiosity... Pacifism by Gandhi, meditation by Mahareshi, and music by Shankar have now solidly entrenched themselves in young America's vocabulary.

Allan Katzman, East Village Other (1968)[1]

God bless you. Let us meditate for one minute for peace and brotherhood.

Yogi Bhajan, opening invocation at the Louisiana Celebration of Life festival, 1971.

Fuck you. Let's boogie!

A member of the crowd's response to Yogi Bhajan.[2]

Swami Satchidananda's address to the Woodstock crowd was not a planned part of the festival programme, nor was it the first evocation of Eastern spirituality at Woodstock: on Friday, for example, before the music started, the Hog Farm's Tom Law sat onstage in the lotus position and demonstrated to tens of thousands of eager and willing audience members how to practice Kundalini yoga.[3] Nevertheless, Satchidananda's address was one of the most unexpected and most memorable events to occur at Woodstock. As is often the case with memorable moments, it actually came about by accident — largely because of the chaotic unfolding of events at the start of the festival. Such were the traffic jams on the roads to Max

Yasgur's Farm that the original itinerary for the opening of the festival quickly fell apart. A band called Sweetwater had been scheduled to open the show, but they were tied up in traffic, so Richie Havens (who had arrived by Friday afternoon) reluctantly agreed to begin proceedings. To kill time, he expanded his set from four to eleven songs, including an improvised song entitled "Freedom (Motherless Child)", whose earnest plea for unity, harmony and liberty helped set the tone for the rest of the weekend. Satchidananda was one of a number of Hindu practitioners to attend the festival, and when he asked the festival organisers if he might address the crowd following Havens' performance, production coordinator John Morris agreed: "Why not?" he would later say.[4]

That such a request would so readily be accepted was not just symbolic of the easygoing nature of the festival, it was also evidence of how eagerly and quickly American youth had embraced Eastern spirituality: just a few years earlier such a request would have been almost unthinkable. Furthermore, less than three hours after Satchidananda addressed the crowd — in effect, giving a kind of blessing to the festival — Indian musician Ravi Shankar made his scheduled appearance on stage, performing a 35-minute, three-song set. Shankar had performed previously at the Monterey Pop Festival in 1967, playing Indian classical music to popular and critical acclaim. His status as Beatles' star George Harrison's sitar teacher raised his public profile, and by 1969 an invite to perform at Woodstock seemed logical and completely normal. The appearance of Shankar and Satchidananda at Woodstock is evidence of the extent to which western audiences embraced and adopted Indian culture at this point.

Before discussing Shankar's appearance at Woodstock, it is important to first consider why young Americans of the counterculture turned to Indian artists for musical and cultural inspiration at this point. It is been well documented that both British and American music artists in the trans-Atlantic pop-rock music community "turned to the East" in the late 1960s, and many writers have drawn attention to the British side of this story[5]; but why and how this phenomenon also occurred in the United States is less well known. At first glance it seems unusual that, at this point in 1969, the United States was such fertile ground for Indian-inspired music: after all, as one commentator has noted, in previous decades the roles assigned to Indians in America had been limited to "a fortune-teller, a snake charmer, a magician or a freak".[6] In the late nineteenth and early twentieth centuries there was nothing in the American imagination of India that made it particularly venerable or attractive. Moreover, anti-Asian racism had been built into the 1924 Immigration Act.[7] Nevertheless, a few American writers and thinkers had expressed intrigue with Indian culture in the pre-World War Two years.[8] It was also the case that the legacy of Mahatma Ghandi struck a chord with many in the United States: his anti-colonial stance resonated with Americans raised on origin stories of overthrowing British rule; and of course Ghandi's advocacy for non-violent resistance to oppression influenced Dr Martin Luther King in his struggle for equal civil rights for African Americans.[9] Moreover, it is notable that between 1941 and 1975 the United States went to war with three different Asian nations — Japan, Korea, and North Vietnam. If it is true that, as satirist Ambrose Bierce once supposedly said, "war is God's way of teaching Americans geography", then these conflicts helped keep South-East Asia in the American public and political sphere.[10] Yet none of these events really explain why Indian music, spiritual life and culture became so central to young Americans in the Woodstock generation of the late 1960s. The answer lies in the very roots of the counterculture that had taken hold at this time, and in its followers' hunger for alternative forms of spiritual, political, and personal ways of living.

The Counterculture and the "turn to the East"

As noted in the Introduction, Woodstock took place at the height of America's counterculture "moment", and a central goal of the counterculture was a quest for alternative forms of spirituality. Until the 1960s, most Americans had belonged to the seven main Protestant churches (and there were also thriving Jewish and Catholic communities), and while the post-war "baby boom" supplied a new population of parishioners for these mainstream churches, it also provided a generation that questioned the traditional roles of organised religion and authority in general.[11] As musicologist Susan Fast notes, "Their attraction to the East came, at least in part, from the countercultural impulse to look somewhere other than the dominant culture for their spiritual and social truths".[12]

This hunger for alternative spiritual and social truths was, in part, a deeply-felt rebellion to the conformity of 1950s American society. Many artists and writers examining the soul of America in this period returned again and again to the idea that America was suffering from staleness, stagnation and stultification. For example, in his 1957 novel *On the Road*, Beat writer Jack Kerouac expressed disillusionment with the United States and felt he had to leave America (for Mexico) to find a taste of the freedom he thought of as his American birthright. When John Steinbeck took a similar journey around the United States in 1960, documented in his travelogue *Travels with Charley in Search of America* (1962), he also became disillusioned with the country's political and cultural conformity, and with the victory of consumerism over values. In 1961, President John F. Kennedy spoke of new frontiers that would keep alive the American spirit of adventure. The nagging question was this: where could Americans find the authenticity and freedom that Kerouac and Steinbeck elegised; and where were these new frontiers?

For many young counterculture enthusiasts, it was the notion of a more spiritual "East" that seemed to offer an alternative to the deficiencies of western consumerism and which provided lessons on "how to live a fuller and spiritually rich life in America".[13] Certainly, some understood Eastern religions to represent forms of pacifist humanism.[14] Furthermore, as the horrors of the Vietnam War played out on American television screens and in the news media, Eastern religions offered an alternative approach to Christian theodicy — the question why a benevolent God would allow such evil to exist. In the 1950s the works of Kerouac, D. T. Suzuki, Alan Watts and others in the Beat Movement marked a distinctive breakthrough in raising the profile of Buddhism in the United States.[15] In addition, Herman Hesse's *Siddhartha* (1922), was published in the States in 1951 and quickly became popular with those looking for an accessible introduction to basic Buddhist themes. And for those interested in hallucinogenic experiences, Timothy Leary's *The Psychedelic Experience; A Manual Based on the Tibetan Book of the Dead* (1964) suggested enlightenment could be found in Tibetan Buddhist writings.

A consequence of this growing interest in the religions of the East was that non-Western religions such as Buddhism and Hinduism developed quickly in America: in 1977 religious anthropologist Harvey Cox counted between forty and fifty "neo-Oriental" religious movements in his hometown of Cambridge (Mass.), including Zen Buddhism, Sufism, Sikhism, Transcendental Meditation, Tibetan Buddhism, Yoga and Tai Chi.[16] He estimated that several million Americans must be following these movements.[17] Religious Studies scholar Jacob Needleman found a similar enthusiasm: "Following upon the great popularity of Timothy Leary, the Maharishi was the first person the alienated masses of young people would listen to", appealing to both the "post-acid generation" and the solid middle-classes.[18] Moreover, this search for the religions of the "East" was not confined to the shores of the United States, as many thousands of young people also embarked on pilgrimages of spiritual and social discovery on the "Hippie Trail" to North Africa and India. These spiritual quests were both internal and external: Harvey Cox noted, in the mid-1970s, "a wave of interest among Americans in Oriental spirituality whose scope and intensity is unprecedented in the history of American religion". Therefore, while earlier transcendentalist poets and thinkers Ralph Waldo Emerson and Walt Whitman had *read* the *Bhavagad Gita*, the new faithful of the late 1960s actually wanted to *practice* Eastern religions.[19] Some did that in the United States while others travelled to India in search of a religious or spiritual experience that was both "authentic" (as opposed to the simulacra of American life) and also an alternative to western religiosity.

This search for alternative forms of spirituality also manifested itself in the popularity of psychedelic drugs in this period. "Psychedelics", asserts cultural historian Nick Bromell, "are powerful and... distinctive": they "do something no other drugs can, and that mysterious something lies very close to the human sense of wonder that is formalized in the world's religions".[20] It was enticing for many young counterculture enthusiasts to believe that hallucinogenic drugs and elevated spirituality were connected: Aldous Huxley made, perhaps, the most articulate case for this in *The Doors of Perception* (1954), suggesting that LSD might alter his "ordinary mode of consciousness so as to be able to know, from the inside, what the visionary, the medium, even the mystic were talking about".[21] Huxley's experimentation muddied the water between science, philosophy, religion and pleasure, and his experiences convinced many to embrace LSD as a catalyst towards raised consciousness and a spiritual or religious pilgrimage. It is perhaps for this reason that many people in the mid-late 1960s tended to amalgamate Indian music and spirituality with drug use, although popular conceptions of India as a stop on the Hippie "Hash" Trail also led to this easy conflation.[22]

Yet it was not only for spiritual awakening that counterculture enthusiasts turned to India for, as in the minds of many young Americans, India offered other attractions too: the best known Indian literature in the United States was probably the *Kama Sutra,* the so-called "bible of sex positions". Historian Theodore Roszak notes how those searching for a religious sanction for sexual permissiveness could find it in the apparently erotic religions of the East.[23] Already-established Orientalist writing referred to a vaguely defined "East", which was supposedly a place of intense sexuality. Some of the best-known examples of Eastern literature in the West were erotic in nature — such as *Arabian Nights* or *Kama Sutra* — and the Western tourist industry promoted India as a romantic or erotic destination with its Taj Mahal "temple of love" and risqué Khajuraho monuments. According to these stereotypes, India was inevitably romantic or erotic in nature, and this resonated with a new generation of Americans who grew up in a more permissive and sexually aware society than had their parents' generation.

Of course, commentators both then and now have picked up on the problems inherent in the counterculture's embrace of the idea of India as a kind of spiritual and sexual Eden. In the first instance, Harvey Cox warned that the Orient could easily become "a convenient screen on which the West projects reverse images of its own deficiencies".[24] And sympathetic, enthusiastic counterculture adherents frequently made mistakes about Eastern religions. For example, historian Carl Jackson pinpoints how beatniks saw Buddhism as a loose, spontaneous, "hip" form of religious faith, and ignored or underestimated the degree of discipline and dedication that Buddhism could demand.[25] Furthermore, it was simply not the case that there was a clear link between Indian spirituality and drug-taking, as many counterculture enthusiasts assumed: indeed, Indian spiritual guides such as Maharishi Mahesh Yogi and Meher Baba insisted that drugs were not required to meditate.[26] The Who's Pete Townshend, a follower of Baba since 1967, recollected: "One minute I was freaked out on acid and the next minute I was into Baba".[27] George Harrison expressed similar sentiments: after meeting Ravi Shankar in August 1967 at Shankar's Kinnara School of Indian Music in Los Angeles, Harrison spoke to journalists. He answered questions about Indian music, and explained that while drugs might help people "see a little bit more", music was in fact the best route to spirituality, and drugs could only interfere with that journey.[28]

Moreover, as Edward Said has noted in his celebrated theory of "Orientalism", Western writers and artists had long liked to imagine "the East" as over-sexualised, primitive and alien[29]: he points out, for example, that many of Rudyard Kipling's admirers spoke of the India he wrote about as a "timeless, unchanging... locale".[30] In so many Western ideas about the "East", Said noted that the rich and diverse histories of Eastern cultures were reduced to a monomyth of exotica, erotica, and danger — or, as Peter Bishop contends in his perceptive study of travel writing about Tibet, "a place of pilgrimage, a spectacle, a totally homogeneous and coherent world of exotic customs, of disturbing yet alluring sensuality, combined with horrific bestiality and perverse morality".[31] Certainly, many elements of counterculture writing and imaginations fell into the "Orientalist" trope that Said depicted. Yet at this point in the late 1960s, music seems to have been both a catalyst and a medium for cross-cultural currents between East and West. In retrospect, it seems apparent that this was something genuinely new, representing a "neo-Orientalist" position; while there remained elements of the counterculture's thinking of India and "the East" that resembled the older, imperialist Orientalism in its tendency to simplify and romanticise the East, arguably it was also different from it in the passionate sincerity of its appreciation for certain Eastern forms. Of course "Orientalisms", whether past or present, often feature admiration for the "other", so this appreciation does not by itself indicate anything new about the turn Eastwards in the 1960s. What, however, is distinct about the neo-Orientalism of the 1960s is that it formed a platform from which to challenge dominant cultural and even political norms within the West; it was also unique in that it was not linked to any colonialist or imperialist project, but instead was rooted in a belief that embracing the music, culture and religions of the "East" could help achieve a deeper knowledge of the human experience.

Moreover, to many counterculture enthusiasts, music was a core, vital platform through which to explore some of these deeper tenets of the human experience, and popular music played a significant role in the "youthquake" of the 1960s. For example, Paul Williams founded music magazine *Crawdaddy!* in 1966 because, he claimed, "music was the most tangible part of our lives".[32] Musicologist David Reck also argues persuasively for the influence of music in the 1960s: "Music", he said, "far from being an ornament on the periphery of... events... was a prime energy center (both in gatherings and private life), an incessant credo hammering out the values and concerns of the counterculture while simultaneously creating new ones".[33] As a "prime energy center" then (to use a yoga term), music was a key language through which to articulate and experiment with ideas in this period. This then begs the question: what impact did this "turn to the East" have on the American music scene in the Woodstock era?

"Raga Rock" — West Meets East.

From around 1965 — concurrent with the development of a trans-Atlantic pop-rock music community — many British and American musicians began to adopt and integrate Eastern spirituality, clothing, instruments and symbols into their music. Bands began to feature Hindu lithographs and Sanskrit writing on their album sleeves, and wore Nehru jackets, robes, beads, and sandals when performing. But more importantly for the purposes of this discussion, many artists began to incorporate Indian musical instruments (sitar, tambura and tabla), rhythms, and themes into their music. Such borrowings became a major ingredient of a new form of psychedelic "Hippie music", which contemporary music commentator Burton Wolfe defined perceptively as a hybrid, "an outgrowth of Negro blues, rock-and-roll, country-western, and finally, ragas from India".[34] This hybrid form quickly acquired the nickname of "raga rock". Referred to by one music journalist, somewhat dismissively, as "rock music based on a few raga ingredients"[35], its typical components, according to the musicologist Jonathan Bellman, were "drones, harmonic stasis, flattened seventh scale degrees, keening vocals, hypnotic beat, ragalike melody, and lyrics that suggest that the singer's inner reality is at least as real as the outer, physical one".[36]

Unlike older generations of musicians, who had only been exposed to performances of Indian music in the Western music hall tradition (or through the theatre, opera, cinema or vinyl records), the 1960s generation actively travelled to find it. Musicians and audiences alike journeyed to North Africa, India and Nepal to experience for themselves what had previously only been available to them mediated through the experiences of others. Amongst those were a handful of dedicated musicians including British folk guitarist Davy Graham (who popularised the DADGAD tuning later used by Jimmy Page in the 1975 song "Kashmir"), Graham Nash, who wrote about his experiences in the song "Marrakesh Express" (which became a huge hit for Crosby, Stills and Nash in 1968), Jimmy Page and Robert Plant of Led Zeppelin, members of the Rolling Stones and Jimi Hendrix, who all visited North Africa; others travelled to India, such as Cat Stevens, Donovan, Wilko Johnson (the guitarist of Dr. Feelgood), Mickey Hart of The Grateful Dead, and most famously The Beatles. While the musicians travelling to India were definitely a minority of "raga rock" artists in this period, their influence was widespread and long lasting. Moreover, even musicians who stayed on American soil found that the spiritual centres of the thriving "Eastern" faiths often created a network of alternative institutions for the musicians of the counter-culture. For example, drummer John Densmore and guitarist Robby Krieger of the Doors met keyboard player Ray Manzarek at a meditation centre in Southern California in 1965.[37]

British artists had originally taken the lead in the forging of this "raga rock" culture in the mid 1960s. David Courtney, who grew up in Houston, Texas, and travelled to India to study tabla-playing, provides a perceptive summary of this new situation:

The explosion began when the Beatles started studying with the Maharishi Mahesh Yogi. Concurrent with this was George Harrison's study of the sitar under Ravi Shankar. Members of ISKCON (aka Hare Krishnas) could be seen proselytising on the street corners... The sitar freely mixed with electric guitars in popular music. The youth regularly sat around in their flats smoking "good old mother nature's best" and listening to Ravi Shankar. Public lectures given by Indian holy men were always well attended.[38]

While several British bands had used sitars or sitar-like sounds in 1965[39], it was the Beatles — specifically George Harrison — who pulled such borrowings into the musical mainstream. During the filming of *Help!* (1965), the Beatles' surreal film about an Eastern cult's search for a magic ring, Harrison was given a sitar as a prop. He became intrigued with the instrument and bought one of his own, which he played later that year on John Lennon's song "Norwegian Wood", from the album *Rubber Soul* (1965).[40] The band took to wearing Nehru jackets on stage, and this garment received massive exposure when the Beatles played Shea Stadium on August 15, 1965.[41]

The following year, Harrison travelled to India to take sitar lessons from Ravi Shankar, which thrust Shankar into the Western counterculture consciousness. For Harrison, Indian music "seemed to have something very spiritual" and he revealed, "it became a stepping stone for me to find out about a whole lot of other things".[42] The *Detroit Free Press* reported further comments from Harrison: "Indian music is hip, yet 8,000 years old… I'd like to see more people interested in it, honestly interested. Not just to cash in on the sitar boom".[43] He deployed his new skills on "Love You To" on the 1966 *Revolver* album. In a *Crawdaddy!* review of that album, Paul Williams wrote: "Harrison's attempt at composing a song in something approximating raga form; as an essentially western piece with eastern influences, it is surprisingly successful and Harrison shows a great deal of respect for the tradition he is working in".[44] Another reviewer observed, "I don't know how the song would sound to eastern ears; but to my western ears — and remember the Beatles are recording for a western audience — it is a lovely and expressive composition".[45] Harrison also played sitar on the Beatles' next album, *Sgt. Pepper's Lonely Hearts Club Band* (1967), and the album artwork included images of four Indian gurus: Sri Yukteswar, Mahavatar Babaji, Paramhansa Yogananda and Lahiri Mahasaya. The influence this album had, and thus the effects caused by their adoption of eastern musical themes, cannot be over-stated. In the late 1960s The Beatles were unparalleled cultural leaders: as musician Neil Innes states, "the Beatles didn't catch the bus, they were the bus".[46] One critic applauded the band for making "old forms new with sitar and raga" and "advancing fifty years of musical development in four. Thank you Sergeant Pepper" [sic].[47]

The Beatles were, though, not the only artists turning to India for new ideas and sounds: American musicians also followed their example. Written in 1966, and released in January 1967, Jim Morrison's "The End" is an early example of the "raga rock" sound, featuring sitar-like guitar by Robbie Krieger. As Peter Lavezzoli notes, Krieger "discovered an interest in Indian raga and modal improvisation [and] utilized many of the same techniques" in this song.[48] Also in 1966, guitarist Roger McGuinn of The Byrds used a 12-string guitar to imitate a sitar in the song "Eight Miles High". Both McGuinn and band mate David Crosby were influenced by the music of Ravi Shankar and of John Coltrane who, since the late 1950s, had been experimenting with different musical structures, including the Indian raga.[49] Crosby's lyrics are about a plane journey to a foreign land, but are also suggestive of a psychedelic drug trip. Mike Bloomfield's guitar work on the Paul Butterfield's Blues Band song "East-West" (1966) is an attempt to emulate the raga drone of Indian classical music.[50] Grateful Dead drummer Mickey Hart began using an 11-count measure that he picked up while studying music in India. According to historian Dominick Cavallo, this was the "first use of this time signature in rock-and-roll".[51] Artists from across the musical spectrum began looking to the East for inspiration. For example, American folk group, Folkswingers, released an album called *Raga Rock* (1966), which featured a sitar.[52] In addition, the cover art of the Jimi Hendrix Experience's *Axis: Bold as Love* (1967) depicted the guitarist as various forms of Vishnu.

Eastern-themed music became closely associated with the hippie movement and with drugs, and for some artists and their followers the sitar seemed to represent a kind of psychic shortcut to some other form of consciousness. For example, Scott McKenzie's 1967 hit "San Francisco (Be Sure to Wear Flowers in Your Hair)" became synonymous with the "Summer of Love" that year: a sitar appears briefly in its middle-eight. Eric Burdon and the Animals signalled their shift from blues-rock to more contemporary psychedelic rock by releasing their *Winds of Change* album. Sitar featured heavily in the eponymous title track, which was a commentary on the state of rock music at that time. Some adopted the sounds of the East without the spiritual baggage. For example, prior to his iconic, career-enhancing appearance at Woodstock in 1969, Richie Havens played sitar on his first three albums and tambura on two of those albums. Havens' background was in folk and blues, but he was one of the pioneers of what would later be known as "fusion" music, combining elements of different musical styles to create new, distinctive sounds. On his 1968 album *Something Else Again*, Havens plays sitar and tambura on a three-minute instrumental track. This was no mere scene-setter: the remainder of the album illustrates Havens' aptitude towards a variety of musical styles — folk, psychedelic, and easy listening jazz. Havens avoided using Indian artwork on his album covers and inner sleeves, and his lyrics were eclectic, ranging from the optimism of "Putting Out The Vibration (And Hoping It Comes Home)", which promised brighter days ahead, to the Orwellian title of his 1968 album *Richard P. Havens 1983*, which was a more sombre affair than previous albums. One song on that album, "Indian Rope Man", suggests Havens was sceptical about the ability of gurus to impart knowledge to westerners. Havens is, therefore, a prime example of a musician in this time period experimenting with Indian musical instruments, but without adopting Indian spirituality.

The eastern influence became more than a musical trend, and the connection these musicians made between Indian music and elevated spirituality set the template for others to follow. For example, The Beatles took an interest in the teachings of Maharishi Mahesh Yogi and in February 1968 visited his ashram in Rishiskesh.[53] Philip Goldberg comments that after the Beatles met the Maharishi, "spirituality in the West would never be the same".[54] The band was "captivated by the Maharishi's promise of bliss without effort", notes Lennon biographer Philip Norman.[55] Their journey certainly raised the profile of Eastern spirituality to a point where the Maharishi actually toured with the Beach Boys in 1968.[56] All four Beatles, at various points, made positive comments about their encounters with Indian culture, and all were sincere in their attempts both to improve their spiritual health through Transcendental Meditation, and to develop their artistic abilities through learning from non-western music. Harrison held the most affirmative view, perhaps best illustrated in a 1969 interview he gave to *International Times*, in which he explained the deep influence of Paramhansa Yogananda's *Autobiography of a Yogi:* "it really explained so much for me", he said, "It filled me in on all sorts of things to do with the physical world and the other existences, the other frequencies — the astral worlds and the understanding of karma".[57] His fascination with Hinduism continued well into his solo career after the Beatles disbanded in 1970.[58]

It is, however, difficult to draw a clear divide between genuine interest in Indian music and the commercial reality that psychedelia was briefly popular among a mainly young, white, middle-class audience. Teen idols jumped on the bandwagon.[59] Even some Elvis Presley songs featured an electric sitar, such as "You'll Think of Me" (1969)[60] and "Snowbird" (1970).[61] Several other bands, including the Rolling Stones and the Moody Blues, made attempts to cash in on the craze for Eastern influences. Moreover, commentators then (as now) also raised critical questions of cultural appropriation and whether British and American musicians of this period were simply re-hashing older invocations of "Orientalism". For example, while critics were generally positive about George Harrison's iteration of Indian music, he was, essentially, being accepted by Western audiences as representing these communities, and so encouraging Orientalist-style fantasies about Indians: they were all spiritual, they all practiced meditation and yoga, and they possessed the secrets of universe. The "hall of mirrors" effect of such visions was not lost on Indian writer Gita Mehta, who observed: "The seduction lay in the chaos. They thought they were simple. We thought they were neon. They thought we were profound. We knew we were provincial. Everybody thought everybody else was ridiculously exotic and everybody got it wrong".[62]

Many trans-Atlantic musicians forging this "raga rock" genre at this time "turned to India" with genuine appreciation of Indian instruments, musical form and spiritual teachings, and strived to reach deeper understandings of the human condition through such borrowings and collaborations. Others, in contrast, used Indian music mainly to expand their musical knowledge, utilising Indian time signatures and instruments to enhance their performances as musicians (for instance, John Lennon); artists in this category were not so deeply interested in Eastern religions or new forms of spirituality. Others still were more commercially minded: these performers used Indian instruments for their novelty value, and their interest in the music of the East was transitory (for example, Traffic's "Hole in My Shoe"). On one hand, the cultural borrowings inherent in the "raga rock" style were celebrated by counterculture enthusiasts and music critics; in contrast, this new genre raised uncomfortable questions of whether this was tantamount to cultural appropriation or whether it indulged in simplistic "Orientalist" romanticism of the "East".

Yet Western musicians of this time generally saw Indian musicians as approximate equals: people who possessed a musical culture as valid and as interesting as their own. The raga rock era took place at a time of intense musical experimentation, when pop groups were attempting to demonstrate that they were different from the previous generation of popular musicians. Instead of being mere crooners, they wanted to convey that they were independent *artists*, capable of producing memorable works of complexity and depth: musicians hoped that music rooted in the "East" conferred a type of legitimacy on the artist, and that the very difficulty of their forms could demonstrate the technical proficiency of the musician. Rather than a simplified, romanticised "other", many music artists instead saw Indian music as a harbinger of high skill and craft. Furthermore, the creation of this new "raga rock" genre was significant not only because it opened an exciting new avenue of musical and cultural exchange; it also catapulted gifted Indian musicians like Ravi Shankar into the American music mainstream.

Ravi Shankar: East comes West

This new appetite for all things "East" had, then, two main manifestations. The first was a quest for spiritual knowledge, either by a physical journey to India to study in an ashram with a guru, or by following the teaching of a guru in the United States. The second manifestation was musical, either westerners adapting to a "raga rock" style, or listening to original Indian classical music, either on vinyl or even live, because this new fascination with Indian music led to Indian classical musicians undertaking regular American tours. For Shankar, who was its best-known practitioner, it opened the door for appearances at American music festivals such as Monterey Pop, Woodstock, and opening the show at the Concert for Bangladesh in 1971.

It was at Monterey in June 1967 that Shankar first made his mark in the American music festival scene. He had been booked initially by the festival's original promoters, Alan Pariser and Ben Shapiro, when it was still planned as a for-profit event: he was, therefore, the only artist to receive a fee for his appearance.[63] Shankar's performance was also the only one not sold out in advance. Shankar performed for four hours and asked the audience not to smoke and photographers not to take pictures during his set as he wanted the audience to be focussed totally on the music. In D. A. Pennebaker's festival film *Monterey Pop* (1968), Shankar's performance is given a prominent position in closing the show. This seems to have enhanced Shankar's reputation and most likely it was a factor in his invitation to perform at Woodstock in 1969. In actuality, California band The Mamas & the Papas closed the Monterey festival.[64] Contemporary reviews of Shankar's performance were mainly positive: for example, Sam Silver of the *East Village Other* claimed that Shankar "held the attention of ten thousand people, for four hours or more".[65] Writing in *Nola Express*, Frank Janusa's review was enthusiastic, if somewhat iconoclastic: Janusa described Shankar as "musically proficient, but he utilizes his proficiency in a neo-religious syndrome". His overall conclusion, "Stimulating it is!" seems to be an attempt to emulate the syntax of an Indian speaking English.[66] However, Robert Christgau pondered why Shankar drew a crowd at all, and he concluded that it was mainly due to curiosity. Christgau poked fun at the audience's ignorance of Indian music, pointing out that after Shankar had finished tuning his sitar, which took around twenty minutes, the audience responded with a round of applause, seemingly unaware that the concert hadn't yet begun. "It isn't likely that a third of those present had more than the most rudimentary understanding of what was going on", Christgau claimed.[67]

]June 1967 was a breakthrough moment for Shankar: as well as his performance at Monterey, he released a collaborative album with classical violinist Yehudi Menuhin entitled *West Meets East*, which reached number one in Billboard's classical album chart. At the 1968 Grammy Awards, the album was successful in the category of Best Chamber Music (this was in the same year that *Sgt. Pepper's* was Album of the Year and Duke Ellington's *Far East Suite* won best Instrumental Jazz performance).[68] Then, in December 1967 Shankar released an album of his Monterey performance entitled *Ravi Shankar at the Monterey International Pop Festival*. This was one of five albums he released that year, and it became a top 50 Billboard hit. Shankar had thus become a commodity in the musical marketplace, with all the sales gimmicks that entails. Describing Shankar as "the soul of India", adverts for the album stressed that it contained a free colour poster and that some record shops stocking the album would be offering a competition to win a free sitar.[69]

After Monterey, Shankar took advantage of the increased exposure his festival appearance generated. He played a concert on August 4, 1967 at the Hollywood Bowl, sharing top billing with sarodist Ustad Ali Akbar Khan, and supported by Bismillah Khan on shehnai, violinist K. V. Narayanaswami, and Palghat Raghu on mridangum (a South Indian drum).[70] The concert, which was two thirds full, began at 8:15pm and ended at 12:45am the next day. Before Shankar's set, many audience members had already left. Not only were they not used to such a long concert, Nat Freedland of the *Los Angeles Free Press* suggested a certain amount of jadedness at the "sheer mass of exotic sounds they had to cope with" and Freedland noted that the standing ovation Shankar received was one of the mildest yet.[71] George Harrison's visit to Shankar's Kinnara School after Shankar's Hollywood Bowl performance, and Harrison's subsequent press conference to promote Shankar's music, helped cement the Indian musician's position as a cultural icon in the United States.

A further series of six concerts took place in August 1967 in New York at the Philharmonic Hall, Lincoln Center. Shankar shared top billing with Bismillah Khan, with each giving separate performances. Reviewing these shows in the *East Village Other*, Ron Mitra, noted the prestigious venue and that Khan was introduced onstage by an Indian diplomat who quoted Shakespeare. Mitra suggested that although classical Indian music had become more familiar in the United States, "performances are being pathetically pushed into a domain of confused stuffiness".[72] While Shankar's familiarity with American audience expectations did give him an advantage over Khan, Mitra bemoaned the audience's lack of patience and focus, marked by "coughing, wheezing and squirming", as well as their limited appreciation of all forms of Indian music and instrumentality. More shows were booked at the New York venue for September 13, 14 and 15, and December 26, 28 and 30. This time, Shankar was top of the bill, with tabla player Alla Rakka second billing.[73] With memories of Monterey still current, Mitra suggested, however, that to experience the full emotional and spiritual effects of Shankar's music, a more informal setting in an outdoor, "natural" venue such as Central Park was desirable. Mitra could not know it, of course, but he would get his wish two years later at Woodstock.

A number of concert reviewers in this time period mention how Shankar's audiences often featured "flower children" — a group Nat Freedland referred to somewhat derisively as "recruits of the Pepsidelic Generation".[74] Peter Kostakis' review of a Shankar performance at the Orchestra Hall Chicago on October 6, 1967 suggests why the musician appealed to this demographic: noting the appearance and "prankish antics" of hippies in the foyer, Kostakis remarked that Shankar's music was "75% improvisation" and its "total spontaniety" demanded the "surrender of all restraints".[75] From the spontaneous prose of Jack Kerouac's *On the Road* (1957) to the street theatre of the Yippies, the notion of not planning ahead, and instead surrendering oneself to the cosmic flow, was a hallmark of the hippie generation that had rejected society's demands for conformity, structure, and routine. Without intending it, Shankar's music was therefore in harmony with some aspects of the counterculture. Not everyone was entirely happy with this development: Richard Goldstein, rock critic for the *Village Voice*, opined that for Shankar's fans, "hip has become mass-cult, and Ravi Shankar finds himself not the prophet of an elite, but the universal guru. His following wants Buddhahood on a long-play record. Tao on tap, a bath in the Ganges without getting wet. And they want Ravi Shankar to sock it to them".[76]

In 1968, demand for Shankar's music was such that he released eight albums that year. He arranged for a number of musicians to travel from India to the United States to contribute to his album *Ravi Shankar's Festival from India*, and in June and July that year he took a number of these musicians on a U.S. tour. They performed as "Ravi Shankar's Festival", and made an appearance at The Northern California Folk-Rock Festival at the Santa Clara Fairgrounds in May 1968. From September 10-15, Shankar took part in a run of shows in New York culminating with two performances at Carnegie Hall. Boosted by good reviews of the Monterey Pop documentary, which had been released in December 1968, and in which Shankar featured prominently, in early 1969 Shankar embarked on a solo tour of the States. Ticket prices give an indication at this point of Shankar's appeal: for instance, on February 14, 1969 Shankar performed at the Santa Monica Civic Auditorium. Ranging from $3.50 to $5.50, the cheapest and mid-priced tickets were comparable to the prices charged by the Rolling Stones on their 1969 tour in the Autumn of that year.

All of these things — Shankar's Indian heritage, his reputation as a virtuoso musician, performances at big outdoor festivals, his relationship with Harrison and subsequent status as a counterculture icon, and even Mitra's suggestion that Shankar's music would be best appreciated in a natural, outdoor setting — paved the way for Shankar's appearance at the Woodstock Festival. Michael Lang thought Shankar's "soft, mellow" vibes would be ideal for the Friday evening slot, which would mostly feature folk music. Lang offered Shankar $4,500 to perform, which Shankar accepted.[77] Shankar took to the stage at around 10pm, and was supported by Alla Rakha on the tabla and MayaKulkarni on the tambura. They played three songs — "Rāga Puriya-Dhanashri (Gat In Sawarital)", "Tabla Solo In Jhaptal", and "Rāga Manj Kmahaj" — lasting around forty minutes in total. Shankar's performance at Woodstock was well received: the final song, "Rāga Manj Kmahaj", took twenty minutes to unfold and it built to a furious crescendo that was appreciated by the crowd. Critic Gilles Malkind asserted that Shankar was "miles above everybody else... He woke up that audience and took them along with him on this soaring musical journey. Nobody else could touch that".[78] Lang claimed that the "vibe was intense" when Shankar performed and that it was a "spiritual moment".[79] However, the rains came pouring down during Shankar's performance and he was forced to leave the stage for a fifteen-minute intermission. Miller Francis Jr. reflected that Shankar "finally got us into some music, but if there was ever an inappropriate time to hear him, it was Friday night at a drizzly, muddy Woodstock".[80] Mike Bourne thought the rain made for "an appalling waste of Ravi Shankar' musical rapture on the mostly rain-fogged stoned crowd".[81]

Shankar too had his concerns. He had played large festivals before, but Woodstock was on a different scale entirely. During the rain intermission he expressed reservations about the size of the crowd and the potential for misadventure. He was also unhappy about the photographers on stage and at one point had asked them to stop using flash photography.[82] Shankar explained that Indian classical music was sacred, and required that nothing should interrupt the free flow of music between musicians and their audience. In a 1999 interview with David Bianculli for National Public Radio, Shankar expressed regrets about the behaviour of stoned American fans "shouting, shrieking and misbehaving" at his concerts. He would challenge them, "when you go to listen to Bach or Beethoven or Mozart, do you behave like that?"[83] Shankar also admitted that the crowd at Woodstock reminded him of the "water buffaloes you see in India, submerged in the mud" and for them "the music was incidental" to having a good time.[84] He bemoaned the fact that the Woodstock audience spent at least some of their time "shouting, smoking, masturbating and copulating — all in a drug-crazed state".[85] Most hurtful perhaps was that Shankar also drew criticism from Indian musicians for his collaborations with western pop stars. Their main concern seemed to be that Shankar had "diluted or betrayed tradition in his attempt to make [Indian classical music] more palatable to Western tastes".[86] There is also some indication that Shankar was unhappy with his performance at Woodstock. When World Pacific Records planned to release it in 1970 as a live recording entitled *Ravi Shankar At the Woodstock Festival*, Shankar insisted that a studio recording of the opening track "Raga Puriya–Dhanashri/Gat in Sawarital" be included instead of the live performance.

Shankar's performance was not included in the Woodstock movie. In part, this was due to the problems caused by the rain interruption. However, it was also difficult to accommodate a static instrumental performance on film without halting the movie's momentum. This was in contrast to Shankar's prominent position in the Monterey film, which depicted Shankar closing the festival. While omission from the Woodstock movie inevitably led to lesser exposure than those artists who were included, it did not noticeably harm Shankar's career. In fact, Shankar was soon involved in what might arguably be considered the high water mark of Western dalliance with Indian music, the Concert for Bangladesh at Madison Square Garden, New York, which was actually two separate performances by a host of artists on the first day of August, 1971. This was a benefit concert organised by George Harrison on behalf of the millions of Bangladeshi refugees stranded following the devastating secession war with Pakistan. The show opened with Ravi Shankar and Ali Akbar Khan performing Indian classical music to an audience of tens of thousands, and later to a greater audience via critically acclaimed and commercially successful audio and cinematic releases.[87] "Everything that was good and famous and beautiful in rock and roll during the '60s came together in a glorious flaring of emotion at Madison Square Gardens" commented one British reporter, suggesting the degree to which Shankar's sitar-playing had become accepted as part of the rock and popular music mainstream.[88]

Shankar was not just a musician, he was a cultural phenomenon. According to American Studies scholars Rachel Rubin and Jeffrey Melnick, he "provided Americans with an occasion to talk about Vietnam, race relations in the United States, religion, drugs, and the meaning of consciousness".[89] He taught George Harrison to play the sitar, and indirectly and inadvertently acted as a kind of guru to many American hippies. That Shankar spoke out against drugs and was unhappy with the over-commercialisation of Indian music did not seem to matter, because for his audiences he was an authentic symbol of the supposed wisdom and superior knowledge of the East. Shankar had the seal of approval of opinion shapers like Harrison, who continued to believe that musical exchange with non-western instrumental composers could facilitate spiritual growth and understanding. In an interview with Barry Miles in *International Times*, Harrison explained that a spiritual person such as Ravi Shankar could transmit his spirituality wordlessly, through his sitar. "Through the music you reach the spiritual", he explained, "It's so attuned to the spiritual scene".[90] To some then, Shankar represented not just Indian music but India itself: and at this time, the United States was particularly receptive to that "authentic" otherness. As cultural theorist Stuart Hall noted, Shankar presented Americans with an opportunity to "return to contemplation and mystical experience".[91]

The Year of the Guru

While Shankar offered a musical path towards spiritual enlightenment, others from the Indian subcontinent offered a more direct route. Indian yogis and holy men such as Jidhu Krishnamurti, Swami Prabhavananda, and Paramahansa Yogananda had travelled to the United States in the years prior to the Second World War and a few established religious societies and spiritual centres. After the war, in a time period marked by new openness to Eastern spirituality, a steady stream of such figures made their way to the United States. The most prominent of these was Maharishi Mahesh Yogi, a practitioner of Transcendental Meditation who, for a time in 1967 to 1968, acted a spiritual advisor to The Beatles. The band travelled to the Maharishi's ashram in Rishikesh in February 1968 and the time spent there proved to be one of the most musically inspiring periods of their career, with twenty songs written in India later appearing on *The Beatles* (White Album) (1968) and two more on *Abbey Road* (1969). Nevertheless, the band left India disillusioned with the Maharishi's behaviour, and cut ties with him in the summer of 1968.

Bhaktivedanta Swami was another guru who made his way to the United States. He founded the International Society for Krishna Consciousness in New York, opening a centre there in 1966 and another in San Francisco in 1967, and Hare Krishna devotees soon became familiar figures at festivals and gatherings. Yogi Bhajan was a practitioner and teacher of Kundalini Yoga. In 1968 he established three ashrams in Toronto, then began teaching in Los Angeles.[92] On July 20-26, 1970 he took part in the "Holy Man Jam" during the Whole Earth Fair and Festival of Peace held at the University of Colorado, Boulder — an event that raised his profile in the United States.[93] A year later, the promoters of the Festival of Life music event, held in McCrea, Louisiana on June 24–27, 1971, invited Bhajan to address the 50,000 crowd at the opening of the festival. This was a clear attempt to emulate Swami Satchidananda's address to the Woodstock audience. A report in *Great Speckled Bird* indicates that Bhajan's plea for "oneness" wasn't entirely adhered to by a crowd that was suffering in sweltering heat, with inadequate water supplies, and high concession prices.[94] A final indicative example is Meher Baba, a Zoroastrian spiritual leader from Poona in India. Baba visited the United States on six occasions from 1931 to 1958: however, it was the series of talks in 1962 that Baba called "The East-West Gathering" that gained him some traction in the United States as Baba invited westerners to come to him for spiritual guidance. In 1966, Baba entered into correspondence with American LSD guru Richard Alpert about the potential pitfalls of the drug. Alpert called Baba the "greatest spiritual luminary in the world today and as a result of his influence, Alpert stopped using LSD and began a journey towards Indian spirituality.[95] In a similar vein, when Pete Townshend came under Baba's influence, the guitarist swore off drugs and instead sought spiritual highs. Townshend dedicated The Who's *Tommy* (1969) to Baba in the year of his death, and when Townshend gave an interview with *Rolling Stone* in 1970, the magazine's front cover was illustrated with an image of Baba.[96] As was the case with numerous rock stars, it took Baba's death to make him famous in the West.

In contrast to some of these prominent and very public gurus, Swami Satchidananda's profile remained modest until his remarkable appearance onstage at Woodstock. He arrived in New York in 1966 as a guest of artists Peter Max and soon attracted a group of supporters, many of whom were intellectuals and artists.[97] That year he made a cameo appearance in Conrad Rooks' anti-drug film *Chappaqua*, which was released the following year. In the film, Satchidananda plays "The Guru" while Ravi Shankar plays the role of "Dieu du Soleil" (Sun God). Shankar also composed the film's soundtrack.[98] In December 1966 he made his first public appearance in the United States, presenting an evening of mantras, chanting and lectures on yoga at a New York church. Beat writer Allen Ginsberg compèred the event, which suggests Satchidananda was already moving in elite hippie circles.[99] Further evidence of this appeared the following year, when the swami gave a lecture and yoga demonstration on September 8, 1967 at the Village Theatre in New York. Among others in attendance was Hugh Romney who in reviewing the event for the *East Village Other* called Satchidananda "Jesus Christ, with lights and make-up" and "truly beautiful".[100]

In February 1968, Satchidananda made his first appearance on the west coast, by way of a yoga lecture at Griffith Park, Los Angeles. An advert for this event in the *Los Angeles Free Press* gives an indication of the appeal of yoga and of the swami: "Yoga is the perfection of mind and body. Yoga is the controlling of all the senses. Yoga is the uniting of all the Religions...

yet it is not a religion. Yoga is the seeking of truth and wisdom". The advert promised an experience "From unreal to real. From darkness to light. From Death to immortality".[101] It is easy to see the appeal in these words and ideas, coming as they did during the political, social and cultural maelstrom of the late 1960s. Further evidence of his appeal was revealed in an interview the swami gave in July 1969 in *San Francisco Good Times*. Satchidananda offered yoga as a cure for the tensions and stresses of city living, an approach that was congruent with the romantic ruralism of the hippies. However, he also warned of the dangers of smoking, drinking and "over-indulgence in sex", which put him at odds with the *San Francisco Good Times*' readership — the "free love", pot-smoking generation of young American hippies. But perhaps overriding that was Swami Satchidananda's promise that yoga could free them from fear, which was a very attractive proposition in an era dominated by worries of nuclear destruction and a savage war in Vietnam.[102]

Earlier that year the swami had shown just how much his teaching was tailored to an American audience when his followers placed a full page advert in *Other Scenes* for a guide to living entitled "Sadhana Tattwa" ("Essence of Yoga Practices").[103] It was aimed at "modern busy householders with fixed hours of work", which very accurately described the American working day. The guide provides 32 instructions under seven "culture" subheadings (Health, Energy, Ethical, Will, Heart, Psychic, Spiritual) and advises readers, in short, to eat moderately and have a balanced diet; give 2-10% of earnings to charity; fast on certain days; practice yoga or do exercise; meditate; reduce possessions; give up vices; do good to others; not to injure anyone; speak the truth; and be honest. Under "Energy Culture", it advises: "Observe celibacy according to your age and circumstances. Restrict the indulgence to once a month. Decrease it gradually to once a year. Finally take a vow of abstinence for your whole life".[104] While overall the guide seemed compatible with the modern American lifestyle, it is unlikely the advice on celibacy would appeal to young hippies. Nevertheless, the advert is illustrated with a photo of Swami Satchidananda in a pose used to advertise almost all of his events: he wears a white robe, sits with crossed legs and with his arms to his sides, palms open and welcoming. He stares straight into the camera, with a friendly, open and honest gaze. Crucially, with his shoulder-length hair and full grey beard, he is the epitome of what Westerners imagine an Indian guru to look like, which, not coincidentally, also resembled how the elite of the counterculture presented themselves at this time, for example the "wise old hippy" appearance of Allen Ginsberg and John Lennon.

There were so many Indian holy men travelling and teaching in the United States that *Time* magazine named 1968 the "Year of the Guru".[105] Satchidananda was one of those holy men interviewed by the magazine. He knew, therefore, that he either needed to find a niche or alternatively appeal to a wide range of Americans. In directing his message towards "modern busy householders with fixed hours of work" — perhaps identifying a "silent majority" constituency around eight months before President Richard Nixon's November speech introduced the term to the general public — and in advocating lifestyle changes that, celibacy aside, were not too challenging, Satchidananda cut an attractive figure. Unlike some of the more evangelical American clergy, he did not proselytise about life after death: instead he advocated common sense lifestyle choices that would act for many Americans as a practical guide to the here and now.

At the end of July 1969, just a few weeks before Woodstock, Satchidananda made an appearance at San Francisco First Unitarian Church, in which he spoke to an audience of 500 people.[106] A few weeks later he would address an audience perhaps one thousand times that size. While Woodstock Ventures' John Morris has indicated the swami asked him for permission to address the crowd, an alternative version of events claims the organisers asked Satchidananda to come from New York by car as they needed someone to keep the crowd calm in light of the overcrowding that disrupted the festival's opening day schedule.[107] While there is only fragmentary footage of the swami at the festival, onstage pictures show him sitting on an elevated platform among an entourage of around twenty white-robed followers, possibly from his Integral Yoga Institute in New York. Satchidananda spoke for approximately twenty minutes about the role music plays in finding peace, happiness and contentment. He expressed his wish that Woodstock's example would lead to further music festivals to spread peace. As President John F Kennedy had done at the beginning of the decade, Satchidananda challenged the young audience to make a difference, and in doing so he hoped that the United States would redirect its energy on world affairs through leadership in spiritual matters.[108] The indirect reference to the Vietnam War here would surely have been unmistakeable to the Woodstock audience. He then led the audience in a minute's mediation, followed by yoga chants. Like the best rock frontmen, Satchidananda instinctively knew that this "call and response" approach is essential in connecting with a large festival audience and in making that audience feel involved in the show. Morris has recalled his first impression of Satchidananda as a small man in a saffron robe with a squeaky voice. However, he was transformed in front of an audience: "he was wonderful", Morris recollected. "It was great. It was part of the calming influence. It was like a blessing. It was like an invocation".[109]

Satchidananda appears briefly in Wadleigh's festival film, being greeted on arrival, walking around backstage, and then onstage for a brief time. The latter scene is introduced in a very effective way: the camera first focuses on an unidentifiable grey mass, then travels upwards to reveal Satchidananda's face. ("From unreal to real. From darkness to light".) While only part of his speech is shown, its effect is evident in the crowd's spontaneous round of applause when the swami spoke of America leading the world in spiritual matters. But perhaps it's the imagery that is most effective: Satchidananda's robes give him an air of dignity and importance, and his tanned appearance, white teeth, charming smile, and full grey beard emanate wisdom and knowledge. His quiet speaking voice draws in the listener, and the elegant simplicity of his words make it difficult to contemplate any argument. The effect of this is that Satchidananda got the same "Woodstock boost" as many of the performing musical acts. In December 1969 and early January 1970 he gave three speaking appearances in the San Francisco Bay area.[110] The *Berkeley Tribe* reported that he had established yoga institutes in Connecticut, Los Angeles, and San Francisco.[111] In 1970 he made speaking appearances in March at the "Whole Earth Week" event at the University of California, Davis, and in July at the "Whole Earth Fair and Festival of Peace" at the University of Colorado, Boulder. The Boulder event attracted two to three thousand people daily, and perhaps 21,000 over the week. As reported in the *Los Angeles Free Press*, a question from the audience asking for his views about psychedelic drugs gave the swami the opportunity to once again make the point that there was no shortcut to nirvana: he replied that drugs "are good to go high (applause), but they won't keep you there. They will drop you down (louder applause). They can never give spiritual height, because that height is not a thing to come from outside. It is in you always".[112]

A cynic might respond to this that Satchidananda, as with other Indian mystics who claimed drugs weren't the answer, was merely eliminating the competition. After all, if the path to enlightenment could be found in a pill, then there was no need for gurus or expensive yoga retreats. And there were plenty of cynics around: in an *East Village Other* article, D.A. Latimer analysed the appeal of Swami Satyananda and concluded that the guru/swami fad was merely a money-making exercise. He suggested Satyananda, newly arrived in the United States, could become the next "Great Shill". The article is illustrated with the Swami's head on a cartoon body, holding a wad of cash.[113] In *Great Speckled Bird*, Kerry Thornley listed a series of complaints about a number of named gurus, including male chauvinism, poor and possibly dangerous advice about breathing exercises, and support for authoritarian politics. Thornley called Maharishi Mahesh Yogi "the biggest cosmic con man of them all", a man who rode around in a Cadillac, used a private airplane, and was worth four million dollars. "So it seems to be with many Masters", she claimed: "They talk like God, but act like Nixon". The article is illustrated with a drawing of a roll of dollar bills on the face of which is a bearded man in a yoga position.[114] And at Woodstock too, not everyone was enamoured with Indian holy men: Joshua White watched Satchidananda from behind the stage as he addressed the festival audience. White opined: "The whole kind of blessed-out spiritualism was beginning to take hold... it was pod-people time... it just scared me".[115]

It's certainly true that Woodstock boosted Satchidananda's profile and he began using his appearance at the festival to advertise forthcoming events. For instance, a three-quarter page advert in *The Rag* for a multiday "self encounter, yoga, [and] sensory awareness" retreat on either March 26-28 or April 9-11, 1971, and organised by the Aquarian Institute of Enlightenment, claimed that the swami "opened the Woodstock Festival". The cost of this event was $25.00, a significant increase in the one or two dollar suggested donations for Satchidananda's usual lecture appearances or yoga demonstrations.[116] In a similar vein, an advert placed by the Integral Yoga Institute publicised a "Yoga Ecumenical Retreat" from June 23 to July 2, 1971 at Annhurst College, South Woodstock, Connecticut. The programme was under the guidance and direction of the Swami Satchidananda, and the cost was an eye-opening $100.[117] It's difficult now to know what attendees got for this substantial fee, or if it was value for money. Probably the only people qualified to make this judgement are the attendees themselves. However, the amount charged speaks for itself: even allowing for the fact that these were multiday events rather than the swami's usual afternoon or evening lecture, and that they may have been dissimilar in other ways, it remains clear that in the aftermath of Woodstock the swami, like many other Woodstock performers, was able to charge a fee for his "performance" that was much higher than before.

There was another benefit of appearing at Woodstock: the swami became a multimedia personality. As well as his role as a guru and his public speaking, Satchidananda had an album of jazz named after him — Alice Coltrane's *Journey in Satchidananda* (1971); he wrote a book, *Integral Yoga Hatha* (Holt, Reinhart & Winston, 1972); and he appeared in the film *Sunseed* (1973), "an exciting film odyssey with several of the world's most respected gurus and their followers of all ages", according to one advert.[118] How all of this should be judged depends largely on whether one is a cynic or an optimist. In an interview *Los Angeles Free Press* journalist Edgar Jones conducted with the swami in 1970, Jones asked the "very warm and understanding Swami" questions about war, individualism, relationships, labour, and wealth that seemed designed to elicit answers that would tally with the values and ideals of the paper's readership. And Jones got what he wanted, as Satchidananda provided a series of trite and superficial answers, short on detail and long on vague truisms.[119] But from a more innocent perspective — perhaps that of the paper's readership and the rest of the Woodstock Nation — Satchidananda's teachings offered a clear path towards a gentler, more purposeful life.

Conclusion

Dilip Basu was a young musician who travelled from Bengal to the United States in 1967 to ply his trade and facilitate understanding of his culture. Fresh from performances at the Fillmore West and at Berkeley's Provo Park, Basu told the Berkeley Barb "he wouldn't be surprised if, in a few years, there were more American than Indian appreciators of classical Indian music".[120] If Basu had gone to Woodstock he would have seen his prediction come true, with perhaps half a million people enjoying the music of Ravi Shankar. One might compare this development with that of American blues music, which also developed a white audience that was at least a step removed from the culture in which that music was created. But it was, at least, a step towards the cross-cultural understanding that the hippies and Indian musicians such as Shankar and Basu both aimed for. By the mid-late 1960s, western musicians were more self-aware, more adventurous, and more open to musical and spiritual influences from outside western culture. They found a receptive audience for their musical experimentation in the era's youthful generation. Because of this, and due also to the popularity of hallucinogenic drugs, the concept of a "trip" had become as much internal as external, and "raga rock" reflected a significant manifestation of the synthesis of eastern and western musical forms. The musical turn to the East took many forms and artists were motivated by a number of musical, spiritual and commercial reasons. At times, the Eastern influence was substantial: some artists deeply immersed themselves in the music of the East, or in the culture, or in both; others saw only an opportunity to cash in on the exoticism of Eastern musical tropes and fashions, to make a quick profit, or to reinvent themselves by jumping on the "Beatles Orientalis" bandwagon. Of the aforementioned artists, a minority went East: Cat Stevens, The Beatles, Donovan, Mickey Hart, and a handful of others. But most were content to imagine the East, sometimes copying it directly from Shankar or second-hand from The Beatles. Most, however, relied on familiar Orientalist tropes, with predictably stereotypical results.

The mystical East was present at the first rock festival, the KFRC Fantasy Fair and Magic Mountain Music Festival, held at Mt. Tamalpais in Marin County, north of San Francisco on June 10-11, 1967. At the fair's entrance, a large inflatable Buddha balloon welcomed festivalgoers.[121] In addition, artist Stanley Mouse's original Fantasy Fair poster featured a Babylonian god, although organisers eventually deemed it not quite right for their purposes.[122] They commissioned instead a new poster depicting an Indian guru on top of a mountain made of flowers.[123] Of course, this festival wasn't the beginning of America's dalliance with aspects of Indian music and spirituality: it simply reflected what was developing at that time. Two years later, no one at Woodstock batted an eye when an Indian spiritual leader took to the stage to bless the festival, or wondered why Ravi Shankar was booked to perform Indian classical music at a rock festival. These points indicate both the extent and depth of the musical "turn to the east" in the decade. The musical results certainly varied: from the crass to the exceptional, from the spiritual to the self-indulgent, from naked profiteering to original, creative work. The extent of these experiments makes the "turn to the east" something arguably more substantial than other musical fashions: it is difficult to think of other movements that had similar musical, spiritual, philosophical and artistic dimensions. Moreover, some of these changes have had permanent effects on musical culture in the West. The idea of "world music" was developed in these years, although the arguments concerned appropriation, borrowing and inspiration continue to circulate, and to frustrate.

By 1971, Indian-inspired music was losing its attractiveness. That year, for example, The Mamas & The Papas released their final studio album, *People Like Us*, which featuring a sitar on five tracks. However, the critical and commercial failure of this album by one of the most emblematic bands of the 1960s suggests the ebbing of the flower power/raga rock musical subgenres. Perhaps this was due to the fickle nature of the music business where new trends and fads quickly replace existing ones. However, it may also be that some of the factors that influenced its growth had now become less prominent and less urgent. The Vietnam War was winding down, for example. The era of the Dr King/Ghandi-inspired Civil Rights Movement was also over: Dr King's assassination in 1968 fractured the movement, which, in any event, was already under challenge from separatist and confrontational "Black Power" ideology. With many of the major battles about voting rights, segregation and education having been won, the movement's main focus shifted to issues of poverty and class division, and these were much more intractable problems that could not be solved simply with the stroke of a pen. The Hippie Trail to the East that had once been the domain of a small number of intrepid travellers was now marked by regular commercial bus routes and mapped by guidebooks. Musically, what was novel and exciting in the mid-1960s had become, by the end of the decade, mercenary and passé: when even Elvis Presley songs now featured a sitar, it was clear the "raga rock" genre was suffering from music's worst possible criticism: it had become "unhip".

The British at Woodstock

"The English Invasion!" is how promoter Bill Graham described the bill at the Fillmore East Festival, New York, a few months before Woodstock. On that occasion, Graham was promoting shows on April 8-9 by Ten Years After, The Nice, and The Family.[124] Graham's description makes reference, of course, to the phenomenon known as the "British Invasion", a term used to explain the extraordinary success of bands such as The Beatles, The Rolling Stones, The Who, The Kinks and The Animals in the United States from around 1964 to 1967. Journalist David Kamp provides some statistics that illustrate the scale of this success: "Prior to 1964, only two British singles had ever topped *Billboard*'s Hot 100 chart — Acker Bilk's 'Stranger on the Shore' and the Tornadoes' 'Telstar,' both instrumentals — and between them they held the No. 1 spot for a total of four weeks. In the 1964–65 period, by contrast, British acts were at No. 1 for an astounding 56 weeks combined. In 1963 a mere three singles by British artists cracked the American Top 40. In 1964, 65 did, and in 1965, a further 68 did".[125] This trend had peaked a few years previously, but Graham's use of the term suggested it still had relevance from a promotional perspective.

However, as we will see, the British bands that performed at Woodstock were somewhat different to their forerunners, more rock-orientated perhaps, and more attuned to the late 1960s' mood. Although defining strict categories is difficult, some of these artists were in the "first wave" of the original British Invasion, which was initially pop orientated, then followed the lead of The Beatles into more experimental music. The Who are a prime example of this trend. Others were part of a "second wave" of British artists who would find chart success in the United States in the late 1960s: included in this group were artists such as Joe Cocker and Ten Years After, who performed at Woodstock, as well as the likes of the Bee Gees, the Moody Blues, Eric Clapton (Cream and Blind Faith), Jethro Tull, Van Morrison, Procol Harum, Deep Purple, Pink Floyd, Traffic, and Led Zeppelin. From this indicative list it is noticeable that only the Bee Gees really fell into the pop category and the main genres of music favoured by popular British artists in America were hard blues rock or progressive/psychedelic rock. That artists such as The Who, Joe Cocker and the Grease Band, Ten Years After, The Incredible String Band, and even the relatively unknown Keef Hartley Band were invited to perform at Woodstock is evidence of the continuing popularity of British music in the United States in the late 1960s; moreover, when taken as a whole, these British performers may well have been more representative of the state of *American* music at the time, and also — for the purposes of understanding the British at Woodstock — a kind of "litmus test" of the general American mood at the time.

For example, the first day of the festival was given over to folk music only because Woodstock Ventures hoped to book Bob Dylan, a man whose status at this time was second only to The Beatles. In his absence the Friday evening line-up looks weak, and for good reason: in the United States the popularity of folk music peaked in the mid-sixties. As incredibly talented and powerful as she was, Joan Baez was more representative of an earlier; perhaps more innocent period of the American 1960s, when people believed change could be affected though mass will. But the war in Vietnam, and the political assassinations of President John F. Kennedy, Robert

Kennedy, Malcolm X, and Dr Martin Luther King, ended that innocence. By the late 1960s even Dylan had given up on folk music. Arguably, then, the aggressive energy of The Who was more representative of the American mood in the late 1960s than the music of many of the American acts; moreover, Alvin Lee's fast but crude electric blues foreshadowed the nihilistic heavy rock and heavy metal era of the 1970s; and Joe Cocker's purposeful emulation of Ray Charles' soulful voice showed how black music and perhaps black culture itself had been co-opted. The British contribution to Woodstock is, then, an often overlooked indicator of the musical zeitgeist, which deserves critical attention.

While it is always difficult to pin down the exact date when a major cultural change occurred, it is possible to trace the origins of the vibrant trans-Atlantic pop-rock music community that developed in the 1950s and 1960s to the early days of rock and roll music, and especially to the popularity in Britain of American artists such as Elvis Presley, Buddy Holly, Little Richard, and Chuck Berry. One indicative and revealing example of this is Presley's first single, "Heartbreak Hotel", which reached number one on the Billboard chart in 1956; such was its impact that when young English band The Quarreymen formed in Liverpool in 1956, "Heartbreak Hotel" became a live staple for them from 1957 until the year after the band changed their name to The Beatles in 1960. Moreover, throughout the Quarrymen/Beatles' career, they played at least 31 Presley songs in their live shows.[126] The Quarreymen's love of American rock and roll was typical of the attraction that young Brits had for this music, and for its remarkable performers. Soon, a new generation of British and American artists featured in pop charts on both sides of the Atlantic, and influences and inspirations flowed back and forth. In the 1950s, American music had a greater impact on Britain than British music did on America; however, from around 1964 to 1967, the momentum shifted the other way, primarily due to the phenomenal success of The Beatles in the United States.

The type of clean cut pop-rock music that developed contemporaneously in Britain and the United States in the post-war years was eagerly embraced by young audiences in both countries. Generally, musicians were well-groomed, besuited and cheerful in the 1950s: surly, nihilistic, long-haired rebels would not appear until the mid-1960s. In the 1950s in the U.K., major artists included Tommy Steele, Marty Wilde, Billy Fury, Adam Faith and Cliff Richard; in the USA, Elvis Presley, Buddy Holly, Jerry Lee Lewis, Eddie Cochran, Little Richard and Chuck Berry held sway. There was no question at that point who was imitating who: musicologist Charlie Gillett notes, for example, that most of Wilde's hits were cover versions of American hits, whereas critic Nik Cohn adjudged Cliff Richard merely as a "sub-Elvis rebel", and Adam Faith "a poor man's Buddy Holly".[127] In his book *Revolt into Style*, which was one of the first attempts at serious critical analysis of this new pop scene, George Melly offered this analysis of the situation: "Early or primitive pop music looked exclusively towards America as its source and inspiration, and while it was true that this America was largely imaginary, it represented the present".[128] This trend continued into the early 1960s. For example, when The Beatles performed in Hamburg in 1962 almost all of their setlist were covers of already released songs by American artists such as Carl Perkins, Chuck Berry and Ray Charles[129]; in later years they would acknowledge American influences such as The Everly Brothers and Buddy Holly.[130] The Rolling Stones had similar American antecedents: their first single release was a cover of Chuck Berry's "Come On", their first U.K. number one a cover of The Valentinos "It's All Over Now", and their first U.S. top ten hit a cover of Irma Thomas's "Time Is on My Side".[131] Out of twelve songs on their debut album release *The Rolling Stones* (1964), only one was not a cover version of an American song.

However, in the wake of the musical "British Invasion" of America from 1964 onwards, this trend shifted when British bands began to influence American music more prominently:

British bands regularly toured the United States, just as American influences continued to flow in the other direction. Jim McGuinn of The Byrds revealed, for example, "we were influenced by The Beatles and other British groups".[132] Joe Walsh of The Eagles claimed it was The Beatles' appearance on the Ed Sullivan Show in 1964 that inspired him to become a musician: "I took one look on The Ed Sullivan Show and it was, 'Fuck school. This makes it!' I memorized every Beatles song and went to Shea Stadium and screamed right along with all those chicks".[133] The exchanges and the rivalry between, for example, the Beatles and the Beach Boys are well known.[134] Other examples of interactions are easily to find. The Byrds' David Crosby considered that the Beatles taught him what a band was supposed to be.[135] Jimi Hendrix first performed as a professional musician in the United States, but it was in Britain, and with a British bass-player and drummer, that he formed his first successful group. John Mayall was born in Macclesfield, England, and first came to public attention with his band, Bluesbreakers (including Eric Clapton) in 1965-66. But by 1970 he was living in Los Angeles, recording with largely American musicians, and singing of the wonders of California and his home in Laurel Canyon.[136] At this point, it became more difficult to decide if Mayall should be judged a British or an American musician.

Furthermore, audiences on both sides of the Atlantic responded to these artists and their music in similar ways, to the extent that Jim McGuinn of The Byrds suggested there was little difference between British and American audiences.[137] Film footage of "Beatlemania" in Britain and America, as well as contemporary concert reviews of Beatles' tours in both countries, support McGuinn's observation in that they reveal no significant dissimilarities in how British and American audiences reacted. Jerry Hopkins described San Francisco in 1965 as "America's Liverpool', whereas the writer George Melly claimed that by 1967 San Francisco had become "the capital of British pop, and British pop became in consequence provincial".[138] These shared tastes of artists and audiences in Britain and the United States suggest that a trans-Atlantic musical community had developed, sharing ideas, sounds, styles and musical traits. Looking back on this era, historian Arthur Marwick adjudged one of its main characteristics as a "participatory and uninhibited popular culture, whose central component was rock music, which in effect became a universal language".[139]

Given that Woodstock took place against the backdrop of this thriving trans-Atlantic musical community, it is perhaps unsurprising that Woodstock organisers prioritised securing British talent for the festival. John Morris recalls a vague idea that the schedule for the festival's opening night would be mellow folk music, performed mainly by American artists; on day two however, the philosophy was "then we'd go England".[140] There was certainly a strong British presence at Woodstock: performers included Ten Years After, The Who, The Incredible String Band, the Keef Hartley Band, Joe Cocker and the Grease Band (including Northern Irish lead guitarist Henry McCullough), Graham Nash of Crosby, Stills & Nash, and Mitch Mitchell (the drummer in Jimi Hendrix's band Gypsy Sun and Rainbows). The Jeff Beck Group, featuring Rod Stewart and Ronnie Wood, were booked to play, but depending on which story to believe, they either cancelled due to illness or split acrimoniously prior to their anticipated Woodstock appearance. Michael Lang hoped Donovan would agree to perform: the Scottish singer-songwriter had been on the Board of Governors for the 1967 Monterey Festival and by 1969 was a significant international star. In the mid-1960s he had developed a style of singing and playing that was similar to Bob Dylan's and perhaps Lang hoped that might offer the audience some kind of compensation if Dylan declined to appear. However, it never came to pass.[141] A number of other British artists were invited to appear, including Led Zeppelin, Jethro Tull and Procol Harum, but for various reasons they declined. The Moody Blues had originally agreed to perform, and they are billed on the advertisements for the event when it was scheduled for Wallkill. However, they pulled out in favour of a concert in Paris instead.[142] The British presence at Woodstock could, then, have been even more substantial if these artists had not declined Woodstock Ventures' invitations to appear.

In addition, Woodstock took place in the shadow of the Beatles, with rumours abounding that the band would perform even though they had stopped touring three years previously. In fact, Michael Lang had written to John Lennon to ask if a live reunion at the festival was possible; however, when Lennon wrote back saying he could only guarantee an appearance by his Plastic Ono Band, Lang made no further efforts to book the band.[143] Nevertheless the Beatles were present at Woodstock by proxy: Richie Havens and Joe Cocker performed cover versions of "With a Little Help from My Friends". Cocker, in fact, had had a U.K. number one hit single with the song the previous November. Havens played a trio of Beatles' songs, adding "Strawberry Fields Forever" and "Hey Jude" to his set. In addition, Crosby, Stills & Nash (and Young) performed Paul McCartney's composition, "Blackbird". That these notable artists would choose to perform cover versions of Beatles' songs in the short time they had on stage and at one of the most important and visible festivals of the era, indicates how influential the British quartet were; and that a significant number of British artists were invited to perform at Woodstock in the last months of the 1960s indicates that the British Invasion lasted longer than is commonly remembered. Moreover, it suggests that music acted as a bridge between the old world and the new which, in the 1960s, was illustrative of shared values and ideas; not perhaps in the traditional sense of a shared language and culture but instead the new "language" of the counterculture — revolt against conformity, antiwar sentiment, pro-recreational drug use, pro-equality, and free love. According to Joel Rosenman and John Roberts, the counterculture — their Woodstock audience —was seeking shelter from "a world gone mindlessly malevolent", and they found refuge in "drugs, naïve mysticism, primal rhythm … and each other".[144]

The transformation of the Who, and Pete Townshend in particular, is indicative of the changes that occurred between the original British Invasion and the British music that was popular in the United States at the end of the decade. Until the release of their 1969 album *Tommy* — an ambitious multi-themed rock-opera — the band was known mainly for their rowdy brand of teenage-rebellion rock, pop and rhythm and blues, as well as for sometimes outrageous on and off stage antics, which included Townshend smashing his guitar at the end of most performances, and on occasion, drummer Keith Moon trashing his drum set or blowing up an amplifier. There is evidence that the band began to tap into wider cultural currents with the 1967 release of their concept album *The Who Sell Out*, their tribute to the pirate radios stations that challenged the BBC's dominance of the radio waves in the U.K. Then in 1968, Townshend began to follow a guru named Meher Baba, who opposed the use of hallucinogenic drugs as "harmful mentally, spiritually and physically". In May of that year, Townshend swore off drugs and developed his fascination with alternative forms of spirituality.[145] Baba was an influence on *Tommy*: for example, the track "The Acid Queen" suggests that while hallucinogens might provide temporary enlightenment, they won't change the essential realities of life (Tommy remains deaf, dumb and blind); and "We're Not Gonna Take It", the album's final track, suggests that alcohol and pot are not holy sacraments, and therefore Tommy's disciples don't need them to follow the guru's teachings. Moreover, Townshend acknowledged that *Tommy* derived from his "new-found spiritual mood".[146] The album's complexity and ambition brought The Who a new fan base in the American counterculture, as well as drawing coverage from the underground press. For example, *Rebirth* newspaper called *Tommy* a "total mind/body trip, a neat balance of Apollonian versus Dionysian rock". Suddenly, Townshend, "esthetic engineer of most of Tommy", was "probably the most intelligent and articulate rock musician around".[147]

It was for these reasons, as well as the band's reputation as an exciting live act, that caused

Woodstock Ventures to push so hard for The Who to perform at the festival. The band initially had little interest. They were nearing the end of a long American tour and wanted to go home. However, Woodstock production coordinator John Morris arranged for Townshend and the band's tour manager, John Wolff, to have dinner at the home of Frank Barsalona, head of Premier Talent agency. Twelve hours later, Morris and Barsalona had finagled an agreement from Townshend and Wolff that the band would play at Woodstock for a fee of $12,500.[148] Townshend would come to regret that decision. He hated everything about Woodstock: it was disorganised, the band was indeed exhausted after their American tour, and he despised the hippies. In addition, the band was initially scheduled to go onstage on Saturday evening but instead had to wait until the early hours of Sunday morning. When rumours began to circulate that the festival was in deep financial trouble, the band demanded their fee upfront, and when that was finally agreed the band took to the stage with a setlist that consisted mainly of songs from *Tommy*, along with a few of their earlier hits.

Reviews of The Who's performance in the underground press were mainly positive. Miller Francis Jr. said it was "one of the great musical experiences" of his life. He called The Who "probably the greatest rock band in the world" and compared *Tommy* favourably with *Sgt. Pepper*. The mainstream press also offered effusive praise: for example, *New York Times* journalist Patrick Lydon called the band's performance "one of the great shows of rock 'n' roll history", with Townshend holding the audience "spellbound" with his dynamism.[149] Townshend was less impressed than the critics: towards the end of the set he recalled thinking "this is a disaster… the vibes were well down. *Tommy* wasn't getting to anyone".[150] The only thing he thought special was that the sun came up at the end of their set, and he was finally able to get a view of the massive crowd in all its ragged glory. He was, however, wrong about the band's supposed failure: despite the early morning slot, they were able to make a connection with the crowd, which sang along during to some of the *Tommy* songs.[151] Moreover, in reviewing the *Woodstock* soundtrack for *New Musical Express*, journalist Richard Green spoke admiringly of the band's performance: "this is positively one of the best Who recordings I've ever heard", he explained.[152]

It was in this dramatic atmosphere that the aforementioned encounter with Abbie Hoffman took place. In an interview with *Rolling Stone* magazine six months after Woodstock, Townshend was in reflective mood about the incident. He explained firstly that he was in a defensive state-of-mind at the festival. His pregnant wife was with him; unlike most of the other performers, he was unable to take a helicopter to the venue and got stuck in a traffic jam for hours; and he unknowingly drank a coffee spiked with acid. Added to that, the band had to follow Sly and the Family Stone, whose set was well received by the tiring audience. In explaining his behaviour towards Hoffman, Townshend wanted to set the record straight about his political stance: "Quite honestly, I mean knock for knock everything Abbie Hoffman said was very fair", he explained.[153]

Most of the other British artists at Woodstock were well-received, thus enhancing both their reputations and their future drawing power. When Woodstock Ventures paid over-the-odds to attract the performers they needed to make the festival a success, they set the bar for future appearance fees. Sociologist R. Serge Denisoff notes, for example, that few of the performers at Woodstock would appear again for less than $10,000 to $20,000.[154] Ten Years After received a significant career boost as a result of their dynamic performance. The English electric blues band played six songs at the festival, four of them cover versions. One of guitarist and lead singer Alvin Lee's original tracks called "I'm Going Home" featured in Wadleigh's concert film and, as a result, brought the band to the attention of mainstream audiences in both Britain and America. While they were not exactly unknown in the United States before Woodstock, having appeared, for example, at the Newport Jazz Festival in 1969, they had enjoyed relatively modest success up to that point. Dave Laing points out, for example, that in 1968 the band played in the United States for the first time and could only secure six gigs in eight weeks. After Woodstock, however, they "were in constant demand for US national tours".[155] Lee claims that after Woodstock Ten Years After did 27 American tours in just seven years, such was the raise in their profile.

By 1969, Joe Cocker had enjoyed some success in the United States, appearing on the Ed Sullivan Show in April that year and performing at the Newport '69 Festival in mid-June, the Denver Pop Festival in late June, and at the Atlantic City Pop Festival in early August. Cocker and his backing musicians the Grease Band, with Northern Irishman Henry McCullough on lead guitar, played eleven songs at Woodstock: a short set, John Morris reflects, but "probably the most effective of his entire life".[156] But Cocker is remembered mainly for his mesmerising performance of The Beatles' "With A Little Help From My Friends", which was the sole song from Cocker's set that Michael Wadleigh and co-producer Bob Maurice chose for the concert film. Cocker's soulful vocals, based on those of Ray Charles, worked in tandem with Cocker's bodily contortions, to produce a captivating and memorable experience. Michael Sciulla was in the audience and his abiding recollection is of Cocker "belting it out".[157] Randy Sheets, another festival attendee, had never heard of Cocker or his music, but he remembers Cocker's sound and band as "amazing!"[158] While Maurice was unimpressed with the performances of some artists, for example Blood, Sweat & Tears, which meant they weren't chosen to appear in the film, he thought Cocker "gave an incredible performance".[159] Reflecting on Woodstock years later, Cocker recalls that while the band played he saw the audience chatting among themselves and eating sandwiches.[160] He remembers that the audience only began to respond when he sang "Let's Go Get Stoned", and that the first real connection happened when he belted out the Beatles' cover.[161] In a May 1969 *Detroit Free Press* article, journalist Mike Gormley wrote: "Joe Cocker isn't the best known name in the land. In fact when it was announced he was coming to town everybody asked, 'Who's Joe Cocker?'"[162] After Woodstock, however, Cocker had a considerably higher profile. He released his second album, entitled *Joe Cocker!*, which reached number eleven in the Billboard album chart, and embarked on a lengthy and successful American tour. Of all the British artists at Woodstock, Cocker probably benefitted most from the exposure the festival brought.

The most notable exceptions to this "Woodstock boost" for British artists were The Incredible String Band and the Keef Hartley Band, whose omissions from the concert film and the *Various Artists Woodstock* vinyl album seems to have sabotaged their potential for fame and fortune. The Incredible String Band was originally scheduled to perform on Friday evening as part of the celebration of folk music planned for the festival's opening day. They were, however, leery of playing in the rain, and Melanie Safka took their place on the bill, while The Incredible String Band played Saturday evening instead. Critics were not kind to the band: Jan Hodenfield witheringly claimed The Incredible String Band "denied the crowd's need for excitement".[163] Joe Boyd, the band's representative, claimed that it was this change in schedule that cost The Incredible String Band the chance to appear on the Woodstock film and album. On Saturday, Boyd claimed, the audience was ready for something "heavy and loud" and instead they got the folk-pop stylings of The Incredible String Band. "They came on and just — died!", said Boyd. Band member Rose Simpson concurred with Boyd's assessment of the situation: "The String Band would have had a different history", she claims, if they had performed on the festival's opening night. "One of our big mistakes really".[164]

Hodenfield was happier with the Keef Hartley Band, which, he says, "did a hard and brassy set".[165] In contrast to Hodenfield's assessment, however, Bill Marion was in the audience on Saturday and was underwhelmed: in the afternoon sweltering heat, he remembers, "the band did not fare well". Guitarist Miller Anderson blames the festival's chaotic organisation for his band's failure to make an impact. He recalls that the band had gone through a line-up change, that they hadn't rehearsed enough, and for reasons unexplained they had to borrow Santana's instruments. "It was a missed chance for the band", he reflected.[166] However, it wasn't the band's performance that caused them to be omitted from Wadleigh's film: Martin Scorsese asked their manager for permission to record the band but in the absence of an advance fee, that permission was refused.[167] After Woodstock the band continued to tour and released a few albums, with moderate success. It never seemed to bother Keith Hartley that Woodstock was a missed opportunity: primarily a musician rather than a rock star, he turned down opportunities to raise his profile with a mainstream audience, preferring instead to play his drum set dressed in a Native American costume and make his own brand of jazz-rock-blues.[168]

Overall, given the diversity of British acts/songs at Woodstock, it is tempting to revise the notion of a peculiarly "British" invasion of the U.S. music scene at this time. In spite of the considerable presence of British musical artists at the festival, it is notable that many British artists were paying homage to American music: Joe Cocker sang the blues and sounded like Ray Charles, Ten Years After played electric blues, which was invented in Chicago, Joplin sang an English group's soul song, and the Keef Hartley band played blues rock, a style of music invented in the United States. Even The Who, the most innovative and original British act on show, were at heart a rock and roll band, and that music genre had an American origin. With the exception perhaps of the Incredible String Band, who had their own peculiar brand of folk-pop, it might be said that these British artists benefitted from two bands which did not appear at Woodstock — the Rolling Stones, who did much to showcase American rhythm and blues music and thereby helped Americans rediscover their roots; and the Beatles who made British/English music cool. What the British bands at Woodstock were doing was what the Stones had been doing for years — playing American music back to an American audience, and doing it better than most American bands.

The British performers at Woodstock were different to their predecessors from the "British Invasion" in that they were more rock-orientated and more in tune with the American mood at the end of the decade. To return again to The Who as an indicative example, Townshend's search for new forms of spirituality and his hunger to "connect" with the crowds in a meaningful way, were in tune with the American counterculture's search for meaning, and their belief that the usual means of communication had failed. Woodstock was both a testimony to the vibrant trans-Atlantic rock music community that still held sway at this point in the late 1960s, and an example of the new musical connections that were being formed between those onstage and those in the audience. At the same time, Townshend's treatment of Hoffman illustrates both the gap between the political radicals, and the dilemma for rock musicians like Townshend: does he speak to the fans or for them? And how can he engage more closely with fans and yet keep the distance necessary for him to perform his music? These self-reflective questions about the role of music in communicating some sort of revolutionary message, while at the same time being embedded in capitalist systems of commerce, were one of the most important and most revealing outcomes of Woodstock. Journalist Miller Francis Jr. eloquently outlined the challenge the trans-Atlantic music community would face in the new decade:

Rock & Roll is more important to young people now than it has ever been... At the same time Rockers are realizing... that Rock & Roll must move beyond its consumer capitalist foundation... It may very well be that understanding the violent confrontation between [Hoffman and Townshend] can help us understand more of what we are and what divides us, what we have to do before we can join in changing the world we live in. If, however, this contradiction among the people is not resolved, and we do not stand united as a Western revolutionary youth movement, then we will not be able to struggle to win a place in the new world. And that's what it's all about.[169]

The international aspect of the new rock festival culture is often overlooked: it represents, for example, a significant shift in American national consciousness, looking outwardly instead of inwards. Nevertheless, a survey of rock festival performers from 1967 to 1969 illustrates that while international representation did increase as the decade progressed, with very few exceptions the internationalism on display was mainly British and Canadian. At the first rock festival of the era, the Fantasy Fair and Magic Mountain Music Festival held in June 1967, there was only one international act, The Sparrows, a Canadian blues rock. At the Monterey International Pop Music Festival later that month, the bill lived up to its name, with non-North American acts performing, such as Hugh Masekela, a South African jazz trumpeter, two British acts, The Who and Eric Burden and the Animals, and of course Indian classical musician Ravi Shankar. At the Northern California Folk Rock Festival in May 1968, Eric Burden and the Animals performed again, as did Ravi Shankar. In August that year, at the 1968 Newport Pop Festival, Eric Burden and the Animals was the only international act to perform. At the San Francisco International Pop Festival in October 1968, José Feliciano (from Puerto Rico), and Britain's Procol Harum, Deep Purple, and Eric Burden and the Animals performed. At the December 1968 Miami Pop Festival, Hugh Masekela, José Feliciano, Britain's Fleetwood Mac, Terry Reid, and Procol Harum, and Canada's Ian & Sylvia, Buffy Sainte-Marie, Steppenwolf, and Joni Mitchell performed. Also in December 1968, José Feliciano was the only international act at the Los Angeles Pop Festival. These examples illustrate that a year and a half after the first rock festival of the era, an increasing number of British and Canadian artists were performing, but only three musicians (Shankar, Masekela, and Feliciano) from outside that English-speaking axis featured at rock and pop festival events. (Feliciano's short-live prominence was due to his chart success in 1968 with a cover of The Door's song "Light My Fire", which reached number three in the Billboard "hot 100" chart.)

This trend continued into 1969: for example, at the Northern California Folk-Rock Festival in May, British acts Eric Burden, Noel Redding, and Led Zeppelin were the only non-American performers. At the Newport '69 event held in June, Canadian acts Steppenwolf and Buffy Sainte-Marie performed, as well as British acts Jethro Tull, Eric Burden and Joe Cocker. Also in June, Joe Cocker was the sole international act to appear at the Denver Pop Festival. In July, Joe Cocker and Ian & Sylvia were the only non-American performers at the Atlanta International Pop Festival. Also in that month, Canadian rock band The Guess Who, and British acts Jeff Beck, Led Zeppelin, Jethro Tull, Ten Years After performed at the Laurel Pop Festival. The Seattle Pop Festival from July 25 to July 27, 1969 featured The Guess Who, Led Zeppelin, and Ten Years After. The Midwest Rock Festival in Wisconsin, held in late July, 1969 probably had the largest proportion of non-American acts on the bill in this era, featured Led Zeppelin, Buffy Sainte-Marie, Blind Faith, Taste, John Mayall & the Bluesbreakers, and Joe Cocker and the Grease Band — six out of the twenty three, or over a quarter of the major acts on the bill.

While the nationalities of the band remained focused on American, British and Canadian acts, the genres of music represented at festivals was evolving. Early festivals had more pop, folk and jazz acts. Indeed, the variety of music on offer was sometimes a festival's major attractions. For example, the 1969 Atlanta International Pop Festival was advertised as "More blues/Psychedelic/Soul/Jazz/Rock greats than ever assembled before anywhere".[170] However, rock music in all its forms was beginning to dominate. Hard rock, blues rock, rhythm and blues, and psychedelic rock had become the main attractions of the big outdoor festivals. For example, in a controversial move, the Newport Jazz Festival, held July 3-6, 1969, featured the likes of Jeff Beck, Ten Years After, Jethro Tull, John Mayall, and Led Zeppelin, all British artists and all — with the exception of Jethro Tull — playing electric blues rock. Moreover, immediately preceding Woodstock, in early August 1969, Ten Years After performed their brand of hard, electric blues at the Atlantic City Pop Festival. The band's performance of this style of rock was popular at Woodstock, and then when the film of the festival appeared in 1970, their sole contribution to that — the electric "I'm Going Home" — was enough to ensure continuing concert and festival bookings.

In the months after Woodstock, as the final year of the decade wound down, there were more festival appearances by British bands and an occasional other international artist. For instance, the Texas International Pop Festival, held on August 30 to September 1, 1969, featured The Incredible String Band, Ten Years After, and Led Zeppelin. On those same dates — that is, on the American Labor day weekend — the New Orleans Pop Festival featured England's Tyrannosaurus Rex with Mark Bolan. At the Palm Beach Pop Festival in November 1969, British acts Spooky Tooth, King Crimson, Terry Reid, and the Rolling Stones featured, as did Canadian-American band Steppenwolf. At the Altamont Speedway Free Concert in December, the Rolling Stones were the only non-American act, and at that month's Miami Rock Festival, which was advertised as the "Last rock festival of the 60's", Hugh Masekela was the only non-American performer. It is a statistical anomaly that only one international act appeared at the first outdoor rock festival of the decade, the Fantasy Fair and Magic Mountain Music Festival, and one featured at the last in Miami, because in the years in between, dozens of performers, mainly British and Canadian, appeared at outdoor festivals. The reasons for this are clear enough — a shared language, and a developing trans-Atlantic (mainly Anglo-American) musical culture. However, Ravi Shankar's appeal suggests deeper currents were in play. For many young Americans, Shankar offered an "authentic", spiritual experience that was missing from modern American life. He offered an alternative to the consumer values, rampant capitalism, violence and discrimination that seemed to mark the American way of life. At the same time, young British musicians were drawn to American electric blues music, which seemed to offer the same lures of authenticity and otherness that Shankar offered to Americans, and therefore, to those young Brits, the blues offered an alternative to the limited opportunities available to them in 1960s Britain.

[1] Allan Katzman, "The Serpent Power", *East Village Other*, Vol 3, Issue 28, Jun 21, 1968, pp. 10-11. At p. 11.

[2] Chet Flippo, "Life Celebration: A Report from the Front", *Rolling Stone*, Jul 22, 1971. Available online at: https://www.rollingstone.com/music/music-news/life-celebration-a-report-from-the-front-40743/

[3] Robert Stephen Spitz, *Barefoot in Babylon: The Creation of the Woodstock Music Festival,* 1969 (New York: Viking, 1979), p. 399.

[4] Mike Evans and Paul Kingsbury, editors. *Woodstock: Three Days that Rocked the World* (New York & London: Sterling. 2009), p. 77.

[5] Jonathan Bellman has argued, for example, that because of London's large Indian community, plus the rich heritage of the Raj "and its resonances in British comedy and music hall (particularly of the satiric, Goon Show variety)", Indian culture was "undoubtedly more familiar in England than it was in the United States. (Indeed, in mid-60s London, exposure to it may have been virtually unavoidable.)" Jonathan Bellman, "Indian Resonances in the British Invasion, 1965-1968", *The Journal of Musicology*, Vol 15, No 1 (1997), pp. 116-36. At p. 117.

[6] Krishnalal Shridharani, quoted in Rachel Rubin and Jeffrey Paul Melnick, *Immigration and American Popular Culture: An Introduction* (New York: New York University Press, 2007), p. 146.

[7] Indians were often employed as cheap labour to build America's railroads, to work in factories, on farms in southern California, on sugar plantations in Hawaii, as miners during the California Gold Rush, in restaurants and laundries in San Francisco, on fishing boats from west coast ports, or as labourers and loggers in the Pacific north west. The low point was after World War One, when a combination of union agitation against cheap labour and "100 per-cent Americanism" campaigns by patriotic groups such as the American Legion and Asiatic Exclusion League, prompted changes in U.S. immigration law. In 1924 the Immigration Act set strict quotas on immigration which favoured north Europeans and almost entirely excluded those from Asian and Pacific countries (See Ronald Takiki, *Strangers From a Different Shore: A History of Asian Americans* (Boston: Little, Brown, 1989); Marcus Duffield, King Legion (New York: Cape, 1931); and Stephen Prothero, "Mother India's Scandalous Swamis" in Colleen McDannell, ed., *Religions of the United States in Practice*, 2 (Princeton, N.J.: Princeton University Press, 2001), pp. 418-432.

[8] For example, in a 1939 essay entitled "The Indian Menace", Christian advocate Mersene Sloan noticed a "considerable craze for eastern things, even to the point of cherishing oriental fabrics, colors, musics and entertainments" (Quoted in Rubin and Melnick, *Immigration and American Popular Culture*, pp. 144-5.) One recurring stereotype was that Indians were more spiritual than westerners, and that particular swamis or gurus such as Swami Vivekananda offered a path to spiritual enlightenment. In 1893, Vivekananda attended the World's Parliament of Religions in Chicago. He then went on a well-received lecture tour and in 1894 established the Vedanta Society, which became the largest Hindu organisation in the United States at this time. Even here though, there was hostility: some American men thought these gurus were "sex-crazed", and that vulnerable women were being taken

advantage of by swarthy foreigners. See Stephen Prothero, "Hinduphilia and Hinduphobia in American Culture" in Anna Lannstrom, ed., *The Stranger's Religion: Fascination and Fear* (Notre Dame, Ind.: University of Notre Dame Press, 2004), pp. 13-37; and Kurt Vonnegut, "Yes, We Have No Nirvanas" in his *Wampeters, Foma and Granfalloons* (London: Grafton Books, 1988 [1976]), pp. 48-57.

[9] On the effects of Eastern-inspired pacifism on one black militant, see: Jan Willis, *Dreaming Me: Black, Baptist and Buddhist: One Woman's Spiritual Journey* (Somerville: Wisdom Publications, 2008).

[10] On an almost daily basis, Americans were exposed to images of combat and suffering. Moreover, the Vietnam War caused huge divisions in American society, leading many to question the state of American values, particularly as the United States remained the only country in the world to use atomic weapons in anger, and against an Asian enemy. Philip Goldberg, an expert on Eastern spirituality, reflects that by the time of the "Summer of Love" in 1967, "a hundred Americans a week were dying in Vietnam, and riots were erupting in Newark and Detroit, and the need for a new kind of consciousness had never been more obvious". See Philip Goldberg, *American Veda: From Emerson and the Beatles to Yoga and Meditation: How Indian Spirituality the West* (New York: Random House, 2010), p. 149.

[11] Neil Campbell and Alasdair Kean, *American Cultural Studies: An Introduction to American Culture* 2nd Edition (London & New York: Routledge, 2006), p. 112.

[12] Susan Fast, *In the Houses of the Holy: Led Zeppelin and the Power of Rock Music* (Oxford: Oxford University Press, 2005), p. 92.

[13] Rubin and Melnick, *Immigration and American Popular Culture*, p. 132. For a more general survey, see: Colin Campbell, "The Easternisation of the West: Or, How the West was Lost", *Asian Journal of Social Science*, 38 (2010), pp. 738-57.

[14] Warren Hinckle, "A Social History of the Hippies" *Ramparts*, Mar 1967, pp. 5-26. At p. 17.

[15] Richard Hughes Seager, *Buddhism in America*. Columbia Contemporary American Religion (New York: Columbia University Press, 2012), p. 4.

[16] Harvey Cox, *Turning East: the Promise and Peril of the New Orientalism* (London: Allen Lane, 1977), p. 10.

[17] Cox, *Turning East*, p. 93.

[18] Jacob Needleman, *The New Religions* (New York: E.P. Dutton, 1977 [1970]), p. 129.

[19] Cox, *Turning East*, p. 9.

[20] Nick Bromell, *Tomorrow Never Knows: Rock and Psychedelics in the 1960s* (Chicago & London: University of Chicago, 2000), p. 62.

[21] Aldous Huxley, *The Doors of Perception and Heaven and Hell* (London: Flamingo, 1994 [1954]), p. 5.

[22] Seth E. Blumenthal, "Nixon's marijuana problem: youth politics and 'law and order', 1968—1972", *The Sixties*, Vol 9, Issue 1 (2016), pp. 1-28.

[23] Theodore Roszak, *The Making of a Counter Culture; Reflections on the Technocratic Society and Its Youthful Opposition* (Berkeley, Los Angeles & London: University of California Press, 1995 [1969]), p. 136

[24] Cox, *Turning East*, p. 149.

[25] Carl Jackson, "The Counterculture Looks East: Beat Writers and Asian Religion", *American Studies*, Vol 29, Issue 1 (1988), pp. 51-70. On the Beatniks' reception of Buddhism, see also Alan W. Watts, "Beat Zen, Square Zen and Zen", *Chicago Review*, Vol 12, No 2 (1958), pp. 1-11.

[26] Timothy Miller, *The Hippies and American Values* (Knoxville: The University of Tennessee Press, 1991), p. 48.

[27] Ira Robbins, "Pete Townshend: What Came Next: Pete Townshend Goes It Alone", *Who Came First* (Rykodisc) 1992 [1972].

[28] Dill Kerby and H Lawrence Lack, "Harrison Expands from Rock to Raga", *Los Angeles Free Press* Vol 4, No. 32, Issue 160, Aug 11-17, 1967, p. 5. Indeed, later that month, at a conference held in north Wales by Indian spiritual guru Maharishi Mahesh Yogi, the Beatles renounced LSD in favour of Transcendental Meditation.

[29] Edward W. Said, *Orientalism* (New York: Random House, 1978). Said's analysis is, of course, much deeper and more nuanced than this short summary can relate. Said also argued, for example, that these attitudes were embedded in serious historical and academic writing, not just in popular literature.

[30] Edward Said, *Culture and Imperialism* (New York: Vintage Books, 1994), p. 134.

[31] Peter Bishop, *The Myth of Shangri-La: Tibet, Travel Writing, and the Western Creation of Sacred Landscape* (University of California Press, 1989), p. 7.

[32] Abe Peck, *Uncovering the Sixties: the Life and Times of the Underground Press* (New York: Pantheon, 1985), p. 166.

[33] David R. Reck, "Beatles Orientalis: Influences from Asia in a Popular Song Tradition", *Asian Music*, Vol 16, No 1 (1985), pp. 83-149. At p. 90.

[34] Burton H. Wolfe, "The New Music and the New Scene" in Jonathan Eisen, ed., *The Age of Rock: Sounds of the American Cultural Revolution* (New York: Random House, 1969), pp. 30-41. At p. 31.

[35] Francesco Adinolfi, "Exoticism" in John Shepherd, David Horn, Dave Laing, Paul Oliver & Peter Wicke, eds., *Continuum Encyclopedia of Popular Music of the World*, Volume 1: Media, Industry and Society (London: Continuum, 2003), pp. 220-23.

[36] Jonathan Bellman, ed.,*The Exotic in Western Music* (Northeastern University Press, 1998), p. 303.

[37] Michael Lydon, "Jim Morrison and the Doors" *New York Times*, Dec 3, 1968.

[38] David Courtney, *An American in Hyderabad: Life in India in the 1970s* (Houston: Sur Sangeet Services, 2012), pp. 8-9.

[39] For example, The Rolling Stones' "Paint it Black" (featuring Brian Jones playing sitar), The Kinks' "See My Friends" (which had an Indian-style drone played on a 12-string guitar) and The Yardbirds' "Heart Full of Soul" (in which a Jeff Beck guitar solo was made to sound like a sitar).

[40] Reck, "Beatles Orientalis", pp. 83-149. At p. 99. Reck finds that some 20 Beatles' songs show Asian influences: one can argue that their borrowings from Indian music were vital to their overall sound.

[41] Annette Lynch and Mitchell D. Strauss, eds., *Ethnic Dress in the United States: A Cultural Encyclopedia* (Lanham, MD.: Rowman & Littlefield, 2014), p. 210.

[42] Nick Jones, "'Beatle George and Where He's At", *Melody Maker*, Dec 16, 1967.

[43] Loraine Alterman, "The Beatles: Four Smiling, Tired Guys Talk About Their Music", *Detroit Free Press*, Aug 19, 1966.

[44] Paul Williams, Rev. of Revolver (USA: Capitol, 1966) in *Crawdaddy*!, No 5, Sep 1966, pp. 3-5. At p. 3.

[45] Williams, Rev. of Revolver, pp. 3-5.

[46] *Arena: The Beatles Magical Mystery Tour part 1.* Dir. Francis Hanly. BBC Arena/Apple Films, 2012. Broadcast BBC Four, Oct 24, 2015.

[47] Don Speicher, "The New Music '68", *Great Speckled Bird*, 1, 4, Apr 26-May 9, 1968, p. 8. Ironically, some decades later, Shankar was asked his opinion about Harrison's sitar performance on this track: he said it was "terrible". See "Ravi Shankar: Remembering A Master Of The Sitar" (1999). NPR Radio transcript, available online at: "https://www.npr.org/2012/12/14/167193821/ravi-shankar-remembering-a-master-of-the-sitar"https://www.npr.org/2012/12/14/167193821/ravi-shankar-remembering-a-master-of-the-sitar

[48] Peter Lavezzoli, *The Dawn of Indian Music in the West* (New York and London: Continuum, 2006), p. 158.

[49] See Carl Clements "John Coltrane and the integration of Indian concepts in jazz improvisation", *Jazz Research Journal*, Vol 2, No 2 (2008), pp. 155-175; and Lavezzoli, *Dawn of Indian Music*, p. 154.

[50] Lavezzoli, *Dawn of Indian Music*, p. 158.

[51] Dominick Cavallo, *A Fiction of the Past: The Sixties in American History* (New York: St. Martin's), p. 160.

[52] Rubin and Melnick, *Immigration and American Popular Culture*, p. 161.

[53] See, for example, Reck, "Beatles Orientalis", pp. 83-149.

[54] Goldberg, *American Veda*, p. 150.

[55] Philip Norman, *John Lennon: The Life* (London: Harper-Collins, 2008), p. 505.

[56] Loraine Alterman, "The Maharishi, the Beach Boys and the Heathens", *New York Magazine*, Mar 6, 1968.

[57] "You can't even say what it was", *International Times*, Vol 1, No 63, Aug 29, 1969, pp. 3 & 5.

[58] For example, the music on his 1973 album *Living in the Material World* was influenced by his spiritual guru, *Abhay Charanaravinda Bhaktivedanta*

Swami Prabhupada. Harrison invited Indian musician Zakir Hussain to play on the album, and the album sleeve artwork was "an exquisitely colorful painting of Lord Krishna driving a chariot in a scene from Bhagavad Gita". See Lavezzoli, *Dawn of Indian Music*, p. 9.

[59]For example, "This Just Doesn't Seem To Be My Day" by The Monkees begins with a sitar solo, although the lyrics are about a relationship break-up rather than a quest for knowledge. Ricky Nelson, a teen idol in the early 1960s, tried to stay relevant late in the decade. His *Another Side of Rick* (1967) featured one song, "Marshmellow Skies", with abstract lyrics and jangling sitar.

[60] Roben Jones, *Memphis Boys: The Story of American Studios* (Jackson: Mississippi University Press, 2010), p. 206.

[61] Michael Jarrett, *Producing Country: The Inside Story of the Great Recordings* (Middletown CT.: Wesleyan University Press, 2014), p. 70.

[62] Gita Mehta, Karma Cola: *The Marketing of the Mystic East* (London: Random House, 1998 [1979]), p. 5.

[63] Brian Hiatt, "Why Monterey Pop Was a Turning Point for Sixties Rock", Rolling Stone, Jul 12, 2007. Available online at: "https://www.rollingstone.com/music/music-news/why-monterey-pop-was-a-turning-point-for-sixties-rock-194407/"https://www.rollingstone.com/music/music-news/why-monterey-pop-was-a-turning-point-for-sixties-rock-194407/

[64] Pennebaker claimed this was a personal, artistic decision: "The chronology was a chronology of my getting into the thing. The element of surprise or revelation for the general audience in Monterey came during Shankar as much as any other act". See Paul Schrader, "A Free Press Interview with: D. A. Pennebaker", *Los Angeles Free Press*, Vol 6, Issue 252 Part Two, May 16, 1969, pp. 26, 32-33, 43-44, 51. At p. 32.

[65] Sam Silver, "Monterey Pop Festival", *East Village Other*, Vol 2, Issue 16, Jul 15-30, 1967, p. 6.

[66] Frank Janusa, "Monterrey Pop Festival", *Nola Express*, No 31, Jun 6-19, 1969, p. 10.

[67] Robert Christgau, originally published as "Anatomy of a Love Festival", *Esquire*, Jan, 1968, pp. 64–66, 147. Available online at: HYPERLINK "http://www.robertchristgau.com/xg/music/monterey-69.php"http://www.robertchristgau.com/xg/music/monterey-69.php

[68] Dr Erik Wallrup, *Being Musically Attuned: The Act of Listening to Music* (Farnham, Surrey: Ashgate, 2015), p. 236.

[69] *East Village Other* Vol 3, Issue 2, Dec 1-15, 1967, p. 20.

[70] "Bowl Hosts Indian Concert", *Los Angeles Free Press*, Vol 4, Issue 159, No. 31, Aug 4-10, 1967, p. 2.

[71] Nat Freedland, "Raga Night at the Bowl", *Los Angeles Free Press*, Vol 4, No. 32, Issue 160, Aug 11-17, 1967, p. 15.

[72] Ron Mitra, "Raga Sutras", *East Village Other*, Vol 2, Issue 17, Aug 1-15, 1967, p. 18-19. At p.18.

[73] *East Village Other*, Vol 2, Issue 18, Aug 5-17, 1967, p. 20.

[74] Freedland, "Raga Night at the Bowl", p. 15.

[75] Peter Kostakis, "Ravi Shankar in Concert", *The Seed* Vol 1, Issue 9, Oct 14 - Nov 3 1967, p. 5.

[76] Richard Goldstein, *Reporting the Counterculture* (Boston: Unwin Hyman, 1989), p. 73.

[77] Spitz, *Barefoot in Babylon*, p. 112.

[78] Qtd. in Michael Lang and Holly-George Warren, *The Road to Woodstock* (New York: HarperCollins, 2009), p. 190.

[79] Joel Makower, *Woodstock: The Oral History* (London: Sidgwick & Jackson, 1989) p. 201.

[80] Miller Francis Jr., "Woodstock", *Great Speckled Bird*, Sep 1, 1969, pp. 12-13, 18-19. At p. 12.

[81] Mike Bourne, "Babycakes in New York", *The Spectator*, Vol 9, Issue 2, Sep 23, 1969, pp. 17-18. At p. 17.

[82] Francis Jr., "Woodstock", p. 12.

[83] "Ravi Shankar: Remembering A Master Of The Sitar" (1999). NPR Radio transcript, available online at: "https://www.npr.org/2012/12/14/167193821/ravi-shankar-remembering-a-master-of-the-sitar"https://www.npr.org/2012/12/14/167193821/ravi-shankar-remembering-a-master-of-the-sitar

[84] Pete Fornatale, *Back to the Garden* (New York: Touchstone, 2010), p. 73.

[85] Mick Brown, "In truth, Ravi Shankar couldn't stand the hippies", *The Telegraph*, Dec 12, 2012.

[86] Rajeev S. Patke, "Music as a Form of Cultural Dialogue: The Case of Ravi Shankar", *European Review* Vol 23, Issue 3 (2015), pp 439-453. At p. 441.

[87] Lavezzoli, *Dawn of Indian Music*, p. 66. David Hepworth, 1971: *Never a Dull Moment* (London: Bantam Press, 2016), pp. 205-37.

[88] Richard Williams, "The Concert for Bangla Desh", *Melody Maker*, Jan 1, 1972.

[89] Rubin and Melnick, *Immigration and American Popular Culture*, p. 132.

[90] "The way out is in", *International Times*, Vol 1, No 13, May 19, 1967, pp. 8-9.

[91] Stuart Hall, "The Hippies: an American moment". Stencilled Occasional Paper. Sub and Popular Culture Series number 16 (Birmingham [West Midlands]: Centre for Contemporary Cultural Studies, University of Birmingham, 1968).

[92] "New Yogi in Town", *Berkeley Barb*, Vol 9, No 6, Issue 208, Aug 8-14, 1969, p. 11.

[93] Jeff Levin and David Stern, "The Whole Earth Fair and Festival of Peace", *Los Angeles Free Press*, Vol 7, No 35, Issue 319, Aug 21, 1970, p. 4a.

[94] Steve Wise, "Celebration of Life?" *Great Speckled Bird*, Vol 4, Issue 27, Jul 5, 1971, pp. 12, 13, & 18.

[95] Arne Passman, "The LSD Conference", *The Realist*, No 72, Dec 1, 1966, pp. 19-23. At pp. 21-22.

[96] Pete Townshend, "In Love with Meher Baba: The Who guitarist confesses his faith in the Indian mystic", *Rolling Stone*, Nov 26, 1970.

[97] Franya J. Berkman, *Monument Eternal: The Music of Alice Coltrane* (Middletown Ct.: Wesleyan University Press, 2010), p. 76.

[98] Advert for *Chappaqua* soundtrack album in *The Seed*, Vol 2, Issue 13, Aug 1, 1968. p. 14.

[99] "Allen Ginsberg Introduces Yogiraj Sri Swami Satchidananda", *East Village Other*, Vol 1, Issue 24 (Nov 15 - Dec 1, 1966) p. 12.

[100] Hugh Romney, "Swami how we love you", *East Village Other*, Vol 2, Issue 21, Sep 15, 1967, p. 15.

[101] Advert for lecture by Swami Satchidananda, *Los Angeles Free Press* Vol 5, No 6, Issue 186, Feb 9-15, 1968, p. 24.

[102] "Free from all that" (Interview with Swami Satchidananda), *San Francisco Good Times*, Vol 2, Issue 29, Jul 31, 1969, pp. 6-7.

[103] Judith and Ike Lasater, "An interview with Swami Vishnu-devananda", *Yoga Journal*, Vol 1, No 5 (1975), pp. 11-12. At p. 11.

[104] "Sadhana Tattwa", *Other Scenes* Vol 3, Issue 2, Feb 1, 1969, p. 10.

[105] Rubin and Melnick, *Immigration and American Popular Culture*, p. 152.

[106] "Utopian Situation", *San Francisco Good Times*, Vol 2, Issue 30, Aug 7, 1969 p. 6.

[107] Rev. Prem Anjali, "A Spiritual Journey: Meeting the Woodstock Guru", in Susan Reynolds, ed., *Woodstock Revisited* (Avon Ma.: Simon & Schuster, 2009), pp. 109-113.

[108] An almost complete text of Satchidananda's speech can be found in Fornatale's *Back to the Garden*, pp. 21-22.

[109] Makower, *Woodstock: The Oral History*, p. 193.

[110] Advert for lectures by Swami Satchidananda, *Berkeley Tribe* Vol 1, Issue 24, Dec 19-26, 1969, p. 10.

[111] "Karma Korn", *Berkeley Tribe*, Vol 1, Issue 25, Dec 26, 1969 - Jan 2, 1970, p. 21.

[112] Levin and Stern, "The Whole Earth Fair and Festival of Peace", p. 4a.

[113] D.A. Latimer, "Miracle of 41st street", *East Village Other*, Vol 3, Issue 30, Jun 28, 1968, pp. 6 & 19. At p. 6.

[114] Kerry Thornley, "Liberated Yoga", *Great Speckled Bird*, Vol 6, Issue 18, May 14, 1973, p. 16.

[115] Fornatale, *Back to the Garden* p. 22. White's "pod-people" remark is likely a reference to Jack Finney's novel *The Body Snatchers* (1955), in which alien pods create unemotional, unthinking duplicates of human beings; or the 1956 film *Invasion of the Body Snatchers*, based on the novel, which transforms Finney's story into a thinly-disguised anti-communist scare story.

[116] "Awareness Retreat", *The Rag*, Vol 5, Apr 22, 1971, p. 15.

[117] Advert for Yoga Ecumenical Retreat, *Quicksilver Times*, Vol 3, Issue 10, Jun 2-16, 1971, p. 17.

[118] Advert for Sunseed, *Los Angeles Free Press*, Vol 10, No 47, Issue 488, Nov 24-30, 1973, p. 15.

[119] Edgar Jones, "Interview with Swami Satchidananda", *Los Angeles Free Press*, Vol 7, No 3, Issue 287 Part Two, Jan 16, 1970, p. 35.
[120] "Bauls Dig Provos, Provos Dig Bauls", *Berkeley Barb*, Vol 5, No. 11, Issue 110, Sep 22-28, 1967, p. 4.
[121] Robert Hurwitt, "Magic Mountain Magic Eyed For Fine Weekend", *Berkeley Barb*, Vol 4, Issue 95, No. 23, Jun 9-15, 1967, pp. 1 & 5. At p. 1.
[122] Jason Newman, "The Untold and Deeply Stoned Story of the First U.S. Rock Festival", *Rolling Stone*, Jun 17, 2014. Available online at: https://www.rollingstone.com/music/music-news/the-untold-and-deeply-stoned-story-of-the-first-u-s-rock-festival-124437/
[123] California Historical Society, "America's First Rock Festival: The KFRC Fantasy Fair and Magic Mountain Music Festival". Available online at: http://summerof.love/americas-first-rock-festival-kfrc-fantasy-fair-magic-mountain-music-festival/
[124] The English Invasion!", *East Village Other*, Vol 4, Issue 18, Apr 2, 1969, p. 18.
[125] "The British Invasion", *Vanity Fair*, Nov 2002. Available online at: http://www.vanityfair.com/culture/2002/11/british-invasion-oral-history
[126] Mark Lewisohn, *The Complete Beatles Chronicles* (London: Octopus, 2006), pp. 361-65.
[127] Charlie Gillett, *The Sound of the City: the Rise of Rock and Roll* (London: Souvenir, 1983), p. 257; Nik Cohn, *Awopbopaloobop Alopbamboom: Pop from the Beginning* (London: Pimlico, 2004), p. 71.
[128] George Melly, *Revolt into Style: the Pop Arts* (OUP, 1989 [1970]), pp. 6-7.
[129] See, for example, The Beatles *Live! at the Star-Club in Hamburg, Germany; 1962* (Germany: Lingasong/Bellaphon, 1977).
[130] Ian MacDonald, *Revolution in the Head: the Beatles' Records and the Sixties* (London: Vintage, 2008), p. 293; Gillett, *Sound of the City*, p. 263.
[131] Gillett, *Sound of the City*, pp. 268-69.
[132] David Griffiths, "The Byrds: "That Criticism Is Fair!"" *Record Mirror*, Aug 21, 1965.
[133] Cameron Crowe, "Joe Walsh, Child of the Silent Majority: Ex-James Gangster Tends His Garden" *Rolling Stone*, Feb 27, 1975.
[134] See Norman, *John Lennon*, p. 480; and MacDonald, *Revolution in the Head*, pp. 214-15.
[135] Marcus Collins, "The Beatles' Politics", *British Journal of Politics and International Relations*, Vol 16, No 2, May 2014, pp. 291-309. At p. 304.
[136] "California" on his *Turning Point* (1969) and "Laurel Canyon Home" on his *Blues from Laurel Canyon* (1968).
[137] Griffiths, "The Byrds".
[138] Jerry Hopkins, Bob Cato, Baron Wolman, and Jim Marshall, *Festival! The Book of American Music Celebrations* (London: Collier, 1970), p 22; Melly, *Revolt into Style*, p. 107.
[139] Arthur Marwick, "Introduction: Locating Key Texts Amid the Distinctive Landscape of the Sixties", in *Windows on the Sixties: Exploring Key Texts of Media and Culture*, edited by Anthony Aldgate, James Chapman, and Arthur Marwick (London: I.B. Tauris, 2000), pp. xi-xxi.
[140] Makower, *Woodstock: The Oral History*, p. 126.
[141] Spitz, *Barefoot in Babylon*, p. 178.
[142] Evans and Kingsbury, *Woodstock: Three Days that Rocked the World*, p. 228.
[143] Spitz, *Barefoot in Babylon*, p. 4.
[144] Joel Rosenman, John Roberts and Robert Pilpel, *Young Men With Unlimited Capital* (New York: bantam, 1989), p. 141.
[145] Townshend, "In Love with Meher Baba".
[146] Mark Wilkerson, *Who Are You: the Life of Pete Townshend* (London: Omnibus, 2009), p. 106.
[147] "Pinball Wizard", *Rebirth*, Aug 20, 1969, p. 8.
[148] Spitz, *Barefoot in Babylon*, p. 185.
[149] Patrick Lydon, "A Joyful Confirmation That Good Things Can Happen Here", *New York Times*, Aug 24, 1969.
[150] Jonathan Cott, "Tea with Townshend: A Post-'Tommy' Chat on Rock 'N Roll, Recording", *Rolling Stone*, May 14, 1970.
[151] Francis Jr., "Woodstock", p. 13.
[152] Richard Green, Review of Various Artists: *Woodstock* (Atlantic, stereo 2663001; 150s), *New Musical Express*, May 30, 1970.
[153] Cott, "Tea with Townshend".
[154] R. Serge Denisoff, *Solid Gold: The Popular Record Industry* (New Brunswick & London: Transaction, 1975), p. 348.
[155] Dave Laing, "The three Woodstock and the live music scene", in Andy Bennett, ed., *Remembering Woodstock* (Aldershot: Ashgate, 2004), pp. 1-17. At p. 9.
[156] Makower, *Woodstock: The Oral History*, p. 283.
[157] Michael Sciulla, "The Little Car That Could", in Susan Reynolds, ed., *Woodstock Revisited* (Avon Ma.:Simon & Schuster, 2009), pp. 153-56. At p. 156.
[158] Brad Littleproud and Joanne Hague, *Woodstock: Peace, Music & Memories* (Iola, WI: Krause, 2009), p. 134.
[159] Richard Whitehall, "Filming at Max's Farm", *Los Angeles Free Press*, Vol 6, Issue 271-Part Two, Sep 26, 1969, pp. 27 & 33. At p. 27.
[160] The film *Woodstock Diaries*, broadcast originally on American television in 1994, features footage not released on Wadleigh's film. It confirms Cocker's recollection of a sedate, seated crowd, which is then energised by Cocker's performance of "Let's Go Get Stoned". See *Woodstock Diaries* DVD. Dir. D.A. Pennebaker and Chris Hegedus. UK: Warner Brothers/Slamdunk Media, 2006.
[161] Makower, *Woodstock: The Oral History*, p. 277.
[162] Mike Gormley, "Joe Cocker: On Stage Joe's Strong Otherwise He's Groggy", *Detroit Free Press*, May 16, 1969.
[163] Jan Hodenfield, "Woodstock: 'It Was Like Balling for the First Time'", *Rolling Stone* Sept 20, 1969.
[164] Pete Fornatale, *Back to the Garden*, pp. 111-12.
[165] Hodenfield, "Woodstock: 'It Was Like Balling for the First Time'".
[166] Fornatale, *Back to the Garden*, p. 111.
[167] Spencer Leigh, "Keef Hartley: Drummer who played with John Mayall and led his own band at Woodstock", *The Independent* Dec 3, 2011. Available online at: "https://www.independent.co.uk/news/obituaries/keef-hartley-drummer-who-played-with-john-mayall-and-led-his-own-band-at-woodstock-6271513.html"https://www.independent.co.uk/news/obituaries/keef-hartley-drummer-who-played-with-john-mayall-and-led-his-own-band-at-woodstock-6271513.html
[168] There is one other British "appearance" of note at Woodstock. Janis Joplin performed "To Love Somebody", a soulful love song written in 1967 by Barry and Robin Gibb of the Bee Gees.
[169] Miller Francis Jr., "Talkin 'bout My Generation", *Great Speckled Bird*, Vol 3, Issue 24, Jun 15, 1970, pp. 12-13.
[170] Advert for Atlanta International Pop Festival. *Los Angeles Free Press*, Vol 6, Issue 258, Jun 27 - Jul 4, 1969, p. 13.

Chapter 3: Woodstock, the Movie: Shaping Woodstock's Popular Memory

Michael Wadleigh's Woodstock is a 3-hour hallusination [sic], a multiple-screen ecstatic mind-blown underground freak movie!... there is finally a movie about us.

San Francisco Good Times[1]

As a documentary, it's terrible. Almost nothing happened the way it's depicted in the film. The film chose to live off the love, peace, eternal beauty, hopes and fantasies of Woodstock Nation, rather than explore its human struggles. It also went to great lengths to avoid criticism of the concert promoters. If nothing else... Woodstock has shown that you do not have to be in Hollywood to make a Hollywood movie.

Mike Jahn[2]

As noted in the Introduction, the Woodstock festival quickly captured the public imagination and was widely reported in the American media. Across the spectrum of views aired in the press, one consistent point of agreement was that Woodstock was more than just a music festival: the mainstream press called it a cultural event, and the underground press described it as a "happening", the biggest yet of the new era of youthful political awareness. Woodstock was both cool and hot, and everyone wanted be part of it, to know more, hear the music, to see the crowds and performers, to reflect on events if they were there, and experience it for themselves if they weren't. Anticipation for the festival film and soundtrack album was, therefore, high, and this potentially would make those releases very profitable for Woodstock Ventures, and for stakeholders in the music and film industries.

When considering the prospect of filming the Woodstock festival, Michael Lang had in mind D.A. Pennebaker's movie *Monterey Pop* (1968), which up until then was the only example of a rock festival film to secure a cinematic release (although other music festivals had been filmed).[3] Despite adjudging *Monterey Pop* a "flop", Lang nevertheless approached David and Albert Maysles to film Woodstock, partly because Albert Maysles had been a cameraman at the Monterey festival. The Maysles brothers declined, but pointed Lang in the direction of Wadleigh-Maurice Productions. Michael Wadleigh had previously filmed live performances by Aretha Franklin and James Brown and was keen on the proposal.[4] Wadleigh put together a team of 18 cameramen and directors who began filming the festival preparations about a month before the scheduled start. They shot all three days of the event, and stayed afterward to shoot some of the clean-up efforts. In total, they shot 120 hours of footage.

When filming *Woodstock,* Wadleigh and his team favoured the "direct cinema" and "cinéma vérité" styles of filming used by D.A. Pennebaker and the Maysles brothers in *Monterey Pop*. Both of these filmic techniques had come about because of new technologies such as handheld cameras which used 16mm film stock, and which, if desired, could make for more unobtrusive film making than had gone before. However, as Aaron Taylor has noted, they were in fact two different and in fact opposing styles.[5] The Maysles Brothers virtually invented the "direct cinema" approach, a term they used to describe their style of objective, observational film making, which made use of a "fly-on-the-wall" approach to hide the camera and encourage the viewer to engage with events as they unfold "naturally" on screen. In so doing, there is an assumption that what is on screen speaks for itself, and that meaning will transfer directly from the screen to the viewer, without being mediated through a third party (the filmmaker). Yet the makers of *Monterey Pop* had also utilised the contrasting "cinéma vérité" approach, in which there is a degree of filmmaker participation, both on screen and in the editing process. With cinéma vérité there is an assumption that the presence of a camera or cameras can influence how events unfold and therefore the filmmaker cannot be objective. With both cinéma vérité and "direct cinema", however, the aim was to utilise cinematic techniques to uncover an essential truth about the events/people being filmed.[6] This was a world away from the hitherto popular Hollywood-style "star vehicle" approach of Elvis or Beatles rock films, wherein the style and intent was mainly to promote performers and their music as a product, not to capture anything essentially truthful or real. In contrast, the "direct cinema" or "cinéma vérité" styles favoured by Wadleigh and his team when filming Woodstock, aimed to reveal something candid and hopefully meaningful.

Given Lang's conviction that *Monterey Pop* had not been a financial success because it didn't capture the spirit and significance of the festival — a view Wadleigh shared — for the Woodstock film, Wadleigh drew on elements of a number of editing techniques that other documentary makers of rock concerts had experimented with to try capture the essence and soul of the music being filmed. For example, Wadleigh borrowed from a split-screen effect that had been first used in the 1960 documentary *Jazz on a Summer's Day*, which documented events at the 1958 Newport Jazz Festival: he thought this technique might help bridge the gap between performer, audience, and later the cinema audience. He arranged a demonstration of this effect for John Roberts, who was impressed by Wadleigh's ideas.[7] The split-screen effect would turn out to be an iconic element of the Woodstock festival film. From the 120 hours of footage, Wadleigh *et al* finally edited it down into a three-hour film which bore the eponymous title *Woodstock*.[8]

Under the terms of the contract between Woodstock Ventures and Wadleigh-Maurice Productions, the film makers agreed to fund the project and find a distributer; Woodstock Ventures would then get a percentage of the producer's royalty. Within a week of agreeing this contract, Maurice contacted John Roberts and asked him to finance the project for $100,000 in return for a much bigger percentage of the film profits. Roberts, however, declined to renegotiate.[9] Maurice then turned to Warner Bros., who agreed to fund and distribute the film. *Woodstock* was a huge financial success: it earned $13.3 million upon release in 1970, and by 1979 it had earned $50 million.[10] This allowed the promoters to recoup their losses on the festival, but because of Roberts' decision, most of the profit went to Warner Bros. Given this huge corporate hand involved in the making and financing of the film, and the high admission fees cinemas charged, many counterculture enthusiasts raged against the seeming contradiction of the Woodstock "free music" paradigm, leading to negative opinion pieces in the underground press, and even protests outside cinemas. Other commentators in the underground press criticised the film as a misleading depiction of what Woodstock meant to those in attendance, and a misunderstanding of Woodstock's significance in the wider cultural context. Notwithstanding its negative reception from sections of the underground press, *Woodstock* the film would go on to shape much of the popular memory of the festival.

Considering the huge commercial success of the film and its central place in creating the popular memory of the festival, few commentators have actually considered *Woodstock* as a "creative construct" — as a film which flagged up certain aspects of the festival, while omitting others. The pages that follow will therefore consider: how was *Woodstock* advertised and to whom? What aspects of Woodstock were made central to the film, and which were left out? Did the film's primary focus on the "alternative lifestyles" of the counterculture — over that of the music and the politics — distort how Woodstock has been remembered in history? And how was the *Woodstock* film interpreted by critics in the mainstream and underground press?

Advertising the Movie: selling a counterculture "dream" of Woodstock

Woodstock Ventures knew that for the movie to be successful it needed to do two things: the first was to appeal to the same generation of young, politicised, counterculture-inspired people who had originally attended the festival; and secondly, it was important that the "Age of Aquarius" image of Woodstock — above all other interpretations of the festival — should be in the foreground of public consciousness. It is likely that Woodstock Ventures was split as to why this should be the case. Footage of Kornfeld and Lang's unrehearsed, unbridled joy as the concert unfolded around them suggests they wanted to ensure the festival was remembered in a positive light, as an example of what the counterculture could achieve, and perhaps even as the "high point" that the festival came to represent; in contrast, Roberts and Rosenman's involvement in the festival was mainly as a financial investment, so maintaining a positive vibe about the counterculture was, for them, likely little more than a smart promotional strategy.

Typically, a major studio film in this time period would be advertised via a trailer shown in cinemas in the weeks leading up to the film's release; advertisements would be placed in newspapers, magazines, and possibly on radio spots; lobby cards would be distributed to cinemas; and posters would be placed on billboards. It is, then, illuminating to consider some of Woodstock Ventures' advertising material in the lead-up to the film's release, in order to see how they went about reaching their target audience and what particular images of Woodstock they honed in on as their main selling point for the festival film. Woodstock Ventures placed at least seven different styles of advertisement in the press[11]; there is a fair degree of similarity in all of these promotional efforts, with the same stock images and terminology reused in most, clearly carefully chosen to resonate with the same youthful audience that had attended Woodstock. Interestingly, a survey of six promotional posters and seven different newspaper advert designs reveals that the most common image (used 6 times) in film advertisements was that of the audience. The second most common image (used 3 times) is a recurring image of Sly Stone; no other performers are shown. One advert in the *Los Angeles Free Press* featured a picture of a couple nude bathing; the same image appeared on one promotional poster. Three pictures showed displays of intimacy — hugging rather than nudity. Two images showed the festival's natural setting; one of these, labelled "grass", served a double purpose, hinting at recreational drug use. There is one picture of the U.S. flag. A final promotional poster, the one most at odds with the others, is an image showing five young people on the bonnet of a car on their way to the festival.[12] One poster of the crowd is captioned "No one who was there will ever be the same. Be there". This poster also amends the original Woodstock advertising by adding the words "and love" to the original text "3 Days of Peace and Music". A second poster with an image of the crowd is virtually identical, omitting only the words "Be there".

Why would Woodstock Ventures decide to focus so much on the crowd in many of its promotional images for the film? The obvious reason is that Woodstock had drawn the biggest crowd in the short history of rock festivals, so advertising the scale of the festival, marking it out as perhaps the pinnacle of the festival phenomenon, was an important selling point for the film. Moreover, the images of the crowd in these posters also depict the idea of the "Woodstock Nation" in all its strength and glory. The sheer weight of numbers is impressive, suggesting this is not so much a counterculture in opposition to mainstream culture but instead this now *is* mainstream culture. The crowd pictures indicate this collection of young people is not a threat — far from it — they show a peaceful community of young people waiting patiently and in good humour for the music to begin. The advertisers thus used these images to reinforce the message that, unlike many other previous mass gatherings (and also in contrast to the behaviour of the police in Chicago in 1968 and the ongoing events in Vietnam), Woodstock was all peace: no violence, only "3 Days of Peace, Music... and Love". Moreover, the emphasis on love in these advertising images does not just have hippie connotations, it also feeds into what might be termed the narcissism of youth, the idea that young people in their innocent naivety believe that love and sex is their domain, and not that of their parents and other old fogeys.

Yet there were also other reasons why Woodstock Ventures placed images of the crowd in its film posters. Advertising that focused on the audience is, perhaps, the 1960s equivalent of a modern day "selfie". By playing on young people's psychology — the idea of "being where it's at" — suggests that to "Be there" is to "Be cool"; this reinforces the idea of fitting in and being hip, which are major impulses of teenage development. So *seeing* crowds in the film posters of loads of other young people "being there" is a clever, if perhaps cynical, and manipulative way to target young people's vulnerability and their need to fit in with their peers. But of course these advertisements did not misrepresent what Woodstock offered: the festival did have many of the qualities of a "be-in" or "gathering of the tribes". All that was missing was a Beatles' "All You Need Is Love" soundtrack. Hog Farm, the hippie commune hired by Woodstock Ventures to help provide security and distribute food and drink, were the most prominent example of this goodwill and communal spirit. Hugh "Wavy Gravy" Romney became the public face of Woodstock, even more than Lang or Kornfeld. His humour and demeanour emanated the goodwill and brotherly love for which the festival became known, and which the advertising strategy focused on. Journalist Andrew Kopkind gave the following account of Hog Farm's behaviour, attitude, importance and impact:

Hip beyond any doubt, they spread the love/groove ethic throughout the farm, breaking up incipient actions against 'the system' with cool, low-key hippie talk about making love not war, the mystical integrity of earth, and the importance of doing your own thing, preferably alone. On the other hand-actually, on the same hand-they were the only good organizers in camp. They ran the free food operation (oats, rice and bulgar), helped acid-freaks through bad trips without Thorazine, and (with Abbie Hoffman) ran the medical system when that became necessary.[13]

Moreover, Romney helped set the tone for the festival and the film in a different way. On the day prior to the festival's opening, many thousands of ticketless young people were already on the festival site. There were no gates or ticket booths, and no serious barrier to entry, so they turned up and chose a place from which to view the show. The only way to charge them for entry would be to clear the site first. When Romney was asked his views on this, he replied: "You want a good movie or a bad movie?" The clear inference here was that if the site was cleared of perhaps 30,000 happy people in order to collect money from them, the bad vibes would set the tone for the rest of the festival.[14] Later that day, when perhaps as many as 110,000 ticketless people were on the site, Wes Pomeroy, the festival's Director of Security, told Roberts and Rosenman the same thing: clearing the site would cause a riot. It was at this point that Roberts and Rosenman realised their investment was likely to end in financial ruin.[15] However, the "free" aspect of the festival would help cement its legend as a seminal countercultural happening.

The promotional film posters didn't just tap into youthful ideas of freedom, of being "where it's at" and of love, it also tapped into another popular idea amongst counterculture enthusiasts: the wonder of "mindfuckery". (That is mindfuckery in its contemporary meaning, describing something as amazing or astounding, rather than our current understanding of this term, to refer to someone psychologically manipulative.)[16] One advert for the movie that appeared in the *Berkeley Tribe,* which again featured a crowd as its core focus, carried two quotes: the first from Richard Ogar of the *Berkeley Barb* is captioned "Woodstock is a real mindfucker"; and the second from *San Francisco Good Times* is captioned, "It'll blow your mind!"[17] Ogar's quote echoes musician John Sebastian's comment in the film, "This thing is a real mindfucker!" An advert in *Street Journal* also made use of review quotes: underneath a picture of Sly Stone, this advert quoted a *Time* magazine review which called the film the "mindblower of all time!"[18] An advert in *Helix* also claimed "Woodstock will fuck-up your mind" and attempted to lure in readers with offers of love, grass, people and "more than 3 hours of continuous music".[19] Another hyperbolic reference appeared in an advert placed in the *Los Angeles Free Press.* This advert included a central crowd picture and a quote from *Rolling Stone* magazine claiming, "Woodstock is a heavy trip. It'll blow your mind!"[20] The purpose of this language was to reinforce the idea that the festival was an unmissable event and that those who were not there to witness it could remedy that by seeing the film instead.

Portraying hip crowds, love-ins and mindfuckery were not the only key ideas that the advertisers tapped into when selling the idea of the festival in the film. Many of the adverts for the film in the press also placed significant emphasis on the pastoral setting. As well as Michael Lang's original vision for a recording studio and de facto artists' community in a rural setting, the original Woodstock festival advertising had emphasised the festival's rural location ("Hundreds of acres to roam on"): this tapped into a powerful, evocative and core idea of the counterculture — that the key to a better life was to return to the land. At this time, many young counterculture enthusiasts embraced the idea of a simpler, rural life, and the natural environment became a celebrated venue for be-ins, happenings and rock concerts. "In the land of the hippies", Abbie Hoffman claimed, "everybody was always 'going to the country' even if they were already there".[21] From the 1967 Fantasy Fair and Magic Mountain Music Festival, held at a natural amphitheatre at Mount Tamalpais, to the concerts held at Golden Gate Park, the idea of a rural festival took hold. "For the counterculture", D.A. Ingram notes, "the rock festival prefigured a new, communal society lived close to a benign natural world, with the Woodstock festival in July 1969 becoming the epitome of such utopian hopes".[22]

The themes inherent in these film posters — the hip crowd, the love-ins, the celebration of mindfuckery and the lofty pastoral ideals — tell us something important about what Wadleigh and Lang were hoping to achieve with *Woodstock* the film. They not only wanted to document the festival, but they wanted to pay homage to the idea of a "Woodstock Nation", to create a film which captured the spirit of Woodstock. This would be a film where the crowd took centre stage; it was the audience, not the musicians that would be the most celebrated aspect of this movie.

Woodstock the Movie: creating a new Eden?

In an April 1970 interview with Miller Francis Jr. of *Great Speckled Bird*, producer Bob Maurice claimed that he and Wadleigh were little more than facilitators helping the audience in the cinema to experience what the Woodstock audience experienced. "We're passing something on", he explained: "we've left out our point of view. We haven't interpreted Woodstock".[23] In a later interview, he added that for many attendees of Woodstock the music wasn't necessarily the main attraction; far more important was the fulfilment of all the pro-revolutionary rhetoric of the previous ten years, and an example of what life would be like "after the Revolution".[24] Maurice's utopian and celebratory interpretation of the Woodstock spirit is a good indicator of the film's final cut. Maurice was insistent that the music, while important, was background, and that the film's main focus would be on the audience. He explained that the on-stage performances would serve as "bridges between the cinema-verite [sic] sections", meaning everything that happened off-stage. Therefore, the filmmakers directed only eight of the eighteen film crews to record musical performances, whereas the majority of crews would film events off-stage.[25] In actual fact then, and contrary to their claim that they had no agenda, the directors actually had a very *clear* agenda: to frame Woodstock as the pinnacle of the counterculture, to celebrate it as the point when alternative lifestyles came to fruition after years of struggle and culmination. How did they go about this?

The *Woodstock* film begins as a study in green — the lush verdure fields of Yasgur's farm, green pasture land — which tapped into the powerful counterculture idea of a return to a simpler, more organic way of life harmonious with the natural world. Perhaps every culture has forms of religious or mythic origin stories which hark back to a simpler age, where humans dwelt in a lost paradise of bucolic bliss, free from the evils of the modern world. Yet ideas of a "return to the land" as being a salve to the terrors of modern life were embedded deeply in American cultural memory.[26] In particular, the idea of the small-scale yeoman farmer had held a sacred place in American national identity ever since being exalted by key "founding fathers" of the American state, Thomas Jefferson and Benjamin Franklin. Indeed, for Jefferson: "Those who labor in the earth" were the "chosen people of God".[27] Moreover, in the 1960s, there was a growing awareness of environmental issues, thanks to Rachel Carson's book *Silent Spring* (1962), which revealed the harmful effects of pesticide use on the natural environment. Carson's work was so influential it effectively started a grass roots environmental movement, increasing awareness of the damage modern humans were doing to the natural world, which in turn would adversely affect human health.[28] By 1969 then, the connection between rock music, hippies, and the natural landscape was well-established. So Wadleigh and Maurice played to this by presenting the Woodstock venue as a bucolic ideal, a kind of lost Edenic paradise made real for three days by smiling farmers and flower children.

The film opens with the aforementioned survey of the luscious green landscape of farming idylls, conveying all the beauty of the land but notably none of the hard grind that is typical of farm work (and which the city folk who made up most of the festival audience and would comprise the main demographic of cinema audiences, will likely not appreciate). There are a few grazing cows, to suggest this is a small family enterprise and not a large-scale industrial farm — making clear that this is a place of yeoman spirit, not corporate enterprise. A dazzling blue lake shimmers in the distance. We see a few Woodstock Ventures' employees working in the fields, driving a tractor, pulling a log, and building the stage: one critic likens them to "worker ants"[29] but it's hard to see how that simile is appropriate as everyone works at a leisurely pace, quite in contrast to the frantic activity that took place after the Wallkill venue fell through. Then we see the first shots of young people arriving. Everyone appears happy: a local man is interviewed and praises the hippies for their good manners; there are shots of hippies on horseback (perhaps another echo to America's cherished notions of a frontier past); a pregnant woman carries a baby; a yellow school bus arrives, painted in psychedelic colours and designs including the phrase "Even God loves America". When a group of nuns arrive and one cheekily flashes a peace sign at the camera, it is as if this great pilgrimage of people has been given official spiritual approval.

The film also opens by depicting farming and farmers as protectors of the pristine natural landscape. As for Max Yasgur himself, Wadleigh and Maurice establish him as a hero, tapping into all the cherished ideas of the humble farmer, speaking for a nation. The film depicts Yasgur addressing the audience from the festival stage with a short but heartfelt speech, which seemed to be an acknowledgement from the older generation that the Woodstock Nation had been born. He said, "the important thing that you've proven to the world is that a half a million kids — and I call you kids because I have children that are older than you are — a half million young people can get together and have three days of fun and music and have nothing but fun and music, and I — God bless you for it!"[30] Wadleigh and Maurice's decision to incorporate Yasgur's address into the film demonstrates how important they believed it was to provide an image of Yasgur as the stout farmer of American legend; a yeoman "father" addressing a sea of young "flower children", giving his blessing to the world they wanted to create.

If the movie leaned towards establishing the Woodstock setting as a bucolic ideal, how did it portray other counterculture ideas of the natural setting, such as the embracing of nudity? Music critic Andy Gordon has linked rock festivals to a folk memory of celebratory festivals connecting people with the natural setting: "In the middle ages English rural villages held May games to welcome in the spring, harvest festivals at which wantonness was encouraged and the renewed fertility of nature celebrated. Woodstock is perhaps our equivalent event".[31] So, if Woodstock was meant to be an iteration of the counterculture's utopian society — what Timothy Leary called, "literally biologically a city of the future"[32] — nudity can be viewed as a form of liberation: as Andy Gordon put it, "in that idyllic context, nudity and sensuality were once again natural, free, and innocent, which they could never be in city streets".[33] So how did the film portray nudity as an idea? Did it fall into the voyeuristic trap of some rock festival documentaries, such as *Jazz on a Summer's Day,* in which the camera seeks out and lingers on attractive young women? In many respects, yes; as Joan Holden of *Ramparts* magazine remarked, *Woodstock* does indeed focus disproportionately on what she called "pretty girls in appealing stages of abandon".[34] Yet this was not the only way in which nudity was explored in the film; it did also offer a glimpse of the freedom in which such undressing could take place without judgement or penalty. For example, when John Sebastian performs, the camera mostly ignores him and instead the cinema audience sees a montage of scenes of young children, some swimming nude with their parents. In another scene a young couple is interviewed, and they discuss sex, living together in a hippie "family", and dysfunctional parental relations. In these indicative examples there is a range of emotion from nudity as sexual titillation, the voyeurism of the male gaze when cameras focus on pretty girls in the festival audience, nudity as a return to nature, intimacy, relationships, family, and love. On balance, the film seems to lean towards titillation rather than present a statement about what all of this means. Ironically, because the nudity included in the film led to it being given a "Restricted" cinema rating, some of those who attended the festival and provided the *mise en scène*, as well as many young people who wanted to identify with the alternative lifestyles on display, could not see the film without being accompanied by their parents.[35]

When it came to portraying another facet of the "alternative lifestyle" of Woodstock — recreational drug use (mainly pot smoking) — the film was similarly nuanced. Aside from arguments about the criminalisation or legalisation of recreational drugs, the freedom to choose an alternative lifestyle was a political challenge to the Establishment, and was embraced at Woodstock. Country Joe McDonald's belief that hedonism was revolutionary[36] reflected a popular view in the decade that "the personal is political", that the way people lived their lives often in opposition to extant value systems or to the law, was a very visible form of protest against those values. And that was certainly in evidence at Woodstock. *Life*'s Barry Farrell called the festival the "great stoned rock show" where "a half-million young Americans spontaneously creating a society based on drugs".[37] While this is not the main focus of the film, Wadleigh and Maurice showed enough of it on screen to make clear to the cinema audience the extent of festival goers' drug use. There is, for example, a montage of around twenty scenes showing groups of people or individuals lighting pipes and joints; fans offer marijuana cigarettes to musicians and festival employees; Jerry Garcia, holds a huge joint, looks into the camera and raps "Marijuana. Exhibit A"; and from the stage, Arlo Guthrie performs "Coming into Los Angeles", whose narrative is about a man smuggling heroin into the United States.

Yet the filmmakers also excluded other elements of the festival drug scene. Kitts notes, for example, the omission of the "infamous Drug Supermarket" and the "thousands treated for bad drug trips".[38] However, it would be an error to overemphasise these omissions: one does not have to see where drugs were sold or who sold them to be aware that many at festival goers had been using recreational drugs. There are plenty of images of drug usage in the film, so it has not been censored. Moreover, while Kitts accurately notes the overdoses, showing the treatment tents would illustrate that the festival organisers made adequate preparation for these medical situations, proving the counterculture was capable of looking after its own. Excluding these scenes could be deemed as politicising events but so too could including them. Either way, they weren't likely to change anyone's minds about drugs.

To give one final indicative example of a drug-related, politically charged moment in *Woodstock*, the filmmakers interview a middle-aged man employed at the site to clean portable toilets. The man goes about his work enthusiastically, remarking that he is happy to do it "for these kids". Then in an off-the-cuff comment, he reveals, "My son's here too. And I got one over in Vietnam too. He's up in the D.M.Z. right now flying helicopters". This scene touches on both the friendliness of the older generation towards the festival spirit, and also the choices many young men faced at this time: Woodstock or Vietnam, fun or patriotic duty. Then a young, long-haired man with a goatee beard exits a toilet with a pipe in his mouth. He has been lighting up in there and he offers some to the camera people. It is a remarkable moment that not only underpins the choices available to young people but which also can be interpreted in light of cinema audiences' political viewpoint: for some, it is a lighthearted scene that perhaps captures the spirit of Woodstock; for others, the juxtaposition of this young man with the soldier in the D.M.Z. flying helicopters and doing his patriotic duty, might only confirm the negative view of the Woodstock Nation.

Overall, Wadleigh and Maurice's decision to depict the legend of the festival is only occasionally balanced out by scenes that undermine that vision. For instance, the "back to the garden" utopia is threatened by counter-images of mounds of garbage that they include in the film; but even then, the filmmakers show the hippies clearing up the mess. Furthermore, Wadleigh ensures the film ends not on anything so mundane as garbage collection: instead a few Edenic scenes from the beginning of the film are replayed, while Crosby, Stills, Nash & Young play Joni Mitchell's "Woodstock". However, what the filmmakers choose to omit is as significant as what they include. "A tractor ran over a sleeping bag and killed its occupant", Ted Franklin reminds us. "There were 25 miscarriages, a fall from a light tower, cases of pneumonia from the cold and hepatitis and typhoid from the bad water, food poisoning, countless minor lacerations when bare feet met the rubbish for which there were no garbage cans, and several hundred bad trips".[39] *San Francisco Good Times* reported three accidental deaths,[40] as did *The Rag*, "one of a burst appendix, one who was run over by a tractor while sleeping, and one of an unexpected overdose or drugs". "Everything's beautiful?" it asked.[41] Only in the film.

Critics' response to Woodstock

What did critics make of the filmmakers' focus on the festival *audience* and their celebration of Woodstock as a key "moment" in the counterculture? And how did musicians, audience members, and critics respond to the idealised world that the *Woodstock* movie constructed?

Some critics were quick to pick up on the inherent problems in the film's portrayal of Woodstock as a bucolic Eden, pointing out that this tapped into only one version of America's cultural memory: the idea of a nation of yeoman farmers tending to a virgin land, thus overlooking the fact that America's lands had already been inhabited by Native Americans, and that many American farms had been worked by slaves. Another of the year's great expressions of the counterculture, the film *Easy Rider* (1969), reminds its audience that the land on which they trod once belonged to Native Americans; yet *Woodstock* steered clear of any such scars on their utopian landscape. Gina Arnold, for example, compared the opening scenes of the *Woodstock* film with ideas of settlers populating the New World but noticed the absence of any unsettling colonial memories: she notes in the bucolic harmony of Woodstock, "no Native Americans are driven cruelly off their land, no slave labour is used to cultivate or build, and no questions of ownership mar the pristine landscape".[42] Arnold is cognisant that the film, in tapping into potent ideals of white American national identity — Yasgur the humble yeoman farmer, uniting young and old in an impassioned speech in gentle rolling hills — was actually peddling a far more conservative message than its makers perhaps cared to admit.

In fact, Yasgur's address to the festival crowd was unplanned: on Sunday afternoon, Director of Operations Mel Lawrence asked him to speak to the crowd, and Yasgur was at first hesitant, but was eventually convinced to do so. The rural idyll depicted was also a far cry from the reality of the tensions with local farmers in the area. For example, having convinced farmer Howard Mills at Wallkill and then Max Yasgur at Bethel to rent land to them to host the festival, Woodstock Ventures then faced opposition from local people including many other farmers who did not want the hassle of thousands of hippies trampling over their land. Many of those farmers were, though, happy to demand cash up front to ease their pain. In the end, opposition from locals at Wallkill caused so many problems for the festival organisers that they conceded defeat and eventually ended up at Bethel, with Yasgur agreeing to host the event on his farm.[43]

Other critics pointed out that the film's portrayal of the "liberating" potential of nudity in this simulacra Garden of Eden was not embraced by everyone in the counterculture: those who wanted revolution saw in this hedonism a lack of purpose, or even behaviour that undermined political action. For example, in *Great Speckled Bird*, Miller Francis Jr. explained the differences between various factions of the counterculture and the underground. He claimed that hippies and political radicals were split on how they viewed rock music in general, and Woodstock in particular: "The hard core 'politicals' wish Rock music were not so loud, so omnipresent, and so goddam *popular* [emphasis in original]; they feel sure that the whole Rock & Roll lifestyle-dope, hair, nudity, communes, music, etc. — are all part of a capitalist diversionary tactic designed to channel energies away from 'building an international socialist movement.' Woodstock — and all it meant — is their NEMESIS".[44]

Moreover, not everyone agreed with the rosy image of the Hog Farm commune that the film portrayed. For example, the Hog Farmers were not popular with other Woodstock Ventures' employees. Spitz notes, for instance, that when the Hog Farmers arrived on-site at Yasgur's farm they immediately drew the ire of those already working on the festival site. They were smelly, complained one worker, disease-ridden, and they stole whatever they could lay their hands on.[45] "They stole everything that wasn't nailed down", one festival aide later told the *New York Times*. John Roberts added: "Everything was taken. The jackets we planned to sell, our walkie-talkies. Even the jeeps disappeared".[46] Some critics went further: referring to "Hog Farm's dubious employment as hip cops at recent rock festivals", *Liberation News Service* claimed that Hog Farm was being used in the same way CIA counter-insurgency programmes set Vietnamese against Vietnamese in Indochina — "using people against people". *Liberation News Service* accused Woodstock security chief Wes Pomeroy of being "a CIA agent or worse", and condemned Hog Farm's supposed naivety: "by being hip police at a rock festival is most likely highly political when your boss is the CIA and when the police departments of all major cities send out observers to see how you do what you do and try to imitate it in their own cities to be of service to $$$$ hip capitalists".[47] None of these criticisms appeared in the final cut of the movie as to do so would undermine the sense of community for which the festival became known, and which the film was determined to show at the expense of a fuller and deeper recounting of events.

Moreover, in a broader sense, a number of reviewers took aim at the film's supposed objectivity. In a mainly positive review, Michael Smith of the *North Carolina Anvil* asserted that the film contained two cinematic styles: the first was cinéma vérité, which provided authenticity; but Smith proposed a second style which he claims was "very much manufactured in the editing and processing. It's subjective and makes use of stills, split screens, mirror images, stop action and fast motion together with such old fashioned techniques as a sing-along bouncing ball and subtitles".[48] For Smith, this combination of styles worked to recreate "some of the magic that was in the air" — the Woodstock spirit. Gina Arnold argues that Woodstock, rather than being simply a record of what happened, contains "a narrative and even an ideology to the event", owing its impact and success to Wadleigh and Maurice's "canny use" of cinematic artistic effects.[49] Arnold points to a number of instances which undermine the film makers' claims of objectivity including the assemblage nature of how the film footage was recorded, and its use of non-diegetic music such as Canned Heat's "Goin' Up The Country", Arlo Guthrie's "Coming Into Los Angeles", and particularly the film's title track, "Woodstock". Written by Joni Mitchell in a New York hotel room about a month after the festival which she did not attend, and performed in the film by Crosby, Stills and Nash, Mitchell's utopian vision did as much as any song to create the Arcadian image of the festival.[50]

Not everyone saw failure in Wadleigh and Maurice's stylistic choices: Richard Ogar called *Woodstock* "the ultimate rock film, and maybe even the ultimate documentary —cinema verite [sic] that picks you up by the scruff of your neck and TAKES you there".[51] Lloyd Steele thought the split screen effect, although overdone at times, was effective in showing the connection between crowd and performers. He points particularly to Wadleigh's depiction of the group Ten Years After on three screens, which lifted their performance from simple, blue-jean blues to something more flamboyant. While Steele expressed concerns that some performers got more screen time than others, overall however, he thought the film had "a spontaneity and a vitality which surmounts its faults".[52] Irwin Silver of *Other Scenes* was also impressed with the results of the split-screen effect, claiming the filmmakers manage to "juxtapose musician and audience, theme and reality, art and life in a marvellously visual counterpoint which is constantly inventive".[53] Writing in *Saturday Review*, Roland Gelatt claimed, "I know of no film that so successfully translates the pulse of music into cinematic images".[54] The main business of cinema is, however, to create make-believe, not authenticity: when musician Neil Young was asked about Woodstock he said it was "bullshit" and blamed the presence of film crews for undermining artists' musical integrity. "No one was into the music", he claimed. "Everybody was on this Hollywood trip with the fuckin' cameras. They weren't playin' to the audience as much as to the cameras... I could see everybody changing their performances for the fucking camera".[55]

These debates raise questions not only about filmmaking but also about who should be the main stakeholder when an event like Woodstock is filmed and released as a cinematic product. Should Wadleigh and Maurice's artistic choices prevail? Should performers have a say? What influence should financial backers have? Most importantly perhaps, to what extent should those who attended the festival and therefore helped create the atmosphere have a say in how they are depicted and represented on screen?

Critics saw many of the shortcomings of Wadleigh and Maurice's film, but many were willing to deem it successful in conveying the "spirit" of Woodstock. Others thought it was either a rip off, or that it depoliticised the event. It is these arguments that the remainder of the chapter will consider.

Woodstock the Movie: depoliticising the festival?

If Wadleigh and Maurice attracted both critical acclaim and fire for their artistic decisions — as to what they included in their film and what they omitted — none caused more controversy than the oft-repeated charge that they ignored most of the festival's political elements. Many critics, especially those from the underground and alternative newspaper scenes, accused the film makers of creating a technically accomplished film which nevertheless misleads in that it presents a politically neutral or even neutered version of events. The consequence of this, the argument goes, is that the film fails to provide the political context in which the festival took place, so it cannot hope then to evoke the "Woodstock spirit".

For example, while acknowledging that there was no single interpretation of what happened *Great Speckled Bird*'s music reviewer, Miller Francis, Jr., was nevertheless unhappy with the film. He asserted that the filmmakers had chosen "the most conservative, least offensive perspective in which to view the three days of 'fun and music'". He lamented this emphasis on "fun and music", arguing it had distorted the political meaning of Woodstock itself. He cited a list of politically charged events at the festival that the directors had edited out altogether, including: Abbie Hoffman's attempt to raise the issue of John Sinclair's imprisonment; political songs like "Volunteers" by Jefferson Airplane; any negative coverage of Woodstock Ventures; and all performances by the Grateful Dead, the Band, and Ravi Shankar. Instead, the author argues, Wadleigh and Maurice chose to show only harmless, sanitised or irrelevant political performances, and he cited Joan Baez and Country Joe and the Fish in those categories. Most damningly perhaps, while there is no footage of police intimidation and arrests outside the boundary of Yasgur's farm, Miller Francis, Jr., accuses the Woodstock film of making every attempt "to portray soldiers, police and representatives of the 'system' as friends of the kids at Woodstock".[56] At the time, Maurice responded evenly to such negative criticism: "Every review that I've read objected to our point of view and criticized us for adopting a view which they see and object to. The interesting thing is that none of the reviewers agree on what our point of view is... Everyone sees a point of view in the film. Well, there really isn't". It is difficult though to reconcile that response with Maurice's utopian view of Woodstock or with his knowledge of cinéma vérité techniques.

Would *Woodstock* have been a more politically charged film if it included, for example, absent performers and songs? If so, were these decisions by design and intent, or accidental happenstance? These are difficult subjects to address, not least because it is unclear in some cases how the festival audience received those performers and the songs that are missing from the film. In fact, for an event so apparently well known and much written about, there remains some doubt even about the festival running order and about some artists' set lists. For example, journalist Robert Spitz claims that after Richie Havens' opening performance, Country Joe McDonald went onstage and performed his famous call and response: "Gimme an F! Gimme a U! Gimme a C! Gimme a K! What's that spell?" Spitz also claimed that John Sebastian followed McDonald's set.[57] In fact, both of these artists performed on Saturday afternoon. In an otherwise excellent study of black music, Craig Werner claims erroneously in his 1998 monograph *A Change is Gonna Come* that the Chamber Brothers performed at the 1969 Woodstock festival.[58] Given these points of confusion though, it is possible to make some basic observations about whether or not *Woodstock* the film was as "politically neutered" as some critics at the time claimed.

Firstly, some critics have argued that certain bands were omitted from the film because they were deemed overtly political. Schowalter observes, for example, that Creedence Clearwater Revival's early morning performance was omitted from the film, and that at the time, this band was "extremely popular and lyrically explicit in their opposition to the Vietnam War".[59] However, closer analysis reveals a different picture of these events. Creedence Clearwater Revival's most prominent anti-war songs were "Fortunate Son", a song not released until a month after the festival, and "Who'll Stop the Rain", which was released about five months later, in January 1970. While the former soon became as a protest song against the Vietnam War and the latter is often interpreted as such, of course neither were played at Woodstock. In fact, the band's image as synonymous with the anti-war movement developed in the time between the festival and the film. It is, therefore, misleading to suggest that Creedence Clearwater Revival's inclusion in the film would have better reflected the festival's political side since that is not what the band was known for at that time.

In this regard, Miller Francis Jr. makes a stronger case in pointing out Jefferson Airplane's omission from the film: he argues this was a missed opportunity to showcase the band's musical shift from Haight-Ashbury hippies to a more militant stance — a development that mirrored wider trends within the movement. "Volunteers" and "Uncle Sam Blues" were overtly political songs played at Woodstock: the former's original title was "Volunteers of Amerika", using the protest spelling as a statement of dissatisfaction with the older generation mentioned in its lyrics, but the song title was shortened to avoid legal action from the organisation Volunteers of America;[60] "Uncle Sam Blues" is an anti-war song about a young conscript who doesn't know why he is being asked to kill. The Airplane also performed the song "Wooden Ships", which Paul Kantner had co-written in 1968 with David Crosby and Steven Stills. The lyrics offer a dystopian vision of a world devastated by nuclear war and in which the narrator dreams of wooden ships on which he can escape the madness. Around 24 hours later, Crosby and Stills would join Graham Nash and Neal Young in performing a shorter and mellower version of the song, but with the same sentiments. The Airplane's "House at Pooneil Corner" would have offered a different challenge to those trying to figure out why Jefferson Airplane was missing from the film: on the one hand it is political in that it offers a vision of a dystopian, almost post-apocalyptic future; yet it also offers a "back to the garden" narrative that fits well with the film's Arcadian vision. Of course any such discussion would have to willfully ignore the fact that it was the band who withdrew their consent to appear in the film, probably because Warner Bros. didn't offer them enough money, so in this instance the film makers had no decision to make.[61]

The inclusion of only two songs from Joan Baez's lengthy set also shows the difficulty in assessing whether the directors deliberately depoliticised the film. The two songs which made it into the film were the left wing political anthem "Joe Hill", and the gospel song "Swing Low Sweet Chariot". An overtly political song entitled "Drug Store Truck Drivin' Man" was sung by Baez as a duet with Jeffrey Shurtleff, while Richard Festinger played guitar; these men were members of the same draft resistance group that Baez's imprisoned husband belonged to. The song is about the Ku Klux Klan, and before they began to play, Shurtleff dedicated it to California Governor Ronald Reagan, whose surname Shurtleff pronounced Ray-gun.[62] The omission of this performance, as well as the civil rights anthem "We Shall Overcome", which Baez also performed, seems evidence of the film makers' depoliticising agenda. Yet, Baez also played The Byrds' track "Hickory Wind", which was written by Gram Parsons. Like Jefferson Airplane's "House at Pooneil Corner", "Hickory Wind's" nostalgic lyrics about a man living in the city who yearns for the rural South Carolina of his youth, would have fitted nicely into the film makers' rural theme. Yet this too was omitted. Furthermore, as David E. James points out, Baez's comments to the crowd about her husband being threatened by prison guards are edited together with her comments about him being moved to another prison, the effect of which is to merge two separate comments from different points in the set into one coherent narrative of political oppression.[63] So again, it is not necessarily the case that politics was deliberately edited out of the film, and even if that were the case, that policy was applied unevenly.

Before the film's release, Richard Whitehall of the *Los Angeles Free Press* asked producer Bob Maurice about rumours that contract difficulties might result in not all the performers appearing in the film. Maurice responded: "The only holdouts now are all of Albert Grossman's people. And that's The Band, Ritchie Havens... I don't know if Janis Joplin is with him or not".[64] (She was.) Of course, neither The Band nor Joplin appeared in the film, but Havens did. As he was not as well known as the others, perhaps Grossman felt that the film would give him much-needed exposure. It appears to be the case, however, that Grossman refused to allow The Band to be included in the film as he thought the fee they were offered to do so was too low.[65] Michael Wadleigh claims there wasn't space to include Creedence Clearwater Revival's performance in the film; in contrast, John Fogerty claims he refused to allow it because technical issues and the 2:00am time slot did not show the band at their best.[66] In the interview with Whitehall, Maurice also made it clear that he and Wadleigh did exercise their editorial power, as Wadleigh explained it, sometimes due to time considerations, and as Maurice explained, sometimes for artistic reasons: he told Whitehall, "We won't have Blood, Sweat and Tears because they gave a bad performance: Really terrible. They were very, very slick and everyone else was informal".[67] However, there was likely also an element of promotion here: spontaneity was hip, whereas planning, schedules, and rules were not. Lang and Kornfeld had developed a somewhat calculated disinterest in many of the organisational and financial problems that drove Roberts and Rosenman to distraction. After all, to do otherwise would have looked uncool. (Similarly, in *Gimme Shelter*, one of the festival organisers said of the chaotic car parking situation, "we're just gonna let it happen. For experimental purposes. You know what I mean?") It was important to Maurice and Wadleigh that if their film was to be successful among their target audience, it had to generate that same air of spontaneity.

Moreover, there are several political elements of the musical performances at Woodstock which *do* make it to the final cut, most notably Country Joe's "I-Feel-Like-I'm-Fixin'-To-Die-Rag" and Richie Havens' "Handsome Johnny". Recorded in 1967, "Rag" became popular among the underground as an antiwar song.[68] Schowalter argues that Wadleigh trivialises the song in the film by superimposing the lyrics on screen and using a "bouncing ball" to emphasise each syllable, allowing the cinema audience to sing along.[69] However, in the actual festival, Country Joe encouraged the crowd to sing along so it might be argued that the filmmakers have accomplished their aim to let the cinema audiences experience what it was like to be at the festival. The song is darkly humorous: it is arranged as an upbeat skiffle, and the lyrics express a deadpan air of resignation about death. It would be difficult then to trivialise a song that already affects a trivial style in order to make a serious point. In that respect, it follows in a long line of satirical literature opposing war, from *Candide* (1759) and *All Quiet on the Western Front* (1929) through *Catch-22* (1961) to *Slaughterhouse-Five* (1969). These novels proved black humour and surrealism were effective techniques to express disapproval of war, so Wadleigh's approach was in line with Country Joe's, and it cannot therefore be argued that this editorial technique depoliticised the original performance. As for its impact in the film, that remains open to debate: Miller Francis Jr. called the song "a gas" but also expressed some of the cynicism that marked the post-Altamont view of festivals and the Woodstock Nation. As a Vietnam protest song, he argued, the song seemed "harmlessly obsolete as far as where our heads are at NOW (and where Amerikan troops and war technology are now)".[70]

As for musician Joe McDonald, he maintained that festivals were an example of effective mass action. Street protests failed because they enable the Establishment to mobilise force effectively against the protesters: in contrast, the Establishment did not know how to respond to Woodstock. Echoing Ellen Sander's critique of Abbie Hoffmann, McDonald claimed that hedonism was probably the most revolutionary thing to do in the U.S. at that point. He said, "The UndergroundEstablishment [sic] is a little bit scared of Woodstock. Abbie Hoffman was totally ignored at Woodstock. That freaked him out. Woodstock had no more to do with Abbie Hoffman than with Richard Nixon".[71] Clearly that was what the promoters wanted: for example, they agreed to Hoffman's demands for cash and an underground presence at the festival not because they necessarily agreed with Hoffman's revolutionary politics, but because having him inside looking out was better than having him outside looking in. Without his support, word-of-mouth on the street might scupper the festival. But Hoffman's support could give the festival the street cred it needed to be successful. It is notable also that none of the festival advertising focused on politics in its usual manifestations. It is for these reasons perhaps that music journalist W. Rexford Benoit adjudged Woodstock "a respite from violent reality… not a revolution".[72] Bob Maurice agreed: speaking to the *Los Angeles Free Press*, he claimed Hoffman's omission didn't matter as most of the Woodstock audience "came to the festival to get away from the battle".[73] So if anything then, for McDonald, it was not that Woodstock was apolitical; it was about a new kind of mass action — a respite from old thinking of "battles" and "revolution" and instead embracing a new kind of cohesion and unity.

Yet the inclusion of Richie Havens' political song "Handsome Johnny" in the movie also suggests that themes of politics and war *were* present in the final cut. Reviewing the Woodstock movie, Alfred B. Packer heard something political in Havens' performance, claiming Havens "brought the war back home" with lyrics about "men marching to war".[74] Since only two of Havens' songs made it into the film Packer must surely have been talking about "Handsome Johnny", a track Havens co-wrote with Lou Gosset Jr., and first heard on his 1967 album *Mixed Bag*. The song tells the tale of Handsome Johnny, a figure symbolic of young men fighting for freedom in different historical time periods, and who participates in battles at Concorde, Gettysburg, Dunkirk, and in Korea and Vietnam. The penultimate verse, which disrupts this seemingly patriotic narrative, has him going to fight in Birmingham, Alabama, although it's unclear if he intends to fight for or against freedom in the civil rights struggle there. In the last verse a hydrogen bomb signals impending doom for everyone. Havens' powerful vocals and impassioned delivery makes "Handsome Johnny" a powerful voice in the Woodstock film for civil rights and against the Vietnam War.

Ultimately, any debate about the filmmakers depoliticising Woodstock has to take account that the film not only included Jimi Hendrix's rendition of the "Star Spangled Banner", but also that Wadleigh made it the film's grand finale. The song's inclusion wasn't automatic: Hendrix played 17-18 songs (depending on how one lists them) and only three were included in the Woodstock movie, so all other considerations aside, it had only about a one-in-three chance of appearing in the film. And while it is not quite the last song to appear in Wadleigh's movie, it certainly feels like its climactic moment. In the original festival setlist, Hendrix played four songs after the "Star Spangled Banner", ending with "Hey Joe" as an encore: but in the film the anthem segues into the song "Purple Haze", and then the end credits begin. Whatever interpretation is placed on it — whether that be anti-Vietnam War, or supportive of his former soldier comrades, or some combination of both — Hendrix's version of the "Star Spangled Banner" is undeniably political, so its inclusion in the film is a powerful rejoinder to those who accused Wadleigh of depoliticising the festival. Nevertheless, the debate is complicated: some political aspects were omitted, yet others were not, and the film makers' decisions weren't necessarily motivated by a deliberate desire to neuter the politics of Woodstock, but were a consequence of a number of competing agendas, as well as by artistic, financial and practical considerations

Reception (protests)

As we recall from the beginning of this chapter, the *Woodstock* film was a stellar financial success. Yet this profitability sat uncomfortably with many of the young Woodstock generation that the movie was marketed to. Many felt this was "their" story, that rock festivals should be free, and that cinemas should therefore screen the Woodstock film for free (or alternatively that a cut of the profits from the film should go back into their community). For some young people, the rock festival had the potential to marry the music of the counterculture with the politics of the underground. For example, Miller Francis Jr. thought festivals might "destroy the capitalist machine" which was exploiting young people. He claimed, "Woodstock proved that selling tickets to hear music is almost an impossibility. Woodstock proved that there are no fences high enough to separate the affluent from those unable or unwilling to produce dollars and cents to hear a music that flows directly out of their experience".[75] The question of ownership loomed large: do those who buy records and attend festivals or concerts have a stake in any media products that music generates? Or was there a fundamental misunderstanding about the music industry, a willing naivety that music is anything other than a product for consumption just like any other product for sale in the marketplace? The resulting impassioned battle over "ownership" of the idea of Woodstock fuelled a spirited movement to undermine the financial success of *Woodstock* the movie.

For some of the young counterculture community advocating the idea of free music, there was an understanding that the festival had a special meaning as an iteration of what the Woodstock Nation supposedly stood for. *Other Scenes*' Irwin Silber called that a "revolution of the mind" that would create a freer society, "unstructured, natural, open and loving".[76] It was, therefore, both a surprise and also a harsh business lesson to learn that the Woodstock film was not going to be free to see, but also that cinemas would be charging an inflated ticket price of $4. "Woodstock will have its national release at Easter", noted the *Madison Kaleidoscope*, before asking its readers: "Did you ever think of going in free?" The *Kaleidoscope* claimed that the festival film and accompanying soundtrack album showed "how Woodstock Nation is being turned into a big profit-making machine" and challenged its readers — "if you let it".[77] "One year later and we're still paying to get in", *The Rag* complained.[78] *The Seed* claimed Warner Bros. had "no right" to charge an entry fee because the movie was "made by the 400,000 who were there, and it belongs to them".[79] Calling the film company "a cold-blooded pig with no interest in the Vision [sic] the film suggests", it urged readers to "slip in, go through a side door, organize mass break-ins". If that was unsuccessful *The Seed* advocated an alternative response, that festival attendees sue Warner Bros. for "actor's equity pay", hopefully forcing the company to pay one million dollars for "the Panther Bail Fund, John Sinclair Defense". The *Ann Arbor Argus* made a similar point, claiming "We are the actors in the film who didn't get paid a cent for making the film".[80] *San*

Francisco Good Times did not object to cinemas charging a fee to see the film, but it considered the $4 ticket price "outrageous, maybe (considering the nature of the film) even sacrilegious".[81] To atone for such profanity, Karen Berg of the *East Village Other* suggested that cinema patrons "mention to the management... that you would like to see part of the proceeds go to the [Chicago 8] Conspiracy, or write Warner Bros. and let them know".[82] In a similar vein, the *Ann Arbor Argus* demanded that the film be shown free or 75% of profits be donated to set up free medical clinics.[83]

One of the responses to these reports was that some radical groups organised protests and pickets at cinemas. These occurred mainly in San Francisco, Los Angeles and New York, and sporadically elsewhere. For example, the *Ann Arbor Argus* organised a protest at the Fox Village Theater in Ann Arbor on June 14, 1970. It's likely no coincidence that *Ann Arbor* is home to the University of Michigan, as universities were hubs for some of the most radical protests, which in turn led to violent repression by the Establishment. For instance, a month previous to this, Ohio National Guardsmen shot dead four student Vietnam War protesters at Kent State University, Ohio, in what became known as the Kent State Massacre. The *Madison Kaleidoscope*, a campus underground newspaper at Michigan State University, called the film "an incredible rip-off" and urged readers not to pay admission fees while "brothers & sisters languish in jail for lack of bail".[84] Protesters picketed the University of California Theater in Berkeley in June to protest the "rip off price" of $3.50. As reported in the *Berkeley Tribe*, the cinema expected to make a gross profit of $400,000 for a 10-week engagement, but the first week of protests led to near-empty showing and 90% losses.[85] The protesters were demanding three extra showings at a cost of $1.50 a ticket, with all proceeds going back into community projects. Their ire was directed at Warner Bros. rather than the cinema or its manager, whom the *Tribe* claimed, seemed sympathetic to the issues raised. Police broke up one demonstration under the pretext of noise complaints.

In Los Angeles, the *Los Angeles Free Press* reported a planned protest against the film showing at the Fox Theater on Wiltshire Boulevard on Friday and Saturday 15-16 of May, potentially the busiest and therefore most profitable days. Picketing had actually begun a month previously upon the film's initial release. On this occasion, protests were preceded by a leaflet campaign targeted at local schools and colleges. One of the organisers was a Yippie named Marc Savin, who claimed Woodstock was "the first movie in the history of Hollywood where the actors can't afford to go see it". The *Free Press* also commented on the "exploitative nature of the film and the industry in general", and pointed to protesters' demands that there be free showings for those who couldn't afford to pay, and donations to the "movement".[86] As Joan Holden pointed out in *Ramparts* magazine, these protests were popular because political radicals of the Woodstock Nation believed they were being exploited. They assumed that Woodstock belonged to them "because we went there, the same way we assume rock is ours because we listen to it".[87] As one protester at the University of California Theater proclaimed, "This is our movie! We didn't get paid for making it. We're the stars and we want to get in to see the movie WE made!"[88]

The protesters' sentiments contrasted markedly with the hard economic reality expressed by Bob Maurice in an interview with *Great Speckled Bird*. Maurice reminded the interviewer: "Warner Brothers is not a benevolent organization; it's a business. It's not interested in rock festivals per se… it's got stockholders. And I was quite willing to make a deal with Warner Bros. because I wanted to make a film, and because I felt that it was important… and I also felt that if the film existed, and people saw it, even if they had to pay, that that was better than its not existing and no one seeing it".[89] In that same interview Maurice was careful to distance himself as a filmmaker and artist from Warner Bros., the film distributer and business enterprise with stockholders. He expressed sympathy for the view that some profits should be funneled back into community organisations or political causes, but claimed that as an artist not involved in finances, that was beyond his control. That was, in part at least, disingenuous, as Maurice was co-owner of Wadleigh-Maurice Productions, also a business which had to turn a profit to keep operating. Nevertheless, his comments demonstrate how out-of-touch some protesters were with the economics of the music business, and indeed the film business.

However, if the protesters demands are viewed as aspirational rather than unrealistic or naïve, they can be considered in a less harsh light. There was no reason why filmmakers could not negotiate in their contracts with big Hollywood studios some degree of profit sharing with community organisations. No doubt the studios would have faced opposition from their shareholders, but if they could be convinced that such demands were in their interests then deals might be done. This was illustrated in an interview *Liberation News Service* conducted with Fred Weintraub, Warner Bros.' Vice President in Charge of Creative Services, and reprinted in *Great Speckled Bird*. Weintraub claimed there were people within the Establishment who sympathised with some of the Movement's concerns but young people would always be ineffective until they learned to use the Establishment, meaning the extant systems of power. Weintraub explained: "What they need is someone who can sit down with bankers. If the bankers think they can profit, they'll play our game".[90]

Aniko Bodroghkozy claims that the underground's response to Woodstock was unambiguous, that "critics supported the film, on the one hand, and raged at Warner Bros., the studio distributing it, on the other".[91] Bodroghkozy makes some astute observations about attempts by Wadleigh and Maurice to position themselves in opposition to Warner Bros. and align themselves instead with countercultural interests. While it's true that the filmmakers were concerned about Warner Bros. editing the film to under three hours, which would enable cinemas to show the film more often, it seems these concerns were unwarranted.[92] Moreover, Bodroghkozy's assertion that the film was "generally above reproach as a document", and that criticism and protest mainly focussed on Warner Bros.' Distribution, seems off the mark. As we have seen, critics were concerned about what they saw as the film's depoliticisation, mostly through a process of excluding acts, songs, and events from the final edit. Overall though, *Woodstock* was a critical and financial success, winning an Oscar in 1971 for Best Documentary Feature. Its use of split-screen, in particular, enabled cinema audiences to connect with the musicians on stage and the festival audience. They were, of course, already connected through the music, their youth, and political ideals, but capturing this on film had, by-and-large, eluded previous filmmakers. Perhaps the only thing missing was the atmosphere and the odour of recreational drugs. If that was the case, *San Francisco Good Times* offered some sage advice: "Get stoned before you go; if possible, get so stoned someone else has to take you to the theater. Eat some hash, or drop a lot of acid".[93]

Woodstock's Legacy

In his influential novel *Fear and Loathing in Las Vegas* (1971), Hunter S. Thompson reflected on the successes and failures of the counterculture. Raoul Duke, a thinly-disguised version of the author, had this to say about the conclusion of the 1960s:

And that, I think, was the handle — that sense of inevitable victory over the forces of Old and Evil. Not in any mean or military sense; we didn't need that. Our energy would simply prevail. There was no point in fighting — on our side or theirs. We had all the momentum; we were riding the crest of a high and beautiful wave. So now, less than five years later, you can go up on a steep hill in Las Vegas and look West, and with the right kind of eyes you can almost see the high-water mark — the place where the wave finally broke and rolled back.[94]

These words were an elegy to the counterculture ideas which, Thompson/Duke claimed, swept eastwards from California in the 1960s, but broke on the shores of Las Vegas, a city the author viewed as the ultimate symbol of the Establishment's capitalist values. Thompson's writing captured a feeling among activists that, even this early into the new decade, the counterculture dream was fading: President Richard Nixon was in power, the Vietnam War was ongoing, and many of the previous decade's struggles over issues such as free speech, gender equality, civil rights, and recreational drug use were still unresolved. As Thompson indicates, the potential of the Woodstock Nation to create a better world and go "Back to the Garden" now started being remembered as a lost opportunity. But what of the *Woodstock* film? We have seen how debates raged about its meaning and importance. We've also considered its mixed critical reception, with many counterculture enthusiasts considering it a rip off or misleading, but which also garnered it an Oscar win that suggests a degree of mainstream approval.

Sometimes an indirect consideration of these events can expose the psychological undercurrents of an era: for example, film is a useful window into the cultural milieu. Perhaps the most interesting insight into how *Woodstock* was understood in the time period shortly after its release can be found in the 1971 dystopian science fiction movie *Omega Man*. While this film could easily be dismissed as B-movie schlock — for example, a contemporary reviewer in *Great Speckled Bird* summarised the plot as, "Christ with a machine gun and a Black Mary Magdelene... Add a hippie, a Black militant, a Head Baddie and Heston crucified and you pretty well have the story"[95] — it nevertheless offers a fascinating insight into how the *Woodstock* film was utilised to explore profound human themes like conflict, survival, identity and hope. But most importantly, *Omega Man* explores the idea of "Paradise Lost" — that Woodstock was a last chance for America's redemption.

Omega Man, loosely based on Richard Matheson's 1954 novel *I Am Legend*, stars Charlton Heston as Robert Neville, one of the few-remaining survivors of a world depopulated and brought to its knees by a devastating biological war. This onscreen post-apocalyptic world is set in 1975, and we learn that Neville survived the apocalypse by injecting himself with an experimental vaccine; others, however, are not so fortunate, and suffer from an acute form of albinism and photosensitivity that condemns them to a perpetual nocturnal existence. These unfortunate souls are led by Matthias, a former television newsreader, and they adopt a violent anti-technology doctrine, which manifests in book burnings, destruction of machinery, and violent retribution against non-believers. Neville calls them "the Family", spending his nights sheltering from them in his fortified apartment, and his days searching for their lair so he can exterminate them. On his lonely quest to annihilate them, he seems doomed to a life of perpetual loneliness, stress and anxiety. At one point, he imagines all the city's telephones ringing at the same time — a hallucination caused by his extreme isolation. He attempts to alleviate this by going to the cinema; and the film that appears before him is *Woodstock*.

Neville observes, with irony, "Great show. Held over for a third straight year". That he can mouth the words as they are spoken on the screen suggests he has seen it numerous times already, and although only a few scenes are shown on screen, it is suggested that Neville watches the film in its entirety, leaving the cinema as the sun sets. The first *Woodstock* scene shows Country Joe and the Fish being introduced onstage to the accompaniment of the crowd chanting "marijuana!" Singer Joe McDonald tells the audience they are in for a taste of "rock and soul music", which is the title of the song they begin to play. Like the Woodstock audience, Neville seems entranced, but perhaps as much by the size of the audience as the onstage performance. This scene shows the world that once existed, with a vast crowd of people free to enjoy the spectacle of a three-day music festival. In contrast, Neville believes he is the only healthy human left alive in Los Angeles. But why does the film focus on Woodstock as the specific paradigm when there were, of course, many films with crowd scenes that were available to choose from? Is there a suggestion that the lifestyle promoted onscreen is the cause of the disaster that has left Neville the sole survivor? Or does Neville's nostalgia for the Woodstock generation suggest a failure on the part of American society to realise the values and lifestyle demonstrated at Woodstock and perhaps this is its punishment?

The way the movie pans out clearly implies the latter interpretation. In using Woodstock and the counterculture as a framework, *The Omega Man* presents two paradigms of a future "family" and ergo a future vision of America: one is pessimistic and one optimistic. The first is Matthias' "Family", which seems to be an evocation of the real-life Charles Manson's Family of followers.[96] This fictional "Family" seem to be Manson's apocalyptic fantasies made real; Manson wanted to instigate a race war between African-Americans and the white middle class, after which, he believed, African–Americans would attain power but then fail to bring order to a new post-apocalyptic society. His "Family" would then come out of hiding to take power.[97] Neville's response to this "Family" in turn echoes the misguided and reactionary approach of modern civilisation to those who do not conform: for example, he refers to the Family as vermin and their lair as a nest; he even captures one of them to experiment on, bringing to mind Nazi depictions of Jews in propaganda newsreels as rats, and subsequent conducting of medical experiments in the concentration camps. There are also reminders of the horrors of Vietnam. Neville is part of the system, politics, society and culture that produced everything from Operation Phoenix to the My Lai massacre. One commentator, for example, refers to Neville's crusade against the Family as a "one-man-search-and-destroy mission", using then-contemporary American military terminology.[98]

Yet the alternative to this "Mansonian future"[99] posed by the Family and Neville's destructive response to them, is offered by the film's other evocation of "family", namely Dutch and Lisa's interracial group of young plague survivors. This family is the epitome of the Woodstock ideal — peace-loving, searching for harmony, and forging new ways of living. Initially afraid of Neville's ultra-violent response to the Family, Lisa then develops romantic feelings for him. In addition, Lisa realises Neville may hold the cure to the plague in his blood and he therefore also represents her ill brother Richie's last chance for survival, as well as that of the group's. Lisa takes Neville to meet her family, and they eventually embrace him, if not quite as one of them, then as someone they can reach an accommodation with. They soon realise Neville is of the old world, but has potential not just to fit into a new world order, but also to be its saviour; that he is "both the cause of and solution to global suffering".[100] When exposed to the possibility of starting over again with this alternative "family", Neville makes the transition from the failed past to a possible utopian future. Previously, by refusing to leave the city and by surrounding himself with consumer items and possessions, he had tried to hold on to the trappings of civilisation. But soon he rejects the urban existence and imagines a new Arcadian life. He tells Dutch and the group that they should seek: "Some place nobody ever bothered with. A river nobody ever dammed, a mountain nobody ever built any bloody freeways to where everything we do will be the first time it ever happened". Dutch responds: "Hey yeah you've got it, that's it. That's it! Just like in the beginning of the world. Like we were starting all over again in the Garden of Eden!"[101]

If the first scene shown from Woodstock serves to demonstrate the beginning of a socially cohesive alternative future — one that has been lost due to the fears and mistakes of old ways of thinking, which culminated in the war that end civilisation — the second Woodstock scene shown in *Omega Man* suggests a way forward if society can be reborn in Dutch's new "Garden of Eden". This scene is of Woodstock organisers Michael Lang and Artie Kornfeld being interviewed. Kornfield says: "These last three days, these last three million years... all of us have undergone a turnabout... and realised, if you can't live together and be happy, if you have to be afraid to smile at somebody, right? What kind of a way is that to go through life?"

Neville repeats his earlier utterance, "Nope. They sure don't make pictures like that anymore", which underlines what the world has lost by not listening to the youthful counterculture. After seeing *Woodstock* and then meeting Lisa, who may represent in the film a new Eve to his Adam, Neville is determined to rebuild the world — no longer hell-bent on eliminating the Family, nor trying to salvage the old order that he at first tried to save, but rather he decides to embrace the multicultural, Edenic future offered by Lisa and Dutch's group. In *Omega Man,* Neville ultimately dies when he returns to the city to find Richie, who has gone there to find the Family in the naïve belief that they will welcome news of a potential cure. Neville dies in a pool of his own blood, arms out-stretched and with his palms facing up, in a Christ-like pose. He sacrifices himself to give his adopted family a chance to start over in a new America.

While science fiction films are often unfairly judged by how well they predict the future, their main value is often as a window into the time period in which they were made.[102] On one level *The Omega Man* reveals some of the existential anxieties of the early 1970s, particularly fear of an apocalyptic war and ecological disaster. But more importantly for our purposes, *The Omega Man* suggests two visions of the future: one is a chance to start again in an Arcadian setting, close to nature, unspoiled by consumerism, and with freedom and equality; the other is the Mansonian future of a powerful cult leader leading misguided young followers towards nihilism and violence. Both imply that the present status quo is untenable. *The Omega Man* clearly suggests that Woodstock offers the best example for the future, representing, as it does, a united family of "freaks" who are truly free, happy, and ecologically aware enough to suggest that a more environmentally sustainable future is possible and indeed necessary if their brotherhood and sisterhood is to survive. As Laurel Westrup notes, in *The Omega Man* the *Woodstock* documentary "comes to function as a memorial to the best and brightest possibilities of the counterculture, now deceased".[103] The scenes from *Woodstock* shown in *The Omega Man* frame the narrative by showing what has been lost but also suggest that society might be reborn in a new "Age of Aquarius", but only if the old society represented by Neville can learn from past mistakes and embrace the change offered by youth.

In 1989, Richard Bernstein wrote a piece for the *New York Times* entitled "Can Movies Teach History?" Noting that "more people are getting their history, or what they think is history, from the movies these days than from the standard history books", he then asked, does "the filmmaker, like the novelist, have license to use the material of history selectively and partially in the goal of entertaining, creating a good dramatic product, even forging what is the sometime called the poetic truth, a truth truer than the literal truth?" Does it matter, Bernstein asked, "if the details are wrong if the underlying meaning of events is accurate?"[104] The *Woodstock* film is about a historical event; added to that, it is also a documentary. As such, historical accuracy seems to be of prime importance. *Woodstock* takes liberties with some basic facts: for example, it changes the running order of the festival. In other ways, of course, it is also "inaccurate" because the process of editing over one hundred hours of film into a 185-minute movie will always mean that reality is distorted by the choices of film makers: some events will seem more prominent than others, some conflation of themes and events will occur, and what is omitted will inevitably draw criticism. There is not space here to fully address wider debates about historical accuracy in movies that explore real-life events, but Bernstein's point about the accuracy of "underlying meaning" is critical to evaluating and understanding *Woodstock*. In some ways it is easy to adjudge accuracy: if all the evidence suggests the band The Who performed early on the Sunday morning of the festival and yet the film has them performing after Joan Baez early on Saturday morning, that is clearly an inaccuracy. However, it is debatable whether an inaccuracy such as this has any real impact on our understanding of the event — its "underlying meaning". Furthermore, such fault finding ignores the fact that the movie was meant to entertain as well as to inform, and therefore if those artistic liberties taken with the running order made the film more entertaining, which in turn led to it being viewed by a larger audience, then perhaps that was a compromise worth making. However, as the events considered in this chapter indicate, Woodstock's "underlying meaning" is not something that can be pinned down with any certainty or consensus. When a society was as fractured as the United States was in the late 1960s, reaching agreement on the meaning and importance of any sizable event was difficult; to reach a consensus on something as impactful and culturally important as Woodstock was probably an impossibility, even when most of those who attended likely shared very similar views many of the cultural, social, and political issues that were relevant to them in that time period. When a movie such as *Woodstock* attempts to depict such an important cultural event as the Woodstock festival, a layer of stakeholders is added — the filmmakers, their financial backers Warner Bros., who were also responsible for distributing the film, movie theatres, movie audiences, and film critics — all of whom had their own interests and their own opinions. In the 1962 movie *The Man Who Shot Liberty Valence*, a reporter turns down a true story, preferring instead to persevere with one that is inaccurate but has become publically accepted as truthful: "When the legend becomes fact, print the legend", he declares. It is clear from his film that Wadleigh chose to "print the legend" of the festival, but did so with the knowledge that the Woodstock legend was almost entirely true.

[1] "Black Shadow", *San Francisco Good Times*, Vol 3, Issue 14, Apr 2, 1970, pp. 10-11.

[2] Mike Jahn, "Recollected in Tranquility: Woodstock", *Music & Artists*, Jun 1970.

[3] There were many other concert films in this period, but none of these made it into cinema screens. Examples include: the 1960 documentary *Jazz on a Summer's Day* which documented events at the 1958 Newport Jazz Festival; Murray Lerner's 1967 film *Festival* which filmed events at the Newport Folk Festival from 1963 to 1965; 1964's televised *T.A.M.I.* Show, which documented a concert held at the Santa Monica Civic Auditorium that year featuring a variety of artists including the Rolling Stones, The Beach Boys, Chuck Berry, and James Brown; and the Beatles featured in a number of promotional cinematic releases such as *A Hard Day's Night* (1964), *Help!* (1965), *Magical Mystery Tour* (1967), and *Yellow Submarine* (1968); *What's Happening! The Beatles in the U.S.A.* (1964) by the Maysles Brothers documented the band's first visit to the United States that year; while D. A. Pennebaker captured aspects of Bob Dylan's 1965 concert tour in England in *Don't Look Back* (1967). Because rock festivals were so new, however, *Monterey Pop* was the only festival professionally filmed and given a cinematic release previous to Woodstock.

[4] Michael Lang and Holly George-Warren, *The Road to Woodstock* (New York: HarperCollins, 2009), p. 147.

[5] Aaron Taylor, "Angels, Stones, Hunters: Murder, celebrity and direct cinema", *Studies in Documentary Film*, Vol 5, No 1 (2011), pp. 45-60. At p. 46.

[6] There are some parallels here with the "new journalism" mode of writing and reporting that developed in the 1960s in that both focused on real subjects, but new journalism utilised literary devices to get at the truth whereas cinéma vérité utilised cinematic techniques to the same aim. For examples of new journalism, see Tom Wolfe & E. W. Johnson, *The New Journalism* (New York: Harper & Row, 1973).

[7] Robert Stephen Spitz, *Barefoot in Babylon: The Creation of the Woodstock Music Festival*, 1969 (New York: Viking, 1979), p. 352.

[8] Miller Francis, Jr., "Woodstock", *Great Speckled Bird*, Vol 3, Issue 18, May 4, 1970, pp. 12, 13, 20, 21. At p. 13.

[9] James E. Perone, *Woodstock: An Encyclopedia of the Music and Art Fair* (Westport, Ct.: Greenwood , 2005), p. 157.

[10] Gina Arnold, "Nobody's Army: Contradictory Cultural Rhetoric in Woodstock and Gimme Shelter" in Sheila Whitley and Jedediah Sklower, eds., *Countercultures and Popular Music* (Farnham: Ashgate, 2014), pp. 123-37. At p. 130.

[11] In addition, due to the continued success of the film after its release, in 1972 Warner Bros. issued an 8-page movie promotional poster/booklet. Woodstock Preservation Archives. Movie Promotion. Available online at: http://www.woodstockpreservation.org/Gallery/MWadleigh/Movie_PromoFlyer.htm

[12] See appendix and Woodstock Preservation Archives online at: http://www.woodstockpreservation.org/Gallery/MWadleigh/MWadleigh.htm

[13] Andrew Kopkind, "Woodstock at Yasgur", *Helix*, Vol 9, Issue 6, 1969, pp. 6-7. At p. 7.

[14] "Lumpy Wavy and the 5 Days of Styrofoam", *Seed* Vol 4, Issue 8, Nov 7-20, 1969, pp. 8-9. At p. 9.

[15] Spitz, *Barefoot in Babylon*, p. 380.

[16] Jesse Sheidlowe, ed. *The F-Word* (Oxford University Press, 2009), p. 213.

[17] *Berkeley Tribe* Vol 2, Issue 46, May 22-29, 1970, p. 18.

[18] *Street Journal* Vol 2, Issue 50, May 1-13, 1970, p. 14.

[19] *Helix*, Vol 11, Issue 20, May 14, 1970, p. 20.

[20] *Los Angeles Free Press*, Vol 7, Issue 301, Apr 24-30, 1970, p. 18.

[21] Abbie Hoffman, *Woodstock Nation: A Talk-Rock Album* (New York: Random House, 1969), p. 20.

[22] D.A. Ingram, "'Go to the forest and move': 1960s American rock music as electronic pastoral", *49th Parallel*, Vol 20 (2006), pp. 1-16. At p. 7.

[23] Francis, Jr., "Woodstock", p. 12.

[24] Francis, Jr., "Woodstock", p. 13.

[25] Richard Whitehall, "Filming at Max's Farm", *Los Angeles Free Press*, Vol 6, Issue 271-Part Two, Sep 26, 1969, p. 27 & 33. At p. 27.

[26] As early as 1893, for example, Frederick Jackson Turner's "Frontier Thesis" hypothesised that east coast cities such as New York were overpopulated with Eastern European immigrants and that the rural frontier offered an escape from urban slums and sin. While Turner's Anglocentric ideas gradually fell out of favour, anti-urbanism and fears of overpopulation did not. To many in the 1960s, large cities seemed to represent everything wrong with the modern world. They were overpopulated, faced high crime levels, and were the hotbeds of capitalist competition, rampant consumerism, and political corruption. Paul R. Ehrlich's hugely popular book *The Population Bomb* (1968) extrapolated from extant population trends to predict a worldwide population explosion, with resultant food shortages and ecological disaster.

[27] Adrienne Koch and William Penn, *The Life and Selected Writings of Jefferson* (New York: Random House, 1944), p. 280. The most heroic depiction of farmers derives from Thomas Jefferson's belied in a nation based strongly on agriculture, a nation comprised mainly of yeoman farmers. He thought that urbanisation led to corruption, laziness and greed; in contrast, he believed that industrialisation would lead to unhappiness and inequality.

Jefferson's notion of the yeoman farmer is a central element of American national identity. Throughout American history a mythic hero figure has been the virtuous farmer who first tames the frontier and then transforms it from wilderness to a beautiful garden. Another foundational American figure, Benjamin Franklin, also championed the farmer as a progressive, heroic figure: in 1741, Franklin remarked with pride that in just a few decades, Pennsylvania colonists had managed to make a "garden of a Wilderness", and as historian Jack P. Green notes, that was "an extraordinarily prolific garden at that". See Jack P. Green, *The Intellectual Construction of American: Exceptionalism and Identity From 1492 to 1800* (Chapel Hill: University of North Carolina Press, 1993), pp. 89-90.

28 Mark H. Lytle, *America's Uncivil Wars: the Sixties Era from Elvis to the Fall of Richard Nixon* (Oxford University Press, 2006), p. 57.

29 Daniel F. Schowalter, "Remembering the dangers of rock and roll: Toward a historical narrative of the rock festival", *Critical Studies in Media Communication* Vol 17, Issue 1 (2000), pp. 86-102. At p. 88.

30 Spitz, *Barefoot in Babylon*, pp. 476-77.

31 Andy Gordon, "Satan and the Angels: Paradise Loused", in Jonathan Eisen, ed., *Altamont* (New York: Avon, 1970), pp. 30-71.

32 "Leary Love Rap", *Berkeley Barb*, Vol 9, No 25, Issue 228, Dec 26 - Jan 1, 1969, pp. 3 & 10. At p. 3.

33 Gordon, "Satan and the Angels", pp. 30-71.

34 Joan Holden, "Woodstock: The Four Dollar Revolution", *Ramparts*, Oct 1970, pp. 60-64. At p. 61.

35 Mary Reinholz, "Woodstock was free — movie should be too", *Los Angeles Free Press*, Vol 7, Issue 298, Apr 3-9, 1970, p. 6.

36 "Fishing for Country Joe", *Berkeley Tribe*, Vol 1, Issue 16, Oct 24-30, 1969, pp. 14-15. At p. 15.

37 Barry Farrell, "Second Readings: Bad Vibrations from Woodstock", *Life* Sep 5, 1969, p. 4.

38 Thomas M. Kits, "Documenting, Creating, and Interpreting Moments of Definition: Monterey Pop, Woodstock, and Gimme Shelter", *Journal of Popular Culture,* Vol 42, No 4 (2009), pp. 715-32. At p. 721.

39 Ted Franklin, "Woodstock: Youth Culture in the Wilderness", *Liberation News Service*, Issue 187, Aug 21, 1969, pp. 1-4. At p. 1.

40 "Wild East", *San Francisco Good Times*, Vol 2, Issue 32, Aug 21, 1969, p. 2.

41 Untitled. *The Rag* Vol 3, Issue 27, Aug 21, 1969, p. 5.

42 Arnold, "Nobody's Army", p. 131.

43 Spitz, *Barefoot in Babylon*, pp. 276-84.

44 Miller Francis Jr., "Talkin 'bout My Generation", *Great Speckled Bird,* Vol 3, Issue 24, Jun 15, 1970, pp. 12-13.

45 Spitz, *Barefoot in Babylon*, p. 330.

46 Richard Reeves, "Mike Lang (groovy kid from Brooklyn) plus John Roberts (unlimited capital) equals Woodstock", *New York Times*, Sep 7, 1969, pp. 34 & 122.

47 "A Leaflet for the Hog Farm", *Liberation News Service*, Issue 193, Sept 11, 1969, pp. 10-11.

48 Michael Smith, "Woodstock combines two fine styles", *North Carolina Anvil*, May 16, 1970, p. 5.

49 Arnold, "Nobody's Army", p. 131.

50 For a fuller discussion of this song, see Amy Kintner, "Back to the garden again: *Joni Mitchell's* 'Woodstock' and utopianism in song", *Popular Music Volume* Vol 35, No 1 (2016), pp. 1–22.

51 Richard Ogar, "A Real Mindfucker", *Berkeley Barb*, Vol 10, No 13, Issue 242, Apr 3-9, 1970, p. 6.

52 Lloyd Steele, "Woodstock or Woodschtick?" *East Village Other,* Vol 5, Issue 9, Feb 4, 1970, p. 17.

53 Irwin Silber, "Woodstock: The Euphoria Was Real", *Other Scenes*, Vol 4, Issue 5, May 1, 1970 pp. 5 & 6. At p. 5.

54 Roland Gelatt, "Was this trip really necessary?" *Saturday Review*, Apr 18, 1970, pp. 42-43. At p. 43.

55 Jimmy McDonough, *Shakey: Neil Young's Biography* (London: Vintage, 2003), p. 320.

56 Francis, Jr., "Woodstock", p. 12.

57 Spitz, *Barefoot in Babylon*, pp. 414-16.

58 Werner, *A Change is Gonna Come: Music, Race and the Soul of America* (Edinburgh: Canongate, 2002), p. 93.

59 Schowalter, "Remembering the dangers of rock and roll", p. 91.

60 Jeff Tamarkin, *Got a Revolution! The Turbulent Flight of Jefferson Airplane* (New York: Atria, 2003), p. 197.

61 Egbert Sousé, "Hollywoodstock", *Berkeley Tribe*, Vol 2, Issue 49, Jun 12–19, 1970, pp. 24-25. At p. 24.

62 Richard Havers and Richard Evans, *Woodstock Chronicles: 3 Days of Peace & Music* (London: Compendium, 2009), p. 80.

63 David E. James, *Rock 'N' Film: Cinema's Dance With Popular Music* (New York: Oxford University Press, 2016), pp. 239-40.

64 Whitehall, "Filming at Max's Farm", p. 27.

65 Evans and Kingsbury, *Woodstock: Three Days that Rocked the World*, p. 195.

66 Quoted in Pete Fornatale, *Back to the Garden* (New York: Touchstone, 2010), p. 162.

67 Whitehall, "Filming at Max's Farm", p. 27.

68 "What's that spell?" *The Seed*, Vol 5, Issue 2, Apr 1, 1970, p. 24.

69 Schowalter, "Remembering the dangers of rock and roll", p. 91.

70 Francis, Jr., "Woodstock", p. 12.

71 "Fishing for Country Joe", *Berkeley Tribe*, Vol 1, Issue 16, Oct 24-30, 1969, pp. 14-15. At p. 15.

72 W. Rexford Benoit, "A respite, not a revolution", *Ann Arbor Argus,* Vol 1, Issue 12a, Sep 17 - October 2, 1969, p. 27.

73 Reinholz, "Woodstock was free — movie should be too", p. 6.

74 Alfred B. Packer, "See You At Mao", *The Rag* Vol 4, Issue 25, May 11, 1970, p. 15.

75 Miller Francis Jr., "Our Park", *Great Speckled Bird*, Vol 2, Issue 28, Sep 22, 1969 pp. 12-13. At p. 13.

76 Silber, "Woodstock: The Euphoria Was Real", p. 6.

77 "Across the nation...What's Goin' Down", *Madison Kaleidoscope*, Vol 2, Issue 7, Apr 8, 1970, p. 3.

78 Packer, "See You At Mao", p. 15.

79 "Woodshock", *The Seed*, Vol 5, Issue 4, May 1, 1970, p. 11.

80 "Woodstock Film Cultural Ripoff", *Ann Arbor Argus*, Vol 2, Issue 22, Jun 10-17 1970, p. 4.

81 "Black Shadow", p. 10.

82 Karin Berg, "Woodstock on Film", *East Village Other,* Vol 5, Issue 18, Apr 1, 1970, p. 6.

83 "Woodstock Film Cultural Ripoff", *Ann Arbor Argus*, Vol 2, Issue 22, Jun 10-17, 1970, p. 4.

84 Mark Knops, "Don't See Woodstock", *Madison Kaleidoscope*, Vol 2, Issue 10, May 19, 1970, p. 5.

85 *Berkeley Tribe,* Vol 2, Issue 48, Jun 5-12, 1970, p. 21.

86 Dennis Levitt, "Woodstock", *Los Angeles Free Press*, Vol 7, Issue 303, May 8-14, 1970, p. 20.

87 Joan Holden, "Woodstock: The Four Dollar Revolution", *Ramparts*, Oct 1970, pp. 60-64. At p. 60.

88 Jef Jaisun, "Stop the Wood Shuck", *Berkeley Barb,* Vol 10, No 21, Issue 250, May 29 - June 4, 1970, pp. 3 & 12. At p. 3.

89 Francis, Jr., "Woodstock", p. 20.

90 Craig Karpel, "Das Hip Kapital", *Great Speckled Bird*, Vol 4, Issue 31, Aug 2, 1971, pp. 6, 7 & 23. At p. 6.

91 Aniko Bodroghkozy, "Reel Revolutionaries: An Examination of Hollywood's Cycle of 1960s Youth Rebellion Films", *Cinema Journal,* Vol 41, No 3 (2002), pp. 38-58. At p. 49.

92 Reinholz, "Woodstock was free — movie should be too", p. 6.

[93] "8Black Shadow", p. 11.
[94] Hunter S. Thompson, *Fear and Loathing in Las Vegas: a savage journey to the heart of the American Dream* (New York: Vintage, 1998), p. 68.
[95] Tom Harper, Rev. Omega Man. *Great Speckled Bird,* Vol 4, Issue 37, Sep 13, 1971, p. 20.
[96] Michael E. Heyes calls Matthia's followers, "Manson-family clones... thinly veiled as a vampiric threat to a democratic, Christian United States". Michael E. Heyes, "Fixing Ground Zero: Race and Religion in Francis Lawrence's I Am Legend", Journal of Religion & Film, Vol 21, No 2 (2017), pp. 1-27. At p. 1.
[97] In *The Omega Man*, which was released just a year after the Manson trial, Matthias' albino Family transcends racial ideology, but their physical racial characteristics remain visible. Matthius thus instructs Brother Zachary, an African-American cult member, to leave behind his old racial prejudices (in this case, against whites) and to fully embrace the Family's anti-technology and anti-knowledge doctrine. See Gerry Carlin and Mark Jones, "Cease to Exist: Manson Family Movies and Mysticism", in Holy Terror: *Understanding Religion and Violence in Popular Culture* by Eric S. Christianson and Christopher Partridge, (London and New York: Routledge, 2016), pp. 53-62.
[98] Mark Sample, "There Goes the Neighbourhood: the Seventies, the Middle Class and *The Omega Man" in Shocking Cinema of the Seventies*, edited by Xavier Mendik (Hereford: Noir, 2002), pp. 29-40. At p. 34.
[99] Carlin and Jones, "Cease to Exist", p. 62.
[100] Mark Gallagher, *Action Figures: Men, Action Films, and Contemporary Adventure Narratives* (New York & Basingstoke: Palgrave Macmillan, 2006) p. 86.
[101] Whereas Woodstock offers an anchor point in *The Omega Man* for a particular vision of the future, Altamont and the documentary film *Gimme Shelter* (1970) are not specifically mentioned or referenced. However, it is possible to read *The Omega Man* as a contrast of both events. For instance, film professor Laurel Westrup claims that in the movie, "dystopian Los Angeles stands in for the dystopian imagery of Altamont popularized by *Gimme Shelter"*. See Laurel Westrup, "Medias Martyrs? Rock 'n' Roll, Film and the Political Economy of Death", Spectator 27 (2007): pp. 33-41. At p. 37.
[102] I. C. Jarvie, "Seeing Through Movies", *Philosophy of the Social Sciences,* Vol 8, Issue 4 (1978), pp. 374-97. At p. 375.
[103] Westrup, "Medias Martyrs", p. 37.
[104] Richard Bernstein, "Can Movies Teach History?", *New York Times*, Nov 26, 1989.

Chapter 4: ANGELS

…nobody who has ever spent time among the inbred Anglo-Saxon tribes of Appalachia would need more than a few hours with the Hell's Angels to work up a very strong sense of déjà vu.

Hunter S. Thompson[1]

It was supposed to be a gathering of the entire culture… It was to affirm faith and proclaim together a new nation. The people and music were there as planned. The nation though, was just as bad as the rest of them.

Paul Glusman[2]

Oh life would be so beautiful if only the bad guys weren't here.

Sandy Darlington[3]

Just a few weeks after Altamont had taken place, *Rolling Stone* magazine published perhaps the most influential contemporary report on the festival.[4] The comprehensive article was authored by Lester Bangs, Greil Marcus, and nine other contributors. As well as offering eye witness accounts and some insightful analysis about the festival, the main thrust of their piece was to list ten mistakes made by the concert organisers which led to an experience that was, in many ways, the total opposite of the ostensible "harmony" of Woodstock (although, ironically, many of their allegations could be also have been made *about* Woodstock). They declared that unlike Woodstock, Altamont had been riddled with practical and technical mistakes (such as poor organisation, planning and publicity), which had led to the festival being hosted at an isolated site that had never hosted a concert of this size before. These faults were compounded by the fact that Altamont Speedway was also situated by an unfinished four-lane freeway which meant there was only one main route in or out. Last but not least, the article vented fire at the festival organisers' decision to ask Hells Angels to act as "security".

Some of the errors noted by *Rolling Stone* were, at least in part, caused by circumstances beyond the control of event organisers. However, the decision to ask Hells Angels to do some security work was made conscientiously and well in advance of the event. It remains one of the most controversial aspects of Altamont. Yet, at the time, engaging with the Angels may have seemed sensible and rational. They had helped at previous festivals, for example. They would probably turn up anyway, so why not keep them close and on side? Members of the Grateful Dead knew some of the Angels, and assured the Rolling Stones, the principal organisers of Altamont, that they could work with them. Not only that, the Angels seemed to share some of the counterculture's ideals: they might, therefore, act as a counterbalance to any violence initiated by police. Lastly, fans often disrupted Stones' concerts by charging onto the stage and, on occasion attacking band members: such was their reputation and demeanour, having Angels around might deter any such behaviour without any need for violence. Grace Slick said of the Angels, "they were good at concert security because people were afraid of them".[5] Besides, the Stones would have their own bodyguards on stage. Furthermore, a standard provision on the Stones tour contract was that the promoter was required to hire at least fifty unarmed guards for crowd control.[6] In fact, Altamont Speedway owner Dick Carter went beyond this requirement, hiring hundreds of plainclothes security guards to protect his property. No doubt, too, there would be undercover police in the audience. While there was always the possibility of disorder at any event that attracted tens of thousands of people, the balance of security forces at Altamont seemed to limit that potential for serious violence. Besides, Woodstock and previous successful festivals indicated that the motivations of festival audiences were, in general, to have fun and listen to good music, and that is what the Stones offered. What, then, could go wrong?

In retrospect, of course, some of these attitudes seem hopelessly naïve, particularly the belief that the Angels might be a force for good. In fact, the evidence was available at the time to suggest that employing a motorcycle gang with a reputation for serious violence — not to mention one that had already expressed its opposition to and distaste for some aspects of the counterculture — was a serious and avoidable error. At the same time, however, the decision did not seem particularly unusual or controversial and that was mainly due to well-established links between the Angels and the San Francisco Bay area music scene. Moreover, even in the immediate aftermath of the deadly events that took place at Altamont, there was not unanimous agreement that Hells Angels were responsible for the violence; indeed, some saw them as the injured party. And there was even a point of view that the Angels did a competent job providing security and it was members of the crowd who incited the violence. The remainder of this chapter will look closer at these events, miscommunications, and tensions with regard to the Hells Angels to try and unearth "what really happened" regarding their mandate with security at Altamont. It will consider the following: the origins of the Hells Angels; the Angels' relationship to the counterculture; the violence at Altamont and the fallout from that.

Origins of Hells Angels

When it comes to the story of the Hells Angels it is difficult to separate myth from truth. Depending on one's point of view and the time period under consideration, the Angels could be viewed primarily as a motorcycle club, a gang of tough outlaws, or a group of organised criminals; it is possible to consider them in any of these lights, or even as some combination of them. Moreover, the image the public sees of them is down in large part to the image the Angels *want* them to see. As one commentator observed, for example, the depiction of the Hell's Angels in "spurious, sensationalized, exploitational movies, magazine articles, one-shot picture books, and so-called responsible news reports", construed them as modern-day outlaws, and inheritors of the wild, brawling spirit of the Old West.[7] The cinematic media, in trying to make sense of the Angels as a new sociological phenomenon in the mid 1960s, depicted the Angels as avatars of freedom and individualism: they were inheritors of the traditions of Billy the Kid, Jesse James,

Buffalo Bill, Wild Bill Hickok, even the Texas Rangers.[8] They were antiheroes, on both sides of the law at the same time; always ready to dispense "frontier justice" when the occasion merited. And if this meant stomping civil rights activists in Oakland or peace demonstrators in Washington or Berkeley, so be it: trying to stop that from happening would be akin to getting between a lion and its prey.

The origin of outlaw motorcycle clubs can be traced to California in the years after World War Two, when bored ex-servicemen joined with like-minded men to form clubs such as the Booze Fighters, Market Street Commandos, and Pissed Off Bastards of Bloomington. Initially their outlaw status was unconnected to criminality: it simply meant they were not affiliated with the mainstream American Motorcycle Association (AMA). Yet soon after, their reputation for hell-raising became notorious when they made a "gypsy run" to Hollister on the July Fourth weekend of 1947, an event traditionally organised by the AMA. Most of the clubs attached to the AMA caused no trouble, but some of the "outlaw" clubs overindulged in alcohol, brawled, and took part in drag races through the streets of Hollister. These improprieties were recorded by journalists from *Life* magazine, and the Hollister story that appeared a few weeks later was illustrated with an image of a drunk motorcyclist, astride his bike, parked among a sea of empty or broken beer bottles. *Life* claimed that bikers terrorised the town, although the story vastly over-inflated the scale of the havoc and damage caused by the motorcycle clubs.[9] In the aftermath of the event, the AMA blamed the disorder on outlaw bikers, the so-called "one percent" who refused affiliation with their organisation and who therefore did not follow their regulations. Outlaw motorcyclists, in turn, thrived on such notoriety and adopted the moniker "one-percenters" to distinguish themselves from anodyne AMA clubs.

The *Life* article brought outlaw motorcyclists to national attention and established their notorious reputation. Hollywood filmmakers saw an opportunity to exploit this new interest in motorcycle gangs and in 1949 *Maniac on Wheels* became the first of a new outlaw biker film genre. However, it was the 1954 film *The Wild One* that was most successful. Starring Marlon Brando and Lee Marvin as rival biker gang leaders; *The Wild One* was based on a short story inspired by the 1947 *Life* photograph. A financial and critical success, *The Wild One* further cemented the reputation of the one-percenters as rebellious antiheroes. When he saw the film, Sonny Barger, who would go on to found the Oakland Hells Angels in 1957, and who would play an important role at Altamont, claimed to identify with Lee Marvin's character Chino rather than with Brando's Johnny. Chino's gang drove American Harleys and Indians, whereas Johnny's bike was British. Aside from Chino's "buy American" patriotism, Barger was attracted to Chino's prickly attitude towards authority: "If you fuck with me, I'll hit back." Barger would reiterate this sentiment after Altamont: the Hells Angels did not initiate trouble; they reacted to it — brutally.

The original Hells Angels club was formed in Fontana in 1948 in the wake of the Hollister event and subsequent press coverage. According to Sonny Barger, it was comprised of at least some former members of the Pissed Off Bastards.[10] In the next few years, a number of clubs calling themselves "Hells Angels" formed independently from each other in the San Gabriel Valley, in Fresno, and in San Francisco. Hunter S. Thompson, a journalist who spent a year riding with the Angels and who wrote the first substantial exposé of the outlaw motorcycle subculture, argues however that the Angels of the San Bernardino (or "Berdoo") chapter, established in 1950, were the "founding fathers" of the organisation. He claimed the San Bernadino group took responsibility in the next decade and a half for authorising all new club charters.[11] In 1954, the Market Street Commandos adopted the Hells Angels name. Ralph "Sonny" Barger, recently discharged from the military for enlisting while underage (and who had a long history of petty crime behind him), helped set up a Hells Angels club in Oakland in 1957, and he became president of that club the following year.

Their original club logo had on it the words "Hells Angels" to indentify the club's affiliation, and "Nomads" to show its location. "Nomads" soon changed to "Oakland", and Barger molded it into a formidable club with a reputation for savage violence. Club rules were designed to emulate top-down systems of authority, and to keep order. For example, each club had a president who set the tone of the club: rules such as no fighting at club meetings were designed to keep order and discipline, and to ensure obedience. However, it was the Angels' ethos about using violence against non-Angels that is particularly relevant to events at Altamont and the death of Meredith Hunter. There was, for example, no such thing as a "fair fight" in the Angels' mentality: instead, their attitude was "One on all, all on one", which meant if someone attacked an Angel under any circumstances, even if that person was severely provoked, all Angels present must join in a "rat pack" against the non-Angel.[12] This tapped into much older conceptions of elite male "honour"; perhaps akin to the equivalent of a "duel", albeit in this case the whole group acting as a pack to destroy the adversary who dared to challenge a fellow Angel's honour. In reality, while the Angels talked a lot about honour, it was brute force that gave them their authority. So when Rolling Stones' road manager Sam Cutler told the band that the Angels "are really some righteous dudes" and they "carry themselves with *honor* and dignity", he was not necessarily misleading the band but instead had accepted the Angels' outward-facing image of themselves.[13] He had, in essence, bought into the Angels' own propaganda of honour and dignity that was designed to deflect attention away from the sheer brutality of how they actually conducted themselves, as well as their alleged ongoing criminal activity.

So for our purposes, the important thing is to identify what the Angels were and how they were seen in the late 1960s, because that provides the context for the decision to invite them to do the security at Altamont, to explain their behaviour, and where possible to assign motives and responsibility.

Hells Angels and the Counterculture: "You Can't Always Get What You Want"

Given the self-styled "macho" image of the Hells Angels then, it might therefore come as a surprise to know that, for a period of time from around 1965 until the end of the decade, it appeared that the Hells Angels and the counterculture shared some ideas and attitudes. Some radicals, hippies, and antiwar activists considered the Angels as a potential counterbalance to police violence. Additionally, some musicians saw potential for the Angels to act at music events as an alternative "security" force instead of the police. By their presence alone, Angels might deter violence. And if violence did occur, the Angels likely would put a stop to it. Besides, the Angels would turn up at many events invited or not, and engaging with them in this way seemed to make more sense than having them act as wild cards.

So why then did elements of the counterculture, and some musicians, see the Angels as potentially useful allies? Initially, the Angels and the counterculture seemed to share a similar rebellious attitude towards authority. As we have seen, the post-World War Two outlaw motorcyclists were looking for thrills, but they also wanted to escape the stifling conformity of the capitalist consumer society that the United States had become by the 1950s. As a result, some of these early outlaw clubs seemed more like beatniks than the violent, guerilla-type imagery more normally associated with Hells Angels. The beatniks were writers and artists active from the late 1950s who, in number of significant ways, prefigured the counterculture: for example, while they remained mostly uninterested in movements and politics, beatniks rejected mainstream society's values, especially the social conformity of the 1950s. Major themes of beatnik literature, as represented in some early, important examples of the genre such as John

Clellon Holmes' *Go* (1952), Allen Ginsberg's *Howl, and other Poems* (1956), and Jack Kerouac's *On the Road* (1957), are alienation from society and rebellion against extant sexual, racial and cultural mores.[14]

Jack Kerouac, the so-called "King of the Beats", is probably the most public face of the Beat literary movement. In *On the Road*, he spends time in the company of the socially stigmatised, including down-and-outs, drop-outs, drug-users and homosexuals. In his novel there are suggestions of homosexual liaisons, with more explicit depictions elided on the suggestion of Kerouac's publisher. This was partly to avoid legal issues, as the book was autobiographical and homosexuality was illegal at this time. Kerouac's friends, Allen Ginsberg and Neal Cassady, slept together, and Ginsberg and Peter Orlovsky were long term lovers.[15] Many beats were homosexual and some gravitated towards San Francisco, which had a gay scene from at least the 1930s onwards, and which would later be home to a number of outlaw motorcycle clubs. Certainly, some Angels clubs mirrored this celebration of homoerotic behavior. An all-male subculture like the Hells Angels would no doubt attract homosexuals: however, journalist Hunter S. Thompson suggested that most of the homoerotic behavior he witnessed was for public consumption — "showbiz" rather that evidence of homosexuality: "[kissing] is a guaranteed square-jolter, and the Angels are gleefully aware of the reaction it gets... The sight of a photographer invariably whips the Angels into a kissing frenzy."[16] Whether true or not, the Angels' apparent connection to homosexuality suggested some shared ideology with the counterculture. This became clearer with the release of Kenneth Anger's *Scorpio Rising* (1963), which was essentially a collage of contemporary pop culture imagery, Nazi iconography, motorcycle leather fetishism, sadomasochistic performance, and homosexual erotica. It wasn't about Hells Angels, but the link was clear enough. For the mainstream media, it was evidence that there was no deprivation the Angels would not indulge in; to the counterculture, however, it was more evidence that the Angels were on their side of the culture war.

Some Angels also seemed to be in harmony with the liberal thinking that characterised other aspects of the beatnik movement and counterculture. Some had liberal views about race: for instance, the Chosen Few club was established in Los Angeles in 1959 as an African-American club, but within a year it had accepted its first white member: it embraced an interracial identity as a badge of strength. Moreover, some Angels clubs seemed in tune with the hippie vibe of the mid-1960s: Hunter Thompson noted, for example, that the Sacremento and Frisco chapters of the Angels "began with a distinctly bohemian flavor".[17] However, a later generation of "baby boom" bikers such as Sonny Barger were more comfortable within a more macho, hierarchical structure. He was responsible for molding the Oakland Hells Angels into a tightly-knit club, with a top-down leadership structure. Club rules advocated conformity and obedience, and this took the form of a written charter, a uniform (club colours), and adopting symbols and ceremonial features akin to a quasi-military organisation.[18]

Hollywood also played a part in linking outlaw motorcycle clubs with the nascent counterculture: in the 1950s, for example, *The Wild One* (1953) portrayed bikers as "beatniks on wheels." In this film, Marlon Brando's Johnny stars as a handsome, brooding rebel who, when asked what he was rebelling against, replied: "Whaddya got?" After *The Wild One*, American etymologist Peter Tamony notes, "Hollywood produced at least one film a year devoted to the low-life pursuits of cyclists — breaking, booze, and broads".[19] The most successful film of this genre, and the one which most aligned outlaw bikers with the counterculture, was *Easy Rider* (1969). In it, Peter Fonda (Wyatt) and Dennis Hopper (Billy) play the roles of drifters who use the profits from a drug deal to finance a motorcycle trip from Los Angeles through the southwest, and the south, towards Florida. The trip's picaresque nature allows viewers to witness the political and cultural divisions in this vast, sprawling country. Essentially a B-Movie biker film, *Easy Rider* was a surprise hit, which seemed to capture aspects of the counterculture that had never before been seen on screen. In an otherwise caustic contemporary review, Paul Schrader said that the underground's identification with the film was "instant and understandable", because it is, as one friend told him, "a picture that doesn't cop out".[20] Wyatt and Billy are California hippies, one cool and existential, the other far out and hedonistic. As film scholar Barbara Klinger points out, these are character types "drawn from the state most recognized as a counter-cultural mecca".[21] Yet they are also recognisable as outlaw motorcyclists. While they may not wear club colours, their behaviour and mode of travel identifies them with the notorious "one-percenters". For example, they drive Harley-Davidson motorcycles rather than cheaper, non-American bikes. Their bikes have been "chopped" — modified and personalised in the tradition of many motorcycle clubs. They are also disdainful of the law, and have been rejected by mainstream society.

Yet in reality, *Easy Rider* did not give a true impression of the lives and behaviour of the Hells Angels clubs. For example, the outlaw motorcyclists in the film don't operate within a club structure; their "colours" or clothing identify them as making individual choices about their attire; their discussions with other characters show they hold liberal views aligned with the counterculture; and unlike the Hells Angels who were traditionally patriotic (for example, in supporting the war in Vietnam), Wyatt and Billy advocate an alternative patriotism based on the notion of real freedom for all Americans, rather than the limited freedom currently on offer. Finally, unlike many real outlaw motorcycle gangs — and particularly the Hells Angels — Wyatt and Billy reject violence as a way of life. So it is not without some truth that Angel Sonny Barger dismissed *Easy Rider* as merely a "movie about two drug dealers who happened to travel across country on bikes", not a bike movie, and certainly not a depiction of the real-life Hells Angels.[22]

Other areas of congruence between the counterculture and the Angels, was their similar use of recreational drugs. In the early 1960s the Angels' drug of choice was alcohol, not pot or LSD — drugs that were more associated with the counterculture. Alcohol dulls the senses, whereas LSD was meant to unlock the mind and expand consciousness;[23] pot tends to mellow out users, whereas alcohol is a depressant and often a catalyst for violent acts. Later the Angels would embrace LSD and virtually any type of drug, but they became "pushers", which is perhaps the ultimate embrace of capitalism and, of course, the opposite of what the counterculture was meant to represent.[24] The Angels' introduction to LSD came in 1965 when author Ken Kesey, the lead figure in the "Merry Pranksters", invited the Frisco chapter of the Angels to an "acid test" party at his ranch at La Honda. This was one of a series of events held at La Honda to which Kesey invited the cream of the counterculture, figures such as Allen Ginsberg, Neal Cassady, Hunter Thompson, Richard Alpert, and the Grateful Dead. Kesey had prepared a welcome for the Angels: when they arrived they were greeted with music and a light show, and a sign saying THE MERRY PRANKSTERS WELCOME THE HELL'S ANGELS.

The Angels were quickly put at ease. Barger said that the Pranksters were, "sort of like us — underground free spirits" but without the motorcycles or violence.[25] It was at La Honda that the Angels first took LSD *en masse*. As Hunter Thompson notes, LSD had similar effects on the Angels as it did everyone else: some mellowed out, and some had bad trips.[26] Word quickly spread to the Oakland chapter and then the rest of the northern California Angels that Kesey was cool and La Honda was a safe place for them to party without much police harassment (in California, police could not enter private property without a search warrant). These "acid tests" became legendary among the counterculture, and since the party invitees were among the coolest figures in the beat movement and the counterculture, the Hells Angels became lumped in with such luminaries. Vaakov Kohn of the *East Village Other*, concluded: "Before Ken Kesey established direct relations with the San Francisco Hells Angels it was taken for granted that there were just a bunch of rightwing redneck punks. Then, suddenly, a change in their image took place. They weren't just beautiful, but groovy too. Suddenly they became glorious pop heroes".[27] Some in the counterculture thus began to see the Angels as potential allies and perhaps even their strong-arm protection against law enforcement.

Yet, despite some of the similarities outlined above, it is also true that the Angels had little in common with the counterculture; in fact, they tended to mimic mainstream power structures. While the press and the film industry portrayed the Angels as modern day cowboys — rugged individualists who fought for and won their freedom from society's mundane constraints — the reality was quite different. Hells Angels were not individualists: they preferred the group experience to the individual, and their violence could not be controlled. Moreover, in spite of some of the seeming shared interests with the liberal counterculture, politically, the Angels were conservative. They supported the war in Vietnam and hated communism. Their Nazi paraphernalia suggested at least ignorance of the Nazi Holocaust, or perhaps even support for it. As Barger told one reporter, "there's a lot about [1930s Germany] we admire. They had discipline. There was nothing chickenshit about em. They might not of had all the right ideas, but at least they respected their leaders and they could depend on each other".[28]

The honeymoon period of fraternity between the Angels and the counterculture ended in October 1965, when the Angels attacked protesters at an anti-Vietnam War march organised by Jerry Rubin and the Vietnam Day Committee, which was to begin in Berkeley and end in Oakland. Despite a heavy police presence, the Angels managed to penetrate a police line to attack protesters, tear up banners, and damage sound equipment, all of which appeared on television news reports.[29] Berkeley police eventually intervened, but not before the Angels had made a significant statement about their relationship to the counterculture. They were happy when it suited them to hang out with the likes of Kesey and Ginsberg, but politically they were poles apart. As Sonny Barger pithily recalled, "We made it clear to the peaceniks, the cops, and the rest of the country where we stood on the war. We dug it".[30]

The Vietnam Day Committee compared the Angels to the Ku Klux Klan. However, in the run up to a second peace march scheduled for November, Barger met with Ginsberg, Kesey, Cassady, and some of the Merry Pranksters in an attempt to smooth the waters. Despite having some personal affection for Ginsberg, Barger's politics and therefore the *de facto* politics of the Oakland Hells Angels, did not align with those of the antiwar protesters. Afterwards, Barger called Ginsberg and other Vietnam War protesters "despicable", "un-American" and "traitors", and in a telegram to President Johnson, Barger offered the services of the Hells Angels as a "crack group of trained gorrillas [sic]" to "demoralize the Viet Cong and advance the cause of freedom".[31] Nevertheless, the second demonstration proceeded with no interference from the Angels. Without irony it seems, the Angels announced: "Our patriotic concern for what these people are doing to our great nation may provoke us to violent acts".[32] Rorabaugh insists, however, that Kesey "bribed them to stay away with a generous supply of beer".[33] More likely, the Angels and particularly Barger had already achieved their goals — look and act tough, stomp some "commies" and intellectuals, appear patriotic, and keep up the reputation of the club for no-nonsense violence. There was therefore no need for the Angels to intervene in the November peace march, which went ahead without incident. Another interpretation is that Barger was won over by appeals from Ginsberg, who was particularly vocal in trying to find common ground between the protesters and the Angels.[34] Nevertheless, Thompson's conclusion about these events was astute and timely: "When push came to shove, the Hell's Angels lined up solidly with the cops, the Pentagon and the Birch Society... The Angels' collective viewpoint has always been fascistic."[35]

"No Expectations": Hells Angels and Be-Ins, Love-Ins, Acid Tests, and Concerts

Despite Sonny Barger's assertion that the anti-Vietnam War march incident in October 1965 marked the end of the Angels' battles with peace demonstrators, if anything, the Angels' position on Vietnam hardened over the next few years. For example, Hells Angels repeatedly vandalised a 33-foot high "Peace Tower" in Los Angeles that was designed and sculpted by hundreds of artists including Roy Lichtenstein, in protest at the Vietnam War.[36] Angels also clashed with protesters at San Jose State College in November 1966, attacking them with baseball bats because the protesters were picketing the College over its links with Dow Chemicals.[37] Angels also announced they would disrupt a Teach-In at the University of California's Berkeley campus, which had been organised by the American Association for the Advancement of Science, and ran from December 26-31, 1966. In the end, however, the Angels limited their protest to a statement that the A.A.A.S. "should volunteer for Vietnam or spend their time making bombs, instead of demonstrating".[38]

Nevertheless, Hells Angels and elements of the counterculture continued to engage with each other on a non-political level. For example, at Ken Kesey's LSD graduation party, held in a warehouse in San Francisco in October 1966, Hells Angels joined "Haight Street Hippies, beautiful pregnant mothers, young girls" as well as Kesey and Neal Cassady for music, a light show, a mock ritual about LSD, followed by a period of meditation.[39] On New Year's Day, 1967, the Diggers and the Hells Angels co-hosted a party to thank Haight residents for bailing two Angels (Chocolate George Hendricks and Hairy Henry Kot) out of gaol a few weeks earlier; they partied along to live music by the Grateful Dead and Janis Joplin.[40] A few weeks later, on January 14, 1967, the first "Be-In" occurred at Golden Gate Park in San Francisco. It was organised by San Francisco artist Michael Bowen, who was friendly with many beat poets, and also with Janis Joplin. Bowen had organised the Love Pageant Rally, held in the Haight Panhandle on October 6, 1966, as a peaceful protest against the criminalistion of LSD. The Grateful Dead and Janis Joplin provided the music, and Hells Angels were in attendance.[41] Buoyed by the success of the Love Pageant Rally, Bowen and beat poet Allen Cohen began drawing up plans for a larger event. With Bowen at the helm, they arranged permits and invited a number of beat writers including Allen Ginsberg, Lawrence Ferlinghetti and Gary Snyder, as well as Timothy Leary and Richard Alpert, with music to be provided by local rock bands including The Grateful Dead, Jefferson Airplane, Big Brother and the Holding Company and Quicksilver Messenger Service. Remarkably, the Hells Angels were invited along to help the event run smoothly, which required the Angels to provide security and even care for lost children.[42] Even more surprisingly perhaps, the Angels did their tasks competently. There were no serious outbreaks of violence, although a fight between Angels did break out close to the stage.[43]

Later that year, in early September, the Angels held a wake in Golden Gate Park for Chocolate George Hendricks, who had been killed in a collision with a car on Haight. The Grateful Dead and Big Brother and the Holding Company provided music for the event.[44] While members of many motorcycle clubs paid their respects, more hippies than bikers attended the event, along with a number of passers-by. Unfortunately one of these passers-by, a cyclist, kicked an Angel's dog and was badly beaten. A week later, Hap Stewart wrote to the *Berkeley Barb* about this event, and reflected on the deeper significance of the mix of attendees at the wake: "I am confused by the hippie-Hells Angels alliance when the fundamental concepts of each group would seem not to coincide … the Hells Angels are not beautiful people. They are, collectively, a group of misfits and assorted morons who, at any given time, are one step away from violence and who will kick the shit out of anyone who happens to displease them (hippies included). I find it very difficult to understand the sheep-like hippie acceptance of the Angels' behavior. Are hippies sheep?" In response, the *Barb* pointed out that hippies are accepting of everyone, and asserted that no other group of non-Angels has better relations with the club.[45]

In the aftermath of Altamont, one commentator declared: "We need the Angels and they need us" but that wasn't necessarily the case.[46] The Angels despised the hippies and exploited them. When one New York Angel ("Spain") was asked if they saw the hippies as brothers, he replied: "Definitely not. The Hells Angels don't consider themselves a part of the Hippie movement. In fact, just about the opposite is the case. The comparison of the two cultures is one of contrast rather than similarity". This tallied with Hap Stewart's summation of the two groups, and his insistence that their respective fundamental concepts did not align. Spain also confirmed Stewart's observation about the Angels use of violence: "The Hippie responds to man's dehumanization with... compassion and kindness... The Bikers, who were an earlier movement, responded by attempting to rip off the false mask of humanity and kindness and get to the real brutal reality of it all".[47] However, that question — are hippies sheep? — would come up again after the violence at Altamont as critics questioned why no one intervened as the Angels brutally beat many fans, and killed Meredith Hunter. As violence raged around and among them, caused mainly by a smallish group of Angels, Sandy Darlington noted the crowd's feeble response: "People all around began to raise their hands in the V sign. That was their big response. It was so fucking pathetic".[48]

What of the argument that simply the presence of Hells Angels at counterculture events would help keep order? One indicative example suggests this was mostly wishful thinking. Approximately 6,000 people attended a love-in at Griffith Park, Los Angeles on Sunday July 23, 1967. The inter-racial crowd included about fifty bikers from various clubs, including the Hells Angels, Satan's Slaves and Galloping Gooses. They had attended previous love-ins at Griffith Park and seldom initiated any trouble. As the *Los Angeles Free Press* observed, "Their attitude towards hippies seems to range from complacent acceptance to total indifference. Many understand that being branded social outcasts by the Establishment gives them far more similarities to hippies than differences". In this instance, however, the Angels' presence gave the police the opportunity to start trouble and then use that as an excuse to break up the love-in. One witness, a non-biker, told the *Los Angeles Free Press* she witnessed a man trying to provoke one of the bikers with verbal insults. When that failed to get the required reaction, the man kicked the biker, who stood up and confronted him. At that point, the attacker pulled out a gun and identified himself as an undercover policeman. This incident gave police the excuse they needed: 75 uniformed officers, and many other plainclothes officers, arrived on the scene and dispersed the crowd by drawing weapons, issuing threats, and hitting out indiscriminately with billy clubs. Elements of the counterculture hoped that the presence of outlaw motorcycle clubs at events like this might deter violence: that their fierce appearance and notorious reputation might be enough, on their own, to keep order. In this instance, however, the motorcyclists' reputation worked against them. Their predictably violent response to being attacked gave police the opportunity to utilise violence against an otherwise peaceful crowd, causing it to disperse.[49]

Nevertheless, after the Golden Gate Park Love-in, the Angels redeemed their reputation as possible strong-arm allies in the fight against "the establishment". A typical example of this sentiment was expressed in the *Berkeley Barb*: "In the Haight-Ashbury, it developed that the Hell's Angels was the military force. And it was really, really strange, fellows, to find out that they would just as well fuck as fight, and just as well get stoned and be friendly as terrorize. Can you dig it?"[50] This was occurring at the same time as the rock music festival scene was beginning to take off, and the Angels appeared, in one form or another, at most of the big festivals held over the next few years. On some occasions they were asked to provide security, and at others they attended as audience members. The first of these was 1967's Fantasy Fair and Magic Mountain Music Festival wherein Canned Heat, The Doors, Country Joe and the Fish, The Byrds and

Wilson Pickett, Smokey Robinson and the Miracles, and Jefferson Airplane were among those scheduled to appear. However, after a one-week delay caused by poor weather, a number of these artists had to cancel. Nevertheless, Michael Goldberg of the *Berkeley Barb* paints an almost idyllic picture of this festival: "around 20,000 hippies came together for a day of fun and sun and 'good vibes.' Admission was $2 and the Jefferson Airplane, Byrds, Doors and Captain Beefheart and the Magic Band were just a few bands present".[51] The event took place over two days on a June weekend at Mount Tamalpais, about thirteen miles north of the Golden Gate Bridge. It was a natural ampitheatre, but with limited parking, so to ensure artists could reach the venue, organisers arranged for busses to take fans from Marin to the event. They called this service "Translove Buslines".[52] Still, there were practical problems: Jeff Blackburn of the San Francisco folk rock duo Blackburn and Snow, suffered a flat tyre, and expressed some disappointment that no one passing by stopped to lend a hand.[53]

While Hells Angels had not been requested to perform any official duties at the festival, they were present, as they were at most sizable music events in Northern California, and they made themselves available to give rides to performers to get them up and down the mountain. Barry Melton, lead guitarist of Country Joe and the Fish, recalls that the Angels were waiting at the bottom of the mountain when the group arrived. After dropping some acid, an Angel calling himself "Broken Dick" took Melton on a wild, hallucinogenic trip up to the amphitheatre.[54] Such benevolent behaviour proved to be great public relations for the club.

Hells Angels also attended the Monterey International Pop Festival, June 16-18, 1967. Often cited incorrectly as the first large rock festival, and more correctly as a major event in the "Summer of Love", Monterey featured some of the most well-known artists of the era, and introduced a few others to a larger audience. While Bob Dylan, the Beatles and the Rolling Stones were absent for various reasons, Janis Joplin, Otis Redding, The Who, and Jimi Hendrix gave eye-catching performances. Hendrix famously set alight his Stratocaster guitar and the Who smashed their instruments. A number of bands from San Francisco who were familiar to the Angels appeared on the bill, including the Grateful Dead, Big Brother and the Holding Company, and Jefferson Airplane. Altogether, the cream of Californian and American rock, pop, and folk music appeared on the bill, as well as some international artists. These included The Byrds and Frank Zappa from Los Angeles, Chicago's Paul Butterfield Blues Band, Simon and Garfunkel from New York, England's Eric Burden and the Animals, and Ravi Shankar from India. Along with 20,000 other fans, a group of Angels camped at Monterey Peninsula College while attending the festival.[55] They were treated to impromptu performances from the Grateful Dead, who entertained fans at the campsite while waiting for their slot at the main venue. D.A. Pennebaker's concert film *Monterey Pop* (1968) contrasts the Monterey police chief's concerns about an influx of Hells Angels with scenes of the Angels getting into the remarkable spirit of Monterey by adopting the trappings of the hippies, and adorning their motorcycles with flowers and incense. Despite helping out at the Fantasy Fair and Magic Mountain Music Festival a week previously, the Angels were not asked to act in any official capacity at Monterey. Given the nature of the event, no one envisaged that they would be needed.

The Newport '69 festival, held on June 20–22, 1969 at Devonshire Downs, near Northridge, Los Angeles, was the first large rock/pop event to experience overt acts of violence. At previous festivals the main criminal activity involved drugs. Here, however, a large number of fans tried to gatecrash the event, in the process fighting with police and "paid-off bikers".[56] These bikers were a group from Los Angeles called the Street Racers, several hundred in number who had been hired by promoter Mark Robinson to act as a security force.[57] The festival had a great line-up, featuring among others, Jimi Hendrix, Janis Joplin, Jethro Tull, Steppenwolf, Creedence Clearwater Revival, Joe Cocker, Marvin Gaye, Ike and Tina Turner, Taj Mahal, Johnny Winter,

The Byrds, and Eric Burden. However, that was part of the problem: far more fans turned up than had tickets — perhaps as many as 180,000 attended.[58] Trouble began on the first evening, a Friday, when fans tore down a section of fence and entered without paying. Some, who were outside the fence at the backstage area, threw rocks at the performers, injuring three members of the Don Ellis Orchestra and sending one to hospital. Despite some scuffles with police and a few arrests, however, violence was minor and damage light.

However, while Saturday was mainly violence-free at the Newport '69 festival, Sunday turned into a horror show. Hundreds of gatecrashers fought for three hours with police and the motorcycle gang. At the end of it all, 67 people had been arrested, fifteen police officers injured, and tens of thousands of dollars of damage caused.[59] Fans inside the fence also caused trouble, partially tearing down a grandstand and lighting bonfires. Someone fired a flare gun at a police helicopter circling overhead. A number of factors instigated this violence, including poor planning, high ticket prices, overcrowding, and some fans who behaved irresponsibly (the *Los Angeles Free Press* called them "a few uptight punks"). However, both fans and musicians pointed the finger at the Street Racers hired to do security. One fan said, ""When people would try to sneak in, the security guys would gang up on them and beat them wildly". Musician Cory Wells of Three Dog Night reflected that the "security was more violent than the audience".[60]

There was further violence that summer at the Denver Pop Festival and Newport Jazz Festival. As with the Newport '69 festival, gatecrashers were mainly to blame and no outlaw motorcycle clubs were involved. However, these events showed that rock festivals were potential powder kegs. They required careful planning to ensure that venues could cope with large crowds. There needed to be adequate sanitary and medical facilities. Entertainment needed to be provided between acts to ensure that fans had something to do, other than causing mischief. Provision of camping sites would ensure fans did not encroach on private property. Promoters needed to judge admission fees carefully, to ensure no one felt ripped off — because when fans did feel ripped off, they would likely try to gatecrash the event. Promoters also needed to consider if security was necessary and if so who would provide it. After his experiences as stage manager at the Denver Festival, E. H. Beresford "Chip" Monck opined that the presence of uniformed police was a catalyst for violence, and suggested a less visible police presence at future festival events.[61] He also argued that all of these practical concerns needed to be resolved before the music was considered, and that was not always the case: often promoters would book a venue, then an act, and then consider such practical concerns.

At Newport '69, for example, promoter Mark Robinson offered Jimi Hendrix $100,000 to appear on the bill, because Hendrix's performance at Monterey had made him hugely popular. Yet, Robinson had failed to consider some practical aspects of the event, such as putting a system in place to allow readmission to the venue. Many fans left the venue, expecting to be readmitted at their convenience, but the organisers had not considered this very basic need, and no practical system was in place to facilitate reentry. As a result, a number of these otherwise law-abiding and peaceful fans joined the gatecrashers. It was prudent also to build a degree of flexibility into event plans. For example, promoter George Wein underestimated how many people would turn up at his Newport Jazz Festival. The bill, featuring for the first time rock and jazz acts, drew bigger and more rowdy crowds than usual. So Wein added 3,000 seats to the extant 19,000, and thus eased some pressure on the event.[62] One simple lesson about festivals was; if the crowd was happy, then it was likely the event would be successful. One of the lessons that required learning was that introducing violent motorcycle gangs into the equation might be asking for trouble.

"Street Fighting Man": Planning for the Hell's Angels at Altamont

It is difficult to get to the bottom of who exactly asked the Angels to do security at Altamont, and what exactly the terms of that agreement were. Unsurprisingly, in the aftermath of the festival, no one was willing to accept full or sole responsibility for the decision, and those involved have since told different versions of events. For example, Ron Schneider, the Stones' business manager, claimed that neither he nor Jagger expected the Hells Angels to be on stage. Schneider inferred that Grateful Dead manager Rock Scully, the Grateful Dead band themselves, and San Francisco "Digger" Emmett Grogan were responsible for the Angels' presence, and he denied that Sam Cutler had cut a deal with the Angels to do security for $500 worth of beer.[63] It was clear, however, in the run-up to Altamont who the band believed were their two main security concerns: the first was the police. Earlier in the tour the Stones were on the receiving end of police harassment. This included cops appearing backstage and forcing band members to pour alcohol into the sink. On another occasion, a female member of the entourage was beaten by a policeman. Police inside venues seemed to be beating up fans not because they were doing anything wrong, but simply because they were having too much fun. In turn, Jagger claimed that the very presence of police often incited fans to attack them.[64] So by the time Altamont came around, the Stones were adamant that they did not want police to do security inside concert venues.[65] However, the other main threat to the Stones' wellbeing was the fans themselves, and if the band did not want police to do security, who would?

Venues usually provided their own security, and during their U.S. tour of 1969, the Stones had hired a few off-duty cops from New York to tour with them. However, while these arrangements might be fine for crowds of between ten to eighteen thousand at most venues, Altamont was an entirely different proposition: would extant security arrangements work with a crowd that might number in the hundreds of thousands? At that point, Stones' concerts were notorious for the behavior of their fans; stage invasions were commonplace, and at times even encouraged by the band. Keith Richards claims that early in their career, stage invasions meant the band did not complete a concert for nearly three years. It got so bad that the band would take bets as to how long a show would last.[66] Fans' rowdy behaviour drew the attention of the press, which kept the band in the media spotlight. They gave journalists something to write about and helped advertise the tour. Fans went as much to see how other fans reacted to Jagger's onstage antics, as they did to listen to the music. But sometimes this got out of hand: equipment was destroyed and on occasion the Stones got hurt. By 1969 fans storming the stage had become a major concern for the band and management. It seemed prudent therefore to get some extra security help.

In engaging with American Hells Angels, the Stones likely thought they knew who they were dealing with. They looked enviously at the San Francisco music scene, which from across the Atlantic looked impossibly vibrant and cool. The Summer of Love began in San Francisco and the Haight-Ashbury scene was happening. Bands like Jefferson Airplane, the Grateful Dead, and Big Brother and the Holding Company were carrying the freak flag, playing exciting music, partying with the hippies, and were on friendly terms with outlaw motorcycle clubs to the point that the Hells Angels were providing security at music events. The idea to approach a local British club of Hells Angels to act as stewards at the Stones' Hyde Park gig in July 1969 probably originated in these fantastic stories emanating from San Francisco. The Hyde Park Angels were, in the main, well-behaved: a report in the British newspaper, *The Observer*, said, "rockers and Hell's Angels acted as stewards. They wore black leather jackets, Nazi steel helmets, dark glasses, and swastikas and crucifixes swinging from neck-chains against their bare chests. Most were gentle and unmilitary and kept order well".[67] Their main job was to protect the stage and the band from invasive fans. In retrospect, however, it is clear that this group of bikers did not have the same modus operandi of their American counterparts, nor indeed did their appearance cause the same consternation. An article in *International Times* noted, for example, that at Hyde Park the Hells Angels, "assembled themselves like a line-up of veteran chorus girls… their belligerence was mainly skin deep as a later incident was to prove, and in countless other ways, their courtesy was as plentiful as it was surprising". This "later incident" occurred when Sam Cutler requested from the stage that the Angels remove all young women from the press section due to lack of space there. Some had exited reluctantly and without fuss but some stubbornly remained and Cutler asked for assistance in speeding this up. However, the bemused Angels took no action against these young women. To the writer this behavior proved that "British Hell's Angels are no more deadly than British policemen".[68]

To return to the Altamont planning, while it was Rock Scully who initially pitched the idea to the Stones of a free concert in San Francisco, the idea of using Hells Angels for the security seems to have originated from a meeting that Mick Jagger had in London with Jefferson Airplane's Grace Slick and Paul Kantner. Slick recalls: "Paul and I were talking to Jagger about how we'd done a bunch of stuff free in Golden Gate Park and the Hells Angels had been our security. And they never hurt anybody... So we said, 'We'll get the Hells Angels to do security,' and Jagger didn't know and said okay".[69] While it is difficult to decipher what specific role the Angels were meant to play at Altamont, and the exact instructions they were given, there are two main sources of information: those directly involved in negotiating with the Angels, and those who heard second-hand accounts, rumours, and wild speculation. Among the former category were the Stones' management, especially their tour manager Sam Cutler, Emmet Grogan, one of the San Francisco Diggers who were involved in many street theatre and music events in the city, Grateful Dead manager Rock Scully, and the Hells Angels. Sonny Barger, who we remember was the founder member of the Oakland Hells Angels, claimed the idea originated from Grogan, who envisaged Angels escorting the Rolling Stones across Golden Gate Park, the proposed original venue for the free concert, and onto the stage. According to Barger, Stones' management made a deal with Pete Knell, vice-president of the Frisco chapter of the Angels, to provide stage security in return for $500 worth of beer. In Barger's recollections, Knell invited other chapters to attend; the deal was that all they had to do was sit on the stage and ensure the crowd did not encroach. Sam Cutler tells a slightly different version of events. Cutler maintains that he, Rock Scully, and Grogan met with Pete Knell, and that in their discussions there had been no suggestion that the Angels would do "security" — rather the Angels would act more as stewards, giving directions, ensuring only those authorised to do so were backstage, and helping people in need.[70] This account has the ring of truth about it, since that was the role of the Hells Angels at the Hyde Park gig a few months earlier, and also the role the Frisco Angels played at previous concerts. It was also the arrangement at a party/concert on New Year's Day 1967 at the Haight Panhandle, featuring the Grateful Dead and Janis Joplin among others, that Grogan had helped organise with Knell.[71]

While it remains hazy then as to who exactly was responsible for the decision to work with the Angels at Altamont — and it is similarly opaque as to whether the organisers had intended for the Angels to act more formally as "security" or more generally as relatively benign "stewards" — what is clear is that the Angels' presence at Altamont would have a profound effect on the outcome of the festival.

"Aftermath": Violence, blame and repercussion

The idea that the Altamont Festival had been *exceptionally* violent was first articulated by *Rolling Stone* magazine. "One thing is most certain", it claimed, "Even the most incomplete medical reports show that this was a festival dominated by violence."[72] *Rolling Stone* reported that volunteer medics treated "dozens of lacerations and skull fractures" and dealt with "an extraordinary number of bad trips", some of which were caused by the violence they witnessed.[73] In addition, the magazine quoted experienced festival photographer Jim Marshall, who also made the case for "Altamont exceptionalism": "The sound was crappy and everybody felt bummed by that. There was no community feeling here at all. There was more violence at this festival than all the other ones I've attended this year. And somehow it relates to the hysteria over the Stones, though I can't really make the connection".[74] Most commentators were clear about who was responsible for this: the Hells Angels, and the Rolling Stones (Mick Jagger in particular) for hiring them.

Was the "bad vibe" and violence of Altamont as vicious as the commentators made out? Certainly, it does seem to live up to its grim reputation. In total, four people died at Altamont: Meredith Hunter's fatal encounter with the Hells Angels is the most well-known, but three others died too. The first was a 19-year-old who drowned in a canal while attempting to sneak into the venue before the music began; the last were two young men (Mark Feiger and Richard Savlov) run over by a stolen car after the festival had ended. As well as the four deaths at Altamont, there were other serious injuries. Denise Jewkes, the heavily pregnant lead singer of local band Ace of Cups, suffered a badly fractured skull after being struck on the head by a beer bottle that had been thrown at her from behind. Marty Balin of Jefferson Airplane was punched unconscious by an Angel after Balin intervened as the Angels beat a fan in front of the stage. The Rolling Stones did not escape injury either: upon arrival at the Speedway, and after Jagger left the helicopter, a fan ran up to him shouting "I hate you, I hate you", before punching Jagger in the face. The Stones' bodyguard Tony Funches in turn punched two Angels unconscious after they directed racist remarks his way.[75] Stanley Booth remembers a particularly shocking act of violence that occurred during "Sympathy for the Devil", the Stones' signature song. The Angels took offence at a young white man dancing close to them. Without warning, they laid into him and the crowd around him, who parted. The man ran away but was caught from behind by Angels who beat him mercilessly, knocking him unconscious with a pool cue. Booth thought the young man had been killed. But even then his ordeal wasn't over. Angels began kicking his prone body, "like kicking the dead carcass of an animal", Booth recalls, "the meat shaking on the bones".[76]

Around 780 people were also treated for drug-related medical problems. However, this was just the tip of the iceberg: tens of thousands of people were tripping on acid and other hallucinogens. There is no reliable figure as to how many were hurt, only many eye witness accounts of the violence: for example, Acers witnessed the Angels take part in "at least ten clubbings of helpless, harmless overdose cases".[77] Those scenes were repeated many times over, but many victims disappeared into the crowd without visiting the medical tent. Andy Gordon witnessed one such example, a young black man beaten almost senseless by the Angels and thrown off the stage: "shirtless, staggering and splitting blood, fighting to stay on his feet, like a punch-drunk boxer about to go down for the count, leaning in a daze against a truck as frightened people stare, until someone hands him his peacoat and he stumbles off".[78]

Even those in sympathy with the Angels offered sobering eyewitness accounts of the extent of the violence: Sonny Barger, in trying to downplay the Angels' brutality, still painted a horrifying picture of almost indiscriminate thuggery. When Barger called the KSAN radio talk show the day after Altamont, he spoke about a small fire that broke out on an Angel's bike. Barger latched on to this story as if it offered an excuse for some of the violence: "Now I ain't saying anything about no Angel hit anybody. I *know* some of them hit people. But they moved them people back out of the way of the bike. And we got the fire put out. In the process, you know what, some people got hit". Barger also shifted responsibility for the violence onto the hapless crowd: he opined that the fire probably began when a crowd crush caused a short circuit on the bike's battery. Of course, the crowd could not avoid the bikes because the Angels had placed them directly in front of the stage, in the process forcing fans to move away from prime spots. Some of these fans had been at the venue since Friday night in an attempt to secure a vantage point near the stage. Barger wasn't interested in the protocols and rituals of music festivals: that's not why the Angels were there. He said of the victims, "some of them people were like maybe them Friday nighters that got that front row, I don't know, but they didn't want to give up that spot even to put that fire out. And they come back fightin'. And when they come back fightin' they got thumped. And a lot of times there were six or seven Angels on one guy".[79]

Two particular incidents demonstrate the ferocity of the violence: one is the Angels' horrendous attack on a photographer; the other is the death of Meredith Hunter. The Angels' attack on the photographer was documented by Jude Acers, a well-respected chess champion, and also the chess columnist for the *Berkeley Barb*. Acers was at Altamont and wrote about his experiences in the *Barb*. At first he praised the Angels for their orderly behavior early in the day; however as the day progressed, he observed that the Angels become more violent. At one point, Acers noted the crowd opening up a space as the Angels chased a photographer:

The photographer was driven to his knees by a dozen blows from sharpened cue sticks that cut deeply. We were forced to watch a man have his whole face shredded. You could see the bone protruding on one side of his face. He was on his knees with arms fastened about his head. The two obviously insane Angels simply stuck their pointed daggers into every hole in the man's head and twisted away ... The Angels even jabbed into the earth to get to the man's mouth and nose.

The Angels ordered him to stand up and empty his camera. Acers saw that he was cut perhaps 50 times and bleeding freely: "There was no visible face, only blood", Acers remembered.[80] It was, however, the death of Meredith Hunter at the hands of the Hells Angels that became the most iconic and damning event of Altamont. That Hunter's death occurred while the concert was in progress, and was captured on film and shown in the documentary *Gimme Shelter* only added to its tragic notoriety. Hunter's death has been the subject of intense speculation, rumour, a police investigation, and jury trial in which Alan Passaro, the Angel seen stabbing Hunter on film, was found not guilty of Hunter's murder on grounds of self-defence.[81] That Hunter's murder was caught on camera gives it a lasting visual legacy: however, the details of his brutal treatment at the hands of Hells Angels best illustrates the hellish events happening at the front of the stage, events that anyone, guilty of innocent, could easily get caught up in.

The *Berkeley Barb* was among the first to go beyond the factual details of Hunter's death by interviewing his girlfriend Patty [sic] Bredehoft, his sister Gwen, and some of his friends.[82] Bredehoft was an eye witness to the assault on Hunter, and its immediate aftermath. She recalls that Hunter was standing on a speaker box on stage right. When the Angels waded into the crowd on one of their many skirmishes, one of them grabbed Hunter by the ear and dragged him violently down off the speaker box. *Gimme Shelter* shows Hunter being pulled away from the stage before pulling out a gun, a long-barreled revolver. Alan Passaro draws a knife from a sheath concealed in his boot and stabs Hunter in a downward motion in the back of the neck, then once again in the back, before the attacker moves stage left and out of view. Bredehoft claimed that Hunter pulled out his gun only after he was attacked by the Angels; whether or not that is true, that action sealed his fate. Passaro reacted instinctively, with overwhelming and lethal violence. This was, in fact, an Angel trait, linked to their "one in, all in" credo. Any threat, any insult, must be met with brutal violence. To act any other way would weaken the Angels' reputation or brand. Passaro's blade inflicted horrific injuries: one deep incision in the neck, below the ear; another four wounds to Hunter's back inflicted, before Passaro was knocked away by other Angels who joined in the attack: one Angel kicked Hunter in the head while he was on his knees, helpless and not offering any resistance; Hunter landed face down, but managed to turn over onto his back; that same Angel picked up a bin and struck Hunter with it, before kicking him again; a group of Angels then began kicking Hunter while he was helpless and dying; someone then stood on his head. Once their blood lust had subsided, the Angels walked off, leaving Hunter to bleed to death. When a helpless Bredehoft asked for help, an Angel told her, "Don't cry over him — he's not worth it".[83]

No one went to Hunter's aid during the assault but a few crowd members took him by the arms and legs and brought him to the stage to try to get help. The Angels quickly pushed them away. Robert Hiatt, one of around 50 medical students who had been rounded up at short notice to provide assistance at the festival, responded to Jagger's onstage plea for medical help. He dragged Hunter around the back of the stage to a Red Cross station. There he noticed the stab wounds and Hunter's swollen face. Blood was flowing freely from the wound to Hunter's neck and Hiatt assumed an artery had been severed. There was probably nothing anyone could do for the injured man at this point.[84] Hunter was put on a stretcher and taken to a medical tent. It was clear if Hunter was to have any chance of survival, he would need to be airlifted to hospital. Dr Richard Fine, one of only eight doctors on site, attempted to commandeer the helicopter reserved for the Rolling Stones, but no one would approve that. Fine pronounced Hunter deceased about half way through the Stones' set.[85]

The horrific violence meted out on Hunter and the slow, inadequate response given to saving his life cast a long shadow over Altamont and this tragic incident also provoked much soul-searching afterwards. Some critics believed that the fact that Meredith Hunter was a black man, attending the concert with his white girlfriend, was linked to the Angels' savage assault on him. Had this offended the Angels' racist code of "honour"? Contemporary critic David Dalton wondered, for example, if Hunter was provoked by "racist Angels who couldn't handle seeing a black man making out with a pretty white girl?"[86] The Angels certainly did contain, among their ranks, racists who required no excuse to be hostile towards blacks. There is, though, no indication of any regulations stopping blacks from joining the Angels (in practice, however, chapter rules stated that if two Angels objected to a new member, that was enough to ensure his application would fail). Angels tended to view African Americans in the same way they viewed hippies, through the lens of a kind of twisted patriotism. Much like Angels developed some links with hippies — despite despising their antiwar and liberal politics — in a similar way, they would hang out with African Americans if it was beneficial to them. For example, Sony Barger's Oakland chapter shared turf with the East Bay Dragons, an all-black motorcycle club formed in Oakland in 1959. Barger professed, "We're not real close [with the Dragons] and we never will be as long as I'm president. But they're different from most niggers. They're our kind of people".[87]

However, black political activism was not something the Angels supported, as from their viewpoint it was unpatriotic. Barger believed that Oakland police viewed the Angels as potential allies in the event of race riots, in which cops would be outnumbered and would require the help of the Angels to restore order.[88] For their part, black activists suspected that the police and Angels were colluding to *instigate* race riots, which explained why the police seemed to ignore some of the Angels' more obvious criminal activity.[89] On occasion, this led to violence between the bikers and the black community. For example, the *Berkeley Barb* reported one incident when a group of around 30 black men attacked seven or eight Angels on the street, with violence spilling over into a local business. This was quite a serious confrontation, with one Angel being hit with a hammer and another with a tyre iron. Afterwards, the Angels vowed to take their own revenge rather than call the police.[90] Similar tensions were evident outside California. In an interview with the *East Village Other*, one former member of the Road Vultures, a club affiliated with New York Hells Angels, explained why there were no blacks in their club: "people in general are basically racists. The same applies to the Hells Angels. We always respected the territory of the blacks and wouldn't go there. They didn't bother us and we didn't bother them".[91]

Some contemporary commentators made a connection between the colour of Meredith Hunter's skin and the assault on him by the Angels. For example, the *Berkeley Tribe* insisted, "It is important that Meredith Hunter was black. What ties the white people of, say, Oakland, to the Hells Angels is their instinctive hatred of the black man".[92] Meredith Hunter's own sister also made the connection. Reflecting on the death of her brother at Altamont, the *Berkeley Barb* asked Gwen Hunter if anyone tried to help Hunter or his partner Patty Bredehoft. She replied negatively: "The majority of people there were white and a white person's not gonna help a black person".[93] In contrast, Bredehoft, Hunter's white girlfriend, did not think racism was the cause of Hunter's death. She reflected: "I don't blame it on race, because like they were hasseling [sic] white people as much as they were hasseling black people... And I don't think it was because he was with me because they didn't know he was with me, even when I was trying to help him they didn't understand who I was. They thought I was just a girl in the audience that didn't like to see a fight. So I don't think it was racial".[94] Like so many situations at Altamont, there is no clear version of events, nor a completely clear-cut apportioning of blame.

Furthermore, another shocking aspect of the behavior of the Angels at Altamont was their willingness to use violence against women. In this respect, they had past form. To give just one indicative example, in 1964, a group of Angels were accused of the gang rape of two Monterey teenagers. According to Hunter Thompson, this incident began as a group sex event in which the two women willingly participated. However, when more Hells Angels indicated they wanted to join in, the women backtracked and the party was over. The next day, however, the women contacted the police and accused a number of Angels of rape. This incident received a lot of media attention, for example in *The New York Times*, *Time* and *Newsweek*, but much of it was hyperbolic. This was not, however, an isolated incident: in 1965 at a party at author Ken Kesey's La Honda ranch, Angels took part in a gang sex assault on a girl friend of Neal Cassady. This incident seemed to start like the one at Monterey, with a degree of compliance from the woman. However, it quickly got out of hand, with multiple gang members taking advantage of the clearly intoxicated victim. When the *East Village Other* asked one ex-biker affiliated to New York Hells Angels what he thought of nonconsensual gang sex, he replied: "Chicks have to be kept in their place... the woman's role is one of total subservience to the man".[95] Eye witness accounts of this incident are somewhat unclear[96]: however, the basic facts of both the Monterey and La Honda incidents indicate that the Angels had little respect for women and that any encounter with them could easily spiral out of control.[97]

While there were no reports of rape at Altamont, there was plenty of evidence that the Angels were busy keeping "chicks" in order. Before the Stones went on stage, Michelle Phillips of the Mamas and Papas told the band that the Angels were beating up fans, including women.[98] When, after Crosby, Stills, Nash and Young had finished their set, but before the Stones took to the stage, Sonny Barger led a procession of motorcycles through the crowd to get to the stage. One female fan protested too loudly and received a smack on the jaw for her trouble.[99] At one point during the Stones' set, and after Meredith Hunter had been stabbed to death, a young women, topless, and likely very high, tried to climb onto the stage. A handful of Angels stopped her, and when Keith Richards protested at how she was being manhandled, Barger walked over and kicked her in the face.[100] The Angels did not set out to attack women at Altamont, and there is also at least two incidences documented by Selvin of women being helped by Angels, but at the same time Angels were not above inflicting violence on women if they felt like it.

"Down the Road A Bit": reflections on the Angels at Altamont

While there is little to be gained from apportioning blame for the violence at Altamont 50 years after it took place, it is illuminating to consider some of the contemporary reflections on this violence. Reactions to the Angels ranged between those who blamed them wholly for all the violence, to those who believed the Angels were stuck between a rock and a hard place — in this case between the stage and the crowd — and were put in an untenable position. In between those opposing viewpoints were those who believed the Angels were partly responsible, but that other factors such as audience provocation and bad planning had also caused many of the confrontations that dogged the festival. Others further blamed the Stones, or more particularly, Mick Jagger.

Perhaps unsurprisingly, in his 2000 biography, Sonny Barger placed blame solely on the Stones. Barger claimed the band deliberately delayed their entrance onto the stage for over an hour until the sun set, to maximise the impact of their arrival. Barger claimed that the crowd, under the influence of drink and drugs, became more and more agitated as time passed. "The Stones' ego trip had turned into our problem", claimed Barger.[101] However, Barger's version of events is one of the least plausible eyewitness accounts. For instance, he ignores the sequence of violent events perpetrated by the Angels well before the Stones were due to take the stage. He claims that he did not see the Angels using pool cues to beat fans; he also denied that he had an agreement with Stones' management that the Angels would park their bikes in front of the stage. Moreover, he insisted that Meredith Hunter opened fire before he was killed, and that it was the Angels who carried Hunter to the medics. Aside from the delayed entrance of the Stones onto the stage, there is no corroborating evidence to support any of these assertions: however, there is plenty of evidence to suggest Barger's comments were self-serving. This section of his book basically rehashes comments he made on a KSAN radio talk show the evening following the concert. During this interview, Barger, high on cocaine, depicted the Angels' behavior as sensible and brave, and he was adamant they acted only in self-defence or to protect the stage and the bands; he also claimed the Stones tricked the Angels. In essence, he was attempting to lay out a semi-plausible defense in the event of legal proceedings against the Angels.[102] "Mick Jagger, he used us for dupes", said Barger. "We were the biggest suckers of anybody. I'm a violent cat when I gotta be, but I don't really wanna: I'm bum kicked. I don't like what happened". But, Barger did also concede that the people who allegedly messed with the Angels' motorcycles "got thumped. They got GOT!"[103]

Some critics in the underground picked up on Barger's obsessive notion that the Angels' motorbikes were somehow sacred, and that anyone messing with the bikes deserved to "got GOT": for example, Todd Gitlin, the president of Students for a Democratic Society, and a regular writer for Liberation News Service (the main news feed for the underground press), mocked Barger's comments as a "parody of the private-property consumer fetish".[104] As for Meredith Hunter's death, Barger simply repeated in his autobiography the longstanding Angels' account of events: that Hunter was high and had planned to shoot Mick Jagger; and when the Angels intervened to protect Jagger, Hunter fired at and grazed an Angel. In stabbing Hunter to death, Barger insisted, the Angels acted bravely and in proportion to the threat Hunter offered.[105]

Many commentators, though, contradicted almost every contention of Bargers' account and put the blame squarely on the Angels. First among these were some of the musicians who had witnessed Angels' violence up-close. For example, during the set by Carlos Santana, the Angels set upon a large, naked Latino man who was stumbling through the crowd and unfortunately ended up too close to the Angels. Bert Kanegson tried to help the man who was being beaten to a pulp, and was himself badly beaten for his efforts. The Angels waded into the crowd with their pool cues a further six times during Santana's short set which lasted less than an hour.[106] Afterwards, Santana blamed the Angels: "The fights started because the Hell's Angels were pushing people around. There was no provocation; the Angels started the whole violence thing and there's no fucking doubt about that",[107] Yet Santana admits that the crowd also played a role in the violence: "There were lots of people just fucking freaked out. During our set I could see a guy from the stage who had a knife and just wanted to stab somebody, I mean, he really wanted a fight. Anybody getting in the way of anybody had himself a fight, whether he wanted it or not. There were kids being stabbed and heads cracking the whole time".[108] Similarly, author Joel Selvin also describes the scene of utter chaos at the front of the stage as "like an overcrowded subway car full of stoned, drunk, and violent people".[109] And a letter to the *Berkeley Barb* summed up the atmosphere: "selfish, hostile, violent, and drunk, grabby, pushy and destructive... each for themselves".[110] So, while there is no question that the Angels used disproportionate and often indiscriminate violence, it is equally clear that violence was instigated by members of the largely high and drunk crowd, particularly those near the front of the stage. This then muddies the waters of placing primary blame on the Angels for the violence of Altamont; there was clearly a bad vibe at the festival, probably exacerbated by the high numbers of "bad trips".

Some bands who played at Altamont were perhaps too afraid to voice criticism of the Angels — particularly those who knew they would be sharing space with them again in future. For example, given that the Angels beat Jefferson Airplane's Marty Balin unconscious twice at Altamont, one might assume this band would have blamed the motorcycle club for Altamont's violence. However, Jefferson Airplane had played at many events where Angels were present. Along with Big Brother and the Holding Company and the Grateful Dead, they comprised the Bay area's big three live music artists, and the Angels usually turned up to any event featuring these three bands. So while the Rolling Stones could return to the U.K. and hope never to see the Angels again, members of Jefferson Airplane were almost certain to share venue space with them in future, and it could be hazardous to their health to bad mouth the club. So in the immediate aftermath of the festival, Jefferson Airplane were either silent or offered only muted criticism of the Angels. Slick chose to blame the crowd, whom she called "a bunch of angry slobs in the mud".[111] *Rolling Stone* magazine asked Balin to comment on the festival but he declined. However, Paul Kantner told the magazine that Jefferson Airplane would not play at any future concerts if the Angels would be providing security.[112]

Unsurprisingly, Mick Jagger blamed the Angels, but went further than other critics in suggesting that the violence was fore-planned. In an interview with Germany's *Der Spiegel*, which was transcribed in English in *The Rag*, Jagger said: "The Hell's Angels had previously been at all the free concerts in San Francisco as marshalls. At these concerts they always maintained themselves well. But this time they wanted to show the people that they were still the strong, violent Hells Angels as they had been known in the past... they are developing into fascists".[113] Like Jagger, Keith Richards saw the violence from the stage and threatened to stop playing if the Angels did not quit beating fans. Later, however, he told journalist Ray Connolly "out of the whole three hundred Angels working as stewards, the vast majority did what they were supposed to do, which was to regulate the crowds as much as possible without causing any trouble. But there were about ten or twenty who were completely out of their minds — trying to drive their motorcycles through the middle of the crowds".[114] In the *Gimme Shelter* film, Stones' drummer Charlie Watts is shown listening to Sonny Barger's KSAN radio interview. After Barger has had his say, Watts comments sarcastically, "Well done Sonny". Yet Watts also praises Angels as "incredible" for clearing a path for the Stones through to the stage, and he refers to some of the Angels as "really very nice". His final conclusion is a downbeat "what a shame". Stones' guitarist Mick Taylor, apparently still in a state of shock about a month after the concert, told *Rolling Stone*, "The Hell's Angels had a lot to do with it... They're just very, very violent people".[115]

Some eyewitnesses in the crowd placed blame firmly with the Angels. Jude Acers, writing in the *Berkeley Barb*, said of the violence, "The Angels did it all, were totally at fault for all the violence I saw the entire day. It was a sport with the Angels"; he went on to call them "a bunch of losers and common punks".[116] Also in the *Barb*, journalist Thomas Klaber wrote that the Angels "did their job with the zealousness of Mayor Daley's finest during the Democratic Convention in Chicago last year".[117] Paul Glusman of the *Chicago Seed* also compared the Angels to the police: "The worst trip was the Hells Angels... They were the security (read police) force. They were there to protect and serve. Like the pigs in uniform they went at their job zealously".[118] As the day progressed, Andy Gordon watched the Angels ingest beer, wine, reds and acid, fighting with each other first before starting on the crowd. "They were out for blood", Gordon concluded.[119] *Rolling Stone* journalist Lester Bangs was also in the crowd at Altamont and concurred with this view. Writing in London's *International Times*, Bangs called the Angels "violent sadists", while excusing the Stones' violent image as essentially harmless and probably even cathartic: Bangs adjudged it "therapeutic and removed to the realm of art".[120] George Paul Csicsery told the *Berkeley Tribe* that the Angels "lost control", which united the crowd in fear.[121] Lester Bangs put it succinctly: "the real source of 90% of the violence was the denim neanderthals washing down reds with wine all over the stage".[122]

It is noticeable, however, that in most of these condemnations of the Angels there remains a grudging, reluctant acceptance that, given the circumstances of the concert — especially the poor planning that meant few provisions were in place for crowd comfort or safety, as well as truly staggering amount of alcohol and drugs ingested by the crowd — the Angels could not be considered solely responsible for the violence. Comments by Jerry Garcia (of the Grateful Dead), illustrate this. Garcia offered a measured response, identifying the nature of the Angels and explaining how it was prudent to walk softly among them:

The Angels... yeah... imagine if there were still sabre-tooth tigers walking around... that's the Angels... busting heads, man, that's the Angels' whole bit... but I mean when you live with them you get cool about the Angels... you learn how to walk... you learn how to avoid em... it's cool... the people that weren't hip, most of the... it was just people... Rolling Stones fans... consumers... 'Get your free Rolling Stones'... not heads... they didn't know about the Angels... they didn't understand... and once the Angels get violent they go all the way.[123]

Of course, Garcia had good reason not to condemn the Angels: they shared the same turf, and no doubt the Angels would take offence at any "betrayal" by the Grateful Dead. But the point to note is that bands like The Grateful Dead, Jefferson Airplane, and Big Brother and the Holding Company knew the Angels' nature and had learned how to act around them. In Garcia's words, they were "hip" to the Angels' scene. When Marty Balin forgot this, he got stomped. The Angels would beat their own if they stepped out of line; they would do the same to musicians they were familiar with; they even mauled Hunter S. Thompson when he forgot the rules. This was just their modus operandi.

So viewed in this light, it perhaps should have been predictable that when thousands of Rolling Stones fans arrived in Northern California from all over the country — fans who were not necessarily "hip" to the Angels — there would likely be confrontations. Emmet Grogan claimed that much of the violence was caused by crowd provocations: he witnessed "bottle-throwers, drunken brawls, attacks upon the sound equipment… attacks upon the Angels' sacred motorcycles… and a lotta people on heavy acid bummers who would not be diverted from their destructive trip by talk alone. The Angels, in their response, were merely being true to their school".[124] Others echoed these sentiments, pointing the primary finger of blame at the antics of the crowd. According to one report in the *Berkeley Barb*: "Hell's Angels did a pretty good job of keeping the roped off section cleared. Most of the bad vibes around the stage area were caused by the jerks who tried to storm the stage. If everyone had sat down quietly, much of the violence that did occur could have been avoided".[125] Another said: "Common sense would seem to preclude blaming the fiasco on the Angels. From reports of those centered around the stage there can be little doubt that the Angels did a lot of shoving, cursing etc., etc., etc. But there were 250,000 other people participating. It is hardly likely that even a group as infamous as the Angels could blanket a festival of a quarter of a million people and turn it into the bummer of the year".[126]

There were other voices that placed the blame primarily on the crowd for the violence at Altamont, and who argued the Angels had rather been provoked, rather than had gone looking for trouble. For example, Sandy Darlington was one of a group of four journalists who travelled together to Altamont; with her was Greil Marcus, Langdon Winner, and Ed Leimbacher. They split up so as to view the action independent of each other, and they planned to compare notes later. Darlington's account of her experiences, published almost a year later in *Great Speckled Bird*, is sardonic and dispassionate. Previously she saw the Angels do security at the 1967 San Francisco Be-In, at the 1968 Santa Clara Rock Festival, and at an Angel birthday party blow-out in 1968 at the Carousel with Big Brother and the Holding Company. Darlington remembered them as "rough people. But within bounds". She foresaw no problems with the Angels doing security at Altamont.[127] However, she hadn't reckoned on the belligerence of the Altamont crowd. She claimed that when Barger's Angels drove through the gathered masses to park their motorcycles in front of the stage, they were quickly swamped with people, many of who had been in that prized spot beforehand. Darlington said, "The crowd got into hating Angels without much trouble".[128] Darlington was firmly on the side of the Angels, blaming the crowd for wanting "Instant Woodstock", without doing anything themselves to attain that. She watched people push their way to the front, act selfishly, and commit acts of violence, such as throwing a smoke bomb onto the stage during the Stones' performance. She praised the Angels for their honesty and absence of bullshit. Perhaps she had here in mind Bob Dylan's lyric that "to live outside the law, you must be honest", or perhaps she was disappointed with the crowd's behaviour, or with her own impotence in the face of the disaster unfolding before her. But mostly, it seems, she was disappointed that the crowd failed to live up to their own hype. The crowd "fucked with" the Angels, she claimed. "The whole day fucked with them. We were frustrated. And we wanted violence. We got it". She ended with a plea not to make scapegoats of the Angels.[129]

Some went further and praised the Angels for their behavior. During the KSAN radio broadcast, Rolling Stones' manager Sam Cutler said: "If you're asking me to issue a general put down of the Angels, which I imagine a lot of people would be only too happy to do, and I'm not prepared to do that. The Angels did as they saw best in a difficult situation".[130] Certainly, there is some evidence of that: Selvin points out, for example, that some Angels were helpful and non-violent and that Angels accompanied film crews as bodyguards.[131] Their presence, on occasion, helped deter violence: for example, Selvin relates an incident when a female marshall on a road leading to the backstage area was harassed by a group of motorcycle riders on Hondas. When a bus carrying Angels from the San Francisco chapter arrived, one joined the marshall on the road to deter any further such behaviour.[132] Andy Carey in *The Seed* said "no one could have expected them to have acted differently from the way they did, and the fact they weren't intimidated by being outnumbered something like 3,000 to 1 is strangely admirable".[133] Even Acers, who ultimately blamed the Angels for the violence, admitted they had done some good work early in the day. "The Hell's Angels arrived quietly", he explained, "and were doing a fine job as informal policemen. I saw them speak to hundreds of people and move them off the stage with no problem before noon".[134]

Still others placed the blame for the violence directly on the Stones and Mick Jagger in particular. *Rolling Stone* commented, for example: "What an enormous thrill it would be for an Angel to kick Mick Jagger's teeth down his throat. They have been watching his dancing and wild gesticulations with disgusted scowls, derisive laughter, elbows in each other's ribs. The looks on their faces read: 'So easy — I could stomp the shit outta this fuckin' sissy *so easy* — I could snuff this motherfucker!'"[135] This is a revealing outburst: despite vilifying the Angels for their behavior at Altamont, *Rolling Stone* still admires their capacity for violence, as long as it is used against the right target. Others pointed the finger at the Stones because of their seeming ignorance of the true nature of the Hells Angels. David Crosby of Crosby, Stills, Nash and Young, for example, griped, "The Stones don't know about Angels. To them an Angel is something in between [*Easy Rider*'s] Peter Fonda and Dennis Hopper".[136] But if that was the case, the Stones were no more naïve than those in the American counterculture who also saw the Angels as kindred spirits. Could the Stones and their management have predicted how the Angels would behave at Altamont? According to Selvin, John Burks of *Rolling Stone* magazine was the first to raise concerns about Hells Angels providing security at the free concert. This was at a meeting at the Grateful Dead's place at Novato.[137] Separately, Bert Kanegson from the Grateful Dead camp also objected to the Angels providing security. Ironically, Kanegson received a beating from the Angels during the Santana set, when he intervened to stop the Angels beating a naked man, high on something that caused him to underestimate the Angels' propensity for violence.[138]

Thus, several of the bands present at Altamont implicitly criticised the Stones and their management's decision to involve the Angels at all. David Crosby concluded: "We didn't need the Angels. I'm not downgrading the Angels, because it's not healthy and because they only did what they were expected to do. I don't know why anyone would expect them to do anything other than exactly what they did. The mistake that was made was in thinking security was needed, and that the Angels should do it". This point was made also by Carlos Santana, who witnessed much of the violence from the stage. Afterwards he said: "the stage has to be guarded by somebody, but you don't need cops and you don't need Hell's Angels. At Woodstock, they had all kinds of cats keeping the stage clear who were all wearing colored jackets and you knew who they were and you didn't need cops or Angels".[139] Point by point, it is hard to argue with this analysis. It is true that the Angels were not required. Like Santana, Crosby was likely thinking about Woodstock, where the Hog Farm hippy community provided some "peace keeping" duties, performing that task professionally, and with compassion and understanding for the fans.[140] That was likely because those fans resembled the Hog Farm hippies, and shared many of their beliefs and habits. John Roberts claimed that a group which "looked, talked, and smelled like the crowd would be both highly credible and highly effective".[141] That wasn't the case at Altamont: Angels shared some similarities with hippies but the resemblance was superficial. Still, Angels had been deployed as security at previous events, sharing the experience with hippies, so there was precedent for the decision. But whether or not it was wise one, remains another matter.

Conclusion: "Stoned"

In the immediate aftermath of Altamont, many commentators turned on the Stones, calling them naïve for misunderstanding the nature of the Hells Angels, accusing them of bullying for insisting on up-front financial guarantees for their 1969 tour, and of being greedy for setting high ticket prices. They were pilloried for playing paid concerts and then again for organising a free concert. Later, they were accused of profiting from the *Gimme Shelter* concert movie and for exploiting the death of Meredith Hunter. A catalyst for this criticism was when Keith Richards compared the behavior of the English crowd at Hyde Park to the behavior of Americans at

Altamont: "The difference between the two countries", he explained, was that at Hyde Park "everybody had a good time, and there was no trouble. You can put half a million young English people together and they won't start killing each other. That's the difference".[142] In response to this, *Rolling Stone* said, "While Richards was satisfying the British press with his incredibly naive view of Western civilization, Meredith Hunter lay dead".[143]

While the Hells Angels were undoubtedly violent — as an organisation overall, but at Altamont in particular — the aforementioned analysis of underground press sources shows that blame for Altamont's shortcomings is not as easily apportioned as many commentators have done, and that a more nuanced approach is required to tease out the truth of what happened and especially why. The Angels may have been partly to blame, but so too was the crowd and the "toxic", drug-saturated atmosphere. Did the Rolling Stones deserve the vortex of post-Altamont fury that they received from the underground press? It is possible to detect more than a hint of xenophobia in some contemporary critiques: it is almost as if American commentators did not like to see themselves reflected in the Rolling Stones. After all, the Stones were paying tribute to American music through the blues, and also playing rock songs influenced by American culture. The Stones were cultural sponges, and they wrote about topical American subjects; for example, during the writing process Jagger updated the lyrics of "Sympathy for the Devil" to include a line about Robert Kennedy's assassination in 1968. The bottom line was that the Stones were fans of America and its rich musical heritage.

Criticism of the Stones' relationship with the Hells Angels is perhaps hardest to understand. The Angels were, after all, an American phenomenon. While it is likely correct that the Stones had a romanticised view of the Angels, albeit one fed by misleading cinematic portrayals that fooled people closer to Angels than were the Stones, the main issue here is that the Stones wanted to be part of the counterculture cool, particularly the San Francisco scene. Jagger perhaps revealed a bit more than he meant to when he spoke at Altamont about "the Grateful Airplane and the Rolling Dead": in merging the Stones with two of San Francisco's biggest and coolest bands, Jagger wanted to associate his band with their counterculture coolness. However, they found out that there was a price to pay for mixing counterculture politics with rock music, and that the space between counterculture cool and the realities of the music business was a minefield of compromises that pleased no one. The Hells Angels were, for a time, part of that hip scene. Andy Gordon offers a useful summary of why the Stones and indeed the northern Californian music scene were attracted to Angels: "Sure they're dangerous, unpredictable and violent, but to the middle-class hip young they have the status appeal of being proletarian and funky. Romantic anarchists! Groovy! Stones, Dead, Angels; a heavy mixture: noise, gasoline, electronic power, celebrity, arrogance, and violence. The worst and the best of the culture".[144]

But of course, the decision to deploy the Angels as a security force was a dangerous gamble. The Stones didn't want police to do security, but that didn't mean the default alternative option was a dangerous motorcycle gang. "Why do we need police", asked *The Rag*, "especially ones orientated towards violence. The Hog Farm would have happily accepted an offer to help".[145] The Stones, however, listened to the Grateful Dead, to Grace Slick, and to Emmet Grogan, all of whom were, anyway, pushing at an open door with the Stones. Jagger wanted to be part of the San Francisco scene, and with that came the Angels, invited or not. But they didn't need to be engaged as a security force. Nevertheless, there was a sense of rolling down hill towards disaster at Altamont. If not the Hells Angels, the *Berkeley Tribe* asked, "what sort of lawman should have been there? The Alameda Sheriffs? The Highway Patrol" The Hell's Angels? Choose your favorite pig".[146]

4: Angels

[1] Hunter S. Thompson, *Hell's Angels: The Strange and Terrible Saga of the Outlaw Motorcycle Gangs* (New York: Ballantine, 1996), p. 156.
[2] Paul Glusman, "Stone Drag", *Chicago Seed,* Vol 4, No 10, 1969, p. 11.
[3] Sandy Darlington, "Let it Bleed", *Great Speckled Bird,* Vol 3, Issue 2, Jan 12, 1970, pp. 20 & 17. At p. 20.
[4] Lester Bangs, *et al,* "The Rolling Stones Disaster at Altamont: Let It Bleed", *Rolling Stone* 50, Jan 21, 1970.
[5] David Browne, "Grace Slick's Festival Memories: Fearing Orgies and Getting Lit", *Rolling Stone,* May 23, 2014. Available online at: http://www.rollingstone.com/music/music-news/grace-slicks-festival-memories-fearing-orgies-and-getting-lit-71111/
[6] Jerry Hopkins, "Kiss Kiss Flutter Flutter Thank You Thank You", *Rolling Stone,* Dec 13, 1969, pp. 1, 6, 54. At p. 54.
[7] Stephen Schneck, Review of Hells Angels by Hunter S. Thompson, *Ramparts,* Mar 1967, p. 52.
[8] Thompson, *Hell's Angels,* p. 56.
[9] "Cyclist's Holiday: He and Friends Terrorize a Town", *Life,* Jul 21, 1947, p. 31.
[10] Ralph "Sonny" Barger, with Keith Zimmerman and Kent Zimmerman, *Hell's Angel: The Life and Times of Sonny Barger and the Hell's Angels Motorcycle Club* (London: Fourth Estate, 2001), p. 30.
[11] Thompson, *Hells Angels,* p. 10.
[12] Barger, *Hells Angel,* p. 39.
[13] Stanley Booth, *Dance with the Devil: the Rolling Stones and their Times* (New York: Random House, 1984), p. 149.
[14] There has been criticism, for example, from Kenneth Rexroth, that Kerouac had a romanticised view of Black culture; in contrast, former Black Panther Eldridge Cleaver saw the Beats more generally as fore-runners of the counter-culture. See Kenneth Rexroth, Rev. On the Road, *San Francisco Chronicle,* Sep 1, 1957; and Eldridge Cleaver, *Soul on Ice* (New York: Random House, 1991 [1968]), pp. 91-93.
[15] For details of both relationships, see Rictor Norton, ed., *My Dear Boy: Gay Love Letters through the Centuries* (San Francisco: Leyland, 1998),
[16] Thompson, *Hells Angels,* p. 197.
[17] Thompson, *Hells Angels,* p. 127.
[18] John Wood, "Hell's Angels and the Illusion of the Counterculture", *The Journal of Popular Culture* Vol 37, Issue 2 (2003), pp. 336-351. At pp. 342-44.
[19] Peter Tamony, "The Hell's Angels: Their Naming", *Western Folklore* Vol 29, No 3 (1970), pp. 199-203. At p. 201.
[20] Paul Schrader, "Easy Rider", *Los Angeles Free Press,* Jul 25, 1969, pp. 26 & 32. At p. 26.
[21] Barbara Klinger, "The Road to Dystopia: Landscaping the Nation in Easy Rider" in Steven Cohan and Ina Rae Hark, eds., *The Road Movie Book* (London: Routledge, 1997), pp. 179-203. At p. 182.
[22] Barger, *Hell's Angel,* p. 133.
[23] See Timothy Leary, Richard Alpert and Ralph Metzner, *The Psychedelic Experience; A Manual Based on the Tibetan Book of the Dead* (New York: University Books, 1964).
[24] Wood, "Hell's Angels and the Illusion of the Counterculture", pp. 347-8.
[25] Barger, *Hell's Angel,* p. 127.
[26] Thompson, *Hells Angels,* p. 234.
[27] Vaakov Kohn, "Laconia '69: State of Hell's Angels Today", *East Village Other,* Vol 4, Issue 30, Jun 25, 1969, pp. 4 & 18. At p. 4.
[28] Thompson, *Hells Angels,* p. 145.
[29] "VDC Reply to Gazette Series", *Berkeley Barb,* Nov 5, 1965, pp. 1 & 3.
[30] Barger, *Hell's Angel,* p. 122.
[31] Thompson, *Hells Angels,* p. 253.
[32] Paul Krassner, "Hell's Angels vs. Berkeley Vietniks", *The Realist,* No 64, Feb 1966, pp. 9-10. At p.10.
[33] W. J. Rorabaugh, *Berkeley At War: the 1960s* (New York: Oxford University Press, 1990), p. 98.
[34] "The New-Right Biker: Violent Voice of Fascism", *Los Angeles Free Press,* Vol 6, Issue 275, Oct 24-31, 1969, p. 1.
[35] Thompson, *Hells Angels,* pp. 244-5,
[36] John Wilcox, "Artists Peace Tower", *East Village Other,* Vol 1, No 7, Mar 1-15, 1966, p. 1.
[37] Karen Wald, "Cops Gas SJS Dow Protesters", *The Movement,* Vol 3, Issue 12, Dec 1, 1967, p. 10; "San Jose's Where the Actions At", *Berkeley Barb,* Vol 5, No 21, Issue 119, Nov 24-30, 1967, p. 7.
[38] "Massive Christmas Teach-In", *Berkeley Barb,* Vol 2, No 1, Jan 7, 1966, p. 1.
[39] "In Kesey's Corner", *Berkeley Barb,* Vol 3, No 18, Issue 64, Nov 4, 1966, pp. 1 & 5.
[40] "New Year's Whale Set To Top Digger's Noel", *Berkeley Barb,* Vol 3, No 26, Issue 72, Dec 30, 1966, p. 3. Also, William Hjortsberg, *Jubilee Hitchhiker: The Life and Times of Richard Brautigan* (Berkeley: Counterpoint, 2012), p. 283. And *The Realist* 74, May 1, 1967, p. 8.
[41] Tony Bove, *Haight-Ashbury in the Sixties!* CD-ROM (1996). Available online at: http://www.rockument.com/blog/haight-ashbury-in-the-sixties/haight-ashbury-videos/
[42] Larry Freudiger, "Hells Angels Babysit", *The Rag,* Jan 30, 1967, p. 7.
[43] "Love is Great, I Love it", *Berkeley Barb,* Vol 4, No 3, Issue 75, Jan 20, 1967, p. 7.
[44] "A Garland for Chocolate George", *Berkeley Barb,* Vol 5, No 9, Issue 107, Sep 1-7, 1967, p. 3.
[45] Hap Stewart, "Letter to Editor", *Berkeley Barb,* Vol 5, No 10, Issue 109, Sep 15-21, 1967, p. 4.
[46] "Million Dollar Bash", *The Rag,* Vol 4, Issue 10, Dec 15, 1969, p. 15.
[47] "Spain" interviewed by Vaakov Kohn, "Laconia '69: State of Hell's Angels Today", *East Village Other,* Vol 4, Issue 30, Jun 25, 1969, p. 4.
[48] Darlington, "Let it Bleed", p. 20.
[49] Elliot Mintz, "It was beautiful until..." and "Blue Skies Cloud Over Into Blue Storm", *Los Angeles Free Press,* Vol 4, No 30, Issue 158, Jul 28 - Aug 3, 1967, pp. 1 & 5. At p. 5
[50] "Mutants Commune", *Berkeley Barb,* Vol 5, No 7, Issue 105, Aug 18-24, 1967, pp. 8-9. At p. 9.
[51] Michael Goldberg, "Zombie Rock: This Ain't the Summer of Love", *Berkeley Barb,* Vol 29, No 23, Issue 708, Aug 23 - Sep 5, 1979, p. 6.
[52] Robert Hurwitt, "Next Time Try the Translove Bus", *Berkeley Barb,* Vol 4, No 21, Issue 93, May 26 - Jun 1, 1967, p. 11.
[53] Robert Hurwitt, "Magic Mountain Fervor Leaves Post-Teen Cool", *Berkeley Barb,* Vol 4, No 24, Issue 96, June 16-22, 1967, p. 5.
[54] Robert Santelli, *Aquarius Rising: the Rock Festival Years* (New York: Dell, 1980), p. 17.
[55] "Looking Back on the Monterey Festival", *Monterey Herald* online, accessed Aug 21, 2018. http://photos.montereyherald.com/2017/06/13/photos-looking-back-on-the-monterey-pop-festival/#8
[56] "The Revolt", SDS *New Left Notes,* Vol 4, No 27, Aug 1, 1969, p. 15.
[57] Jerry Hopkins, "Crashers, Cops, Producers Spoil Newport '69", *Rolling Stone,* Jul 26, 1969. Available online at: https://www.rollingstone.com/music/music-news/crashers-cops-producers-spoil-newport-69-120810/
[58] Paul Cabbell and Jerry Applebaum, "Devonshire Downer, It wasn't Newport, Pop, or even a festival", *Los Angeles Free Press,* Jun 7, 1969, pp. 2 & 14. At p. 14.
[59] Santelli, *Aquarius Rising,* pp. 90-91.
[60] David Wharton, "The Lost Love-In: It was the Woodstock they forgot: Newport '69, Los Angeles' own weekend of music, masses and mayhem", *LA Times,* Aug 6, 1989. http://articles.latimes.com/1989-08-06/entertainment/ca-315_1_los-angeles
[61] Norma Coates, "If anything, blame Woodstock. The Rolling Stones: Altamont, December 6, 1969" in Ian Inglis, ed., *Performance and Popular*

Music: History Place and Time (Aldershot: Ashgate, 2006), pp. 58-69. At p. 60.
[62] Santelli, *Aquarius Rising*, p. 103.
[63] Ralph J. Gleason, "More Questions For Rolling Stones", *San Francisco Chronicle*, Dec 12, 1969.
[64] *Crossfire Hurricane*. Dir. Brett Morgen. Milkwood Films/Tremolo Productions, 2012.
[65] Selvin, *Altamont*, p. 242.
[66] *Crossfire Hurricane*. Dir. Brett Morgen. Milkwood Films/Tremolo Productions, 2012.
[67] John Gale, *The Observer*, Jul 6, 1969, p. 1. Available online at: http://www.theguardian.com/music/2018/jul/01/observer-archive-the-rolling-stones-in-hyde-park-5-july-1969
[68] "Free Concerts-The Aftermath", *International Times* 61, Aug 1-14 1969, pp. 10-11.
[69] David Browne, "Grace Slick's Festival Memories: Fearing Orgies and Getting Lit", *Rolling Stone*, May 23, 2014. Available online at: http://www.rollingstone.com/music/music-news/grace-slicks-festival-memories-fearing-orgies-and-getting-lit-71111/
[70] Selvin, *Altamont*, p. 87.
[71] Hjortsberg, *Jubilee Hitchhiker*, p. 283.
[72] Bangs, "Rolling Stones Disaster at Altamont".
[73] Bangs, "Rolling Stones Disaster at Altamont".
[74] Bangs, "Rolling Stones Disaster at Altamont".
[75] Selvin, *Altamont*, p. 170.
[76] Booth, *Dance with the Devil*, p. 359.
[77] Jude Acers, "Exile to Altamont", *Berkeley Barb*, Vol 20 Issue 466, Jul 19-25, 1974, pp. 12-14. At p.13.
[78] Andy Gordon, "Satan and the Angels: Paradise Loused", in Jonathan Eisen, ed. Altamont (New York: Avon, 1970), pp. 30-71.
[79] Bangs, "Rolling Stones Disaster at Altamont".
[80] Acers, "Exile to Altamont", p. 13.
[81] "Hell's Angel Acquitted in Rock Slaying", *Washington Post*, Jan 15, 1971, p. A3.
[82] "'Mert' Hunter: the kid they killed at Altamont", *Berkeley Barb*, Vol 9, Issue 24, No 227, Dec 19-24, 1969), pp. 1, 5, 6, 13, & 17.
[83] Selvin, *Altamont*, pp. 216-17.
[84] Santelli, *Aquarius Rising*, pp. 159-60.
[85] Selvin, *Altamont*, pp. 219-20.
[86] David Dalton, "Altamont: An Eyewitness Account", *Gadfly*, Nov 1999.
[87] Thompson, *Hells Angels*, p. 239.
[88] Thompson, *Hells Angels*, p. 238.
[89] "Hells Angels Rumor Bugs the Ghetto", *Berkeley Barb*, Vol 1, No. 15, Nov 19, 1965, p. 1.
[90] "Brief Skirmish Between Blacks and Angels", *Berkeley Barb*, Vol 4, No 23, Issue 95, Jun 9-15, 1967, p. 3.
[91] "Spain" interviewed by Vaakov Kohn, "Laconia '69: State of Hell's Angels Today", *East Village Other*, Vol 4, Issue 30, Jun 25, 1969, pp. 4 & 18. At p. 4.
[92] "Altamont", *Berkeley Tribe*, Vol 2, Issue 76, Dec 18-25, 1970, p. 9.
[93] "'Mert' Hunter: the kid they killed at Altamont", pp. 13 & 17.
[94] "'Mert' Hunter: the kid they killed at Altamont", p. 17.
[95] "Spain" interviewed by Vaakov Kohn, p. 4.
[96] See Thompson, *Hells Angels*, pp. 14-15; and Tom Wolfe, *The Electric Kool-Aid Acid Test* (New York: Farrar Straus and Giroux, 1968), pp. 173-187.
[97] Barger, *Hell's Angel*, pp. 99-101.The alleged rape at Monterey led directly to an investigation by California Attorney General Thomas Lynch and his findings, published in 1965 as the Lynch Report, gave the Angels a publicity boost that was good for both their ego and for recruitment, but also brought them the unwelcome attention of law enforcement for years to come. Lynch's report is a mixture of fact, half-fact, rumour, and myth. As Thompson points out, many of Lynch's sources were exaggerated media accounts of the lewd and violent behavior of California's outlaw motorcycle gangs. Thompson notes that the Lynch Report gave the Angels "coast-to-coast infamy" and turned them into "all-American bogeymen" (Thompson, *Hell's Angels*, p. 39). Despite the errors in the Lynch Report, and in media accounts, it was clear the Angels were not to be trifled with. Lynch sent questionnaires to over a hundred law enforcement officials and they documented numerous occasions of violence and criminality (Hunter S. Thompson, "The Motorcycle Gangs: A portrait of an outsider underground", *The Nation*, May 17, 1965, pp. 521-526).
[98] Selvin, *Altamont*, p. 202.
[99] Selvin, *Altamont*, p. 199.
[100] Barger, *Hell's Angel*, p. 164.
[101] Barger, *Hell's Angels*, p. 163.
[102] Todd Gitlin, "Woodstock West", *The Spectator* Vol 9, Issue 13, Jan 7, 1970, pp. 7-9. At p. 8.
[103] Ralph J. Gleason. "Who's Responsible For the Murder?", *San Francisco Chronicle*, Dec 18, 1969.
[104] Gitlin, "Woodstock West", p. 8.
[105] Barger, *Hell's Angels*, pp. 165-66.
[106] Selvin, *Altamont*, pp. 163-65.
[107] Bangs, "Rolling Stones Disaster at Altamont".
[108] Bangs, "Rolling Stones Disaster at Altamont".
[109] Selvin, *Altamont*, p. 184.
[110] George, "Let Him Who Hath Not Sinned", *Berkeley Barb*, Vol 9, No 24, Issue 227, Dec 19-24, 1969, p. 17.
[111] Alice Echols, *Scars of Sweet Paradise: The Life and Times of Janis Joplin* (New York: Holt., 1999), p. 264.
[112] Bangs, "Rolling Stones Disaster at Altamont".
[113] "A Little Tea and Sympathy", *The Rag*, Vol 5, Issue 8, Dec 7, 1970, p. 5.
[114] Keith Richards, interview with Ray Connolly. *Evening Standard*, Dec 1969. Available online at: http://www.rayconnolly.co.uk/pages/journalism_01/journalism_01_item.asp?journalism_01ID=74
[115] Bangs, "Rolling Stones Disaster at Altamont".
[116] Acers, "Exile to Altamont", pp. 13-14.
[117] Thomas Klaber "At his Satanic Majesty's Request", *Berkeley Barb*, Vol 9, No 23, Issue 226, Dec 12-18, 1969, p.3.
[118] Paul Glusman, "Stone Drag", *Chicago Seed*, Vol 4, No 10, 1969, p. 11.
[119] Gordon, "Satan and the Angels", pp. 30-71.
[120] Lester Bangs, "500 Mile Pilgrimage To A Hell's Angel Death Festival", *International Times* 72, Jan 28, 1970, p. 11.
[121] George Paul Csicsery, "Stones Concert Ends It: America Now Up For Grabs", *Berkeley Tribe*, Vol 1, Issue 23, Dec 12-19, 1969, pp. 1 & 5. At p. 5.
[122] Bangs, "500 Mile Pilgrimage", p. 11.
[123] James Lichtenberg, "Dark Star", *East Village Other*, Vol 5, Issue 7, Jan 21, 1970, p. 9.
[124] Anon. "Shake", *Berkeley Tribe*, Vol 1, Issue 23, Dec 12-19, 1969, p. 13.
[125] "A stony thing", *Berkeley Barb*, Vol 9, No 23, Issue 226, Dec 12-18, 1969, p. 2.

[126] "A murderous thing", *Berkeley Barb*, Vol 9, No 23, Issue 226, Dec 12-18, 1969, p. 2.
[127] Darlington, "Let it Bleed", p. 20.
[128] Darlington, "Let it Bleed", p. 20.
[129] Darlington, "Let it Bleed", p. 17.
[130] Bangs, "Rolling Stones Disaster at Altamont".
[131] Selvin, *Altamont*, p.146 & p.168 respectively.
[132] Selvin, *Altamont*, pp. 134-5
[133] Andy Carey, "Gimme Shelter", *The Seed*, Vol 6, Issue 9, Mar 1, 1971, p. 20.
[134] Acers, "Exile to Altamont", p. 13.
[135] Bangs, "Rolling Stones Disaster at Altamont".
[136] Bangs, "Rolling Stones Disaster at Altamont".
[137] Selvin, *Altamont*, p.108
[138] Selvin, *Altamont*, pp. 163-64.
[139] Bangs, "Rolling Stones Disaster at Altamont".
[140] Approximately 276 off-duty New York Police Department employees provided a more traditional security presence at the festival, albeit one that was unarmed and under strict instructions to avoid conflict with concert attendees. See Robert Stephen Spitz, *Barefoot in Babylon: The Creation of the Woodstock Music Festival, 1969* (New York: Viking, 1979), p. 378.
[141] Joel Rosenberg, John Roberts and Robert Pilpel, *Young Men With Unlimited Capital* (New York: bantam, 1989), pp. 95-96.
[142] Keith Richards, interview with Ray Connolly. *Evening Standard*, Dec 1969. Available online at: http://www.rayconnolly.co.uk/pages/journalism_01/journalism_01_item.asp?journalism_01ID=74
[143] John Burks, "In the Aftermath of Altamont", *Rolling Stone*, Feb 7, 1970.
[144] Gordon, "Satan and the Angels", pp. 30-71.
[145] "Million Dollar Bash", *The Rag*, Vol 4, Issue 10, Dec 15, 1969, p. 15.
[146] Anon. "Shake", *Berkeley Tribe*, Vol 1, Issue 23, Dec 12-19, 1969, p. 13.

A provisional performance schedule for Woodstock, drafted before the final line-up was confirmed

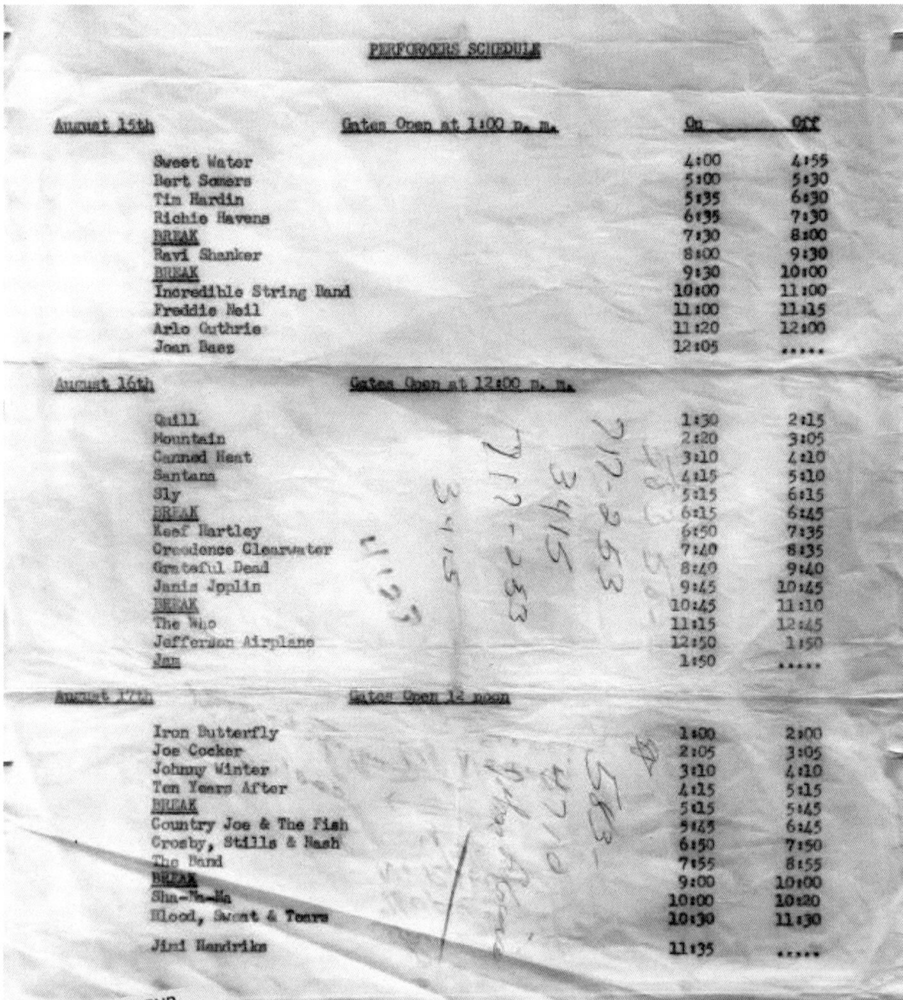

PERFORMERS SCHEDULE

August 15th	Gates Open at 1:00 p. m.	On	Off
	Sweet Water	4:00	4:55
	Bert Somers	5:00	5:30
	Tim Hardin	5:35	6:30
	Richie Havens	6:35	7:30
	BREAK	7:30	8:00
	Ravi Shanker	8:00	9:30
	BREAK	9:30	10:00
	Incredible String Band	10:00	11:00
	Freddie Neil	11:00	11:15
	Arlo Guthrie	11:20	12:00
	Joan Baez	12:05	.....
August 16th	**Gates Open at 12:00 p. m.**		
	Quill	1:30	2:15
	Mountain	2:20	3:05
	Canned Heat	3:10	4:10
	Santana	4:15	5:10
	Sly	5:15	6:15
	BREAK	6:15	6:45
	Keef Hartley	6:50	7:35
	Creedence Clearwater	7:40	8:35
	Grateful Dead	8:40	9:40
	Janis Joplin	9:45	10:45
	BREAK	10:45	11:10
	The Who	11:15	12:45
	Jefferson Airplane	12:50	1:50
	Jam	1:50	.....
August 17th	**Gates Open 12 noon**		
	Iron Butterfly	1:00	2:00
	Joe Cocker	2:05	3:05
	Johnny Winter	3:10	4:10
	Ten Years After	4:15	5:15
	BREAK	5:15	5:45
	Country Joe & The Fish	5:45	6:45
	Crosby, Stills & Nash	6:50	7:50
	The Band	7:55	8:55
	BREAK	9:00	10:00
	Sha-Na-Na	10:00	10:20
	Blood, Sweat & Tears	10:30	11:30
	Jimi Hendrix	11:35	.....

Richie Havens was the opening act at the Woodstock festival.
(Globe Photos/ZUMAPRESS.com)

Hippies 'On the Bus' at Woodstock.
(United Archives GmbH / Alamy Stock Photo)

Joan Baez 'beautiful and pure'. (Everett Collection Inc / Alamy Stock Photo)

Janis Joplin had an off night at Woodstock but was still incredible, claimed The Who's Pete Townshend.(Jason Laure, Frank White Photo Agency)

Sly and The Family Stone: one of the few interracial acts at Woodstock.(United Archives GmbH / Alamy Stock Photo)

Fans scaled light and sound towers to get the best view of the stage.
(Granger Historical Picture Archive / Alamy Stock Photo)

Woodstock's elevated stage gave the fans a good view of performers and also provided a physical barrier to deter potential stage invasions. (Entertainment Pictures / Alamy Stock Photo)

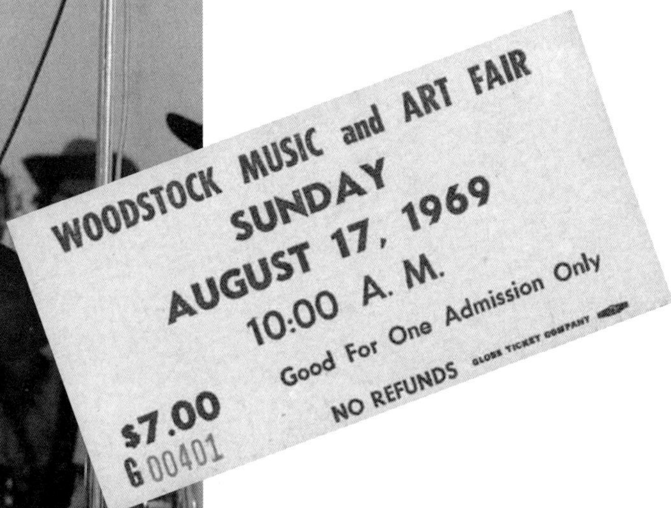

Grace Slick 'doesn't smoke, she smoulders', claimed one observer.
(Jason Laure, Frank White Photo Agency)

A novel use for this Volkswagen Beetle.
(Granamour Weems Collection / Alamy Stock Photo)

The Who's Roger Daltrey strikes a dynamic pose during the band's set at Woodstock.
(United Archives GmbH / Alamy Stock Photo)

Jimi Hendrix closed the show early on Monday morning with a lengthy and dynamic set which included his iconic version of the 'Star Spangled Banner'.
(Doug Marks, Frank White Photo Agency)

Flying a peace flag at Altamont.
(Mira / Alamy Stock Photo

Hippies 'On the Bus' at Altamont.
(Bob Kreisel / Alamy Stock Photo)

Fans packed tightly together at the front of the stage during The Rolling Stones' set at Altamont.
(Everett Collection Inc / Alamy Stock Photo)

Hells Angels at Altamont enforcing order with sawn-off pool cues.
(PictureLux / The Hollywood Archive / Alamy Stock Photo)

Mick Jagger on stage at Madison Square Garden, New York during the Stones' 1969 US Tour.
(Granger Historical Picture Archive / Alamy Stock Photo)

Chapter 5: Demons

There are black magicians who think we are acting as unknown agents of Lucifer and others who think we are Lucifer. Everybody's Lucifer.

Keith Richards[1]

In trying to understand why the Altamont festival failed to live up to its billing as "Woodstock West" and became forever synonymous with violence, most analysis has focused on practical decisions (such as proceeding with the festival at the somewhat unsuitable venue of Altamont Speedway, or building a stage so low it was virtually impossible to separate the band from the audience) and poor planning (such as employing Hells Angels as security). Yet interestingly, most accounts of the festival have not actually considered the obvious: that unlike at Woodstock, the Rolling Stones were at the heart of Altamont. This is surprising, because many contemporary commentators in the late 1960s noted that the Stones were a band that did little to refute their reputation that violence followed them wherever they went; and that in many respects, violence was in fact "inherent in their music".[2] They were also a band touched by tragedy with the recent, mysterious-seeming death of Brian Jones. Indeed, such was the band's dark reputation by this point in 1969 that many contemporary commentators suggested the Stones were enthralled by Satanic or demonic influences, and some even went so far as to argue Meredith Hunter's death at Altamont was part of some Satanic plot by Mick Jagger. Why did so many commentators make a diabolic connection between the band and Altamont's tragic violence? And how did the Stones' sinister reputation come about?

In a sense, there is a fairly straightforward answer to this: the band cultivated a Satanic image for dramatic effect, and it was therefore an accessible and colourful metaphor that contemporary commentators could utilise. Given their flirtation with demonic imagery and occultism — and that they were also renowned for their deliberately provocative, violence-laden songs — it perhaps seems obvious why so many contemporary commentators portrayed the Stones at Altamont as devils in human form. When added to the already explosive mix of the misery wrought by the poor festival planning, the staggering number of "bad trips", and the controversy of the Hells Angels, Altamont seemed to represent hell on earth. Yet, as we will see in the pages that follow, this is only part of the story. There were also other factors at play, which were rooted in the Rolling Stones' creative debt to the blues, and particularly Robert Johnson, who, by this point in the late 1960s was remembered as one of the greatest American blues artists. It was the Stones-Johnson connection that helped fuel the idea that Altamont was a kind of high alter of devil pacts and sacrifice. This is because, as well his outstanding music that the Stones greatly admired, Robert Johnson was also famous for his link with the "crossroads myth" — the legend that he had sold his soul to the devil at a crossroads in exchange for outstanding musical skills. While he died in relative obscurity in his own lifetime, Johnson's music left a lasting impression on the Stones and other prominent white musicians, on their fans, and on music critics such as Greil Marcus, who once claimed that, "a good musical case can be made for Johnson as the first rock 'n' roller of all".[3] And given the Stones' paid tribute to Johnson at Altamont with their rendition of "Love in Vain", it was perhaps the "crossroads myth" ghost of this founding father of rock 'n' roll which cast a shadow over interpretations of the dark atmosphere of the Altamont festival. As we shall see, the idea of a pact between musicians and demons has a long and colourful history, and in the late 1960s the connection between Johnson's music, its discovery mainly by white rock musicians in that era, and events at Altamont provide a powerful lure for those looking for answers to the festival's troubled atmosphere, and subsequent violence.

Demonic Pacts: Faust, Paginini, and the American Gothic

In Western culture, the Faust legend is perhaps the main origin of the "demonic bargaining" yarn, wherein a man sells his soul to the Devil in exchange for wealth and fame. The Faustian legend, in turn, was rooted in Christian parables of good versus evil, particularly those which stressed the perilous consequences of renouncing God's gift of an immortal soul and entry into Heaven in favour of earthly pleasures. The Christian Church has a long history of persecuting those who have been suspected of demonic pacts or witchcraft, most famously witch trials in Europe in the 17th century and the Salem Witch Trials in Colonial America. No one was above suspicion, from the highest Christian nobility to the lowest peasant: for example, rumours abounded that Pope Sylvester II (946–1003) made a compact with a female demon to help him ascend to the Papacy. The *Malleus Maleficarum* (1487) treatise on witchcraft considered that all witches and warlocks were in league with demons or with Satan. Many innocent people were tortured and put to death in line with the philosophy and teachings of the *Malleus Maleficarum*, with women especially singled out. In America's most notorious case, the Salem Witch Trials in Massachusetts in 1692-3, twenty people were executed, sixteen of them young women.

The Faust legend, loosely based on a real-life historical figure named Johann Georg Faust (1480–1540), narrates that the eponymous anti-hero bargained away his soul to Satan's representative, Mephistopheles, in exchange for worldly knowledge. This German folklore story has been depicted in significant works of literature, opera, and symphonic music. It is unclear why Johann Georg Faust, in particular, was depicted in lore as forging a pact with Satan: in reality, Faust was a travelling scholar (who once studied at Heidelberg University) and who described himself variously as a physician, astrologer, alchemist and magician. At one point he was condemned by the church as a blasphemer in league with the Devil. He met a violent death, possibly caused by a chemical explosion during his alchemy experiments, but essentially there is little in his recorded life that would suggest a demonic pact. Nevertheless, around 47 years after his death, German printer Johann Spies published *Historia von D. Johann Fausten*, the first "Faust book", whose author remained anonymous. It is possible that the legend had been passed down orally before this first written instance. This first tale of Faust focused on the physical benefits that Faust gained from his demonic pact, including consumption of Europe's finest wine, food and women; it also described his violent death, smashed to pieces by the Devil in the most gruesome fashion. *Historia von D. Johann Fausten* was the basis for further written instantiations of the Faust legend, including English playwright Christopher Marlowe's *The Tragical History of Doctor Faustus* (1592), in which Faust gains knowledge rather than physical pleasure. A further development in the legend appeared in Johann Wolfgang von Goethe's play *Faust* (1808) wherein it is Mephistopheles rather than Faust who initiates the bargain between them. Furthermore, Faust's soul is saved when angels intervene to thwart Mephistopheles.

Given the extent that the Faust legend permeated Western culture, perhaps due to its value as a morality tale, it proved adaptable enough to be applied to almost anyone with a degree or knowledge or talent; but it has been to musicians especially that the devil pact legend has most often been applied.[4] Music has, of course, long been deemed sacred in the Christian Church; the music of angels after all is the heavenly harp. Yet as with most aspects of Christian doctrine, the heavenly also has its evil opposite — and in this case, the music of the Devil has often been portrayed as the fiddle/violin. For example, in Nikolaus Lenau's poem "Faust" (1836), Mephistopheles and Faust attend an inn where a wedding party is in progress. Mephistopheles tempts Faust to seduce the innkeeper's daughter, but Faust declines. The wily Mephistopheles picks up a violin and plays a demonic refrain that drives the dancers into a frenzy, at which point Faust and the innkeeper's daughter retire into the woods, where they obey Mephistopheles's salacious bidding. The violin, then, was clearly linked to distraction, frenzy, deception and ultimately lust. Lenau's poem was the basis for Franz Liszt's Mephisto Waltz (The Dance in the Village Inn) (1859-62), which gave musical voice to Lenau's prose. Liszt's composition, according to one music critic, "includes a marvelously devilish tune and lots of instrumental flourishes".[5] The poet Lenau was no doubt influenced by stories of two notorious Italian virtuoso violinists, Giuseppe Tartini and Nicolo Paginini. Tartini would regale anyone who would listen that the origin of his most famous composition, the "Devil's Trill Sonata", was in a dream he had in 1713 wherein he made a compact with the Devil, who would be at Tartini's disposal when needed. Tartini handed the Devil his violin and asked him to play, whereupon the Devil played a mesmerising and beautiful piece. Tartini was so surprised that he awoke from the dream and immediately took up his violin and tried to recreate what he had heard. Much to his frustration he was unsuccessful; instead he composed a piece inspired by the dream entitled "Devil's Sonata", but the haunting music he heard in his dream remained tantalisingly out of reach. This story attained legendary status and remained popular throughout the nineteenth century.[6]

Given these associations between Satanic compacts and violin virtuosoism it is perhaps unsurprising that the infamous nineteenth century Italian virtuoso violinist Nicolo Paginini was accused of demonic influences. A child prodigy, and a star in his native country, Paginini would in his later years tour Europe extensively, at one point in the 1830s playing 151 concerts in France and the British Isles in a 12-month period.[7] Lurid, outlandish rumours began to circulate in Italy about the source of the artist's extraordinary skill. As rock biographer Stephen Davis explains, eyewitnesses "soberly related having seen Satan guide Paganini's hands during a concert in Milan, while in France supposedly creditable witnesses swore that they saw emissaries from hell driving away from the concert hall along a road that was not even there".[8] However, it was during his time abroad that more open accusations became commonplace. As musicologist Maiko Kawabata recounts, the most popular labels given to Paginini were magician or conjurer — professions associated with the dark arts. In Berlin in 1829 he was called "Hexensohn" (son of a witch), "Hexenmeister" (witch-master), "Goethe's Mephisto" and "Dr. Faustus". In Vienna in 1831 he was accused of being the "Devil's spawn". In that same year in Weimar he was referred to as "demonic" and in Paris they called him "Mephistopheles". Visual depictions of Paginini reinforced the demonic connection: for example, Johann Peter Lyser's "Karikatur auf die Wiener Konzerte" (c. 1828) depicts Paginini inside a magic circle playing his violin, while skeletons dance around him. The image also features Satanic, supernatural, astrological and occult symbols such as a black cat, a pyramid, a snake wrapped around a staff, the Star of David, a possessed nun, and a number of ethereal creatures. Kawabata concludes that Lyser's caricature "provides a visual expression of the famous legend that Paganini had sold his soul to acquire superhuman powers on the violin".[9]

Musicologist Robert Riggs suggests that the popularity of Johann Wolfgang Von Goethe's *Faust* (1805) made comparisons between Paginini and both Mephistopheles and Faust a natural consequence.[10] No doubt Paginini's extraordinary and innovative musicianship contributed to this perception but so too did his scandalous and troubled private life. Paginini was tall and lean, with long black hair; he wore tight-fitting trousers when he performed, causing women in the audience to "scream and faint".[11] He never married but had a number of passionate relationships, one of which gave him a son whom he took custody of when the relationship ended. Paginini also had a gambling addiction and at one point allegedly wagered away his violin, but his rare talent and prolific concert appearances made him a wealthy man.[12] European Christian fears about Satanic pacts, combined with virtuoso musical talent, scandalous lifestyles, sexual promiscuity, and attainment of (what must have seemed to most ordinary people) obscene wealth, set the template for the rock stars of the latter half of the twentieth century. For example, in the 1950s, rockers such as Elvis Presley and Jerry Lee Lewis were accused of producing "devil music". Presley, a Christian with a passion for gospel music, never understood the allegation. As far as he was concerned, he was channeling something righteous and powerful, but not something evil. But other artists openly spoke of the diabolic aspects of their music and lifestyle: for example, in a moment of repentance, Little Richard declared that his music career was being "directed and commanded by...the power of darkness".[13]

In the United States, there was, however, another source and template for the *maleficus* — a person who makes a pact with Satan (as opposed to someone possessed by the devil or by a demon) — and this was rooted in African-American lore. Ideas of the *maleficus* had a complex history, one intertwined with the institution of slavery in the American south (slavery being present in the U.S. from the its earliest colonial days and prohibited only after the defeat of the secessionists in the American Civil War). While historians have argued about the extent to which slaves retained aspects of their African heritage under the bondage of slavery,[14] many agree that a kind of "religious syncretism" became the norm, with the first generation of slaves adopting some aspects of Christianity alongside older African beliefs and superstitions. Music historian Elijah Wald suggests, for example, that in some slave communities the Christian notion of the Devil tempting the righteous to commit sin was placed alongside the African spirit of Elegua, who was a "spirit of crossing paths".[15] Blues scholar Adam Gussow points to the "cultural utility" of this African supernatural being in the South, who could, in turns, be representative of the Christian Devil, the white slave-owner, a supernatural trickster, or even a humorous figure. In his most potent form, Gussow argues, Elegua could be "highly phallic, highly mobile, devil-affiliated, good-and-bad culture hero associated with the crossroads",[16] and also, most importantly, someone with whom one might do business. For example, in the 1930s Harry Middleton Hyatt, an Anglican minister, travelled through the south to collect folklore. He found the lore of "the deal with the Devil" to be still in evidence, as indicated by the following examples he collected:

> *"The devil will give you power to do evil things, if you sell yourself to him."*
> *"You can talk to the devil face to face, if you sell yourself to him."*
> *"Boil a black cat until all the meat comes off and take the bones to the four corners of the road and you will meet the devil. Then talk to him and you will have good luck all your life."*[17]

Thus, these core ideas of the Devil-Elegua hybrid — and significantly the idea of devil pacts and the symbolism of crossroads (already long associated with death because of the tradition of public executions at crossroads) — in turn percolated down to the popular music of African Americans: blues and jazz. Blues musicians used this powerful imagery as inspiration for some of their lyrics and also to boost their public image. For example, William Bunch, a blues musician originally from Arkansas, used the stage name Peetie Wheatstraw, which was derived from African-American folklore and referred to the evil half of a twin personality. On occasion, he called himself "The Devil's Son in Law" or the "High Sheriff of Hell".[18] Demonic inspiration can also be found in the titles of songs such as Clara James's "Done Sold My Soul to the Devil"

(1924), Skip James's "Devil Got My Woman" (1931), and Lonnie Johnson's "Devil's Got the Blues" (1938), to give just a few indicative examples. Perhaps the most well known figure connected to such legends back then was blues musician Tommy Johnson, who told his brother, Reverend LeDell Johnson, that he had sold his soul to the devil in exchange for his musical gifts. Tommy Johnson said:

If you want to learn how to play anything you want to play and learn how to make songs yourself, you take your guitar and you go to where a road crosses that way, where a crossroad is. Get there, be sure to get there just a little 'fore twelve o'clock that night so you'll know you'll be there. You have your guitar and be playing a piece there by yourself... A big black man will walk up there and take your guitar, and he'll tune it. And then he'll play a piece and hand it back to you. That's the way I learned to play anything I want.[19]

There was, though, nothing particularly demonic about Tommy Johnson's music, lyrics, voice or behavior: but what claims like his *did* do was cement the connection between African American blues artists and the "crossroads pact" myth — the idea that only the Devil/Elegua himself could grant such exceptional musical gifts to those willing to sell their soul.

Robert Johnson and the Crossroads legend

Yet it wasn't Tommy Johnson who became most closely associated with the crossroads myth; in fact it was the black blues musician Robert Johnson (no relation to Tommy). In his own lifetime, Robert Johnson suffered the fate of many great artists — he was a relative unknown and his musical talents were not recognised until long after his death. He had been born outside of wedlock in Hazelhurst, Mississippi in May 1911, and although little is known of his early life, one story has it that he suffered violent abuse from one of his mother's husbands. By his teens he had become a travelling blues musician, spending much of his time in the Mississippi Delta region. However, he also travelled to make a living, to places like Memphis, St. Louis, Chicago, Detroit, New York and as far as Canada. By 1930 he had married and lost his first wife, a sixteen-year-old who died during childbirth; he remarried in 1931. As a bluesman, he failed to make much of an impact on the music scene, locally or nationally. He recorded 29 songs in total, along with a number of alternative takes. Only one of these songs, "Terraplane Blues", had any commercial success, becoming a minor regional hit when it was released as a 78 rpm single on the Vocalion label in March 1937. Johnson may have been on the verge of some popular recognition in 1938, when a Johnson fan and music producer called John H. Hammond Jr. sought to feature Johnson in a Christmas show at Carnegie Hall which would be advertised under the name "From Spirituals to Swing". Unknown to Hammond, however, Johnson had died of unknown causes in August of 1938 and was already buried in a pauper's grave by the time Hammond's representative arrived in the South.

It was probably Son House, an established and respected blues musician, who first introduced the Robert Johnson legend to modern audiences: this came about in 1966, when Pete Welding of *Downbeat* magazine interviewed House for an article about Johnson. House had known Johnson before he was well-known, and observed that while Johnson could play the harmonica quite skillfully, he had limited guitar skills. In fact, as House put it rather brutally, Johnson was so untalented on the guitar that the noise he made would scare off House's paying customers! House and Johnson parted company for a while (reports vary between six months and two years), but when they saw each other again, House found Johnson's guitar playing had improved exponentially, leading to rumours that he had sold his soul at the crossroads in return for exceptional musical prowess.[20] It is instructive that House said this — that Johnson "sold his soul to the devil in exchange for learning to play like that"[21] — almost as an after-thought, as if he thought everyone already knew that was the way blues singers got their mojo. A school friend of Johnson named Willie Coffee added fuel to the fire of these crossroads rumours, claiming that Johnson had admitted to him that he had sold his soul to the devil (albeit Coffee conceded that he had probably been simply joking around).[22] Johnson, of course, did little to dispel these rumours; he was an almost unknown musician, struggling to make a name for himself; reports of supernatural skills could only enhance his reputation, and hopefully fatten his wallet.

Although Johnson died in obscurity, with little recognition of his musical talents, a few decades after his death Johnson would be considered one of the most talented blues artists of all time, a major influence on the likes of Bob Dylan, Keith Richards, Jimmy Page, Peter Green and Eric Clapton, and a figure of interest to historians as well those interested in music. Historian Marybeth Hamilton states, for example: "Over the last forty years, Robert Johnson has come to dominate the agenda of blues scholarship. Accounts of his brief, violent, mysterious life are given pride of place in most blues studies".[23] How did a commercially unsuccessful, almost unknown blues musician become so famous? And how did he become so closely associated with the crossroads' legend? The answer lies in the folk and blues revival of the 1950s and 1960s, which would also play a huge impact in shaping the Stones' music and Altamont Festival.

American folk and blues revival

The discovery of Johnson as an outstanding blues musician is located in the American folk and blues revival of the 1950s and 1960s. In this context, "revival" refers mainly to the exposure this music had among a white, mainstream audience, which resulted in increased sales of folk and blues music, the concurrent growth in media coverage of this music and its musicians, and recognition of both genres by The Recording Academy — for example, the Kingston Trio winning the first Grammy for Best Folk Performance in 1959. Blues music was often considered a subcategory of folk or jazz music and not a genre in its own right. There was nothing unusual, for example, in blues musicians Memphis Slim, Odetta, Sonny Terry and Brownie McGhee appearing on the bill at the inaugural 1959 Newport Folk Festival, while John Lee Hooker performed at the 1960 event; furthermore, Hooker, Otis Spann, and Muddy Waters performed at the 1960 Newport Jazz Festival.

This revival took place against the backdrop of the Cold War and the explosion of anti-communist paranoia, particularly in the early part of the 1950s. This period was characterised by a "Red Scare" which saw the trial and execution of atomic spies Julius and Ethel Rosenberg, as well as the devastating Korean War and the unfolding of the McCarthy hearings. This was a time of national hysteria: sedition laws were enacted and there were 25,000 FBI investigations into suspected communist sympathisers; many state employees such as teachers and university lecturers were asked to sign loyalty oaths (approximately 600 teachers and lecturers were blacklisted for their political beliefs); universities banned "radical" speakers and fired lecturers who came under suspicion; and in total, 1500 TV & radio producers were fired, 300 actors blacklisted, 2,700 federal employees fired and 12,000 resigned.[24] Musicians also entered the line of fire. Folk music in particular came under suspicion due to the historic ties between the music, left-wing politics, and labour union activism. When the backlash came from mainstream America, it hit hard. For example, The Weavers, featuring Pete Seeger, had a number of hit singles in the early 1950s but when Seeger was accused of being a communist the band's record label, Decca, dropped them. During the McCarthy era, there was a general media blacklisting of folk artists whose loyalties were deemed questionable.

Much like the Beat movement, which had grown in response to the stifling conformity of 1950s America, the revival of both folk and blues was also partly a response to the toxic atmosphere of domestic politics and perceived cultural stagnation — folk and blues seemed to offer something "authentic" about America. As the renowned folk singer Pete Seeger put it, there were five main reasons for the revived interest in folk music in this time period:

1. Americans wanted to learn more about their culture.
2. It was a reaction to the "couch potato" mentality that television was supposedly producing.
3. There was renewed belief in the excellence of American folk songs, and their authenticity proved particularly attractive in an era increasingly dominated by advertising and the mass media.
4. Folk songs documented and sometimes celebrated marginalised social groups, but they never looked down upon them as inferior.
5. Folk songs provided an opportunity to discuss current events, such as the threat of atomic war, the Civil Rights Movement, and America's policy towards Vietnam.[25]

The blues revival also began towards the end of the 1950s, caused mainly by the same factors that instigated the folk revival. Blues expert Jim O'Neal points to the blues as an "alternative" culture and "the voice of an alienated and oppressed people". It attracted white Americans because it was "erotic, sweaty, hypnotic; it dealt on the level with the battle of the sexes... In the eyes of the rebel youth, blues was sung by guitar-slinging outlaws and macho antiheroes".[26] O'Neal notes also that a particular style of blues was favoured in this revival, and that was "prewar down-home blues", which celebrated "that genre's direct descendants — for example, practitioners of the Chicago blues [like Muddy Waters, Howlin' Wolf, Junior Wells, Otis Rush, Buddy Guy and Sonny Boy Williamson]".[27] The "prewar down-home blues" seemed, to many fans, to be the more "authentic" version of the genre. Some critics argue, however, that there is a false distinction between different forms of the blues: Marybeth Hamilton asserts, for example, that blues historians, chroniclers and collectors have created a false divide between "authentic" blues (rural, male, sad) and "inauthentic" blues (more often urban, salacious/sexual — even pornographic — and sung primarily by women, although by no means exclusively so).[28] Elijah Wald, too, decries any attempt to form a distinction between what is authentic and inauthentic: "Such standards framed my own introduction to blues... I now consider them pure romanticism, an outsider's perception that has virtually no bearing on the realities of the music".[29] Bearing in mind this "false divide" then, it is important to understand that it was more this idea of the "authentic" blues — rural, male, non-commercial, and sorrowful — that was "discovered" by whites in the 1960s, and this created the opportunity for Robert Johnson to emerge as a "lost" blues legend, guitar virtuoso, and troubled spirit.

Robert Johnson: Crowned King of the Delta Blues Singers

As we noted earlier, just before the end of Robert Johnson's life, the music producer John H Hammond Jr. — a big fan of Johnson's music — had hoped to invite him to perform at Carnegie Hall, but Johnson died before he could be reached. By the 1960s, Hammond was working for Columbia records, who owned the rights to 1930s and 1940s recording artists after buying labels such as Vocalion and ARC.[30] Hammond was the driving force behind the release of *King of the Delta Blues Singers* (1961), a compilation album which included much of Johnson's recorded output and which exposed his work to a modern record-buying audience for the first time. Previous to this, Hammond had signed Bob Dylan onto Columbia and he gave Dylan an acetate of the *King of the Delta Blues Singers* album. In his autobiography *Chronicles*, Dylan recalls seeing Johnson for the first time via an artistic rendering on the album cover. Dylan thought the guitarist was "fiercely intense" and "electrifying", and from that moment on Dylan claimed to be "possessed" by Johnson.[31] Johnson's music also had an immediate impact on Dylan: "From the first note the vibrations from the loudspeaker made my hair stand up. The stabbing sounds from the guitar could almost break a window. When Johnson started singing, he seemed like a guy who could have sprung from the head of Zeus in full armor. I immediately differentiated between him and anyone else I had ever heard".[32] Dylan listened to the record repeatedly and made a second supernatural reference to describe the impact of Johnson's music: "it felt like a ghost had come into the room, a fearsome apparition".[33] Dylan utilised "five or six" of Johnson's song structures, as well as writing "hundreds of lines" of lyrics inspired by Johnson, mentioning specifically that "Highway 61 Revisited" owes a particular debt to the bluesman.[34]

Music artist Eric Clapton recorded a similar visceral response to Johnson's work. In the sleeve notes to the Robert Johnson vinyl box set entitled *The Complete Recordings* (1990), Clapton explained:

I don't think I'd even heard of Robert Johnson when I first found [King of the Delta Blues Singers]. I was around fifteen or sixteen, and it came as something of a shock to me that there could be anything that powerful... It was almost as if he felt things so acutely that he found it almost unbearable... At first it was almost too painful, but then after about six months I started listening, and then I didn't listen to anything else. Up until the time I was 25, if you didn't know who Robert Johnson was I wouldn't talk to you... It was as if I had been prepared to receive Robert Johnson, almost like a religious experience.[35]

Much like Dylan then, Clapton also described Johnson's work as almost supernaturally sublime. In his autobiography, Clapton testified: "It was hardcore... I realised that, on some level, I had found the master, and that following this man's example would be my life's work".[36] He was true to his word: Clapton's first recorded lead vocal was on the Johnson song "Ramblin' on my Mind", which appeared on the John Mayall & the Bluesbreakers's 1966 album *Bluesbreakers with Eric Clapton*. Clapton later recorded a version of Johnson's "Cross Road Blues" with English blues band, Cream, which incorporated lyrics from "Traveling Riverside Blues". And in "Layla", which Clapton recorded with his group Derek and the Dominoes (and which was released on the 1970 album *Layla and Other Assorted Love Songs*), Clapton included the Johnson lyric "all my love's in vain". As Greil Marcus has noted, in the tortured lyrics of "Layla", in which Clapton writes of his feelings for Pattie Boyd (aka "Layla"), who was then the wife of Clapton's friend George Harrison, Clapton may have come the closest to emulating his idol Robert Johnson.[37] Polydor released a box set of Clapton recordings in 1988, entitling it *Crossroads*. Clapton organised five music festivals between 1999 and 2013 under the name "Crossroads Guitar Festival". Johnson has remained an influence on Clapton's music throughout his career, with Clapton releasing an album of cover songs in 2004 entitled *Me and Mr. Johnson*.

Others were equally affected by *King of the Delta Blues Singers*. Both Jimmy Page and Robert Plant heard the album and became "obsessed" with Johnson.[38] When they formed Led Zeppelin, they played live renditions of Johnson's "Traveling Riverside Blues", and on their second album their composition "The Lemon Song" incorporated lyrics from "Traveling Riverside Blues". In a 1966 interview with Steve Barker, Jimi Hendrix claimed Robert Johnson, along with Muddy Waters and Elmore James, as early influences on his music.[39] The Butterfield Blues Band included the Johnson track "Walkin' Blues" on their 1966 album East-West; and Peter Green's Fleetwood Mac recorded "Hellhound on My Trail" on their 1968 debut album.

It is remarkable that after the release of just one retrospective album, Johnson had gone from obscurity to being essential listening for the cream of rock and blues artists on both sides of the

Atlantic. Why was this? No doubt, Johnson was a talented guitarist and singer, who wrote moving and evocative lyrics. Equally, though, it could be said that he was not the most talented blues guitarist of his era, nor the most powerful singer: Wald makes the case, for example, that Charley Patton, Skip James and Son House — all Johnson contemporaries — were "among the greatest musicians this country has produced". In contrast, Wald considers Johnson someone who had a "broad grasp of the popular styles of his day", and a commercial performer who often played cover versions of popular songs to appease his audiences.[40] While not understating Johnson's considerable musical attributes, Wald attributes Johnson's modern-day popularity mainly to the fact that Johnson's music was recorded and preserved in decent quality and was therefore available in 1961 for reissue on the new 33 rpm "long play" vinyl record format. This gave the opportunity to modern listeners to hear and appreciate Johnson's music, which had immediate and profound effect on the likes of Dylan, Clapton, and the other aforementioned musicians. While it is easy to detail how technical achievements contributed to Johnson's "discovery", it is more difficult to explain what it was about the man and his music that was so affective. And what was it that made him particularly attractive to white musicians and a white audience?

Both Dylan and Clapton mention the *power* of Johnson's music, and Clapton makes particular reference to its evocation of Johnson's pain, being a poor black man born in the American South; perhaps his music also evokes the pain of an entire race that had been enslaved and transported to the Americas, and which then endured generations of Jim Crow segregation, discrimination, and racial violence. Marybeth Hamilton argues that for blues revivalists, authenticity was key, and the most authentic bluesman "was a tormented soul who found in his suffering a kind of transcendence: driven by demons, as legend held Robert Johnson had been, but generating through his torment the blues' highest art".[41] Looking more broadly at how white men, in particular, have reacted to black masculinity, social historian Eric Lott has suggested fascination with "blackface" is linked to appropriation and subjugation of blacks. It developed out of racial desire and also features homoerotic undertones.[42] Lott argues that blackface minstrelsy developed because of white fascination with, and fear of, black males. Furthermore, he contends, whites were obsessed with the black body and therefore projected their own masculinity onto it. Whites admired the supposed spontaneity, everyday existentialism, and "primitiveness" of African-Americans. They sought to be part of black culture, while always having the option to still be white.[43] This "racial desire" (using Lott's term) is perhaps one of the reasons why the blues became prominent in the white imagination during the revival of the late 1950s and 1960s, offering, as it seemed to do, more "authentic" experiences than those available to whites in an America geared towards consumerism and where conformity and homogeneity was often required to be successful.

Yet perhaps it wasn't solely the tragedy of Johnson's life — and the way he fitted in to the "authentic" model of blues singers that white male rock musicians seemed to prefer in their "rediscovery" of blues music — that accounted for his posthumous success. Perhaps it was also in large part due to the fact that his story had become cemented with the "crossroads" legend, from which he became synonymous with mysterious devil pacts and intrigue. For example, while the album sleeve of *King of the Delta Blues Singers* makes no direct reference to any deal with the devil, it does add that Johnson "lived the life he sang about and which ultimately killed him... [he] died of poison, administered by an unknown woman, most likely in a drink". The implication is clear: he "lived the life he sang about" (devil pacts, selling his soul), and his sinful life killed him, when he was caught out by poison "administered" by an "unknown woman" (an unambiguous reference perhaps to a witch-like character). As we have seen, it was in 1966 that this legend was first committed to print, during the Pete Walding interview with Son House, and Johnson's friend Willie Coffee then added fuel to the fire of these rumours. It seems very likely then that this cementing of Johnson's talent with the "crossroads" legend contributed greatly to the aura of mystery and the idea of the supernatural power of his music. In turn, this was, at least in part, a reason for his musical rediscovery in the 1950s and 1960s.

Certainly, Johnson's actual music suggests that he had been aware of his so-called link with a Faustian deal, and he explored this through his work. Song titles such as "Cross Road Blues", "Preachin' Blues (Up Jumped the Devil)", "If I Had Possession Over Judgment Day", "Hell Hound on my Trail", and "Me and the Devil Blues" clearly hark to this. But it is his lyrics which provide the best insight into how aware he was of his connection to the "crossroads legend". In "Cross Road Blues" Johnson physically locates himself at the place where, as the lore tells it, one can do a deal with the devil. In the song, not only the sun but Johnson himself is "sinkin' down", having signed away his soul in return for his musical ability. In "Hell Hound on my Trail", Johnson is pursued by a demonic figure; in one of the few contemporary reviews of Johnson's music, published just a few years after his death, Rudi Blesh referred to "Hell Hound on my Trail" as "the expression of uncanny and weird feelings… Johnson's voice sounds possessed like that of a man cast in a spell".[44] In "Me and the Devil Blues" Johnson completes the sad story of his downfall when Satan knocks on his door to collect on his side of the deal. Johnson goes with him, knowing that he is doomed, making one final request that he be buried by the side of the road. Of course, there are other, less fanciful but perhaps equally terrifying, interpretations of these lyrics. For example, in "Cross Road Blues" Johnson is on the open road as night falls, which is not a good place to be in the Jim Crow South. In reality it is not the devil he is likely to meet there, it is white people.[45] In the language of the blues, they were often interchangeable.

The Stones and African-American blues: "What can a poor boy do?"

In his autobiography *Life*, Keith Richards explains that it was Brian Jones who introduced him to Robert Johnson through Johnson's *King of the Delta Blues Singers* album.[46] While it is not known when Richards first became aware of the Johnson legend of a deal with the devil, it clearly influenced his thinking about the music business and about fame and fortune. For example, in his autobiography, when Richards mused on the transition the Rolling Stones made from the relative obscurity of playing in small-scale London blues clubs to their international fame as rock stars, he reflected: "It's not that easy being famous; you don't want to be. But at the same time you've got to be to do what you're doing. And you realise you've already made the deal at the crossroads… You're now set on the path, along with all those people you wanted to follow anyway, like Muddy Waters, Robert Johnson. You've already made the fucking deal. And now you have to follow it, just like all your brothers and sisters and ancestors. You are now on the road".[47] Richards saw a lot of his own struggles in life mirrored by the strife, hardship and tragedy that had befallen Johnson.

Richards, a working class man born in post-war Britain, was keenly aware of the choking restraints placed on his life by class and poverty. England was still rebuilding after World War Two; food rationing didn't end until 1954, the class structure of British society was still deeply entrenched and few working class British men saw any chance to improve their lot in life. Working class people often lived in cramped, squalid conditions. In London especially, the high rises built on former bomb sites fell quickly into disrepair, and were without proper facilities, green space, or adequate safety provisions. Many working class men were employed in labour-intensive industries, in factories, steel mills, shipyards and coalmines, often in dangerous conditions. For young people like Keith Richards, whose dad Bert was a "fucking hardworking man" who grew up during the depression of the 1930s, music was a potential pathway out of this life. He referred to his dad as a "great bloke" but also as a "silly sod" for working so hard for so little reward.[48] When Richards was expelled from school, Bert was angry and disappointed;

he wanted Keith to get a job. Keith, however, considered him the "most unambitious man in the world" and asked sarcastically if he should get a job "making lightbulbs". Richards confessed, "I was a kid and I didn't even know what ambition meant. All I felt was the constraints".[49]

To Richards and many young men like him, making a living from music — and its attendant promise of social mobility, good money and an itinerant lifestyle — had a particular attraction in the 1960s. As cultural historian John Scanlon points out, the Rolling Stones became "so enamored of the 'on the road' experiences of two generations of American blues singers who had seemed destined never to stay in one place — and who sang mostly about the highs and lows of such a life — that they would turn the life that their songs conjured into their own kind of culture".[50] Indeed, before *Exile on Main Street* (1972), Keith Richards wrote the majority of the band's music while on the road in the United States.[51] Richards and his band mates had thus looked enviously at the travelling and touring culture of itinerant blues artists like Johnson, who like them, had desperately wanted to avoid the poverty, daily grind and stultifying boredom that seemed all that was on offer to them. These blues artists had proved they were not tied to the land, as their parents had been; they were not only geographically mobile but also upwardly mobile — when they earned any money, they spent it on looking good. They wanted to be and to look successful, and they believed those two things went hand-in-hand. All of these ingredients freed them from what would be an otherwise mundane and unremarkable existence — seemingly the lot of black people in the United States and particularly in the Jim Crow South. They chose a life "associated with all manner of fast living and ungodly pursuits — a veritable underworld of promiscuous sex, drinking, here-today-gone-tomorrow hell-raising, gambling and generally living the life of a drifter".[52] Johnson chronicled this life in songs like "Rambling on my Mind", "Walkin' Blues" and "Traveling Riverside Blues", with his turbulent relationships with women being a recurring theme. As Werner notes, Keith Richards was just one of many white musicians to "bear witness to how black music helped them escape the suffocating communities they grew up in".[53]

Of course, the question remains as to whether it is either accurate or morally right for white working class English people to equate their life experiences with those of blues musicians like Robert Johnson, who were born black in an era when that simple fact of nature condemned one to a life of inequality, discrimination, and sometimes brutal violence. Phil Spector thought so. In an interview with *Rolling Stone* magazine, he claimed:

I believe that the English kids have soul. Really soul. When I watch Walter Cronkite or Victory at Sea, or You Are There — any of those programs, I see bombs flying all over England and little kids running. Now that's probably Paul McCartney running. You know, 'cause that's where the bombs fell. They say soul comes through suffering. Slavery for the blacks. And gettin' your ass bombed off is another way of gettin' some soul, so I would say that these English cats have a lot of soul legitimately.[54]

Whether or not this is true, artists like Keith Richards, Eric Clapton, and Jimmy Page, arguably were not so much trying to equate their experiences with the likes of Robert Johnson, as much as to recognise them as kindred spirits with somewhat similar troubles, and to pay them tribute. Keith Richards mused, for example, that in their early days the Rolling Stones' aim was simply to "turn other people on to Muddy Waters and Bo Diddley and Jimmy Reed".[55] In other words, what the Rolling Stones did was to help pave the way for Americans to rediscover their own musical culture.

Perhaps there was a selfish and cynical side to this, to bask in the reflected cool of authentic blues artists. Writing in *Rolling Stone* magazine in May 1969, San Francisco music critic Ralph Gleason suggested that in Cream's forthcoming tour if the US, they should not only pay homage to the black blues artists that inspired them, but also share some of the profits by employing these artists as part of the bill.[56] The underground magazine *Great Speckled Bird* also saw the problematic aspects of white artists playing traditionally black music, noting ironically of the Ann Arbor Blues Festival, August 1-3, 1969, "Would you believe a BLACK blues festival? [emphasis in original], before providing a list of the festival's all-black line up.[57] However, the Stones saw in the blues a pure form for expressing emotion: they were drawn to the kind of authentic, rural music they deemed modern consumer culture had not corrupted. They loved Elvis and Chuck Berry, and saw correctly that the roots of that music were in the compositions of earlier blues artists. They also saw the potential for their music to connect people together. Richards wrote: "We realised that the guys we were playing, like Muddy Waters, had also grown up with Robert Johnson and translated it into a band format. In other words, it was just a progression... What I found about the blues and music, tracing things back, was that nothing came from itself. As great as it is, this is not one stroke of genius. This cat was listening to somebody and it's his variation on the theme. And so you suddenly realise that everybody's connected here".[58]

Richards' point also addresses the equally valid criticism as to whether white artists like the Stones were able to understand Johnson's body of work and his life, in a way that did not romanticise the black experience as something to be consigned to the past, as non-commercial, and confined to the rural South. This was, after all, the 1960s, when the Civil Rights Movement was at its most active since the 1920s, and also when lynching was at its devastating height. Some historians are adamant that this was appropriation rather than celebration. Hamilton states, for example: "Blues revivalists privileged an obsolete form of rural black culture in an era when most African-Americans lived in cities, and towards contemporary black music they were at best ambivalent, if not overtly hostile. Some black musicians drew a blunt conclusion: whites were prepared to laud black creativity only when it was old and decrepit. As blues guitarist Lonnie Johnson put it when [anthropologist Charles] Keil approached for an interview: 'Are you another one of those guys who wants to put crutches under my ass?'"[59] Yet there were also positive practical results of white fascination with the blues. In the 1960s, there were more blues records in the charts and on the radio than ever before. Moreover, blues artists received royalties when white artists covered their songs: for example, Robert Wilkins benefitted financially when the Rolling Stones recorded his song "Prodigal Son" on their 1968 album *Beggar's Banquet*. "Black bluesmen have been incomparably better off since the coming of the British blues than they were before", noted the *Berkeley Barb*.[60] And there were benefits other than financial: whereas B.B. King had been popular among black audiences for a generation before his music was discovered in the mid-1960s by white audiences, King recognised the cultural value of such mainstream success: "We're beginnin' to be treated among them as stars, with respect, the same as they would give any other artist".[61]

The Rolling Stones at Altamont: Sympathy for the Devil?

In addition to the profound impact of African-American blues artists on the Stones' music, sound, and attitude, the Stones — and other British bands like The Beatles, Black Sabbath and Led Zeppelin — also enjoyed flirting with the "crossroads legend" that had added irresistible mysterious appeal to artists like Robert Johnson.[62] As Paginini's example makes clear, there is a kind of alchemy that creates the particular circumstances wherein accusations of demonic pacts can gain traction. The first French edition of Goethe's "Dr Faustus" appeared in 1814, and it quickly became a sensation: over the next few decades stage shows, operas, and other iterations of the story appeared. As Kawabata points out, "Paganini's Parisian audiences were thus primed for a "Mephistophelean" performer before he had even set foot in the city".[63] In a similar way in the long 1960s, circumstances combined in popular music to create fertile ground for speculative tales about Satanic pacts, Devil worship, or evil influences.

Even before Altamont, the Stones had acquired a reputation for using occult imagery in their music and identity. For example, in 1967 the Stones released an album entitled *Their Satanic Majesties Request*; and the opening track on their 1968 album *Beggars Banquet* is entitled "Sympathy for the Devil". When the Stones performed "Sympathy for the Devil" for their *Rock 'n' Roll Circus* (1968) project, Jagger removed his shirt to reveal devil tattoos on his chest and upper arms. There seems little doubt that in this time period, Jagger, and some acolytes of the band, dabbled with black magic, Satanism and the occult. For example, Jagger and Richards befriended Kenneth Anger, an American underground filmmaker and occultist. Indeed, Anger was a collector of the works of English occultist Aleister Crowley, and a follower of Crowley's religion, Thelema. He was also friendly with Anton LaVey, founder of the Church of Satan. Jagger agreed to play the synthesizer soundtrack to Anger's short film *Invocation of My Demon Brother* (1969), a film in which LaVey played a minor role. Perhaps in homage to Jagger's physical appearance in *Rock 'n' Roll Circus*, magical tattoos appear on Anger's arms in *Invocation of My Demon Brother*. Anger also wanted Jagger and Richards to star in his forthcoming film *Lucifer Rising*, wherein he hoped Jagger would play Lucifer with Richards as Beelzebub. That never came to pass, but Anger did cast Jagger's girlfriend Marianne Faithfull as the goddess Lilith and his brother Chris Jagger as a minor character. The Stones' connection to Anger thus gave them a reputation as associates of the dark arts. This suspicion deepened with allegations that Anita Pallenberg, Richards' partner at the time, was a practitioner of black magic. Rumours spread that she was a witch, a point Marianne Faithfull seemed to confirm in her autobiography: "Anita eventually took the goddess business one step further into witchcraft", Faithfull wrote.[64] Tony Sanchez, Keith Richards' personal assistant at this point, claimed Pallenberg was "obsessed with black magic" and performed rituals and spells.[65]

Adding to the Stones' dark reputation at this period in the late 1960s was the tragic drowning death of Brian Jones in July 1969, just a few months before Altamont. Jones died about a month after he had been expelled from the band, at the age of 27, just like one of his heroes, the blues guitarist Robert Johnson. Fellow band members Richards and Jagger were also fascinated with Johnson, and would go on to record Rolling Stones' versions of Johnson's "Love in Vain" for their 1969 album *Let it Bleed*, and "Stop Breakin' Down Blues" (as "Stop Breaking Down") for their 1972 album *Exile on Main St.* Richards recalls his first exposure to Johnson through the *King of the Delta Blues Singers* album: "I was astounded at what I heard. It took guitar playing, songwriting, delivery, to a totally different height".[66] Johnson was, of course, known not only for his music but also for the legend that he sold his soul to the devil at a crossroads in return for his musical gifts. It was likely this pact that "Detroit Annie" made reference to in the *Berkeley Tribe* just after Altamont: "Mick and the boys, you see, have signed this pact with the devil: First of all, they get the Power — just enough to pull off a few pranks and fantasies — have some fun, you understand. But don't waste your sympathy on the devil. He ain't trustworthy".[67]

However, the Stones (and those close to them) would later deny that there was anything serious in their passion for the occult in this period. Mick Jagger pointed out, for example, that "Sympathy for the Devil" "was only one song... It wasn't like it was a whole album, with lots of occult signs on the back".[68] Marianne Faithfull also reiterated this, claiming Jagger and Richards were "utterly contemptuous of... satanic hocus pocus". Instead of being a disciple of Satan, Faithfull describes Jagger as a "devotee of satin", someone "far too sensible and normal ever to have got seriously involved with black magic". She claims "Sympathy for the Devil" was "pure pápier-mâché satanism".[69] Prince Rupert Lowenstein, the band's long-time financial advisor, agreed with Faithful. He opined: "As a committed Catholic, to be working so closely with the Rolling Stones, a band who had recorded a song called 'Sympathy for the Devil' and released an album called *Their Satanic Majesties Request*, might seem to pose a dilemma, but I always felt that the public perception of the band was somewhat skewed... The church... sees Jagger as a purveyor of satanified obscenity, which is not so: the group has always been saucy but not satanic. A Halloween pumpkin satanism".[70] From people who knew the Stones intimately then, the Stones' dalliance with the dark side was just that; a harmless dabble into "pumpkin satanism". Nevertheless, these rebuttals were made years after the fact: at the time Altamont took place, this connection between the Stones and the occult — much like Johnson and the "crossroads legend" — was solidly established.

When reporting on Altamont, both the underground and mainstream U.K. and U.S. press were buzzing with claims that the festival had been a kind of rock-music "ritual of death" ceremony. For example, Thomas Klaber of the *Berkeley Barb* claimed, "There are a few who swear that what they saw at Altamont was a Ritual Death — a human sacrifice for His Satanic Majesty, Mick Jagger". Klaber then cites an audience member named "Eagle" who claimed Hunter's death was "planned and executed by the Hells Angels and Mick Jagger as a 'Black Mass' ritual murder to give Jagger 'satisfaction'".[71] Writing in the *New York Times*, Albert Goldman echoed this view, calling Jagger the "Prince of Darkness", and similarly opined that Hunter's death bore a striking resemblance to a "ritual murder".[72] Todd Gitlin of *The Spectator* also made reference to diabolic rituals, claiming: "The Stones copy the form of the Black Mass, which is celebrated human sacrifice".[73] Likewise, Andy Gordon, who was an eye-witness to events at Altamont, referred to Hunter's death as a "blood sacrifice" and to Jagger as the "the prince of darkness leading his black mass".[74] David Goodman, another eye-witness who was in the crowd at the front of the stage, seems to corroborate Jagger's alleged complicity in Hunter's death. Goodman claims: "Jagger was really into the whole thing. Like the cat getting killed... He could have stopped it if he'd wanted to".[75] Leonard Brown from the *Los Angeles Free Press,* also talked of "The demonic revelation of Altamont, with its implications of ritual sacrifices".[76] In that same organ, Gene Youngblood spoke of his "realization that the Stones actually are evil as their image" and of the "demonic aura that is unmistakable Mick Jagger".[77] Mary Strong opined in *NOLA Express* that the Stones "wrap themselves in evil cloaks".[78] As reported in the *Berkeley Tribe*, another festival attendee screamed at the stage, "Christ died on the cross. Mick Jagger is the devil".[79] Indeed, *Berkeley Tribe* reporters could not resist making supernatural references to explain events at the festival: for instance, George Paul Csicsery claimed that the role of the Hells Angels was to protect Mick Jagger, "their diabolic prince".[80] Another claimed that "300,000 people went to Altamont "to see if Mick Jagger embodies the rough beast, rocking and rolling toward Bethlehem to be born".[81] And in a *Rag* review of the documentary *Gimme Shelter*, the reviewers make reference to the "insane, demonic intensity and fury" of "Under My Thumb", the song the Stones played as Hunter was killed.[82] According to *Rolling Stone* magazine, even Jagger's clothes were infused with evil: they describe his attire as a "demonic orange and black satin cape/robe" which somehow "gleamed wickedly" while he performed onstage.[83]

Contemporary reports on Altamont were thus awash with claims that Jagger was the devil in human form. Andy Gordon, for example, turned to classical literature to describe Altamont, quoting from John Milton's *Paradise Lost* in a section of Jonathan Eisen's book *Altamont* entitled "Satan and the Angels at Altamont". Also in the *East Village Other*, Lloyd Steel describes the scene as the Hells Angels attacked Hunter: "the music was loud and the devil screamed from the stage".[84] Don MacLean's epic song-poem "American Pie" (1971) blames Jagger, not the Hells Angels, for Hunter's death at Altamont, with Jagger portrayed as Satan casting a murderous spell from the stage. San Francisco music critic Joel Selvin claimed, "Jagger wanted to be filmed strutting the stage as the emissary of the Dark Lord".[85] Timothy Leary, in an interview with the Berkeley Barb, called Jagger the "great Satanic figure".[86] If the Stone's fans and musical peers made these diabolic connections, it is no surprise that Christian groups also saw the Stones as a force for evil. Winding his way through a ten-mile traffic queue to get to Altamont, Andy Gordon was handed a leaflet accusing the Stones of "collusion with the forces of Lucifer: chaos, anarchy, and revolution". The leaflet was signed, "Christian World Liberation Front".[87] Other commentators also pointed out that it was not just the Stones themselves that seemed to convey this demonic aura: the Stones may have been the ones at the sacrificial table of the stage, but to Grateful Dead musician Jerry Garcia the crowd was awash with devil-worshipers too. In an interview in the *East Village Other*, for example, Garcia claimed walking through that crowd "was like going through the circles of Dante's Inferno".[88]

Some critics made the connection between the Stones and Robert Johnson as a cause for the festival's dark tone: a few suggested, more convincingly, that Stones' set was saturated with references to violence, death and suffering. For example, as well as Johnson's "Love in Vain" and the now-notorious "Sympathy for the Devil" (in which Jagger identifies with Satan), the Stones' setlist for Altamont seemed designed to be deliberately provocative. For example, they performed songs such as: "Midnight Rambler", a song about the Boston Strangler; "Under My Thumb", a blatantly misogynistic track; "Gimme Shelter", with its dark themes of war and violence; "Street Fighting Man", which was inspired by the 1969 street protests in London and Paris; "Stray Cat Blues", about a man lusting after an underage girl;[89] and "Brown Sugar", a song about race, slavery, sex, and rape. In reviewing *Gimme Shelter* (1970) for *The Rag*, Mike Saunders claimed: "Any band that pleads with the crowd to cool it, and then goes into "Under My Thumb", is practically asking to get offed [sic] themselves".[90] Not all critics agreed however. In his review of the Altamont concert film, *Rolling Stone* magazine journalist Lester Bangs warned against blaming the Stones' music for what happened. Bangs said, "It has become fashionable lately to lay most of the blame for Altamont… as the inevitable product of music like 'Midnight Rambler' and 'Sympathy for the Devil,' but *Gimme Shelter* seems to reveal them in a more realistic light, as the pawns of circumstance equally as confused and bemused as anyone in their audience".[91]

Moreover, instead of one of the "supernatural" songs that Robert Johnson wrote and performed, the Stones chose instead one of his more innocuous tracks, "Love in Vain". It is essentially a love song about a relationship in trouble, with the male protagonist left watching from the station platform while his partner leaves on a train. Greil Marcus called "Love in Vain" one of those Johnson songs that is a "two-minute image of doom that has the power to make doom a fact".[92] In this piece about Johnson, however, Marcus, tends towards the hyperbolic. More judiciously, Elijah Wald adjudges the song (as recorded by Johnson) romantic, beautiful, sad, and mournful.[93] Furthermore, in both the recorded version of the song on *Let it Bleed*, and in live performances on their 1969 U.S. Tour, the Stones performed it at a slower tempo than Johnson's original version, and on those live shows "Love in Vain" serves as a lull in the frantic pace of the set — a breathing space for both the onstage performers and the crowd. Wald claimed that the Stones "were giving a demonstration of a music they loved, showing their audience how the blues used to sound in the old days, before returning to the roar and clash of the present".[94]

Yet the connection between the Stones and Johnson's demonic legend existed, and was in fact encouraged by the band and then, as we've seen, the press. Furthermore, the disturbing tone set by songs such as "Midnight Rambler", "Under My Thumb", "Gimme Shelter", and the other aforementioned songs they performed at Altamont, helped form an image of the band as controversial, on the edge, dark, and dangerous. This is what the audience came to see, not necessarily the acoustic pop-rock stylings of Crosby, Stills, Nash and Young, or the country-rock of The Flying Burrito Brothers, but instead the dark and dangerous rhythm and blues of the "greatest rock 'n' roll band in the world". With "Midnight Rambler", they wanted to hear Jagger sing about a serial killer and to watch him slam his studded belt onto the stage in an attempt to whip the crowd into a frenzy. "Street Fighting Man" allowed them to connect vicariously with the violent protests that inspired the song. And in "Brown Sugar" they were introduced to a new song in which Jagger takes pleasure at the prospect of interracial rape and other misogynist violence. Whether this instigated aggression or was instead cathartic is impossible to adjudge: certainly, there were other more tangible and more convincing reasons for Altamont's violence — and a particular song or songs probably didn't convince Hells Angels to beat people with pool cues — but, as we've seen, many commentators noted the audience's dark mood, especially when contrasted with the Woodstock crowd's harmonious reputation. In any event, the Angels were as likely to direct their violent energy towards Jagger, as they did with Jefferson Airplane's Marty Balin, so they weren't taking their lead from the Stones' music or Jagger's reputation. The *Berkeley Tribe* offered a levelheaded conclusion as to these events: "The Midnight Rambler lives in each of us. That's so obvious it's trite. Jagger didn't invent rape, and doesn't sing about it to promote it. He sings about it because it IS. I'm convinced that Jagger knows it is more dangerous to shut out those deep passions than it is to acknowledge them".[95]

The Hell-raising Stones: the bad boys of British Rock

Yet even all this — the Stones' dalliance with demonic imagery and occultism, their love-affair with American blues music and lore, and the strong Johnson-Stones "crossroads legend" connection made by many commentators at the time — still only tells part of the story of why Altamont became remembered for its violence. The other part of the story is simply that the Rolling Stones was a controversial band whose appearances often led to violence, and whose public image was closely associated with danger. In short, long before their interest in "the demonic", they had already become known as the "bad boys" of British rock.

As is well known, the Stones began as a cover band, playing mostly American rock and blues songs like "Route 66", "Time Is on My Side", "It's All Over Now", "Susie Q", "Little Red Rooster", and "Get Off of My Cloud". However, from their album *Aftermath* (1966) onwards, the Jagger/Richards writing partnership dominated. This was partly due to their natural evolution as musicians and partly an attempt to emulate the Lennon and McCartney writing partnership that proved so successful for The Beatles. In fact, these intensely rival bands matured at roughly the same time: 1964-65 was the era of "Beatlemania" in which The Beatles had twelve successive number one hits[96], the majority of these being simple love songs (which owed a great debt to 1950s' rock stars such as Buddy Holly and The Everly Brothers). Beatles concerts were frenetic affairs, during which neither the band nor the audience could hear much of the music. However, in 1966 the Beatles stopped touring to concentrate on albums. They broke new ground from 1965-67 with critically acclaimed albums like *Rubber Soul* and *Revolver*, which were notable for musical experimentation and more advanced lyrical compositions. In a similar vein, the Stones also began to produce their own original work. They were usually just a step behind the Beatles though, and when they released *Their Satanic Majesties Request* in December 1967, some critics saw its psychedelic themes as derivative of the Beatles' well-received *Sgt. Pepper's Lonely Hearts Club Band*, which had been released earlier that year in June of 1967.[97]

In the early 1960s, the Stones were a kind of bad-ass mirror image of clean cut Beatles: as Maureen Cleave wrote in the *Evening Standard,* "Just when we'd got our pop singers looking neat and tidy and, above all, cheerful, along come the Rolling Stones".[98] The Stones' rough and roguish image took a number of forms, and was manifest in their music, in how audiences reacted to the band, and in the behaviour of band members. In their music, the Stones took on dark themes. In 1965, for example, the track, "Play With Fire" is about a relationship between a man and a high society woman, wherein the man warns her to watch her step in how she treats him, or else; in a similar vein, also from that same album, the lyrics of "Under My Thumb" suggest strong animosity towards women, with derogatory lyrics about control and objectification. *Between the Buttons* (1967) features the songs "Let's Spend the Night Together", which seemed designed to provoke outrage among the prudish, and the more experimental track "Ruby Tuesday" was a song about a groupie. *Beggars Banquet* (1968) was somewhat of a return to their blues-rock roots, after the relative failure of *Their Satanic Majesties Request*, and it features songs such as "Sympathy for the Devil" and "Street Fighting Man". "Sympathy for the Devil", featuring a hypnotic samba beat, provoked accusations of Satanism, and "'Street Fighting Man", which was inspired by Jagger's attendance at an anti-war rally in London, was banned by Chicago radio after the riots at the Democratic Convention. "Gimme Shelter", which features on the 1969 album *Let It Bleed*, seemed to be about the Vietnam War, and expressed general unease about modern society's tendency towards violence. Also from *Let it Bleed*, "Midnight Rambler" is about serial killer Albert De Salvo, the so-called "Boston Strangler", who attacked, raped and terrorised women in the Boston area in the early 1960s.

If the Stones' lyrics explored dark themes of misogyny, violence, sex, orgies and politics, then their concerts were similarly controversial: "physical violence. That's the kind of trouble we get into", Jagger told Stanley Booth in 1969.[99] He was not exaggerating. Their first U.K. tour began in October 1963 and, as Rich Cohen points out, their shows "became increasingly chaotic, even violent, as the Stones gained fame".[100] The Stones began the tour at the bottom of the bill, but as Keith Richards recollects, within six weeks they had girls screaming in the audience to the point where no one could hear the music. Richards reflects: "We got bigger and bigger and more and more crazy, until basically all we thought about was how to get into a gig and how to get out... The only question was how it would end, with a riot, with the cops breaking it up, with too many medical cases".[101]

Yet in these early tours, it was largely a case of too many female fans trying to get close to the band, and perhaps grab a souvenir. Future tours would see male violence of a different type and intensity: for instance, Ian Stewart, the Stones' keyboard player and road manager, told Stanley Booth that at a gig at the Empress Ballroom in Blackpool in July 1964, there was a bad atmosphere caused by a group of aggressive males in the audience who had an "anti-Stones thing going on". When someone in the audience spat on Keith Richards, the guitarist kicked out at him, which incited a riot. The Stones were ushered quickly from the stage while the police dealt with the troublemakers. Afterwards, the band discovered that most of their onstage equipment had been destroyed.[102] Four thousand pounds worth of damage was caused to the arena and Blackpool Council banned the Stones from playing there again. In addition, the bill for damages caused by the Stones gig at the Palace Theatre in Paris that year amounted to £1400. This was proving to be an expensive tour, but the value to their reputation as the "anti-Beatles" more than compensated for some financial losses.

From that point onwards, trouble at concerts was almost a trademark of the Stones. At their gig at the Adelphi Theatre in Dublin on September 3, 1965, for example, crowd frenzy reached such proportions that about a dozen fans jumped on stage and wrestled with band members.[103] The following year in 1966 hundreds of fans stormed the stage at their first gig at the Royal Albert Hall.[104] Keith Richards was thrown to the stage floor and Jagger grappled with fans, while Jones and Wyman took to their heels. Bouncers and members of the Stones' entourage ran onto the stage to help and order was only restored when it was announced that the concert would be abandoned unless the stage was cleared.[105] It was the same everywhere the band went. At a gig in at the Kurhaus in Scheveningen, Holland on August 8, 1964, fans rioted and the concert was cut short. Their stadium concert at Ratcliffe, Fresno U.S.A. on May 22, 1965 had to be abandoned when fans stormed the stage. The Stones entered and left the stadium in an armoured car.

Such was the Stones' reputation at that point that when they played in Münster, Germany on September 11, 1965, armed British and Dutch military police provided support for local police. Water cannons were on hand in case of crowd trouble. Thankfully, that did not materialise. However, four days later, at the Waldbühne ampitheatre in Berlin, crowd trouble did erupt: the Stones' concert there had to be abandoned after fans once again climbed on to the stage (fans then fought police, and badly damaged the venue).

Typically, it was fans' attraction to the Stones which led to trouble rather than any attempt to cause serious physical harm. Disorder and sometimes violence usually involved fans invading the stage, throwing things at the band, damaging equipment or furnishings, or chasing after the band when they tried to exit the venue. In the process, fans would get hurt and the police also often suffered injuries as they attempted to keep order. Such offstage activities matched the Stones onstage persona. Their co-manager Andrew Loog Oldham called it "Aggressive… they don't play nice-mannered music; it's raw and masculine".[106] Stanley Booth maintains that it was "Part of the Stones charm was that they lived in an atmosphere of danger, and one came near them at one's own peril".[107] While there is a degree of truth in these comments, in retrospect, Booth and Oldham have omitted an important reason for the Stones' notorious reputation. In the context of the time period, they represented not just a rowdy "anti-Beatles" rock band, but they were also staunchly anti-authoritarian and anti-Establishment: the Stones' wore their rebellious, violent image like an epaulet of honour.

In his book *1965: The Most Revolutionary Year in Music*, Andrew Grant Jackson makes the case that the Stones were both part of, and also representative of, the changes that were taking place in the 1960s. To provide just one instance of this, Jackson claims that Jagger's androgynous image helped kick start the gay rights movement. Jagger's demeanour, his long hair, his stage moves, and the way he spoke in a slightly camp and effeminate English accent, made Jagger attractive to men as well as women. For Jackson, rock stars like Jagger were "walking science experiments for the wholesale reconsideration of values in Western society: which limits were worth breaking (racism, sexual repression, homophobia) and which perhaps made sense (restrictions against harder drugs)".[108] Moreover, it was not just Jagger in the band who attracted male attention; Richards and Jones were also targets of male lust. For example, at the Royal Albert Hall gig, when fans invaded the stage, one young man took the opportunity to kiss Keith Richards before security managed to throw him back into the audience. Indeed, Peter Whitehead, who filmed that gig, and another in Dublin a short time later, believes repressed homosexuality helps explain at least some of the violence at Stones concerts: he claims "those boys who get up on that stage, they want to kiss Mick Jagger and Brian Jones, but when they get there they feel so damned silly, they don't know what to do, so they hit them".[109] To further confuse their fans, and perhaps also outrage society's "squares", the whole band posed in drag for the U.S. cover of their 1966 single "Have You Seen Your Mother, Baby, Standing in the Shadow?" At the time, Richards claimed, "The photograph was just a laugh. There's no deeper interpretation to be placed on it than that", but it is unlikely the band would not have anticipated the implications of its impact.[110]

The off-stage behaviour of band members also contributed to the band's notorious reputation, particularly their disdain for the countless petty rules and regulations that governed everyday life, their run-ins with law enforcement, and their use of recreational drugs, all of which meant they were rarely out of the headlines and often in court. Stanley Booth points to 1969 as the year the Stones started taking drugs seriously, or more serious drugs, to help them cope with touring schedules.[111] The main exception to this was Brian Jones, who developed a serious drug habit (which negatively affected his song writing, playing, and availability for concerts and media appearances) much earlier. It is likely his use of harder drugs began when he started dated

Anita Pallenberg in 1965; Richards claimed that is when Jones began taking LSD.[112] Jones was arrested twice for drugs possession, in May 1967 and again in May 1968, and well-publicised court cases made the public aware of his drug problems.

It was, however, the infamous Redlands drug bust that established the reputation of the Stones as both stoned hell raisers and sexual deviants. In brief, this was when the West Sussex police raided Richards' house, Redlands, while a party was going on; they had been tipped off by a member of the public who was quite possibly a *News of the World* journalist. The paper had the band under constant surveillance after Jagger sued them for an earlier story which attributed to him a quote wherein he admitted smoking marijuana and taking speed.[113] No one offered any resistance while the police searched the house. At one point a policewoman asked Marianne Faithful to go upstairs so she could be searched. Faithfull had just had a bath and had only a rug wrapped around her. As she moved towards the stairs, she briefly lowered the rug, giving everyone a glimpse of her nude figure. The police found little of interest — some cannabis resin and a few pills. They missed an entire suitcase full of drugs that dealer David Schneiderman brought to the party, some of which had been ingested earlier by Jagger and Richards. However, art dealer Robert Fraser was found in possession of heroin jacks, tiny white pills which dissolved in water in preparation for injection. Jagger, Richards and Fraser were charged with various drug offences. The Stones pleaded not guilty and elected for a jury trial. Fraser admitted his guilt and was sentenced to six months in gaol. The trials of Jagger and Richards took place in July and both were found guilty, with Jagger given a six month sentence and Richards a year. They were both sent to prison until their appeals were heard a few days later. On appeal, Richards' sentence was overturned and Jagger was given a conditional discharge instead of imprisonment.

The impact and significance of Redlands goes far beyond the rather tame sequence of events — a peaceful drug raid, dignified trials, and short sentences which were, in any event, overturned on appeal. In fact, these events symbolised the changes happening in British society, and the challenge of the new order to the old. That everything unfolded in public did much to cement the Stones' notorious image. In reporting this story, the British press routinely sensationalised an event that was in reality very polite and good-humoured. During the trial, a headline in the *London Evening News* screamed "NAKED GIRL AT STONES PARTY" and rumours soon began that when the police burst in (they didn't: they knocked the front door and entered when Richards opened it and invited them in) Jagger was engaged in a lurid sexual act with Faithfull (known as Miss X in newspaper reports) involving a item of confectionary; although this was untrue, it became the stuff of legend, and while Jagger and Richards were set free, Faithfull was tried in the press and the court of public opinion, found guilty, and given a life sentence of having to endure endless smutty innuendo about her character and morals.

How did the Stones' respond to their brush with the law? Jagger was shocked at his sentence and at having to spend a night in gaol before his appeal was to be heard; Richards endured it more phlegmatically. Onlookers and fans admired how they conducted themselves in court. When asked by the prosecutor if he thought Faithfull's behavior was "normal", Richards replied, "We are not old men. We are not worried about petty morals".[114] This seemed to offer the clearest summation yet of the yawning gap between 1960s' youth and the older generation. The Stones' musical peers offered solidarity: for example, The Who issued a press release announcing that they would release a single containing covers of two Stones' songs "The Last Time" and "Under My Thumb". They declared that the Stones were scapegoats for the drug problem and these songs would help keep the Stones in the public eye until such time as the band was able to record again.[115] Supportive articles appeared in London-based underground magazines such as *International Times* and *Oz*.[116] And street protests were held outside the *News of the World*"s offices in London. The Stones won not only their court appeals but a new coolness factor. They took on the establishment and won. “Before Redlands they were a great band”, Cohen notes. “After Redlands, they were the dark lords of rock ‘n’ roll”.[117]

Long before Altamont then, the Stones had a notorious reputation, but the violence at their concerts consisted mainly of stage invasions by over-excited boys and girls, or were the result of crowd control issues at the entrances and exits of the concert venues. As we saw in the previous chapter, Hells Angels dealt with potential stage invasions in a much more violent way than did British “bobbies” (police) or venue security in the U.K. Furthermore, the Stones’ devilish interests weren’t really taken seriously in Britain, as Marianne Faithfull’s aforementioned comment about Jagger being a devotee of satin rather than Satan attests to. It was only when the Stones toured the United States that their “Satanic” attribution was taken more seriously. We return then to the weird alchemy of people and circumstances that facilitates and encourages rumours of demonic pacts. If a President can be assassinated in a wicked criminal conspiracy (as many Americans believed), if a man could walk on the moon, if people like Charles Manson and the Hells Angels could exist, then it wasn’t difficult to believe that anything was possible, that strange, dark magic was afoot and that demons might be walking the Earth. Jagger deliberately molded himself into a polysemic figure — a jester, magician, sex symbol, and trickster — but he thought it was just showbiz: an odd and amusing part of his rock and roll lifestyle that he could discard when it bored him. However, at Altamont people took him seriously, and at a terrible cost.

Conclusion

That so many commentators turned to the supernatural to explain Altamont is, therefore, rooted in a combination of circumstances, not least the Stones’ association with diabolic forces, their strong musical bond with Robert Johnson and their reputation for violence. Just as Paginini’s demonic image was created by the press and by rumours about his hedonistic lifestyle, the Stones’ off-stage activities fuelled interest in such rumours. Like Paginini, the Stones cultivated an emaciated appearance, to the extent that Ian Stewart was expelled from the band because he did not look as thin as everyone else; and also like Paginini, they grew their hair long, wore tight-fitting trousers, and had multiple sexual partners. They played the blues with passion and skill, citing Robert Johnson as a hero. And when they started writing songs about the Devil and about serial killers, the stars had aligned to facilitate the “imaginary dark world of the Stones” coming to life at Altamont.[118]

The Stones were, however, shocked by what happened at Altamont, and after the festival, they toned down their rebellious image to a degree, and shifted to one that was more slick, funny, and camp. The dark forces that seemed to surround them became, as Prince Rupert Lowenstein asserted, akin to Halloween tomfoolery. Interestingly, soon after, other bands exploited the occult to better effect: Black Sabbath, Alice Cooper, and, to an extent, Jimmy Page, boosted their careers by associating themselves with occult and demonic forces. And in the late 1970s and into the 1980s, heavy metal bands such as Dio, Ozzy Osbourne and Iron Maiden took this imagery to a level unimagined and surely unattainable by the Stones. So when, in 1972, the Stones released the album *Exile on Main St.*, their cover of Robert Johnson’s “Stop Breakin’ Down Blues” created no special attention. And when the track “Dancing with Mr D” appeared on their album *Goats Head Soup* the following year, its supernatural themes and lyrics about voodoo, death, graveyards and skulls caused barely a raised eyebrow. While the commercial benefit of the occult was still apparent, everyone was now in on the act.

Consequently, when the *Berkeley Barb* reviewed a Stones’ show at the San Francisco Winterland Ballroom in 1972, they wrote: “Being demonic is a business, like anything else. Jagger does it, carefully, conscientiously, with enormous energy, like the very professional, conscientious artist he is. And what’s more surprising is that... people really don’t expect much more than that... The Rolling Stones... are just another rock band bigger and better, but just musicians. The Stones figured this out some time ago, and made their peace with it".[119] On their 1972 American tour, the demonic energy had dissipated from the Stones' setlist. They played "Love in Vain", "Midnight Rambler" (and the rather odious "Brown Sugar", which had its live debut at Altamont but was not released until 1971 when it appeared on the album *Sticky Fingers*), but as the *Berkeley Barb* review notes, just 30 months after Altamont, no one took any special note of these songs' dark reputations. "Sympathy for the Devil" was, though, notably absent from the band's 1972 tour set list. Wrongly attributed as the song that played while Meredith Hunter was killed at Altamont (that was, in fact, "Under My Thumb"), the Stones had been badly burnt by its reputation and did not want to repeat that experience. Jagger quoted Nietzsche in the film *Performance* (1970). Perhaps he was aware also of Nietzsche's warning: "if thee gaze long into an abyss, the abyss will also gaze into thee".[120]

[1] Robert Greenfield, "The Rolling Stone Interview: Keith Richards". *Rolling Stone*, Aug 19, 1971. http://www.rocksbackpages.com/Library/Article/the-irolling-stonei-interview-keith-richards

[2] "Gimme Shelter", *Great Speckled Bird*, Vol 4, Issue 18, May 3, 1971, p. 19.

[3] Greil Marcus, *Mystery Train: Images of America in Rock 'n' Roll Music. Fourth edition* (London: Penguin, 1991), p. 21

[4] For example, as well as musical tributes, the Johnson Crossroads legend has generated storylines and plot twists in numerous film and television scripts, and in popular literature. The 1986 movie *Crossroads* showed the Johnson legacy was compelling enough to warrant a full-length feature film, and in a particularly memorable scene a young guitarist — who had been mentored by Johnson's friend and fellow Delta Blues musician Willie Brown — takes part in a duel with a demonic figure. In the popular film *O Brother, Where Art Thou?* (2000) the character Tommy Johnson is a blues guitarist who is picked up by the "Soggy Bottom Boys" while hitchhiking. He claims to have sold his soul to the devil in exchange for his skill on the guitar. He shares his name and story with Tommy Johnson, a blues musician with a mysterious past, who is said to have sold his soul to the devil at the Crossroads (a story more often attributed to Robert Johnson). The American television series *Supernatural* (2005-) retells the Johnson legend in an episode from 2006 entitled "Crossroad Blues"; in the television series *Timeless* (2016-18) features Johnson in an episode entitled "King of the Delta Blues". Johnson appears as himself in Sherman Alexie's 1995 novel *Reservation Blues* (1995). A final indicative example is J.M. Dupont's *Love in Vain* (2016), which tells the Johnson story in the form of an illustrated graphic novel.

[5] Ben Arnold, ed., *The Liszt Companion* (Westport, CT: Greenwood, 2002), p. 270.

[6] Robert Riggs, *The Violin* (Rochester: Uni of Rochester Press, 2016), p. 16

[7] Riggs, *The Violin*, p. 18.

[8] Stephen Davis, *Hammer of the Gods: Led Zeppelin Unauthorised* (London: Pan, 2006), p. 6.

[9] Maiko Kawabata, "Virtuosity, the Violin, the Devil ... What Really Made Paganini 'Demonic'?" *Current Musicology*, 83 (2007), pp. 85-108. At pp. 87-88.

[10] Riggs, *The Violin*, p. 19.

[11] Davis, *Hammer of the Gods*, p. 6.

[12] Riggs, *The Violin*, p. 20.

[13] Charles White, *The Life and Times of Little Richard* (London: Omnibus, 2003), p. 206.

[14] Slaves transported to America were from different cultures and spoke many languages, but slave-owners required them to abandon their belief systems and learn English. There is, though, some consensus that the slaves retained some aspects of their heritage, for example in the design of domestic materials, in funeral rites, music, and religion. The latter two categories are most relevant to this discussion: in the early colonial period both slaves and colonists resisted the attempts of wandering preachers to bring Christianity to the slaves. By the middle of the Eighteenth Century however, slaves had become more receptive to Christian teachings. Often this was for practical reasons: it gave slaves the opportunity to meet not under the gaze of their slave masters. It also gave them the opportunity to learn to read and write, which were valuable tools in resisting slavery. For their part, slave-owners began to see the potential benefits of religion as a method of controlling and pacifying slaves.

[15] Elijah Wald, *Escaping the Delta: Robert Johnson and the Invention of the Blues* (New York: Amistad, 2005), p. 271. As Ayana Smith notes, Elegua "exists under different names in many West African cultures and throughout the Americas, including Legba, Exú, Echu-Elegua, Papa Legba, and Papa La Bas". See "Blues, criticism, and the signifying trickster", *Popular Music* Vol 24, Issue 2, (2005), pp. 179-191. At p. 184.

[16] Adam Gussow, *Beyond the Crossroads: The Devil and the Blues Tradition* (Chapel Hill: University of North Carolina Press, 2017), p. 12.

[17] Harry Middleton Hyatt, *Folk-Lore from Adams County Illinois* (New York: Alma Egan Hyatt Foundation. 1935), p. 455.

[18] Paul Garon, *The Devil's Son-in-Law: The Story of Peetie Wheatstraw and His Songs* (Chicago: Charles H. Kerr, 2003), p. 32.

[19] David Evans, *Big Road Blues: Tradition and Creativity in the Folk Blues* (Berkeley and Los Angeles: University of California Press, 1982), p. 115.

[20] Patricia R. Schroeder, *Robert Johnson, Mythmaking, and Contemporary American Culture* (Urbana and Chicago: University of Illinois Press, 2004), p. 27.

[21] Pete Welding, "Hell Hound on his Trail: Robert Johnson", *Downbeat Music '66* (Chicago: Maher, 1966), pp. 73-74, 76, 103. At p. 76.

[22] Wald, *Escaping the Delta*, p. 275.

[23] Marybeth Hamilton, "Sexuality, Authenticity and the Making of the Blues Tradition", *Past & Present* 169 (2000), pp. 132–160. At p. 136.

[24] Terry H. Anderson, *The Sixties*. Second edition. (Pearson Longman, 2004), pp. 1-18.

[25] Richard Crawford, *America's Musical Life: A History* (New York & London: Norton, 2005), p. 745.

[26] Jim O'Neal, "I Once Was Lost, But Now I'm Found: The Blues Revival of the 1960s" in *Nothing but the Blues: the Music and the Musicians*, edited by Lawrence Cohn (New York: Abbeville Press, 1993), pp. 347-387. At p.378.

[27] O'Neal, "I Once Was Lost", p. 363.

[28] Hamilton, "Sexuality, Authenticity", p. 134.
[29] Wald, *Escaping the Delta*, p. xiv.
[30] Bob Dylan, *Chronicles*. Vol. 1 (New York: Simon and Schuster, 2005), p. 280.
[31] Dylan, *Chronicles*, p. 281.
[32] Dylan, *Chronicles*, p. 282.
[33] Dylan, *Chronicles*, p. 283.
[34] Dylan, *Chronicles*, pp. 287-88.
[35] Robert Johnson, *The Complete Recordings* (Columbia, 1990), p. 22.
[36] Eric Clapton, Clapton: *The Autobiography* (New York: Broadway, 2007), p. 40.
[37] Marcus, *Mystery Train*, p. 34.
[38] Mick Wall, *When Giants Walked the Earth: a biography of Led Zeppelin* (London: Orion, 2009), p. 74.
[39] Steven Roby, ed., Hendrix on *Hendrix: Interviews and Encounters with Jimi Hendrix* (Chicago: Chicago Review Press, 2010), p. 6.
[40] Wald, *Escaping the Delta*, p. xv.
[41] Hamilton, "Sexuality, Authenticity", p. 160.
[42] Eric Lott, "Love and Theft: The Racial Unconscious of Blackface Minstrelsy", *Representations* 39 (1992), pp. 23-50.
[43] As Ulrich Adelt notes perceptively, to "take everything but the burden from Black culture". Ulrich Adelt, *Blues Music in the Sixties: A Story in Black and White* (New Brunswick, NJ: Rutgers University Press, 2010), p. 59.
[44] Rudi Blesh, *Shining* Trumpets (New York: A.A. Knopf, 1946), p. 121.
[45] Marcus, *Mystery Train*, p. 25.
[46] Keith Richards and James Fox, *Life* (London: Orion, 2012 [2010]), p. 105.
[47] Richards and Fox, *Life*, p. 163.
[48] Richards and Fox, *Life*, pp. 41-2
[49] Richards and Fox, *Life*, pp. 72-3.
[50] John Scanlon, *Easy Riders, Rolling Stones: In the Road in America from Delta Blues to '70s Rock* (London: Reaktion, 2015), p. 129.
[51] Thomas Thompson, "The Stones Blast Through The Land", *Life*, Vol 73, No 2, Jul 14, 1972, pp. 30-37. At p. 33.
[52] John Scanlon, *Easy Riders, Rolling Stones: In the Road in America from Delta Blues to '70s Rock* (London: Reaktion, 2015), p. 30.
[53] Craig Werner, A *Change is Gonna Come: Music, Race and the Soul of America* (Edinburgh: Canongate, 2002), p. 65.
[55] Jann S. Wenner, Phil Spector: The Rolling Stone Interview Nov 1, 1969.
Available online at: https://www.rollingstone.com/music/news/the-rolling-stone-interview-phil-spector-19691101
[55] Richards and Fox, *Life*, p. 122.
[56] Ralph Gleason, "Let's Spread the Goodies Around", *Rolling Stone* 32 (May 3, 1969), p. 22.
[57] "Festivals, 1969", *Great Speckled Bird*, Vol 2, Issue 19, Jul 21, 1969, p. 9.
[58] Richards and Fox, *Life*, p. 105.
[59] Hamilton, "Sexuality, Authenticity", pp. 156-7.
[60] Barret Hansen, "British bring the blues back to the US", *Los Angeles Free Press*, Vol 6, Issue 251-Part Two, May 9, 1969 pp. 45-47. At p. 45.
[61] O'Neal, "I Once Was Lost", p. 367.
[62] For some bands, their borrowings from blues music simply resulted in them carrying on the legends of old, particularly the trope of selling one's soul in return for success, wealth and fame. Others, though, deliberately chose the language of Satanic pacts themselves, either through simple hyperbole or descriptive metaphor: some had a genuine interest in the occult, the supernatural, or alternative forms of spirituality and others made a calculated effort to develop a Satanic image to increase interest in their work. In the first category is John Lennon, who in 1965 told fellow musician Tony Sheridan "I've sold my soul to the devil" (Ray Coleman, Lennon: *The Definitive Biography* (New York: McGraw-Hill, 1985), p. 256). A year later, Lennon claimed that The Beatles were "more popular than Jesus", a remark which caused uproar in some parts of the United States while the band toured there in August of 1966. The Beatles were further implicated in supposed anti-Christian activities when the image of English occult figure Aleister Crowley was included on the cover of the band's 1967 album *Sgt. Pepper's Lonely Hearts Club Band*. In the second category was Jimmy Page of Led Zeppelin. Page was an avid collector of Aleister Crowley books and memorabilia, and in 1971 he took his hobby as far as to buy Crowley's former residence in Scotland, Boleskine House. Page insisted that a Crowley mantra, "Do what thou wilt", should be etched in the vinyl run-off groove of side two of the album *Led Zeppelin III* (1970). However, it was Page's unusual, off-stage behavior that caused the biggest stir. Stephen Davis, author of an unauthorised biography of Led Zeppelin entitled *Hammer of the Gods*, retells lurid accounts from groupies of "invocations and gyromancy" which led to accusations that "Led Zeppelin sold their souls to the Devil in exchange for their instant success, their addictive charisma, their unbelievable wealth" (p. 2). David Bowie also had an interest in the occult, as well as ideas garnered from science fiction novels, and from New Age spirituality. Bowie mentioned both Aleister Crowley and the magical order to which he belonged, The Hermetic Order of the Golden Dawn, in the song "Quicksand", from Bowie's album *Hunky Dory* (1971), and went on to develop an otherworldly persona by way of his alter ego, Ziggy Stardust.
[63] Kawabata, "Virtuosity, the Violin, the Devil", p. 91.
[64] Marianne Faithfull and David Dalton, *Faithfull: An Autobiography* (New York: Rowman & Littlefield, 2000), p. 159.
[65] Tony Sanchez, *Up and Down With the Rolling Stones* (London: John Blake, 2010), p. 159.
[66] Richards and Fox, *Life*, p. 105.
[67] Detroit Annie, "You always get what you want", *Berkeley Tribe*, Vol 1, Issue 23, Dec 12-19, 1969, p. 5.
[68] Interview with Mikal Gilmore, *Rolling Stone*, Nov 5 - Dec 10, 1987. Reprinted in David Nathan and Susan Gedutis Lindsay, eds., *Inside the Hits* (Boston: Berklee, 2001), p. 227.
[69] Faithfull and Dalton, *Faithfull: An Autobiography*, p. 186.
[70] Prince Rupert Loewenstein. *A Prince Among Stones* (London: Bloomsbury, 2013), pp. 167-8.
[71] Thomas Klaber, "At his Satanic Majesty's Request", *Berkeley Barb*, Vol 9, Issue 23(226), Dec 12-18, 1969, p.3.
[72] Albert Goldman, "Movies", *New York Times*, Jan 3, 1971, p. D9.
[73] Todd Gitlin, "Woodstock West", *The Spectator*, Vol 9, Issue 13, Jan 7, 1970, pp. 7-9. At p. 9.
[74] Andy Gordon, "Satan and the Angels: Paradise Loused", in Jonathan Eisen, ed., *Altamont: Death of Innocence in Woodstock Nation* (New York: Avon, 1970), pp. 30-71.
[75] "The David Goodman Story", *International Times* 86, Aug 27 – Sep 10, 1970, pp. 7 & 10. At p. 10.
[76] Leonard Brown, "Jagger's Performance Devastating", *Los Angeles Free Press*, Vol 7, Issue 301, Apr 24-30, 1970, p. 8.
[77] Gene Youngblood, "Nasty Habits: A Nihilist Spasm Disguised As A Rolling Stones Record Review", *Los Angeles Free Press*, Vol 7, Issue 288 Part Two, Jan 23, 1970, p. 43.
[78] Mary Strong, "Give Me Shelter: who could hang a name on you", *NOLA Express*, Issue 82, Jun 3, 1971, p. 38.
[79] Anon. "Shake!", *Berkeley Tribe*, Vol 2, Issue 29, Jan 24-30. 1970, p. 17.
[80] George Paul Csicsery, "Stones Concert Ends It: America Now Up For Grabs", *Berkeley Tribe*, Vol 1, Issue 23, Dec 12-19, 1969, pp. 1 & 5. At p. 5.
[81] Anon. "Shake!", *Berkeley Tribe* Vol 2, Issue 29, Jan 24-30, 1970, p. 20.
[82] Mike Saunders *et al*., "Juke Box Jury: the Rolling Stones Gimme Shelter", *The Rag*, Vol 5, Issue 22, Apr 19, 1971, p. 4.
[83] Lester Bangs et al, "The Rolling Stones Disaster at Altamont: Let It Bleed", *Rolling Stone* 50, Jan 21, 1970.

[84] Lloyd Steele, "Woodstock or Woodschtick?", *East Village Other,* Vol 5, Issue 9, Feb 4, 1970, p. 17.
[85] Joel Selvin, *Altamont: The Rolling Stones, the Hells Angels, and the Inside Story of Rock's Darkest Day* (New York: HarperCollins, 2016), p. 317.
[86] "Leary Loves Rap", *Berkeley Barb,* Vol 9, Issue 25 (228), Dec 26 - Jan 1, 1969, pp. 3 & 10.
[87] Gordon, "Satan and the Angels", pp. 30-71.
[88] James Lichtenberg, "Dark Star", *East Village Other,* Vol 5, Issue 7, Jan 21, 1970, p. 9.
[89] In the recorded version of the song the girl is fifteen years old but on some live versions of the song on their 1969 American tour, for instance at the LA Forum, Jagger changed the girl's age to thirteen. See Jerry Hopkins, Jerry, "Kiss Kiss Flutter Flutter Thank You Thank You", *Rolling Stone*, Dec 13, 1969, pp. 1, 6, 54.
[90] Saunders *et al.*, "Juke Box Jury", p. 4.
[91] Lester Bangs, "Fractured at the Stones Flick: Wondering Where to Lay the Blame", *DOOR* Vol 2, Issue 21, Mar 17-31, 1971, pp. 13-14. At p. 14.
[92] Marcus, *Mystery Train,* p. 33.
[93] Wald, *Escaping the Delta*, p. 183.
[94] Wald, *Escaping the Delta,* p. 246.
[95] "Shake!", *Berkeley Tribe*, Vol 1, Issue 24, Dec 19-26, 1969, p. 18.
[96] These hits included "Please Please Me", "She Loves You", "I Want To Hold Your Hand", "Can't Buy Me Love", "A Hard Day's Night", "I Feel Fine", "Ticket to Ride", "Help!", "Day Tripper", "Paperback Writer", and 'Yellow Submarine'.
[97] An alternative point of view was presented by film maker Jean-Luc Godard. As Nora Alter points out, in February 1968, Godard "announced that the Rolling Stones were even more relevant than the Beatles. Pronouncing the Rolling Stones' 1968 album, *Their Satanic Majesties Request*, "very advanced", Godard explained during a panel discussion in Los Angeles that "The Rolling Stones are very important because they are popular and intellectual at the same time. That is good. That is what I am trying to do in the movies". See Nora M. Alter, "Composing in Fragments: Music in the Essay Films of Resnais and Godard", *Substance* Vol 41, No 2, Issue 128 (2012), pp. 24-38. At p. 33.
[98] Maureen Cleave, "The Rolling Stones: This Horrible Lot — Not Quite What They Seem", *Evening Standard*, Mar 21, 1964.
[99] Stanley Booth, *Dancing with the Devil: the Rolling Stones and their Times* (New York: Random House, 1984), p. 153.
[100] Rich Cohen, *The Sun & the Moon & the Rolling Stones* (London: Headline, 2016), p. 80.
[101] Richards and Fox, *Life*, p. 152.
[102] Booth, *Dancing with the Devil,* p. 159.
[103] See Charlie is my Darling*: Ireland 1965*. Dir. Peter Whitehead and Michael Gochanour. ABKCO, 2012.
[104] Barry Miles, "Pop... Pop... Ouch!" [The Rolling Stones/Ike & Tina Turner: Royal Albert Hall, London], *International Times,* Issue 1, Oct 14, 1966, p. 11.
[105] Norrie Drummond, "Dynamite! Ike & Tina Turner warm up the Albert Hall before the Stones set the stage alight" *New Musical Express,* Sep 30, 1966.
[106] Cleave, "The Rolling Stones: This Horrible Lot".
[107] Booth, *Dancing with the Devi*l, p. 160.
[108] Andrew Grant Jackson, *1965: The Most Revolutionary Year in Music* (New York: St. Martin's, 2015), pp. 214-15. At p. 282.
[109] Whitehead, qtd in Victor Coelho, "Through the Lens, Darkly: Peter Whitehead and The Rolling Stones", *Framework: The Journal of Cinema and Media*, Vol 52, No 1 (2011), pp. 170-191. At p. 179.
[110] Keith Altham, "The Rolling Stones: Stones Reveal Secrets", *New Musical Express*, Sep 23, 1966.
[111] Booth, *Dancing with the Devil*, p. 148.
[112] Richards and Fox, *Life*, p. 213.
[113] David Dalton, "Redlands: The Drug Bust of The Rolling Stones", *Gadfly*, May 1999.
[114] Richards and Fox, *Life*, p. 252.
[115] "Should we defend the Stones?" *Freedom Anarchist Weekly*, Vol 28, No 20, Jul 8, 1967, p. 1.
[116] "Time is on our side", *International Times* Vol 1, Issue 17, Jul 28 – Aug 13, 1967, p. 3; John Wilcox, "Jagger Saga", Oz 6, Aug 1967, p. 16.
[117] Cohen, *The Sun & the Moon & the Rolling Stones*, p. 157.
[118] Selvin, *Altamont*, p. 225.
[119] "Stones Cold: Whose Jig's Up? Jag's or Rock's?" *Berkeley Barb*, Vol 14, No 23, Issue 356, Jun 9-15, 1972, p. 5.
[120] Nietzsche, Friedrich Wilhelm. *Beyond Good and Evil: Prelude to a Philosophy of the Future*. Translated by Helen Zimmern. Vol 12 of *The Complete Works of Nietzsche*. 1923. Reprint, Forgotten Books, 2008, p. 54.

Chapter 6: Gimme Shelter: the Altamont movie

They're just trying to make it all seem like there was nothing they could do to stop the shit going on at Altamont. It's not at all a real representation of what happened

Sioux Shannon[1]

If critics had a field day pinning the blame for the violence at Altamont on the Rolling Stones in the aftermath of the festival, then the release of the concert documentary film *Gimme Shelter* gave them a second opportunity to pillory the band. In the wake of the film's release, criticisms came thick and fast: it was accused of distorting the portrayal of the death of Meredith Hunter, it was deemed exploitative, and it was lambasted for absolving the Stones of any guilt for events at Altamont. Moreover, as with the *Woodstock* film, critics also called for profits made from the film to be distributed to worthy causes such as Hunter's family, or to select charities. Another recurring, if perhaps more minor criticism was that fans had somehow been duped into becoming unwilling cast members in the concert film, and had become just another stakeholder like the Hells Angels who, they claimed, had been exploited by the Stones. *Rolling Stone* magazine said, for example, "It may surprise many of the people who suffered Altamont to discover that they were, in effect, unpaid extras in a full production color motion picture".[2] These disputes overshadowed the concert film, which is unfortunate because the film is a remarkable visual documentary about the Stones and fascinating window into the era.

Unlike the *Woodstock* movie, where the Woodstock Festival was the core subject of the film, *Gimme Shelter* was instead a documentary film about the Rolling Stones' 1969 American tour: therefore, only the second half of the film is devoted solely to Altamont. The idea of filming the tour first arose midway through it, after the plan for a free concert was announced in November 1969. This is an important point, because critics such as *Rolling Stone* magazine pointed to the fact that it was antagonism over the film distribution rights that had been responsible for the hastily rearranged change of venue from Sears Point to Altamont Speedway (as we recall, Filmways, the owners of Sears Point, wanted distribution rights for the concert film and had certain financial demands; the Stones and their management refused). *Rolling Stone* said: "the real reason for the free concert was to make a sort of *Woodstock West* movie. Jagger was eager for the movie to be rush-processed, edited as quickly as possible, and hurried into release to beat the real Woodstock film to the punch".[3] In fact, the plan to film the tour was made hastily, and without much thought or planning. The band missed an opportunity to appear at Woodstock, and they knew a Woodstock festival film was going to be released in 1970. Jagger, in particular, saw an opportunity for the Stones to release their own tour or concert film before the *Woodstock* film came out, and while memories of their own tour were still fresh. There was also money to be made: as we recall, the Stones were almost broke and a film could potentially be very profitable. But the Stones were artists too: they recognised the power of the medium and they had already dabbled in promotional films and movies. *Gimme Shelter* was an opportunity for publicity and profit, but also an outlet for their music and for visual creativity. So how did the movie come about? Who were the producers and stakeholders, and what kind of film did they strive to make? Equally important, what parts of the Altamont story did the producers want to flag up in the film, and what did they decide to leave out?

"Performance": the Stones on Screen

The Stones were not new to engagement with filmmakers and had appeared in concert movies and other films before. Their first was *Charlie Is My Darling* (1965), which had been directed by Peter Whitehead; almost a rehearsal for *Gimme Shelter,* this film follows the band's tour of Ireland, mixing concert footage with sequences of intimate, off-stage interactions (due to legal wrangling it was not released in its entirety until 2012). Whitehead also directed *Tonight Let's All Make Love in London* (1967), which was his effort to capture the essence of "swinging" London: in this film, a soundtrack by Pink Floyd is interspersed with interviews with Jagger, actress Julie Christie, and artist David Hockney, among others. The Stones also appeared in the French director Jean-Luc Godard's *One Plus One (Sympathy for the Devil)* in 1968. Dipping his toe into the cultural politics of the 1960s, Godard's film featured documentary footage of the Stones recording "Sympathy for the Devil" at Olympic Sound Studios, which he mixed with a montage of staged scenes with actors. Arguably, some of the fictional scenes in this film sit uneasily with the recording process. For example, the footage which documents how the song "Sympathy for the Devil" evolved from its early origins to the markedly different track that ended up on *Beggars Banquet*, is fascinating. In contrast, scenes relying on actors to depict the Black Panthers seem forced, and hopelessly out-of-touch with the culture Godard was commenting on. Reviewing it in the *East Village Other*, James Lichtenberg said, "it's really two movies, and neither of them come off".[4] Yet *One Plus One* does tell us something significant about the Stones. In his autobiography, Keith Richards expressed his dissatisfaction with Godard's approach; and when their manager Alan Klein saw the footage, he insisted the film's title be changed from *One Plus One* to *Sympathy for the Devil*. Without Godard's permission, some scenes were cut from the film, and the full album version of the song "Sympathy for the Devil" was added to the film's final scene.[5] Thus, *One Plus One* morphed from a film about left-wing politics to one that was really an extended advertisement for the Rolling Stones and their new album.

The Stones were also the core band in *Rock 'n' Roll Circus* (1968), directed by Michael Lindsay-Hogg. For this film, the band invited rock luminaries such as John Lennon, The Who, Jethro Tull, Eric Clapton, and Taj Mahal to perform. The film's theme of the circus top gave the artists space for visual expression, and an invited audience performed choreographed routines in costume (much like *Charlie Is My Darling, Rock 'n' Roll Circus* was not released until many years later). Jagger was particularly in demand for visual performances: he appeared in Kenneth Anger's *Invocation of My Demon Brother* (1969) and also composed and performed the score on a moog organ. All of these films are noteworthy due to the engagement of avant-garde filmmakers with the young and hip Stones.

The Stones also made some striking films to promote their record releases. For example, in 1966 they dressed as women for a short film to promote the 45 vinyl single "Have You Seen Your Mother, Baby, Standing In The Shadow?" Whitehead directed the promotional film for the band's 1967 single "We Love You", which depicts the 1895 trial of Oscar Wilde, and seems influenced by the Stones' arrest at Redlands and subsequent trial for drug offences. The band made two films in 1968 to promote their song "Jumpin' Jack Flash", the most interesting of which is a performance video with the band in heavy make-up. Jagger's face is illustrated with red, black and white stripes, a tribal design reminiscent of a Native American shaman (or perhaps a Hollywood version of same); Brian Jones' face is totally covered with silver make-up and he wears sun glasses with a bright green frame; Richards wears black bubble sun glasses; Bill Wyman wears white make-up; and Charlie Watts wear eye-liner and his forehead is adorned with a triangular symbol. The overall glam effect predates the glam scene by a few years. Michael Lindsay-Hogg directed a few promotional films for the band too, including "She's a Rainbow", "2000 Light Years From Home", "Child of the Moon" and "Angie". Of these, "2000 Light Years From Home" is the most interesting, with Jagger again in face paint, and with the film making use of coloured lighting for a psychedelic effect.

By the time of the Stones' 1969 American tour, the band therefore had experience of performing in promotional films, of acting in movie roles, of working on soundtracks, and in planning and staging performances. The Altamont concert film was a natural progression of their visual output, as well as an outlet for their colourful and exciting visual ideas.

Their Satanic Majesties Request: the Stones' and the Maysles Brothers

When it came to the idea of filming some of their 1969 U.S. tour, the driving force for a concert film seems to have been Jagger. The Stones travelled to the United States about a month before their first scheduled tour date; they wanted time to acclimatise, and they also hoped to cut some tracks at Muscle Shoals studio in Alabama. Jagger probably had it in mind to emulate acclaimed music documentaries such as *Don't Look Back* (1967), about Bob Dylan's 1965 English tour, and *Monterey Pop* (1968), which was the first festival film to secure a cinematic release. Jagger approached D.A. Pennebaker, who directed both of the aforementioned films, but Pennebaker turned down the offer. Jagger then approached Haskell Wexler, director of the acclaimed film *Medium Cool* (1969). However, Wexler also turned down the chance to work with the Stones. Wexler, however, recommended Albert and David Maysles. Albert Maysles had worked on *Monterey Pop*, and the brothers were developing a reputation for documentary film making; as we recall, they had turned down the offer to film the Woodstock Festival, but they were keen to meet the Stones.[6] Jagger met the Maysles brothers on November 26, with eleven of the seventeen tour dates already completed. The Maysles rushed to Baltimore to see that night's show, and although they missed most of it, they were impressed by what they saw of the Stones' performance and the excitement it engendered in the audience. The next day they signed a contract with Stones' business manager Ronnie Schneider and, remarkably, given the short time span, they began getting a team together to film the Stones' performance that same day at Madison Square Garden, New York City, footage of which would later appear on *Gimme Shelter*.

After the Madison Square Concert, the Maysles brothers understood they had completed their part of the agreement, which they believed was just to film the Stones in New York. However, when Jagger announced at a New York press conference that there would be a free concert in San Francisco in the first week of December, the filmmakers were intrigued: they tasked Stanley Goldstein, Albert Maysles' audio engineer at Madison Square Garden, to proceed to San Francisco to put together a film crew. They also contacted Baird Bryant, a Los Angeles-based filmmaker, with the same request. Meanwhile the Maysles travelled to Boston for the shows on November 29, to Florida for the Palm Beach Pop Festival, November 28-30, and they then followed the Stones to Muscle Shoals where they shot some footage from December 2-4 of the band recording new songs "Brown Sugar", "Wild Horses", and a cover of an old blues song called "You Got to Move". Maysles claims that it was at Muscles Shoals that he had final confirmation the free concert would go ahead at Altamont Speedway.[7] Such was the speed of events that the Maysles brothers only travelled to San Francisco on the Friday night before the concert. They were able to make a brief visit to the Altamont Speedway venue, where they met some of their new crew for the first time, but it was not until midday on Saturday that the a full film crew meeting took place at the Altamont site. The crew consisted of a number of UCLA film school graduates gathered by Bryant, while Goldstein had recruited some young film makers from Francis Ford Coppola's company American Zoetrope. Twenty two camera operators are listed in *Gimme Shelter*'s credits, and fourteen sound crew. Among the camera operators was a young George Lucas. The Maysles told their film crew to do interviews and film the crowd. A Hells Angel was assigned to each team of cameraman and sound recorder.

At Altamont itself, the mainly young camera crews were left to their own devices; a few of the young filmmakers took LSD, while some others unknowingly ingested alcohol spiked with LSD.[8] Only a few of the camera crews followed the Maysles' instructions to interview fans, and some of that ad hoc footage can be seen in *Gimme Shelter*. During the day they captured scenes of "dancing people, sleeping people, bad trips, sweet highs, Hell's Angels and spaced-out cats".[9] Albert Maysles, who had put himself in charge of filming the Stones' performance itself, positioned himself in front of the stage. However, he was right behind a father holding a small child: the man was apparently afraid the camera might fall on his kid and he told Maysles rather ominously that if Maysles didn't move he would kill him. Such was the vibe of the crowd at Altamont. This meant most of the Stones' performance, and also most shots of the crowd during the Stones' set, are seen not from the central point of Maysles' choosing, but from camera positions behind or to the sides of the stage. While seemingly a disadvantage, it worked in the Maysles' favour in two significant ways: it allowed the filmmakers to capture footage of the Stones and the Angels in the same frame; and more poignantly, or some may say voyeuristically, it was an excellent vantage point from which to witness Hunter's death.

All in all, in the relatively short time period they spent with the Stones, the Maysles shot around 100,000 feet of film, and although some of that was unusable, it was still much more than the Maysles would normally shoot. They explained this was due to the nature of the tour, the requirement to shoot the whole Madison Square Garden gig, their desire to capture lots of off-stage footage, to film at Muscle Shoals, and to capture as much of the Altamont festival as possible. They did indeed capture footage of much of the music on stage at Altamont, although only some of that made it into *Gimme Shelter*. The Flying Burrito Brothers' set consisted of nine songs, but only "Six Days on the Road" appeared in *Gimme Shelter*. Jefferson Airplane played ten songs but only one featured in the film. Crosby, Stills, Nash & Young played four songs, and Santana played seven, but neither of these groups were included in *Gimme Shelter*. The Stones played fifteen songs at Altamont but only four are shown. The film also changes the order of performances, with The Flying Burrito Brothers appearing onstage ahead of Jefferson Airplane: in reality the Airplane appeared before the less well known Flying Burrito Brothers. It is possible that Keith Richards' close friendship with Gram Parsons led to the Flying Burrito Brothers getting a more prominent position. The final cut of *Gimme Shelter* came to around 91 minutes, which suggests some tight editing given that the New York gig alone was around that duration. Condensing a timeframe of around a month into a movie of an hour and a half of course meant a lot of omissions and a carefully created narrative. So what creative process did the Maysles brothers put in place? What was the story of Altamont that they chose to tell in *Gimme Shelter*; and what was their narrative agenda?

As we will recall from the chapter about the *Woodstock* film, the makers of concert-movie films in this era favoured the "direct cinema" and "cinéma vérité" styles of filming. The former, used particularly by the Maysles brothers in *Monterey Pop,* was a kind of unobtrusive, fly-on-the-wall kind of filming, which almost hides the camera to encourage the viewer to engage with events as they unfold "naturally" on screen; the latter shares the same quest for authenticity, yet places more emphasis on the editorial process in shaping a story. While the Maysles were known for the former, *Gimme Shelter*, in fact, seems to sit more comfortably in the cinéma vérité style because the Maysles make clear interventions on screen and in the editing process to convey to the audience a particular way of seeing and making sense of Altamont.

For example, film critic Paul Schrader, who would later go on to write the screenplay for Martin Scorsese's *Taxi Driver* (1976), mused that there were four obvious directorial interventions that mark *Gimme Shelter* as an artistic interpretation of events rather than an objective documentary. These are: (1) artificially created suspense (2) montage clichés (3) parallel cutting (4) a bogus sense of perspective.[10] Moreover, there is one obvious use of special effects in *Gimme Shelter*, when the Maysles use slow motion to create mood during the Stones' performance of "Love in Vain". Schrader was scathing about what he deemed to be the Maysles' "second rate artistic vision" in capturing events at Altamont but failing to give them meaning. In fact, though, as Schrader's own analysis shows, there *is* meaning in the film, and in part it is formed by the Maysles' careful framing of events, particularly making Altamont the centerpiece of the tour, and making Hunter's death both the film's climax and its main focus. Furthermore, the editing process creates a narrative of Altamont that is just one of many that could have been created. In short, the Maysles' film creates a narrative which defends the Stones from most of the criticism that was directed their way; instead, it puts that blame mainly on the shoulders of the Hells Angels, but also on the crowd. As film expert Aaron Taylor notes, "while the band members are not always on their best behaviour, many of the concertgoers appear in an even worse light".[11] In particular, however, *Gimme Shelter* portrays Meredith Hunter as a potential assassin who caused his own death by drawing a revolver, which led to his demise at the hands of the Angels.

Given that *Gimme Shelter* was originally meant to be a documentary record of the last part of the Stones' 1969 U.S. tour, in the actual film, there are only a few short excerpts of the Madison Square Garden gig included, along with some scenes from Muscle Shoals, and some backstage and off-stage footage. Thus, although Altamont was not part of the original tour itinerary, and it took place after the tour had ended, *Gimme Shelter* situates Altamont as the tour's central point. It is Altamont that gives meaning to the events that preceded it, and also what comes afterwards. Overall, the Maysles structured the film in three parts: it first captures the atmosphere of the rock festival culture of the Stones' tour; the second part illustrates preparation for the Altamont festival; and the third part of the film focuses on the horror of Altamont and Meredith Hunter's death. The second half of the film is therefore devoted solely to Altamont. To a large extent, the structure remains chronological, which gives it a veneer of veracity and diverts the viewers' attention away from the directorial interventions indicated by Schrader. To fully understand the implications of these directorial and artistic choices — and most importantly to see how this created a very specific pro-Stones narrative of Altamont —

it is helpful to get a sense of how *Gimme Shelter* flows from beginning to end. What follows, therefore, is a "plot summary" of the film, with analysis and commentary on how the Maysles present key scenes to the viewer, and the effects of that artistic license. It is particularly revealing to judge the film against the Maysles' assertion that at the heart of what they aim for in their films is "letting what happens happen without interfering in any way".[12]

"Talkin' About You": the Mayles' focus on the Stones

Gimme Shelter begins in the darkness of New York and ends at daybreak on the Sunday after the Altamont concert. The film opens with Sam Cutler getting the Stones' gig at Madison Square Garden underway: Cutler announces, "Are you ready? For the first time in three years, the greatest rock 'n' roll band in the world, the Rolling Stones!" Instead of the concert though, we then see Charlie Watts dressed as a knight and riding a donkey. (An image from this scene would later be used for the cover of the Stones 1970 album *'Get Your Ya-Ya's Out!' The Rolling Stones in concert.*) In one of the cleverest segues in the film, Jagger takes Watt's "stars and stripes" top hat, and in the next frame is seen putting it on his own head, onstage at Madison Square Garden, as he begins to sing "Jumpin' Jack Flash". This is a clear directorial intervention, so already we see this should be judged as an artistic or stylised version of events. This becomes even more evident in the next scene, wherein the band watch themselves on editing monitors performing "Jumpin' Jack Flash" onstage at Madison Square Garden. This then cuts to Charlie Watts listening to post-Altamont comments by Sam Cutler on KSAN radio about the Angels, and Sonny Barger's remarks about Angels defending their motorcycles from vandalism. While the viewer is still seeing real-life events unfold — in this case the Maysles capturing band members' responses to the footage — it has an unsettling effect on the viewer. Firstly, it disrupts the linear narrative of events, making it difficult to ascertain if we are seeing past or contemporary present. In addition, it puts the Stones in a privileged position of being able to respond to what they see, when no such opportunity is given to anyone else; the Stones are thus positioned as observers to their participation in events, which of course allows them to pass judgment on those events and on their own behaviour. And crucially, in doing this, the filmmakers are allowing the Stones to guide and influence the viewer, with a view to absolving themselves of any responsibility for events.

The film then cuts back to Madison Square Garden, where the Stones perform "(I Can't Get No) Satisfaction". Viewers then see Jagger watching that performance on a monitor, before there is a quick segue to a press conference in New York wherein a female journalist asks Jagger if he is any more satisfied than he was when he wrote that song. Jagger provides a light-hearted sound bite in reply, accepting the invitation to respond in kind to the risqué innuendo in the question. The film then returns us to the studio where Mick says "rubbish" in response to his reply to the reporter. In this short scene there is a lot to unpack. First we see the band at their strongest, on stage performing one of their hits; Jagger has the audience in the palm of his hand, and the band are tight and on form. Then the Maysles use the song title to segue to the journalist's question: the journalist is female and her question causes sniggers from the male journalists around her. Jagger's risqué response reminds viewers that he is a sex symbol, but it can be viewed as disrespectful to women, especially a professional woman such as this reporter for whom it is likely that earning the respect of males has been a difficult task. As many Stones' songs remind us though, chicks should be seen and not heard.

This technique — of blending actual footage with pre-recorded (and thus to a certain degree, staged) footage of the Stones watching themselves on monitors and giving their response/verdict — is replicated with aplomb to provide a truncated and selective narrative of events that led to Altamont. Next, the Maysles take us back to the New York press conference where Jagger announces the free concert. This then cuts to footage of Stones' lawyer Melvin Belli talking by phone to the owner of Sears Point Raceway, and then we see Jagger and Watts watching footage of this conversation. There is, however, no footage to show why the Stones offered to do a free concert, and of course because this is "direct cinema", there is no voice over narrative to explain what is happening off the screen. The images alone must provide the narrative. This is, of course, impossible, since only selective images are shown, and what is on screen cannot therefore provide a full or truthful account of events. Furthermore, in shifting the viewers' gaze to Belli's negotiations, it shifts blame onto Belli. He admits, for example, he has never met any of the Stones. No one likes lawyers, and his attempts at humour fall flat. He is a pantomime villain, in contrast to the Stones' rock star cool. The narrative frame here then is that Belli is symbolic of mainstream America, business interests, and capitalism — in short, a representative of the structures of power the counterculture had in its sights, and an easy target for blame when reflecting on Altamont. If this was the filmmakers' intention — to shift the blame onto corporate America — then it is was rather disingenuous. Because in order to function, bands required business and road managers, lawyers and accountants, promoters and organisers, law enforcement and security. And all of this costs money, so like every other enterprise, the Stones needed to turn a profit to stay in business. Entry to the concert may have been free, but the concert itself was not, and neither were the Maysles' services, or the film and sound crews they hired. Aaron Taylor claims that the Maysles alone were paid $14,000 for filming the Madison Square Garden concert, and a further $129,000 for Altamont.[13] In turn, the Maysles claim that *Gimme Shelter* cost more than half a million dollars to make, and they bore much of that financial burden.[14]

The next important scene shows the band checking out of a Holiday Inn and travelling to Alabama to record some tracks at Muscle Shoals Sound Studios. Viewers are not privileged to see the actual recording sessions, but in a surprisingly poignant scene, the band are shown listening to playback of a demo of the track "Wild Horses". Jagger's delicate vocals on this slow-paced song are combined with a montage of shots showing the band relaxing. In a long tracking shot, the camera captures Richards, wearing snakeskin cowboy boots like some demonic outlaw, but singing along softly with Jagger's voice, while Jagger intermittently swigs from a whisky bottle. This is an "artist-at-work" scene, showing the artistry of the band, but it also advertises their outlaw image.

We next see the Stones checking into a new hotel, as if to remind viewers of the band's life on the road as travelling troubadours. In a hotel room, Jagger and Richards dance in response to the sound of "Brown Sugar" from their Muscles Shoals recording session. It is unclear if this scene was staged, or if the musicians' reactions are natural. Either way, it is a remarkable scene: Jagger dances off-stage as he does on-stage, perhaps suggesting it is not a performance for the camera but simply an extension of his personality. Despite its distasteful lyrics, the song's rhythm is irresistible. It swings! But not for long: this is, after all, an unreleased track, soon to be one of the highlights of their new album, and since *Gimme Shelter* might be released before the album, we hear only a part of the song before it cuts off and we see the band board a helicopter, presumably on their way to prepare for the Altamont gig. However, the next scene takes us back to footage of the band onstage at Madison Square Garden again, playing Robert Johnson's "Love in Vain". The Maysles use slow motion effect to emphasise the importance of the song: as we recall from the previous chapter, Johnson was an influence on both Richards and Jagger, and he had become a legendary blues figure after being "rediscovered" in the 1960s. However, the timing of this song, coming right after the racially insensitive lyrics of "Brown Sugar", is noteworthy. The Stones occasionally made clumsy remarks about race: for example, on the evening before Altamont, Jagger told tour chronicler Stanley Booth about his plans to go to the East, possibly touring Africa. Jagger wanted to make a concert film that would include "African music, oriental music, native things"; yet he follows this by discussing Bangkok prostitutes, which is a typical Orientalist thought process — Africa and the East equals sex.[15] In these comments, Jagger is unwittingly advocating that the Stones appropriate the music of other cultures to advance their own musical development. There is also little doubt that "Brown Sugar" is, at best, lyrically insensitive — while Aretha Franklin was singing about respect and James Brown about being black and proud, the Stones were fantasising about slave-owners having sex with slaves. But perhaps this is too uncharitable: they were young English men negotiating their way through the minefield of American racial history and politics, and their respect for blues artists was genuine. Perhaps the placement of "Love in Vain" at this point in *Gimme Shelter* was an effort to remind viewers of this.

Following their performance of "Love in Vain" at New York, the film then cuts back to images of Belli talking to Altamont Speedway owner Dick Carter about using his property to host the concert. It then cuts to images of Charlie Watts watching this footage, with an enigmatic smile on his face. As this is the pivotal moment in the story, the image of Watts' smile seems to say so much — the editorial decision to depict Watts, the band member, watching in hindsight as the lawyer Belli negotiates their concert, implies the Stones were simply carried along to Altamont by their coterie of advisors, lawyers, and managers. This is reinforced by the following scene, which shows Woodstock organiser Michael Lang at a news conference announcing that the concert can go ahead at Altamont. If it had Lang's seal of approval, *Gimme Shelter* seems to be suggesting, if he had spread some of his Aquarian fairy dust on proceedings, then surely no one — especially the Stones — could have foreseen the problems ahead. A little later, the film cuts back again to Watts watching footage of Belli in his office; this time, Watts watches as Carter enquires about the car parking capacity at Altamont. Again, this suggests that the band had no responsibility for the logistical failures of proceedings.

While it is true that the Stones left the actual logistics of the event to subordinates, as most large rock bands would, what the film *doesn't* explore is whether the band had responsibility for larger problems at Altamont — such as why they refused to meet Filmways' conditions for hosting the free concert at Sears Point, which was a more suitable venue than Altamont. The *mise-en-scène*, which positions the band passively watching events as they unfold, suggests the Stones played no role in these decisions, thus absolving the band for any responsibility of what went wrong at Altamont. Yet at the same time, while the film makes clear that the Stones should not be apportioned any of the blame, it is occasionally edited in such a way to suggest that the Stones did learn from their experience. For example, among the next few scenes we see Jagger giving a press conference at Altamont while standing in the doorway of his backstage caravan. The film then cuts to Jagger watching this press conference on a monitor, seemingly a bit annoyed about his "Grateful Airplane, Rolling Dead" remark. There is, of course, no reason to be annoyed: it was a clever sound bite, which kept the press happy. Jagger is watching it in retrospect, however, which provides this older and wiser man the opportunity to judge his jovial and naïve younger self. Regret is evident, but no acceptance of responsibility.

Before we come to the Altamont section of the film, one more scene of *Gimme Shelter* is worthy of note, because it gives an insight into how the Maysles Brothers used the editing process to enhance and protect the Stones' image — if ever proof was needed that the Stones are the stars of this film, then this is it. Before turning to Altamont, the film shows a scene of Ike and Tina Turner, one of the support acts at Madison Square Garden, performing Otis Redding's "I've Been Loving You Too Long" (a song also covered previously by the Stones). Tina Turner is mesmerising: her overtly sensual performance, using a microphone as a phallic symbol and her voice to arouse, drove the crowd wild. Stanley Booth, for instance, wrote that when he watched her perform while he was under the influence of heroin, he was entranced by her "mad nigger poses" which caused him to lust after her "black cunt"; if we can look past the inherent racism and sexism in these detestable comments, the point to make is that Turner was incredible on stage.[16] In *Gimme Shelter,* footage of Turner's captivating onstage performance is interspersed with footage from the Stones' backstage dressing room, until it switches back to the studio where Jagger says "It's nice to have a chick occasionally". Perhaps this was meant as a compliment, but a *Berkeley Tribe* review of the film offers an alternative point of view: "Tina had the whole audience with her, moaning. When it was over, Mick kind of scowled ... He seemed to be a little pissed that someone, especially a woman, could do his act as well as he could, and that it wasn't he who had control over the situation".[17]

Given Jagger's deadpan comment about Turner, and the obvious effect her performance had on him, it seems likely he was jealous of her onstage skills and ability to captivate the crowd. It is significant, then, that in *Gimme Shelter,* the very next scene the film cuts to is New York footage of the Stones performing "Honky Tonk Woman" — a song about a stripper/prostitute. In this footage, some female fans (and one male) jump onstage and are removed by security (mainly Tony Funches) before they can reach Jagger; moreover, between songs, Jagger is shown teasing fans about a broken button on his trousers which may cause them to fall down. So in showing "Honky Tonk Woman" immediately after Turner's performance, the Maysles seem to be attempting to diminish her — by reminding viewers that "chicks" are useful primarily for sex but are otherwise a drag. In essence, the Maysles seem to be agreeing with Jagger: they will not let him be upstaged by a black woman, and the trouser-button scene drives home the message that it is Jagger, the sex symbol, the audience is meant to focus on, not Turner. In this diegetic narrative she has to be punished because she has subverted the order of things — "chicks" must be passive, after all. Paul Schrader was scathing in his review of this scene, saying it was "the Maysles' most irresponsible artistic intervention". Schrader claimed the Maysles' parallel cutting technique made Turner into an "obscene caricature", and he called it "the most vicious, demeaning treatment of a person I have ever seen in a documentary".[18]

Much of the rest of *Gimme Shelter* is concerned with events at Altamont and an important change takes place in the editing style henceforth. As we have seen, up until now, to tell the story of the tour, the Maysles brothers use the technique of editing actual footage of the tour together with crafted, post-event shots of the Stones reacting to events. But once we get to Altamont, the Maysles allow the images to speak for themselves far more, and cut much less to footage showing the reactions of members of the band. This, again, has the effect of showing the Stones as helpless victims, caught up in events that were spiraling out of control. The shift in tone then is deliberately marked. Up until Altamont, the Maysles portray the Stones as being in control of their tour, as the editing sequences make clear; once we get to Altamont, however, the Stones are portrayed in a more passive vein, as if they were caught up in a vortex of forces beyond their control. The message is clear: Altamont was "done" to them; they had no part in its "doing".

"Play With Fire": Altamont on Screen

The sense of chaos begins as soon as the film sequence opens at Altamont: the first shots are of footage taken from a helicopter of hundreds of cars parked on the road to the venue, and thousands of fans on a grim pilgrimage across the barren, brown landscape. It is then revealed that the band are in the helicopter, as Jagger is shown looking down on the speedway where the crowd is gathering. When the helicopter lands and the band alight, without any warning a man runs at Jagger and punches him in the face. This foreshadows what is to come. On screen we increasingly see images of Hells Angels, stoned fans, and acts of violence. Instead of the Stones or their representatives being in control of events, the Angels and the audience begin to become the story of *Gimme Shelter*.

The sense of being trapped in a sequence of events beyond their control is highlighted further by a shift to quick edits between scenes. On screen we see in quick succession a girl handing out flowers, a stage announcement from Sam Cutler warning fans not to climb on scaffolding, people urinating, a man selling LSD, couples kissing, a man tripping, another downing a large bottle of wine, a huge bong, a woman crying out that a "chick's having a baby", a woman collecting "contributions to Panther Defence Fund", a naked woman, a man with a head injury, a request for bandages, Cutler demanding all unauthorised people onstage and backstage be removed, motorbikes, Hells Angels on top of yellow school bus, a huge naked man, and Angels sitting on stage. This montage of scenes ends with Cutler thanking everyone who helped set up the stage, and his pronouncement: "I'd like to point out to everybody here that this can be the greatest party of 1969 that we've had. Let's have a party, and let's have a good time". Given that most of the audience watching *Gimme Shelter* would know already what happened at Altamont, Cutler's comments come across as deeply ironic and even bathetic. Once again, this emphasises the idea that the Stones and their management had only the best intentions; here was their manager, calling on fans to make real the promise of a great party — the implication being that it was the crowd and the Angels who let the side down.

When the film shows the music kicking off at Altamont, it does not so much relieve the tension but act as a trigger for more unfortunate events. Out of the Flying Burrito Brothers' set, the Maysles chose to show them play just one song, "Six Days on the Road". The film depicts the audience as being in a happy mood at this point, and we see fans throwing miniature frisbees, lots of smiles, a teenage girl blowing bubbles, people grooving to the music, one man crowd surfing (and some people pushing him more roughly than required to keep him moving). However, the shots also make clear how overcrowded it is, with people crammed around the side of the stage, and others sitting on speakers. As the song ends, one scared, panicking woman runs towards the camera and we then see the first instance of Hells Angels beating someone with a sawn-off pool cue. It could be the crowd surfer. The film then shows footage of the Angels as they drag his unconscious body around the side of the stage, while onstage there is a plea for non-violence. Cutler announces that they need a doctor presumably to help this man. At this point, the mood of the film changes: while the opening shots of Altamont had shown the potential for chaos — the overcrowding, the punching of Jagger — the Angels' violent attack is the first move which makes real the potential for disaster. So the film establishes straight away that it was the both the crowd and the Angels' overreaction that set Altamont on its doomed course. In reality, there were no attacks of this kind during the Flying Burrito Brothers set: and moreover, the band's easy listening brand of country rock seemed to calm both the crowd and the Angels.[19] The violence had actually begun during the preceding set by Carlos Santana, but since that performance was omitted from *Gimme Shelter*, the Maysles clearly took some artistic license at this point, which doesn't sit well with claims of historical veracity. Nevertheless, within the contained limits of *Gimme Shelter* as an artistic rendering of events, their main point seems to be to emphasise that the violence started as soon as the music started.

In the altered timeline of the film, Cutler's warning about "people on and around the stage who should not be here" is shown next; again, this foreshadows forthcoming eruptions of violence. Cutler introduces "The Jefferson Airplane" who begin to play. The scenes that the Maysles now depict of the crowd are very different to the snapshots we saw earlier: people are acting strangely. A man dances wildly on roof of a truck; a young topless woman dances in the crowd, barely noticed by those around her; a bare-chested man crowd surfs, unhurt, but looks very stoned. Then the Hell's Angels eject someone from the stage. Suddenly they are beating someone in front of the stage. A black man gets violently yanked backwards. The Angels push someone around onstage now, all while Grace Slick tries to calm everyone, saying "Easy, easy, easy..." into the microphone. The Airplane stop playing and Marty Balin goes to the front of the stage. He throws something at the Hells Angels as they beat someone in the crowd. Balin then jumps down into the melee. We don't see what happens next (although we know with hindsight that Balin is knocked unconscious by an Angel). The Maysles then show Airplane guitarist Paul Kantner announcing to the crowd: "I'd like to mention that the Hell's Angels smashed Marty Balin in the face and knocked him out for a bit. I'd like to thank you for that". Remarkably and ominously, Frisco Angel William Fritsch, known usually as "Sweet William", moves to a different microphone and says "You're talking to my people. Let me tell you what's happening. You! Are what's happening". This section of the film make clear: this is where the line between performer and Angel has been crossed. The Angels are now completely in control, and driving events. As if to emphasise this, the Maysles cut to an Angel hitting someone with a pool cue and we hear the horrific wooden sound of it connecting with the man's skull.

Given that two bands that played at Altamont were entirely left out of the film, it is perhaps significant that the Maysles find space to include a scene featuring the Grateful Dead — a band scheduled to play, but who then backed out when told of the Angels' attack on Marty Balin. Of all the musicians present at Altamont, the Dead were the ones most closely associated with Hells Angels. When they were told of the Balin incident, they were dumbfounded: in all of their previous dealings with the Angels at concerts, the Angels had never attacked a musician. They decided not to play. "Let The Stones go on", said Dead bassist Phil Lesh, "this is *their* madness".[20] Garcia agreed, and the Dead flew back to San Francisco. There is no compelling need for the Maysles to show the moment the Dead found out about the Angels' treatment of Balin, and they don't show the band leaving Altamont. So why include this in the film? It might be because it raises questions about the different reactions of the Grateful Dead and the Rolling Stones, particularly given the violence — should the show proceed? "In front of the biggest audience of the band's career", adjudged Selvin, "under the most harrowing and fearful conditions the group had ever faced, these five rock and roll musicians were going to go out on that stage and play their set. No matter what. The show must go on".[21] Selvin makes it sounds like a brave and honorable decision.

In fact, the Stones had sheltered in their caravan backstage for most of the day and the sporadic reports of violence they heard were a bare sketch of what was really happening. Members of Crosby, Stills, Nash & Young had earlier faced the same dilemma: they knew too that the Grateful Dead had declined to perform. They decided to do their set anyway, as to do otherwise might risk further violence. Earlier, from her position in the crowd, Sandy Darlington watched the Angels attack Marty Balin and she wondered why his band chose to continue: "Why didn't the Airplane walk off stage then? I doubt they could have. They were at bay".[22] The Grateful Dead took off before they had to face the Angels, but like Jefferson Airplane, the Stones were cornered and refusing to play was not a serious option. Besides, how could they face their fans and the press afterwards? This was their gig. They owned it. They were the bad boys of rock 'n' roll and it was time to face the music. Because *Gimme Shelter* was released almost a year to the day after the concert, most viewers would likely know that the Grateful Dead declined to play. But in eliding the decision-making process behind that option, and the alternative choice made by the Stones, the Maysles let the audience fill the gap: the Dead ran away, whereas the Stones lived up to their outlaw reputation by choosing to enter the gladiatorial arena. Reflecting on Altamont a few weeks later, even Garcia seemed to believe this: "I've got to hand it to Jagger... the music was OH FUCKIN' KAY... GOOD SHIT... JAGGER IS A HEAVY DUDE, MAN".[23]

After this footage showing the Grateful Dead refusing to play, the film then cuts back to shots of the crowd: we see agitated, nervous looking people. Then we are shown the source of their fear: footage of a group of Angels, led by Sonny Barger, who ride their motorcycles through the crowd to the front of the stage. Angel reinforcements. And it's getting dark. The movie then shows Jagger and Richards climbing onto the stage; it implies that far from the big entrance the Stones had intended, the Stones have been upstaged by the Angels on their motorcycles. After this shambolic entrance, footage then switches to shots of the Stones weaving their way through the backstage crowd and through Hells Angels "security" to climb onto the stage through any space they can find. The film then shows a clip of Jagger telling the audience at the front to "be cool and don't push around. Keep still. Keep it together". Interestingly, in the film, the Maysles edit out the first two songs that actually began the show, namely "Jumpin' Jack Flash" and Chuck Berry's "Carol", and instead in the film the Stones' set begins with "Sympathy for the Devil", whose lyrics ruminate on the nature of evil and conclude that the Devil exists in us all. In this context, it shares the blame of Altamont's evil among the Stones, but crucially also among the Angels and the crowd.

As the Stones begin "Sympathy for the Devil", the film cuts almost immediately to a disturbance at the front of the stage, where footage shows the Angels charging into the crowd to clear a space. The film then cuts to shots of Jagger asking Richards to "cool it" (stop playing), before declaring: "I will try and stop it". He says to the audience, "Brothers and sisters, c'mon now. That means everybody, just cool out!" At this point there is a cut to Jagger looking at footage of himself on stage. Someone tells Jagger "A bike blew up man". The Maysles sequence suggests that the disturbance ends and the band continues.

Yet in the scenes that follow, the film shows the atmosphere growing increasingly bizarre, somber and dangerous. A German Sheppard dog walks across the stage in front of Jagger, which is such an odd occurrence that it should provoke comment, but so many odd things are happening that it just adds to the gloomy atmosphere. Then a large, naked woman pushes her way through the crowd towards the stage. In the face of this madness, the Stones are shown on stage, seeming to falter a bit, before the film again switches to footage of the crowd. Some look upset; some are shaking their heads; one woman is crying, although it is not clear why. A few are still grooving to the music but there is so little space at the front of the stage that all most people can do is nod their heads. As the song plays on, the film shows another disturbance beginning in the crowd: an unconscious man is lifted onto the stage and Angels carry him off stage left. The film then cuts to Jagger, sounding irritated, helpless:

"Uh, people, who's fighting, what for?
Who's fighting, and what for?
Why are we fighting?
Why are we fighting?
We don't want to fight.
Come on!"

We then see shots of Richards, Jagger and Cutler standing at the front of the stage. Richards points into the crowd and says: "Look, that guy there, if he doesn't stop it, man... Listen, either those cats cool it, or we don't play". Given what happened to Balin a few hours earlier, this seems a brave or foolish act on Richards' part. The film clearly implies that there is a real sense that something terrible is unfolding in front of everyone and there is nothing anyone can do to stop it. The sense is that everything has been building towards this.

We then hear someone shouting "We need a doctor!", followed by an Angel taunting the crowd, growling into a microphone: "If you don't cool it, you ain't gonna hear no music! Now, you wanna all go home or what?" More calls for a doctor follow. The film then shows Jagger looking confused: he is used to commanding the stage but now it is clear he was *never* in charge here. Yet as the film makes clear — and which is something he is not often given credit for — he does try to help. Like Grace Slick addressing the crowd earlier, Jagger does what little he can to soothe the savage beasts:

I cannot see what's going on. I just know that every time we get to a number, something happens. I don't know what's going on, who's doing what. It's just a scuffle. All I can ask you, San Francisco, is like the whole thing. Like, this could be the most beautiful evening we've had for this winter, you know, and we've really... Why don't... Don't fuck it up, man. Come on, let's get it together. I can't do any more than just ask you, beg you, just to keep it together. You can do it. It's within your power. Everyone, Hell's Angels, everybody, let's just keep ourselves together. You know, if we are all one, let's show we're all one.

It is during Jagger's impassioned speech that the film shows shots of Meredith Hunter for the first time. We see he is tall, dressed in a lime green coat and dark ruffled shirt. The contrast between Jagger's words and the appearance of a man the viewers know will soon die creates a sense of tragic drama. The film then shows the Stones beginning to play "Under My Thumb" but the camera focuses not on the band but instead on an Angel making his way through the crowd to a motorcycle which appears to have fallen or been pushed over. Jagger stops singing as if he has been distracted by something. The camera focuses on a man stage right of Jagger. Clad in denim, with long hair and a beard, he appears stoned; he is probably an Angel, but maybe not. Another Angel notices him, grabs him and pushes him from the stage. What's remarkable here is that there is so little focus on the band as the camera tracks Angels rather than the "the greatest rock 'n' roll band in the world", as Sam Cutler usually introduced them. The Stones are used to being the centre of attention but they have been usurped by Hells Angels. "The whole stage was just full of Angels," said eyewitness David Goodman, "so many Angels you couldn't see anyone else. It was their stage. No stage crew could possibly remove them. It was their stage… and they knew it".[24] The film reflects this, in this scene in particular: the shots are not of the Stones, but of the Angels, with their wild beards and hair, their colourful garb (one wears a road-kill animal of some sort on his head), and their tight-knit togetherness. Viewers know what is to come, although they aren't entirely sure what the Maysles have captured on film. Is there footage of Hunter's death and the events that led to it? Will *Gimme Shelter* finally reveal what happened?

When making *Gimme Shelter,* the Maysles clearly struggled with this responsibility. As film historian Jonathan B. Vogels points out, they faced a problem in that viewers already knew about Hunter's death, and they also know it had been filmed; so perhaps there was an expectation that it be included. But how should they consider the moral implications of showing his death, and also ensuring it did not overshadow everything else? Vogels claims that the Maysles showed Hunter's death out-of-sequence to reduce the "tension of building toward it", a strategy Vogels admits is not entirely successful.[25] In fact, however, almost every directorial choice the Maysles make has the effect of building up tension towards Hunter's death. However, when it comes it is anticlimactic. The scenes capturing Hunter's death begin by being framed as just another disturbance in the crowd. The film then shows Hunter being dragged around by an Angel; it then cuts to footage showing Hunter pulling out a gun, followed by him being stabbed twice by an Angel (Alan Passaro). The next shots are of Keith Richards trying to intervene: he says, "We're splitting if those cats don't stop beating everybody up in sight. I want them out of the way, man". However, the film then cuts to an Angel telling Richards: "A guy's got a gun out here, and he's shooting at the stage". Interestingly, the film then switches tack — we return again to a sequence of the post-Altamont Stones watching this footage on a monitor: we see Jagger asking David Maysles to roll back the tape on the monitor. They watch Hunter's death unfold again. Maysles stops the recording to show Hunter's pistol clearly silhouetted against his girlfriend's white clothing, and Jagger is shown looking thoughtful and serious. He says, "It's so horrible". The film then cuts back again to actual Altamont footage, where Hunter's body is shown being loaded onto an ambulance, with a witness telling a policeman that Hunter had a gun which the Angels took away from him.

This sequence of events, carefully edited by the Maysles, suggests Hunter was responsible for his own death. By showing an Angel accusing Hunter of trying to assassinate Jagger, and offering no counter analysis, *Gimme Shelter* discards any pretence at neutrality and comes down firmly on the side of the Stones. The implication is clear: they weren't responsible in any way; nor were the Angels necessarily responsible for Hunter's death as they were simply protecting Jagger; moreover, Hunter is portrayed as just another dangerous freak, one of many shown in the film. The Maysles were surely aware of other versions of events. For example, *Rolling Stone* magazine's prominent article "The Rolling Stones Disaster at Altamont: Let It Bleed", published in January 1970, began with an eye witness account which claimed the Angels provoked and physically assaulted Hunter to the point that he felt it necessary to draw his gun to protect himself. There is no evidence, aside from testimony from Angels, that Hunter had any intention of shooting Jagger or anyone else. In fact, those were his final words. Furthermore, while he was a gang member who carried a gun for protection, there was no evidence in Hunter's pre-concert behavior to suggest he had planned to assassinate anyone. The Maysles ignore this: indeed, they go further and anonymise him by refusing even to provide his name. The only effort to show any sympathy for him is when the Maysles show footage of his girlfriend Patti crying, "they can't hear his heart" and when she asks to go with him in the helicopter to the hospital. It's a tragedy in a number of senses: Hunter lost his life and left behind grieving friends and family. But in the literary sense, a tragedy is often caused by the weakness of the victim: a character flaw or a mistake brings about their downfall. Perhaps this is how *Gimme Shelter* depicts Meredith Hunter — the tragic victim of his own mistakes.

After this sequence, the narrative cuts back to the stage where the Stones play "Street Fighting Man". While this happens, Angels throw flowers into the crowd. These flowers were a rehearsed part of the show: at a certain point in the set, Jagger would normally disperse them into the crowd, but the Angels had clearly decided they were as much a part of the show as the Stones, and they beat him to it. In contrast to Jagger, who would normally throw individual flowers to the audience and make it part of the theatre of the show, the Angels dump them into the crowd unceremoniously and without artistry. The symbolism is clear: the Angels were not flower children; and more importantly, they were in control, daring anyone onstage or in the crowd to challenge them. But no challenge came. Moreover, in the film, it shows the Stones' set ending with "Street Fighting Man", as the next scene cuts to show them leaving in a helicopter. In reality, the Stones' set at Altamont consisted of fifteen songs, nine of which they played after the attack on Hunter. *Rolling Stone* magazine claimed that these later songs were "amazing" and "miraculous" … "the Stones were playing their asses off. Jagger is incredible. They all look like they'd rather be *anyplace* else. But it's getting better and better".[26] Why end the film with this song in particular? Perhaps the Maysles did this to make Hunter's death both the focus and climax of the film. It is interesting to note, for instance, that "Street Fighting Man" perhaps not coincidentally contains the lyric "I'll kill the king": perhaps this is another indication of the Maysles' support for the allegation that Hunter planned to assassinate Jagger. Was Hunter a street fighting man who met his match in the Angels, the counterculture's real street fighting men? While any interpretation is possible, given the absence of a clear narrative from the Maysles, what appears on screen seems to suggest some of the negative critical reviews of the film were germane and accurate.

While Hunter's death is the final act of the film, it is not quite the final scene. By the time the concert ends it is almost completely dark. With only lighting from the stage to guide them, the film shows fans beginning to leave Altamont, stumbling down a hillside. The Maysles cut back to Jagger watching this on the monitor. "See you", he says and then looks directly into the camera. There is a freeze frame at this point, and the camera then slowly zooms in on his face. Then, for the closing shots of the film, it cuts ahead a few hours to daylight, and closes with footage of fans leaving en masse to the accompaniment of the live version of the song "Gimme Shelter". (This track also plays over the credits.) The implication is clear then: out of the horror of the night, when violence and death had erupted, the daylight brings a sense of hope, of optimism — we are back with the music, which is what Altamont had wanted to be about, and see crowds ambling home peacefully. Yet in actual fact, the ending of *Gimme Shelter* was intensely contested, and in itself reveals a lot about who was pulling the strings in this film.

Who was responsible for this final edit? David Maysles wrote to Jagger in June 1970, indicating his desired ending would be a freeze frame of the scene wherein fans stumble down the hillside as they leave the concert venue.[27] Aaron Taylor claims, however, that the freeze frame of Jagger's face was meant to end the film. If the freeze frame of Jagger had been meant to end the film, the narrative of the film would have begun and ended with the Stones, which perhaps implied they bore some responsibility for what went on in between. Yet as we have seen, the Maysles brothers editing of *Gimme Shelter* had consistently downplayed any attempt to blame the band for the horror of Altamont, so this would have been a contradiction. Another source points to Charlotte Zwerin, who had been recruited by the Maysles to edit the film (she is listed as a co-director); in this version, it was she who decided she did not want "the finger pointing squarely at Jagger's nose" and that she instead chose to end on happier "sunrise" ending of the departing crowds.[28] Most damningly, in another version of events, Stanley Goldstein claims that the final edit was made at Jagger's request.[29] Certainly, David Maysles' letter to Jagger indicates that the singer raised objection to an early cut of the film which was too much of a downer — "a horror, shocker leaving the audience drained" — so it is possible that Maysles "preferred" ending was a compromise to placate Jagger. After all, the film required Jagger's approval for release, and the Maysles indicated in *Filmmakers Newsletter* that there were many problems getting various permissions. Perhaps then, in this and many other artistic decisions made by the Maysles, they were only too aware that the Stones would not allow themselves to be portrayed in an unsympathetic or negative light. This was later proven by the legal action taken by the band to stop the release of Robert Frank's *Cocksucker Blues* (1972), which provided graphic details of the Stones' 1972 tour, including drug use, violence, and sex. In contrast, *Gimme Shelter* "portrays the Stones as workaholics and perfectionists. There's no sex, no drugs, just rock and roll".[30] In any event, ending as it does, with the crowd leaving in daylight rather than with the camera pointed at Jagger, *Gimme Shelter* allows the singer and the band to elide responsibility for events.

Given what we have seen from the narrative sway of the film, was the Maysles' creation of *Gimmer Shelter* true to the cinéma vérité and direct cinema approaches they claimed to advocate? In one sense, cinéma vérité is more honest than direct cinema in that it accepts that there are multiple points of view and multiple "truths", whereas direct cinema leans towards the idea that there is an objective truth out there that can be captured on film. In the former, the filmmakers are honest in saying this is *their* version of the truth, whereas in the latter, filmmakers adopt a neutral or ambivalent position with regard to the object of their view. The Maysles didn't quite seem certain what they had created, as they insisted the final product was objective, while still containing their view of events: "Our feelings about Altamont are in the film," they insisted in a tetchy letter to the *New York Times* and in response to a negative Vincent Canby review.[31] Critics like Vogels, however, were clear that the *Gimme Shelter* film had a didactic aim, and that the Maysles were attempting to instruct viewers not to believe everything they see, especially when what they see is incomplete.[32] Perhaps that was their aim: if so, they have never discussed it. Furthermore, in the absence of information to explain that approach, the viewer will likely take *Gimme Shelter* at face value. Vogels perhaps gives the Maysles too much credit for intent and implementation: but if that was what they intended, as with many artistic endeavours, the result of their efforts was not as planned. Overall, as we have seen, *Gimme Shelter* clearly had a narrative mission: to give artistic space to the Rolling Stones to distance themselves from responsibility for Altamont's violence.

"Look What You've Done": the reviews

Gimme Shelter appeared in cinemas in December 1970 and took longer to release than anticipated. Jagger's hope that it would be released before the *Woodstock* concert film was dashed: Woodstock opened in March 1970, and at over three hours long, it gave audiences visual and audio evidence of the legendary concert, making it one of the big cinema events of the year. How would *Gimme Shelter* compare to this hugely successful movie? How was it advertised and then received by reviewers?

Unlike the advertising material for the *Woodstock* film, which had tapped into the most popular images of the counterculture, the official trailer for *Gimme Shelter* struck a different tone. It opens with the Rolling Stones performing "Sympathy for the Devil" at Altamont, which indicates two things immediately: firstly that its focus will be on Altamont rather than the tour, and secondly that this is all about the Stones (unsurprisingly given that this was their movie). In that first scene also are the Angels, who feature prominently in the trailer, and whose motorcycles are seen in its last scene. Although a few flower children appear in the trailer, nods perhaps to the "Woodstock Nation", *Gimme Shelter* focuses on the Stones' darker image, as well as Altamont's notoriety, as its main selling points.

This is true also of advertisements placed in underground magazines. For example, an advert placed in the *Los Angeles Free Press* proclaimed, "This movie is so powerful because it shows what really happened", and according to two out of the three images that appear in the advert, what happened was that the Hells Angels beat people.[33] "You feel the tremendous impact when you watch people caught in an event gone completely out of control", it goes on, stressing violence and disorder as voyeuristic selling points. A variation of this advert appeared in the magazine *Fifth Estate*, and the text is slightly different: "This movie is so powerful because what it shows really happened". This version also adds some statistics: "four died, hundreds were hurt", which again suggests that violence is the main attraction of the movie.[34] Another advert design shows the band onstage. The point of view is to the rear, stage left, and the band is lit from the front only. It is a dark, gloomy, almost secretive image — like the setting for some weird Satanic ritual. It seems to capture the sinister energy of the band. The text reads, "Altamont changed a lot of people's heads", which suggests common knowledge of events among potential viewers.[35] Another design features a double silhouette of Jagger holding a microphone. The text reads, "The suspense builds and builds and builds until you find yourself wanting along with Mick Jagger and the Stones to scream — GIMME SHELTER".[36] A further ad shows eight images, three of which feature Hell's Angels (and in one of those images the Angels are beating fans); only two images concentrate on the Stones, which suggests to potential viewers that the Angels are the focus of the film.[37] A final indicative example is an advert which appeared in *San Francisco Good Times*, which shows a studded belt placed diagonally across the page. The text states: "Stones, Airplane, Mick Jagger, Ike & Tina, Hells Angels, Vibes, Hypnotic, Ecstatic, Hysteria".[38] It's a rare advertisement for a concert film that omits one of the artists from the event (The Flying Burrito Brothers) in favour of the group hired to do security, but of course the Angels were no ordinary security guards. The cumulative effect of these adverts suggests that at least some of the accusations of exploitation and sensationalism leveled against *Gimme Shelter* had some validity.

When it came to the reviews, one of the main charges levied against the film was the idea that events had been calculated and planned in advance. Usually the Stones are blamed; on occasion it's the Maysles brothers; or less often it's both parties. For example, *San Francisco Good Times* said: "In Mick Jagger [the Maysles brothers] found their ideal hero; At Altamont, for $81,000, they constructed their set; a supporting cast of Hell's Angels were hired; 300,000 people came and were turned ugly by arrangements the brothers (and the Stones) played a good part in making. The cameras were turned on, the film was cut… and we have 'Gimme Shelter', the ugliest thing I have ever seen on screen".[39] The review suggests a degree of calculation, that if all the right (or wrong) ingredients were put in place then the Maysles and the Stones would get the violence they supposedly hoped for. In a similar vein, *New York Times* film critic Pauline Kael was also highly critical of the film and the role the Maysles played. She claimed, "The free concert was staged and lighted to be photographed, and the three hundred thousand people who attended it were the unpaid cast of thousands. The violence and murder weren't scheduled, but the Maysles brothers hit the cinéma-vérité jackpot".[40] Yet as we have seen, in fact, not much planning was done at all, which was the main problem with the free concert. As indicated earlier, the Stones hired the Maysles brothers to film the Madison Square Garden shows, and after those occurred the Maysles stayed on, with the Stones' consent, to witness the rest of the tour. At some point during that short space of time, and as the likelihood increased of a free concert going ahead in San Francisco, the Stones asked the Maysles to film it, and gave them funding to do so. So the haphazard reality of how the filming idea came about is far from the cold, calculating plan that some critics accused the Stones of following. There is also no evidence that anyone prepared the venue for filming: in fact, the opposite is true — Jagger insisted there would be no concessions to filming. The Maysles would have to shoot what was happening and work around any problems that caused. David Maysles said, "We had no special lighting... We didn't ask the Stones to change the lighting... Chip Monck (Stones' lighting man) and I never even talked".[41] In a *Salon* interview many years later, camera operator Stephen Lighthill insisted that, "*Nothing* [emphasis in original] was done to accommodate the movie, everything was working against the purposes of filming".[42]

The *San Francisco Good Times* was, though, on firmer ground when it implicated the Maysles in the venue change from Sears Point to Altamont: it says the "squalid, mercenary struggle" over film rights between Filmways and the Stones/Maysles was the main reason for the relocation to Altamont and "the move, and the confusion and desperate improvisation that the move produced was responsible for much of what went on there". Most accounts blame Jagger for the refusal to negotiate over film distribution rights but *San Francisco Good Times* also implicates the Maysles brothers, as does Aaron Taylor, who is even firmer in assigning responsibility: Taylor claims it was David Maysles, "in his role as the film's producer", who refused Filmways' demands.[43] It may well be that neither the Stones nor the Maysles were prepared to hand over distribution rights to Filmways, nor pay the $100,000 Filmways wanted in lieu of those rights. Whoever had been the ultimate driving force in rejecting the Filmways contract, it was this fateful decision which led to the move to the site of Altamont, which, as we have seen, was simply not equipped for the volume of people that the Festival attracted.

Critics were also agitated about who would benefit from any profits the film made. Like Ralph Gleason, whose well-publicised concerns about high ticket prices on the tour likely acted as motivation for the Stones' decision to proceed with a free concert no matter what, they seemed especially concerned about fans being "ripped off". For example, *San Francisco Good Times* said: "the people who made Altamont will soon be asked to pay $3 a head to observe the spectacle of their own degradation. The money is going back to the filmmakers and to all the other people who produced the catastrophe, the very people most responsible for the insanity are the people who will be getting rich from it".[44] There is, of course, a contradiction in that statement: if the fans are the people who made Altamont, they share responsibility for its outcome. Here, however, *San Francisco Good Times* absolves fans of responsibility and places it firmly on the Maysles and the Stones.

Other reviews were more mixed. While opining that *Gimme Shelter* lets the Stones off the hook about Hunter's death, *East Village Other*'s "Honest Bob" column, written by journalist Robert Singer, praised the film as "a great rock 'n' roll movie about the best rock 'n' roll band in the world".[45] Later that month, however, "Honest Bob" was a bit more critical of the Maysles for ignoring the link between big business interests and the music scene: "A film about rock that does not make these connections", Singer claimed, "is either ignorant or in bad faith. I don't consider the Maysles brothers ignorant".[46] Somewhat ironically, Singer's comment about *Gimme Shelter* being a "great rock 'n' roll movie" was then quoted on a cinema advert for the film — a development which indicates how connected film and music critics are to the networks of financial power they criticise.[47] In his lament about the Maysles' reluctance to face the relationship between big business and the music industry, Singer was reiterating the astute critiques of earlier, more influential critics such as Michael Lydon who wrote for the radical, San Francisco-based *Ramparts* magazine. In June 1969, Lydon wrote an influential piece entitled "Rock for Sale", in which he pointed out that from its beginnings in the 1950s, rock music had always been a commercial venture. And while there was much talk in the late 1960s that rock and the counterculture shared similar values, or at least that rock music might help the counterculture achieve its aims, Lydon pointed out that the fallacy of those beliefs: "rock, rather than being an example of how freedom can be achieved within the capitalist structure, is an example of how capitalism can, almost without a conscious effort, deceive those whom it oppresses. Rather than being liberated heroes, rock and roll stars are captives on a leash".[48] Lydon also pointed out how advertising campaigns co-opted the language of the counterculture, how rock bands made artistic compromises at the behest of the huge corporations they worked for, and how *Rolling Stone* magazine had thoroughly ingratiated itself within capitalist systems of power. In fact, a year after *Gimme Shelter*'s release, a group calling themselves the Rock Liberation Front, broke into and occupied the offices of *Rolling Stone* in New York to protest against the magazine's alleged attempts to "turn revolutionary energy into product consumption", and against its allegiance to mainstream values.[49]

To return to *Gimme Shelter*, the implication of Singer's criticism about big business interests was that the Stones were not part of the counterculture, which, given Jagger's attempts to place the band within that context, was perhaps the most hurtful criticism of all. Jerry Garcia's condemnation of the Maysles was also a thinly-veiled jab at the Stones: "They filmed the murder... if the Mayseles had any sense or cool they would burn the film... (the Maysles flew back to San Francisco with the developed film to be used as evidence for indicting the offending Angels)... that'll stir them up... The Maysles fly out... but we have to live with them".[50] Promoter Bill Graham made the same point the day after Altamont, but aimed it at directly Jagger: "what right did you have to walk out onstage every night with your Uncle Sam hat, throw it down with complete disdain, and leave this country with $1.8 million? And what right did you have in going through with this free festival… What right did you have to leave the way you did?"[51]

Continuing on this theme, critics questioned whether the Stones and the Maysles should forego all profits from *Gimme Shelter* and instead perhaps those profits should be donated to charitable causes, or to Meredith Hunter's family. Ironically, one of the conditions attached to the hire of the original Sears Point venue was the charitable question: Craig Murray had only agreed to the Stones using his venue if all profits went to "Vietnamese War Relief".[52] This arrangement was null and void when the venue changed to Altamont Speedway: Altamont owner Dick Carter was completely unaware of his strong negotiating position when he gave permission for the Stones to use his property. All he wanted at that point was the publicity, whereas he could have imposed more onerous conditions. Nevertheless, the Stones had indicated that profits from the film would be donated to charity, so it was a natural topic for journalists to pick up on, especially given events at Altamont.[53] *Life* magazine's Richard Schickel also speculated about film profits: "one imagines proceeds from the film helping defray cost of concert, since even philosopher kings like Jagger don't work for nothing, whatever their faithful followers like to think".[54] When asked by *Rolling Stone* journalist Robert Greenfield if the profits from *Gimme Shelter* were destined to go to Meredith Hunter's family, Keith Richards replied: "I don't know, man. As far as I know, the Maysles, the cats who made it, told me that the premiers in various cities have been to help street clinics... I don't know about the Meredith Hunter scene because it's all litigation. It's all lawyers. I've never met his mother. They should get something from somebody".[55] When John Carpenter asked David Maysles if money from the film would be going to charity, Maysles replied: "There will be a share. I don't know which yet. I am thinking of the Free Clinic in San Francisco".[56] It is not known, however, if any money from *Gimme Shelter* went to charitable causes, or to Hunter's family.

While Schickel's "philosopher king" comment drips with sarcasm, it is perhaps deserved, given Jagger's sense of noblesse oblige. He had expected everything to fall into place, and that any criticism would wilt in the glow of his and the Stones' star power. As John Scanlon notes, "The ability to simply announce a free concert and believe that it would happen reflects something of the Stones' status".[57] There was a degree of truth in Jagger's expectations: for example, virtually no one close to the band was willing or able to make their concerns known about the short-notice change of venue from Sears Point to Altamont. In Altamont's wake, however, everyone connected to the concert was fair game for criticism, and the Stones' arrogance and reputation, which previously had worked to their benefit, now worked against them.

By far the most damning criticism was that *Gimme Shelter* exploited Hunter's death, while concurrently absolving the Stones and the Maysles brothers of any responsibility for it. Len Schafer of Detroit's *Fifth Estate* newspaper said, "'Gimme Shelter' tries to scape-goat the violence at Altamont. It portrays the Angels as violence-loving drunken 'bad guys,' while the let's-put-on-a-free-concert-and-think-of-the-promotional-value Rolling Stones are the helpless 'good guys'".[58] Writing in the *New York Times*, Albert Goldman claimed *Gimme Shelter* uses "brightly colored footage to whitewash the Rolling Stones, who must share some of the responsibility for the disaster".[59] *New York Times* film critic Vincent Canby opined, "The depressing thing about the movie is... the exuberant opportunism with which it exploits the events".[60] The Maysles were robust in their response to these allegations, turning criticism back on their critics: "Was the stabbing in the film 'exploiting murder,' as some have suggested? We never judged it as a 'murder.' Those who did could not wait for the jury trial which concluded a verdict of 'self defense,' not premeditated homicide".[61] While perhaps a valid point, it was also a very narrow defense, which ignores the series of events which led to Passaro's attack on Hunter and denies the possibility that any other explanation existed for his murder; it was also a defense which ignored allegations of the poor planning, abrupt change of venue, short-notice preparations, and of course engaging the Angels as a security force.

As well as "Honest Bob" Singer's judgement that *Gimme Shelter* is "a great rock 'n' roll movie about the best rock 'n' roll band in the world", there were other positive reviews of the film. Carpenter called it a "traumatic experience", but also a "major film".[62] *Sight and Sound*'s David Pirie called *Gimme Shelter* "disturbing", but also "easily the most important result so far of the fusion between cinéma vérité (in its loosest sense) and pop music".[63] Writing in *Vogue*, Arthur Schlesinger Jr. proclaimed it, "aurally and visually an exciting film".[64] Even Canby's mainly negative review in the *New York Times* still praised the Mayles brothers for their skill in photography and editing. However, Lester Bangs was perhaps the most effusive with praise, saying, "*Gimme Shelter* is... everything you could want in a rock 'n roll movie... that you'll probably want to see again and again. After the lethal boredom of *Let it Be* and suffocating narcissism of *Woodstock* we finally have a film about rock 'n roll and about the counter culture that's true to both, pandering neither to Hollywood sensationalism nor to the self-righteous pieties of 'our' people. And that means something".[65] Mostly, however, *Gimme Shelter* has been remembered as a document of an elegiac moment, the end of the 1960s. And although that too is a false memory, like the film itself, it does not matter what is real, because reality is only a point of view, it only matters what people believe.

[1] Sioux Shannon, *"Gimme Shelter"*, *DOOR* Vol 2, Issue 21, Mar 17-31, 1971, p. 13.
[2] Lester Bangs, *et al*, "The Rolling Stones Disaster at Altamont: Let It Bleed", *Rolling Stone* 50, Jan 21, 1970.
[3] Bangs, *et al*, "The Rolling Stones Disaster at Altamont".
[4] James Lichtenberg, "Sympathy for the Audience", *East Village Other*, Vol 5, Issue 19, Apr 7, 1970, pp. 9 & 18. At p. 9.
[5] Nora M. Alter, "Composing in Fragments: Music in the Essay Films of Resnais and Godard", *SubStance* Vol 41, No 2, Issue 128 (2012), pp. 24-39. At pp. 32-33, 35.
[6] Joel Selvin, *Altamont: The Rolling Stones, the Hells Angels, and the Inside Story of Rock's Darkest Day* (New York: HarperCollins, 2016), pp. 55-56.
[7] John Carpenter, "An interview with David Maysles. '*Gimme Shelter*': the Stones, fantastic and no bullshit", *Los Angeles Free Press*, Vol 8, Issue 348, Mar 19-25, 1971, p. 31.
[8] David and Albert Maysles, "*Gimme Shelter* Production Notes", *Filmmakers Newsletter*, Vol 5, No 2, Dec 1971, pp. 28-31. At p. 29.
[9] Paul Schrader, "*Gimme Shelter*", *Cinema*, Vol 7, No 1, Fall 1971, p. 52.
[10] Schrader, "*Gimme Shelter*", p. 52.
[11] Aaron Taylor, "Angels, Stones, Hunters: Murder, celebrity and direct cinema", *Studies in Documentary Film*, Vol 5, No 1 (2011), pp. 45-60. At p. 55.
[12] David and Albert Maysles, "*Gimme Shelter* Production Notes", p. 31.
[13] Aaron Taylor, "Angels, Stones, Hunters: Murder, celebrity and direct cinema", *Studies in Documentary Film*, Vol 5, No 1 (2011), pp. 45-60. At p. 54.
[14] David and Albert Maysles, "Gimme Shelter Production Notes", p. 31.
[15] Stanley Booth, *Dance with the Devil: the Rolling Stones and their Times* (New York: Random House, 1984), p. 223.
[16] Booth, *Dance with the Devil*, p. 128.
[17] "Stones/Gimme Shelter", *Berkeley Tribe*, Vol 4, Issue 85, March 5-12, 1971, pp. 16-17. At p.16.
[18] Paul Schrader, "Gimme Shelter", p. 53.
[19] Selvin, *Altamont*, p. 183.
[20] David Dalton, "Altamont: An Eyewitness Account", *Gadfly*, Nov 1999.
[21] Selvin, *Altamont* p. 205.
[22] Sandy Darlington, "Let it Bleed", *Great Speckled Bird*, Vol 3, Issue 2, Dec 1, 1970, pp. 20 & 17. At p. 20.
[23] James Lichtenberg, "Dark Star", *East Village Other*, Vol 5, Issue 7, Jan 21, 1970, p. 9.
[24] "The David Goodman Story", *International Times*, No 86, Aug 27 – Sep 10, 1970, pp. 7 & 10. At p. 10.
[25] Jonathan B. Vogels, *The Direct Cinema of David and Albert Maysles* (Carbondale & Edwardsville: Southern Illinois University Press, 2010), pp. 85.
[26] Bangs, *et al*, "The Rolling Stones Disaster at Altamont".
[27] Michael Chaiken, Steven Kasher and Sara Maysles, editors, *A Maysles Scrapbook: Photographs/Cinemagraphs/Documents* (New York: Steidl/Kasher, 2008), pp. 236-37.
[28] Vogels, *Direct Cinema of David and Albert Maysles*, p. 94.
[29] Aaron Taylor, "Angels, Stones, Hunters: Murder, celebrity and direct cinema", *Studies in Documentary Film*, Vol 5, No 1 (2011), pp. 45-60. At p. 55.
[30] Amy Taubin, "Gimme Shelter: Rock-and-Roll Zapruder", The Criterion Collection, Dec 2, 2009. http://www.criterion.com/current/posts/103-gimme-shelter-rock-and-roll-zapruder
[31] David Maysles, Albert Maysles, and Charlotte Zwerin "But the Killing Happened", *New York Times,* Dec 27, 1970, p. 77.
[32] Vogels, *Direct Cinema of David and Albert Maysles*, pp. 76-77.
[33] *Los Angeles Free Press*, Vol 8, Issue 350, Apr 2-8, 1971, p. 25.
[34] *Fifth Estate*, Vol 5, Issue 23, Mar 18-31, 1971, p. 28.
[35] *East Village Other*, Vol 6, Issue 2, Dec 7, 1970, p. 15.
[36] *Berkeley Tribe*, Vol 4, Issue 89, Apr 2-9, 1971, p. 16.
[37] *Berkeley Tribe*, Vol 5, Issue 91, Apr 17-24, 1971, p. 11.
[38] *San Francisco Good Times*, Vol 4, No 13, Apr 2, 1971, p. 12.
[39] "The Nature of my Game", *San Francisco Good Times*, Vol 4, Issue 9, Mar 5, 1971, pp. 2-3.
[40] Pauline Kael, "The Current Cinema: Beyond Pirandello", *The New Yorker,* Dec 19, 1970, p. 112.
[41] Carpenter, "An interview with David Maysles", p. 31.
[42] Michael Sragow, "'*Gimme Shelter*': The true story", *Salon,* Aug 10, 2000. Available online at: http://www.salon.com/2000/08/10/gimme_shelter_2/
[43] Taylor, "Angels, Stones, Hunters ", p. 55.
[44] "The Nature of my Game", *San Francisco Good Times*, Vol 4, Issue 9, Mar 5, 1971, pp. 2-3. At p. 3.
[45] *East Village Other*, Vol 6, Issue 2, Dec 7, 1970, p. 14.
[46] *East Village Other*, Vol 6, Issue 3, Dec 15, 1970, p. 20.
[47] *Fifth Estate*, Vol 5, Issue 22, Mar 4-17, 1971, p. 20.
[48] Michael Lydon, "Rock for Sale", *Ramparts*, Jun 1969, pp. 19-24. At p. 24.
[49] "Yi-Pentagon Peepers: Rolling Stone", *Berkeley Barb*, Vol 13, No 22, Issue 330, Dec 10-16, 1971, p. 8.
[50] James Lichtenberg, "Dark Star", *The East Village Other* Vol 5 Issue 7. 21 Jan 1970, p. 9.
[51] Quoted in Selvin, *Altamont*, p. 246.
[52] Selvin, *Altamont* p. 109.
[53] Vincent Canby, "Making Murder Pay?", *New York Times*, Dec 13, 1970, p. 117.
[54] Richard Schickel, "Apocalypse at Altamont: *Gimme Shelter*", *Life*, Jan 29, 1971, p. 11.
[55] Robert Greenfield, "The Rolling Stone Interview: Keith Richards", *Rolling Stone,* Aug 19, 1971. http://www.rocksbackpages.com/Library/Article/the-irolling-stonei-interview-keith-richards
[56] Carpenter, "An interview with David Maysles", p. 31.
[57] John Scanlon, *Easy Riders, Rolling Stones: In the Road in America from Delta Blues to '70s Rock* (London: Reaktion, 2015), p. 144.
[58] Len Schafer, "Gimme Shelter", *Fifth Estate*, Vol 5, No 23, Mar 18-31, 1971, p. 18.
[59] Albert Goldman, "Movies", *New York Times*, Jan 3, 1971, p. D9.
[60] Vincent Canby, "Making Murder Pay?", *New York Times*, Dec 13, 1970, p. 117.
[61] David and Albert Maysles, "Gimme Shelter Production Notes", p. 31.
[62] Carpenter, "An interview with David Maysles", p. 31.
[63] David Pirie, *Sight and Sound*, Vol 40, No 4, Fall 1971, pp. 226-27. At p. 227. .
[64] Arthur Schlesinger Jr., *Vogue*, Vol 157, No 4, Feb 15, 1971, pp. 86-87. At p. 86.
[65] Lester Bangs, "Fractured at the Stones Flick: Wondering Where to Lay the Blame", *DOOR*, Vol 2, Issue 21, Mar 17-31, 1971, pp. 13-14.

Afterword

It's been a long time comin' — but that's where we're at now. The events of our time bear witness to the death throes of an outworn civilization, and the apocalyptic vision is writ large in contemporary life and thought. Needless to say it is one of the main currents in rock music. Altamont and Woodstock are the symbols that define it

International Times[1]

It's been 50 years since Woodstock and Altamont took place, and undoubtedly this special anniversary year of 2019 will be marked by much coverage in the media about these landmark festivals. To give a sense of perspective, 50 years is the period of time separating 1969 and 1919: in that year, Americans went to the Paris peace talks to formally end World War One, Eugene Debbs was sent to prison for protesting against that war, women in the United States were fighting for their suffrage rights, left wing radicals mailed bombs to prominent figures, May Day riots took place in Cleveland, Ohio, and race riots occurred in South Carolina, Chicago and Arkansas. Some events of 1919 would therefore have been familiar to young people in 1969, many of whom were themselves protesting against an unpopular war or fighting for their civil rights, or both. Other aspects of 1919 were less familiar: for example, alcohol prohibition took effect that year, and marijuana use was legal. While the vast majority of young people who went to Woodstock or Altamont weren't born in 1919, many of those who attended these festivals are still alive today. (And remarkably, some of those who performed at Woodstock and Altamont are still playing music today.) The young people of the Woodstock/Altamont generation grew up in a world that would become dominated by the technology of computers, mobile phones, and the Internet. Information about almost anything is available with the push of a button or swipe of a screen. Films and books about Woodstock and Altamont are now a simple click away.

Moreover, "music festival culture" is now firmly embedded in the mainstream cultural landscape of both Britain and America: in 2018, for example, the Association of Independent Festivals estimated that music festivals had contributed £1 billion in revenue to the U.K. economy in the years between 2014 and 2017 alone.[2] In North America hundreds of music festivals are now held each year. When Forbes tallied up the five most lucrative festivals held in 2014, they arrived at a total gross just short of $183 million in ticket sales.[3] Music festivals are now, in fact, *the* thing to do for both the young millennial generation and also their older forebears, the "young at heart" generations who have watched festival culture grow exponentially in recent years. Newspapers and social media are now awash with guides for festival-going fashion, and terms such as "glamping" (posh camping, making the mud and grime of festivals more palatable to the middle classes) have entered common parlance. In short, festivals have now become part of the mainstream. Festivals like Woodstock and Altamont then, have now seeped into cultural memory — and in doing so, they have perhaps become tinged with the idea that they were emblematic of the "true" festival culture of '69. Time has perhaps enhanced them with an epaulet of "authenticity", which is rather ironic, given that this book has shown that many criticisms levied at festivals today — that they are "cashing in" on youth culture, for example —

were also present in contemporary critiques of Woodstock and Altamont in 1969. Yet tantilising questions about both festivals remain unanswered. How does one make sense, for example, of people wallowing in mud and rain at Woodstock, going hungry and without sleep, yet still claiming that Woodstock was a mystical experience and for some, the best time of their lives? At Altamont, how could a crowd of hundreds of thousands proffer ineffectual peace symbols and yet not interfere while a group of perhaps 20-30 Hells Angels assaulted fellow audience members with broken pool cues?

As indicated in the previous chapters, the particular dynamics of each festival help explain what happened and why. However, to this point I've resisted imposing a particular theoretical approach that would explain "festival culture". That's partly because I haven't found one that can explain events at Woodstock and Altamont when a similar set of ingredients led to such different outcomes. In addition, comparing and contrasting any of these events is only useful when what's being compared is relevant, and there were too many dissimilarities between festivals to make any single analytical approach of any value. Yet the work that I believe comes closest to explaining the special memory accorded to festivals like Woodstock and Altamont is found in Mikhail Bakhtin's book, *Rabelais and His World*. Here Bakhtin studies the role of festivals and rituals in the European Middle Ages, and his ideas and insights are surprisingly relevant to the festival cultures that developed in the decades since the end of the Second World War. In his book, he suggests that inherent in many medieval European festivals and rituals was a "carnivalesque" spirit, which he called "the people's second life"; this second life was based around an all-consuming spirit of laughter, and a profound sense of the linked qualities of birth, death, and renewal. Bakhtin explained that carnivals and festivals represented a unique time in which this "spirit" could be temporarily unleashed: it briefly allowed people to subvert the existing hierarchy of power relations and allowed for the evocation of alternative discourses. These cultures were marginalised and discouraged during the Age of Enlightenment but, argues Bakhtin, they never disappeared. While, of course, few modern music festivals followed the exact model evoked by Bakhtin, his ideas help explain how, for example, radical politics and music festivals developed contemporaneously in the 1950s and 1960s. As we have seen particularly with Woodstock, the festival was seen as a "moment" when the counterculture ideals — ideas that were on the fringes of society at the time — could be made real for three days, where people could temporarily live out their dreams of free love, harmony and alternative lifestyles. We can also see Bakhtin's ideas in the way in which events such as the Newport Folk Festivals, Monterey, Woodstock, and Altamont were described; particularly when critics and commentators explained these events in terms of a cosmic balance, where "birth, death and renewal" were played out — if three people [sic] died at Altamont, and a rumoured three babies were born, claimed one *Tooth and Nail* journalist in 1970, then the universe was in balance.[4]

This idea of music festivals as modern-day equivalents of medieval carnivals also helps explain the reaction of the "Establishment" to them: which in essence, was either to stop them from taking place, or to control them. Between 1967-71 there were over 300 large rock festivals in the U.S., attracting a combined audience of around 3 million.[5] 1969 has often been named the "year of the festival", mainly because of Woodstock, but also because of other large music events held in Atlanta in July, Atlantic City in August, Texas (30 August - 1st September), and Altamont in December.[6] "Country Joe" McDonald claimed that Woodstock was a "template for every successful festival since"[7] but while it and other events were largely joyous and peaceful, evoking Bakhtin's "all-consuming spirit of laughter", such huge gatherings of people often had a negative impact on local communities and raised health, safety, as well as security and environmental issues for organisers, local authorities, and law enforcement. Leaving aside Woodstock and Altamont, the most headline-grabbing complaints about festivals in 1969 concerned violence and lawlessness: at the Newport Pop Festival, held that year at Devonshire Downs, California, gate crashers kicked down sections of the perimeter fence and clashed with a motorcycle gang who had been hired to provide security. Police were called in and dozens of gatecrashers and police were injured.[8] The 1969 Denver Pop Festival at Mile High Stadium also saw violence from a group of up to 350 gatecrashers who fought with riot police amidst a fog of tear gas.

However, as Country Joe indicates, it was usual to look mainly to Woodstock and Altamont respectively for lessons about how to organise and conduct a successful outdoor festival, or for what to avoid. For local authorities new health and safety laws and restrictions seemed to be the answer. As music scholar Michael Ethen points out, "rural communities and legislators attempted to contain the festival industry by ratifying laws intended to increase their own security or, in some cases, to prevent rock festivals outright". Ironically, given the scale of violence that unfolded at Altamont, the batch of laws that ensued were dubbed the "Woodstock Laws" — not the "Altamont Laws", which is reminder to us that Woodstock had also been viewed as chaotic and problematic. Ethan argues this new swathe of "Woodstock Laws" threatened the future viability of the festival industry."[9] They obstructed access to rural land-use permits, were punitive and severe, and also had a moral aspect, with some new legislation requiring that drugs check points be set up at the perimeter of festival grounds. The result of these laws, claimed underground newspaper *Helix*, was that festivals "are being killed by people with little or no vision".[10]

Yet organisers and promoters knew the financial potential of rural rock festivals so they continued to organise them into the early 1970s, sometimes successfully and sometimes with disastrous results. Many looked upon Woodstock as their ideal template. For instance, the second Atlanta Pop Festival, staged in Byron on the July 4th weekend, 1970, was an attempt to emulate Woodstock. Held in a rural location, with a variety of rock acts billed, it attracted 200,000 people. However, it suffered from poor organisation, not least holding a concert in such stifling heat with not enough water or medical facilities available. And remarkably, given that the terrible violence at Altamont had led to much soul-searching in its aftermath, the lessons learnt from it — that a combination of poor planning, an ill-equipped venue and the hiring of dubious organisations like the Hells Angels to do security/stewarding, led to disastrous consequences — didn't seem to have sunk in. In addition to the poor planning, for example, the Atlanta organisers hired a motorcycle gang for security. At one point, when hundreds of ticketless fans threatened to gatecrash the event and were facing up to the motorcycle gang outside the venue, the organisers intervened and declared it a free festival. *Washington Post* reporter Michael Kernan estimated that only 45,000 out of 200,000 festival-goers actually paid to attend. Kernan wondered if this would be the end of festival culture as he doubted that promoters could bear the financial burden of further non-profitable events.[11] The underground press was split in its views about the festival, to the extent that Atlanta's *Great Speckled Bird* could not agree if it was a "triumph" because it was "an occasion to do all the dope we wanted to in total freedom, a chance to get naked, and a moment of meditation but — and this is absolutely basic — as a people's assembly in, of, and for Woodstock Nation";[12] or a rip off due to overpaid performers, "shit" music, festival "hype", food shortages, and the aforementioned motorcycle gang.[13]

Kernan was incorrect though, as the second Atlanta Pop event of 1970 was not the last big outdoor festival; the following summer of 1971 saw the "Celebration of Life" Louisiana Festival near McCrea, Louisiana take place. Yet again, this festival seemed hell-bent on repeating all of the mistakes of both Woodstock and Altamont. As reported by David Fenton in the *Ann Arbor Sun*, the Louisiana festival originally was to be held in a rural location, on an island in the middle of the Mississippi, which would have ensured perimeter security and deter gatecrashers.

When that bizarre plan fell through, the festival was relocated to a barren location near McCrea. Organisers hired three Louisiana motorcycle clubs to provide security, with, as Fenton notes, predictable results: "The bikers ended up shaking people down for money, food and dope, beating skinnydippers with chains, fighting amongst themselves, and finally hassling with the state police, who forced them to leave at gunpoint after at least 29 persons were injured." The lessons of Altamont had thus not been learned. In addition, there were shortages of toilets and water, over-priced food, and bare minimum medical facilities. Three people died during the event. From these events, Fenton concluded: "What a mess. Another indication that as long as our people's festivals are put together by big-money people (even the 'hip' ones) who are more interested in gobbling down their profits than providing a good time for all, they will continue to end up as this one did".[14]

Canny festival organisers responded to the new "Woodstock Laws" in ways that would change the nature of rock music festivals in the 1970s. They recognised that careful planning pertaining to containment, size, and duration of rock festivals could mitigate or remove entirely most of the problems of large multi-day outdoor events. By erecting fences, limiting crowd sizes and shortening events, most of the logistical problems of Woodstock were avoided. More emphasis on controlling the perimeters of venues ensured that non-ticket holders could not access venues, and gave greater control on crowd numbers and also enhanced profit maximisation. While "free music" was a mantra of some elements of the counterculture, and, as Michael Ethen notes, that point of view had some support from artists such as The Grateful Dead, MC5, Fleetwood Mac and Deep Purple — all of whom blamed record companies and promoters for exploiting artists and fans through unfair contracts and high prices — large, free concerts like Altamont remained the exception. Even then, the Altamont experience provoked a response from the California legislature to pass a law against outdoor rock festivals.[15] In response to these new laws and restrictions, promoters began to organise music events in urban stadiums rather than rural arenas. Such arenas were designed to accommodate large numbers of people in a safe environment with a secure perimeter; after all, relatively little effort was required to turn a sports arena into a music venue. This became the template for most rock festivals in the 1970s but it came at a cost to counter-cultural ideas: it undermined the idea of "free music" and it reversed the Arcadian impulse towards rural music venues.

Attempts were, however, made to capture the Woodstock spirit or even to recreate it. The first of course, was Altamont which was meant to be "Woodstock West". The Woodstock name was a totem and was used numerous times to evoke goodwill and "must see" demand. For example the Cosmic Carnival concert at Atlanta Stadium on June 13, 1970 was advertised in *Great Speckled Bird* with the line "Sound by Hanley — the people who made Woodstock".[16] Russ Gibb, co-organiser of the Cincinnati Pop Festival, held on March 26, 1970, advertised it as, "as groovy as Woodstock but without the hassles".[17] A series of concerts at Mountaindale in Sullivan County New York in July and August 1970 was advertised as "a combination of Woodstock, Provincetown, Tanglewood and Greenwich Village".[18] Even music events that predated Woodstock such as the 1969 Harlem Cultural Festival were retrospectively renamed, in this case "Black Woodstock". The 1972 Sunbury Pop Festival was promoted as "Australia's Woodstock"; and *Oz* magazine claimed the Aquarius Festival in May 1973 was an attempt to produce an "Antipodean Woodstock".[19] In Valle de Bravo, Mexico, the 1971 Festival de Avándaro came about, as one musician recalled, because "we loved rock and roll and Mexican bands wanted to have a festival similar as the Woodstock festival... We protested with music. Our instruments were our weapons to tell the youth that the government was bad".[20] In England, the second (1969) and third (1970) Isle of Wight festivals emulated the "peace and love" vibes from Woodstock. And perhaps the most iconic British festival — Glastonbury — also managed to retain some of the Woodstock spirit from its early days in 1970 until the early years of the 21st century, when organiser Michael Eavis finally agreed to commercial sponsorship masquerading as "partnerships". In addition, Woodstock anniversary concerts were organised in 1979, 1989, 1994, 1999, 2009, and a 2019 50th anniversary concert has been proposed. Although, interestingly, at the time this book goes to print, the 50th anniversary of Woodstock has become a bitterly contested battleground, in which two rival festivals are claiming to be the true "Woodstock 50" festival. On one side, original Woodstock co-founder Michael Lang (who has the legal right to use the name "Woodstock") claims *his* event, to be hosted at Watkins Glen (and which he promises will feature original Woodstock artists), is *the* Woodstock 50 festival; a claim refuted by Scott Cullather and the organisers of the "Bethel Woods Music and Culture Festival", who will hold their festival on the original grounds of Woodstock site at the same time (and who promise a line up of both original Woodstock bands and current music talent).[21] Even now then, debates as to who has "ownership" of the memory of Woodstock and who gets to make claims to its hallowed sense of "authenticity" continue to play out.

Woodstock has also been remembered in various ways in popular culture, often with humorous intent. For example, in 1973 the American satirical magazine *National Lampoon* put together a stage show called "National Lampoon: Lemmings", which consisted of sketch comedy and also a musical parody of Woodstock called, "Woodshuck: Three Days of Peace, Love and Death". Among other performances, comedian John Belushi did an impression of Joe Cocker that he would later repeat when he became a regular cast member on the popular American television show *Saturday Night Live*. A further indicative example of Woodstock parody is the 1993 film *Wayne's World 2*. In this movie, rock fans Wayne Campbell and Garth Algar attempt to organise a rock festival in a local park (Adlai Stevenson Memorial Park) in their home town of Aurora: they call it "Waynestock". To obtain the necessary permits they approach the City of Aurora Parks & Recreation Department, and there face an unctuous and hostile official. This humourless bureaucrat tells them that they will need an "application for authorisation, approval from the guilds and unions, you'll need some release forms, the decibel level... You both realise there are certain jurisdictions you'll need to follow? I'm assuming of course you have the five thousand dollar occupancy permit or you wouldn't even be here? Fine. Then all forms and applications must be filled out in triplicate and returned to this office no later than ten working days before the event, with the money." In its own humorous way, this scene gives an indication of how the world has changed, but also how oddly alike it is to 1969. The organisers of Woodstock and Altamont had to deal with similar red tape. They faced local opposition, logistical difficulties, people problems, and shake downs. In the end, greasing the wheels with money proved to be the main way of dealing with these hassles at both festivals. Woodstock Ventures, for example, responded to Abbie Hoffman's open threats by paying a bribe for him not to interfere. In contrast, at Altamont, it was Mick Jagger's refusal to submit to Filmways Corporation's demands that ultimately denied them the use of Sears Point for their concert, which then had to be hastily rearranged at Altamont Speedway instead. It would be impossible for that hasty relocation to happen with today's health and safety requirements.

Woodstock's success was also, ironically, the beginning of the end for large, rural rock festivals. They were soon under threat from both the "establishment" (particularly state law enforcement agencies) and the underground; the establishment instigated the so-called Woodstock Laws, whereas the underground wanted control and money. For example, the Powder Ridge Festival in Middlefield, Connecticut was cancelled after locals successfully petitioned the State Superior Court. (Fifty thousand young people turned up anyway.)[22] The proposed "Wild West" festival, a non-profit event organised by some well-known San Francisco music figures such as Bill Graham, Ralph Gleason, Rock Scully, and Jan Wenner and due to be held in Golden Gate Park in late August 1969, fell through after local community and political groups refused to support it unless their demands for consultation and money were met.[23] In 1970, Abbie Hoffman and the Yippies demanded 50% of the proceeds of a proposed New York State rock concert, which also resulted in it being cancelled.[24]

Furthermore, following Woodstock's example, musicians realised they could ask for large appearance fees, while promoters knew they had to pay them to get the marquee artists who would guarantee a large crowd. Realistically, entrance fees were the only way to pay for this new development. Potential movie money could not be counted on and corporate sponsorship would not normally be sought until well into the next decade. As concerts and festivals moved away from rural venues towards city stadiums, gate-crashing became a small scale issue. Yet a consequence of this was that festivals also lost their spontaneity and their potential for political protest. Moreover, many of the protest issues on the 1960s had, by the mid-1970s, disappeared or become less urgent. Conscription into the U.S. Armed Forces ended finally in 1973; American troops left Vietnam in 1973 and the war ended in 1975; and the Civil Rights Movement seemed to have won most of its political objectives. In 1970, one festival goer explained: "Festivals have become... representative of the type of lifestyle of government under which we wish to, and will live. A free flowing communal anarchy with no hard laws and rules, governed by a sense of feeling of brotherhood, of common destiny, and of love. We have been shown a path, we have seen the light".[25] However, even as those words were written, festivals had become less a "gathering of the tribes" and more a visible iteration of the relationship between rock music and consumer culture. Like many of the brightest musical stars of the 1960s, the light that shined brightest, burnt quickest, and at the height of their popularity the free festival movement and the moment of the rural, multi-day rock festival was, essentially, drawing to a close.

[1] "Missions of The Apocalypse-Altamont/Dylan/Hendrix", *International Times*, 111, Aug 26 - Sep 9 1971, pp. 13-14. At p.13.

[2] "Independent Festivals Contributed Over £1Bn to UK Economy in Last 3 Years – Report", Nov 6 2018, Music Business Worldwide, accessed at: http://www.musicbusinessworldwide.com

[3] These were: Stagecoach, held in Indio, California, which earned over $18.5 million; Outside Lands, held in San Francisco's Golden gate Park, brought in $19 million; Lollapalooza, held in Chicago's Grant Park, generated $29 million; the Austin City Limits festival collected $38 million in ticket sales; and Coachella garnered $78 million. See Hugh McIntyre, *America's Top Five Music Festivals Sold $183 Million In Tickets In 2014*. Mar 21, 2015. Available online at: http://www.forbes.com/sites/hughmcintyre/2015/03/21/americas-top-five-music-festivals-sold-183-million-in-tickets-in-2014/#34b81b4f54ac

[4] "Altamont Rock Festival", *Tooth and Nail*, Vol 1, Issue 4, Jan 1, 1970, pp. 16-19. At p. 17.

[5] Robert Santelli, *Aquarius Rising: the rock festival years* (New York: Dell, 1980), p. 2.

[6] Santelli, *Aquarius Rising*, p. 87.

[7] Sean O'Hagan, 'The Year of Living Dangerously' *The Guardian*, May 17, 2009. Available online at: https://www.theguardian.com/music/2009/may/17/woodstock-altamont-40th-anniversary-hippie-generation

[8] Santelli, *Aquarius Rising*, p. 90.

[9] Michael Ethen, "The Festival is Dead, Long Live the "Festival", *Journal of Popular Music Studies*, Vol 26, Issue 2–3, pp. 251–267. At p. 255.

[10] "John!! Do It! (or Mick will)", *Helix*, Vol 11, Issue 15, Apr 9, 1970, p. 13.

[11] Michael Kernan, "Washington to Byron", *Washington Post*, Jul 7, 1970, p. B1.

[12] "What Beast is this that crawls to Byron to be born?", *Great Speckled Bird*, Jul 7, 1970, pp. 2-3. At p. 2.

[13] Michael Hill, *Great Speckled Bird,* Vol 4, Issue 29, Jul 20, 1970, pp. 12, 13. At p. 12.

[14] David Fenton, "Sellebration of Life", *Ann Arbor Sun*, Issue 11, Jul 9-23, 1971, pp. 4-5.

[15] Joan Holden, "Woodstock: The Four Dollar Revolution", *Ramparts*, Oct 1970, pp. 60-64. At p. 64.

[16] *Great Speckled Bird*, Vol 3, Issue 24, Jun 15, 1970, p. 17.

[17] "Pig Festival", *Ann Arbor Argus*, Vol 2, Issue 23, Jun 18-25, 1970, p. 13.

[18] *East Village Other*, Vol 5, Issue 31, Jun 23, 1970, p. 25.

[19] *Oz* 46, Jan-Feb 1973p. 11.

[20] Qtd. in *The Rolling Stones: Olé Olé Olé*. Dir. Paul Dugdale. Eagle Rock, 2016. See also "A Letter from Jim Hougan to Dave Wagner", *Quixote*, Vol 6, Issue 9, 1971, pp. 56-8. At p. 57.

[21] Edward Helmore, "Rival Woodstocks compete to keep the 60s hippy dream alive", *The Observer*, Feb 2, 2019; Andy Greene, "Three-Day Woodstock Festival from Original Organizer Coming This Summer", *Rolling Stone*, Jan 9, 2019.

[22] Santelli, *Aquarius Rising*, pp. 195-201.

[23] "Wild West Fucked", *Ann Arbor Argus*, Vol 1, Issue 12a, Sep 17 – Oct 2, 1969, p. 29.

[24] Santelli, *Aquarius Rising*, p. 190.

[25] "John!! Do It! (or Mick will)", *Helix*, Vol 11, Issue 15, Apr 9, 1970, p. 13.

Appendix

Festival Attendance

YEAR	NAME	VENUE	TICKET PRICE	ATTENDANCE
June 10-11, 1967	Fantasy Faire and Magic Mountain Music Festival	Mount Tamalpais, California	$2.00	20,000[1]
June 16-18, 1967	Monterey International Pop Festival	Monterey, California	$3.00 to $6.50[2]	45,000[3]
May 18-19, 1968	Northern California Folk-Rock Festival	Santa Clara County Fairgrounds, San Jose	$4.00 daily	
August 3-4, 1968	Newport Pop Festival	Costa Mesa, California	$4.50 daily advance. $5.50 on the day	100,000[4]
Dec 28-30, 1968	Miami Pop Festival	Hallandale, Florida	$6.00 advance. $7.00 on the day[5]	100,000
June 20-22, 1969	Newport '69	Devonshire Downs, Northridge, L.A.	$7.00 daily[6]	150,000
July 4-5, 1969	Atlanta International Pop	Atlanta International Raceway	$6.00 daily $15.00 whole show[7]	140,000
August 1-3, 1969	Ann Arbor Blues	Fuller Road Flatlands, Ann Arbor	$2.00, $5.00 & $14.00 whole show[8]	20,000[9]
June 27-29, 1969	Denver Pop Festival	Denver, Colorado	$6.00 daily or $15.00 all three[10]	50,000
July 3-6 1969	Newport Jazz Festival	Rhode Island		78,000
August 15-18 1969	Woodstock Music & Art Fair	Bethel, White Lake	$7.00 daily, $13.00 two days $18.00 three days[11]	400,000
Aug 30 to 01 Sept, 1969	Texas International Pop Festival	Lewisville, Texas	$7.00 daily	120,000
Dec 1969	Altamont Speedway, Free Festival	Altamont Speedway, California	FREE	250,000
March 27-29, 1970	Winter's End	Miami	$20.00 for weekend[12]	
June 13, 1970	Cosmic Carnival	Atlanta Stadium	$3.00 to $7.00	
June 21-28, 1971	Celebration of Life	McCrea, Louisiana	$28.00 eight-day ticket $20.00 three-day ticket[13]	50,000
July 3-5, 1970	Second Atlanta International Pop Festival	Byron	$14.00	200,000
July 28, 1973	Summer Jam	Watkins Glen Grand Prix Raceway	$10.00	600,000

1 Michael Goldberg, "Zombie Rock: This Ain't the Summer of Love", *Berkeley Barb* Vol 29, No 23, Issue 708 (Aug 23- Sep 5, 1979), p. 6.
2 Robert Christgau, originally published as "Anatomy of a Love Festival," *Esquire*, January 1968, pp. 64–66, 147. Available online at: http://www.robertchristgau.com/xg/music/monterey-69.php
3 Spitz, *Barefoot in Babylon* p. 22.
4 Robert Santelli, *Aquarius Rising: the Rock Festival Years* (New York: Dell, 1980). Unless stated, all other data is from this source.
5 "Miami Pop Festival", *Kaleidoscope* Chicago Vol 1, Issue 1, Nov 22 - Dec 5, 1968, p. 5.
6 Jerry Applebaum and Paul Cabbell, "Devonshire Downer", *Los Angeles Free Press* Vol 6, Issue 258, June 27 - July 4, 1969, p. 14.
7 *North Carolina Anvil* Vol 3, Issue 112 (12 July 1969), p. 9.
8 *North Carolina Anvil* Vol 3, Issue 112 (12 July 1969), p. 9.
9 Alan Glenn, "Singin' the Ann Arbor Blues", *Ann Arbor Chronicle* August 27, 2009. Available online at: http://annarborchronicle.com/2009/08/27/column-singin-the-ann-arbor-blues/
10 *The Seed* Vol 3, Issue 13, Jun 1, 1969, p. 22
11 Joel Rosenberg, John Roberts and Robert Pilpel, *Young Men With Unlimited Capital* (New York: Bantam, 1989), p. 49.
12 *East Village Other* Vol 5, No. 13 (March 3, 1970), p. 19.
13 Advert for Celebration of Life festival. *Great Speckled Bird* Vol 4, Issue 22, May 31, 1971, p. 26.

Woodstock Performer Fees

Performer	Fee $
Jimi Hendrix Experience	18,000*
Blood, Sweat & Tears	15,000*
Creedence Clearwater Revival	10,000*
Joan Baez	10,000*
The Band	7,500*
Jefferson Airplane	7,500*
Janis Joplin	7,500*
Sly and the Family Stone	7,000*
Canned Heat	6,500*
The Who	6,250*
Richie Havens	6,000*
Arlo Guthrie	5,000*
Crosby, Stills, Nash and Young	5,000*
Ravi Shankar	4,500*
Johnny Winter	3,750*
Ten Years After	3,250*
Country Joe	2,500*
Grateful Dead	2,500*
The Incredible String Band	2,250**
Mountain	2,000**
Tim Hardin	2,000**
Joe Cocker	1,375**
Sweetwater	1,250**
John B. Sebastian	1,000**
Melanie	750**
Santana	750**
Sha Na Na	700**
Keef Hartley	500**
Quill	375*
Paul Butterfield Blues Band	unknown
Bert Sommer	unknown

*"Woodstock Revisited", *Berkeley Barb*, Vol 9, No 19, Issue 222, Nov 14-20, 1969, p. 13.

** *Variety* magazine, reprinted in Robert Santelli's *Aquarius Rising: The Rock Festival Years* (New York: Dell, 1980), p. 153.

Woodstock Running Order

FRIDAY	SATURDAY	SUNDAY
Richie Havens	Quill	Joe Cocker
Speach by Swami Satchidananda	Country Joe McDonald	Country Joe & The Fish
Sweetwater	Santana	Ten Years After
Bert Sommer	John B. Sebastian	The Band
Tim Hardin	Keef Hartley Band	Johnny Winter
Ravi Shankar	The Incredible String Band	Blood, Sweat & Tears
Melanie Safka	Canned Heat	Crosby, Stills & Nash (and Young)
Arlo Guthrie	Mountain	Paul Butterfield Blues Band
Joan Baez	The Grateful Dead	Sha Na Na
	Creedence Clearwater Revival	Jimi Hendrix
	Janis Joplin	
	Sly & The Family Stone	
	The Who	
	Jefferson Airplane	

Woodstock Set Lists

FRIDAY

Richie Havens
From the Prison
Get Together
From the Prison (Reprise)
The Minstrel from Gault
I'm a Stranger Here
High Flying Bird
I Can't Make It Anymore
With a Little Help from My Friends
Handsome Johnny
Strawberry Fields Forever / Hey Jude
Freedom (Motherless Child)

Sweetwater
Motherless Child
Look Out
For Pete's Sake
Day Song
What's Wrong
Crystal Spider
Two Worlds
Why Oh Why
Let the Sunshine In
Oh Happy Day

Bert Sommer
Jennifer
The Road to Travel
I Wondered Where You Be
She's Gone
Things Are Going My Way
And When It's Over
Jeanette
America
A Note That Read
Smile

Tim Hardin
(How Can We) Hang on to a Dream
Susan
If I Were a Carpenter
Reason to Believe
You Upset the Grace of Living When You Lie
Speak Like a Child
Snow White Lady
Blues on My Ceiling
Simple Song of Freedom
Misty Roses

Ravi Shankar
Raga Puriya-Dhanashri (Gat In Sawarital)
Tabla Solo In Jhaptal
Raga Manj Kmahaj

Melanie Safka
Close to It All
Momma Momma
Beautiful People
Animal Crackers
Mr. Tambourine Man
Tuning My Guitar
Birthday of the Sun

Arlo Guthrie
Coming into Los Angeles
Wheel of Fortune
Walking Down the Line
Arlo Speech: Exodus
Oh Mary, Don't You Weep
Every Hand in the Land
Amazing Grace

Joan Baez
Oh Happy Day
The Last Thing On My Mind
I Shall Be Released
No Expectations
Joe Hill
Sweet Sir Galahad
Hickory Wind
Drug Store Truck Driving Man
I Live One Day at a Time
Take Me Back to the Sweet Sunny South
Let Me Wrap You in My Warm and Tender Love
Swing Low, Sweet Chariot
We Shall Overcome

SATURDAY

Quill
They Live the Life
That's How I Eat
Driftin'
Waitin' for You

Country Joe McDonald
Janis
Donovan's Reef
Heartaches by the Number
Ring of Fire
Tennessee Stud
Rockin' Round the World
Flying High
Seen a Rocket
"Fish" Cheer / I-Feel-Like-I'm-Fixin'-To-Die Rag

Santana
Waiting
Evil Ways
You Just Don't Care
Savor
Jingo
Persuasion
Soul Sacrifice
Fried Neckbones And Some Home Fries

John B. Sebastian
How Have You Been
Rainbows Over Your Blues
I Had A Dream
Darlin' Be Home Soon
Younger Generation

Keef Hartley Band
Spanish Fly
She's Gone
Too Much Thinkin'
Believe In You
Rock Me Baby
Medley: Sinnin' For You (Intro) / Leaving Trunk / Just to Cry / Sinnin' for You

The Incredible String Band
Invocation (Spoken Word)
The Letter
Gather 'Round
This Moment
Come with Me
When You Find Out Who You Are

Canned Heat
I'm Her Man
Going Up the Country
A Change Is Gonna Come / Leaving This Town

I Know My Baby
Woodstock Boogie
On the Road Again

Mountain
Blood of the Sun
Stormy Monday
Theme for an Imaginary Western
Long Red
For Yasgur's Farm
Beside the Sea
Waiting to Take You Away
Dreams of Milk and Honey
Blind Man
Dirty Shoes Blues
Southbound Train

The Grateful Dead
St. Stephen
Mama Tried
Dark Star
High Time
Turn On Your Lovelight

Creedence Clearwater Revival
Born on the Bayou
Green River
Ninety-Nine and a Half (Won't Do)
Commotion
Bootleg
Bad Moon Rising
Proud Mary
I Put a Spell on You
The Night Time Is the Right Time
Keep on Chooglin'
Suzy Q

Janis Joplin
Raise Your Hand
As Good as You've Been to This World
To Love Somebody
Summertime
Try (Just a Little Bit Harder)
Kozmic Blues
Can't Turn You Loose
Work Me, Lord
Piece of My Heart
Ball and Chain

Sly & The Family Stone
M'Lady
Sing A Simple Song
You Can Make It If You Try
Everyday People
Dance To The Music
Music Lover
I Want To Take You Higher
Love City
Stand!

The Who
Heaven and Hell
I Can't Explain
It's a Boy
1921
Amazing Journey
Sparks
Eyesight to the Blind (The Hawker)
Christmas
Acid Queen
Pinball Wizard
Do You Think It's Alright?
Fiddle About
There's a Doctor
Go to the Mirror
Smash the Mirror
I'm Free
Tommy's Holiday Camp
We're Not Gonna Take It
See Me, Feel Me
Summertime Blues
Shakin' All Over
My Generation
Naked Eye

Jefferson Airplane
The Other Side of This Life
Somebody to Love
3/5 of a Mile in 10 Seconds
Won't You Try / Saturday Afternoon
Eskimo Blue Day
Plastic Fantastic Lover
Wooden Ships
Uncle Sam Blues
Volunteers
The Ballad of You & Me & Pooneil
Come Back Baby
White Rabbit
The House at Pooneil Corners

SUNDAY

Joe Cocker and the Grease Band
Who Knows What Tomorrow May Bring
40,000 Headmen
Dear Landlord
Something's Coming On
Do I Still Figure in Your Life
Feelin' Alright
Just Like a Woman
Let's Go Get Stoned
I Don't Need No Doctor
I Shall Be Released
Hitchcock Railway
Something to Say
With a Little Help from My Friends

Country Joe & The Fish
Rock & Soul Music
(Thing Called) Love
Not So Sweet Martha Lorraine
Sing, Sing, Sing
Summer Dresses
Friend, Lover, Woman, Wife
Silver and Gold
Maria
The Love Machine
Ever Since You Told Me That You Love Me (I'm a Nut)
Short Jam (instrumental)
Crystal Blues
Rock & Soul Music (Reprise)
"Fish" Cheer / I-Feel-Like-I'm-Fixin'-To-Die Rag

Ten Years After
Spoonful
Good Morning Little Schoolgirl
Hobbit
I Can't Keep from Crying Sometimes
Help Me
I'm Going Home

The Band
Chest Fever
Don't Do It
Tears of Rage
We Can Talk
Long Black Veil
Don't You Tell Henry
Ain't No More Cane on the Brazos
This Wheel's on Fire
I Shall Be Released
The Weight
Loving You Is Sweeter Than Ever

Johnny Winter
Mama, Talk to Your Daughter
Leland Mississippi Blues
Mean Town Blues
You Done Lost Your Good Thing Now > Mean Mistreater
I Can't Stand It (with Edgar Winter)
Tobacco Road (with Edgar Winter)
Tell the Truth (with Edgar Winter)
Johnny B. Goode

Blood, Sweat & Tears
More and More
Just One Smile
Something's Coming on
More Than You'll Ever Know
Spinning Wheel
Sometimes in Winter
Smiling Phases
God Bless the Child
And When I Die
You've Made Me So Very Happy

Crosby, Stills & Nash (and Young)
Suite: Judy Blue Eyes
Blackbird
Helplessly Hoping
Guinnevere
Marrakesh Express
4 + 20
Mr. Soul
I'm Wonderin'
You Don't Have to Cry
Pre-Road Downs
Long Time Gone
Bluebird Revisited
Sea of Madness
Wooden Ships
Find the Cost of Freedom
49 Bye-Byes

Paul Butterfield Blues Band
Born Under a Bad Sign
No Amount of Loving
Driftin' and Driftin'
Morning Sunrise
All in a Day
Love March
Everything's Gonna Be Alright

Sha Na Na
Get A Job
Come Go With Me
Silhuettes
Teen Angel
Jailhouse Rock
Wipe Out
Blue Moon
(Who Wrote) The Book of Love
Little Darling
At The Hop
Duke Of Earl
Get A Job (Reprise)

Jimi Hendrix
Introduction
Message to Love
Getting My Heart Back Together Again / Hear My Train a-Comin'
Spanish Castle Magic
Red House
Mastermind
Lover Man
Foxey Lady
Beginning / Jam Back at the House
Izabella
Gypsy Woman
Fire
Voodoo Child (Slight Return)
Stepping Stone
Star Spangled Banner
Purple Haze
Woodstock Improvisation
Villanova Junction
Hey Joe

Altamont Set Lists

Santana
Savor
Jin-go-lo-ba
Evil Ways
Conquistadore Rides Again
Persuasion
Soul Sacrifice
Gumbo"

Jefferson Airplane
We Can Be Together"
The Other Side of This Life
Somebody to Love
3/5 of a Mile in 10 Seconds
Greasy Heart"
White Rabbit
Come Back Baby
The Ballad of You and Me and Pooneil
Volunteers"

The Flying Burrito Brothers
Lucille
To Love Somebody
Six Days on the Road
High Fashion Queen
Cody, Cody
Lazy Day
Bony Moronie

Crosby, Stills, Nash & Young
Long Time Gone
Down by the River
Sea of Madness
Black Queen
Pre-Road Downs

The Rolling Stones
Jumpin' Jack Flash
Carol
Sympathy for the Devil
The Sun Is Shining
Stray Cat Blues
Love in Vain
Under My Thumb
Brown Sugar
Midnight Rambler
Live with Me
Gimme Shelter
Little Queenie
(I Can't Get No) Satisfaction
Honky Tonk Women
Street Fighting Man

Index

About the Author

Dr Brian Ireland is the author of three books of modern history, as well as numerous journal articles, book chapters, essays, and reviews. He has written about such diverse topics as the US military in Hawaii, hippies, travel narratives, public monuments and museums, horror and science fiction stories, and comic books. Among the publications his work has appeared in are Studies in Travel Writing, American Studies Today, BBC World Histories Magazine, the Western Mail, and 2000AD. He has given talks at Honolulu's East-West Center, Queen's University, Belfast, the Cardiff Story Museum, the Felixstowe Book Festival, and at the Victoria and Albert Museum in London.

Acknowledgements

Many thanks to Penelope James for constructive criticism of the manuscript. I'm very grateful for her advice, which helped generate ideas and which allowed for a deeper analysis of events. Her input about pacing and context has been invaluable. Thanks too for her diligent editing and meticulous proof reading. Without this input this would be a much poorer book. If any errors remain, they are mine.

Some material in this book previously appeared in different form in the Journal of American Studies (Cambridge University Press). My thanks to the journal, and also to Dr Sharif Gemie, for granting permission to use this material here.

Dedicated, with love, to Myles, Morgan, and Penny.

For Stephen, Janice, Louise, Andrew, and Paul.